Introduction to Korean Law

Korea Legislation Research Institute
Editor

Introduction to Korean Law

Springer

Editor
Korea Legislation Research Institute
Seoul
Republic of Korea (South Korea)

ISBN 978-3-642-31688-3 ISBN 978-3-642-31689-0 (eBook)
DOI 10.1007/978-3-642-31689-0
Springer Heidelberg New York Dordrecht London

Library of Congress Control Number: 2012953279

Printed on acid-free paper

Springer is part of Springer Science+Business Media (www.springer.com)

Preface

As the president of the Korea Legislation Research Institute I take great pride in the recent publication of *Introduction to Korean Law*. In particular, I would like to emphasize two aspects of the publication.

First, the Korea Legislation Research Institute has made various efforts to introduce Korea's advanced legal systems to the rest of the world, and the publication of *Introduction to Korean Law* is a significant contribution to such efforts.

Since its establishment, the institute has clarified 'disseminating information about Korean law to the world' as one of its three principal mission statements. The institute has uploaded English translations of Korean statutes and decrees on its web site (http://www.klri.re.kr) so that anyone can have easy access to the information.

In 2010 we published *Einführung in das Koreanische Recht*, the first book to introduce the Korean law in German. Our publication of *Introduction to Korean Law* is a continuation of such endeavors.

Second, I would like to praise the book's academic excellence. *Introduction to Korean Law* examines Korean law in nine chapters discussing the historical background of Korean law, constitutional law, administrative law, civil law (including civil procedure law), private international law, commercial law, economic law, labor law, and criminal law (including criminal procedure law). The nine authors who have participated are all prominent scholars who have provided their expert knowledge for the project. I guarantee that the book will be a great source of information and insight into our legal framework.

In this global era, understanding a country's legal system is a great avenue to understanding the country. I hope this book will spread awareness of our outstanding legal systems throughout the globe, as an authoritative source of legal information for other countries.

I extend my deepest gratitude to the book authors and advisor of this project, emeritus professor Kwon Young Seol of Chung-ang University Law School. I would also like to show my appreciation to everyone who worked on the publication for their sincere concern and hard work. Thank you.

Seoul, October 2012

Yoohwan Kim
President
Korea Legislation Research Institute

Contents

Overview

Kipyo Kim

1 Introduction

The purpose of this chapter is to give an overall picture of Korean legal history and legal system and to give some insight on essential aspects of these areas of Korean law.

This chapter begins with a brief overview of the history of Korea and the development of Korean law with a view to understanding current features of the Korean legal system and legislative process.

Part II provides an overview of the history of the development of Korean law, aiming at providing readers with relevant background information concerning Korean legal history. Part III presents a general overview of the legal system of Korean law and legal institutions of Korean government. Part IV explains the role of Korean law in the development of Korea's successful achievement of democracy and economy. Part V explains the legislative process of Korean laws and regulations in the Legislative and the Executive. Part VI consists of a summary and conclusion of this chapter and prospect of Korean law in the future.

The purpose of this chapter is to introduce an outline and main aspects of the legal system of the Republic of Korea (hereinafter "Korea") and to provide readers with general information on Korean law. To understand Korean law, it is essential to have knowledge about Korean legal history, legal system and legislative process in general. These areas of Korean law cover a wide range of subjects.

Foreigners may find the Korean legal system difficult to understand because it has its own unique and traditional legal history and system different from those of Western and other countries. It is more difficult for them to understand the overall concepts of the legal system and legislative process of Korea without knowing Korean language and history. This chapter is designed to help readers, especially for foreign readers who are interested in Korean law, understand and become

K. Kim (✉)
Kyonggi University, Suwon, Republic of Korea
e-mail: kpkim26@hanmail.net

Korea Legislation Research Institute, *Introduction to Korean Law*,
DOI 10.1007/978-3-642-31689-0_1,

familiar with the Korean legal history and system, and present the legislative process of Korean by giving an overall picture on essential aspects of Korean legal history and system in plain English.

Although Korean traditional legal system had no separation of powers and the judicial function was incorporate with the executive function, Korea had its own legal system even before the modern judicial system was first introduced to Korea at the end of the nineteenth century.

The legal system of Korea and contents of Korean law have undergone drastic procedural and substantive reform from the late nineteenth century of Joseon Dynasty to the present. There have been many significant changes and development in the Korean legal system since the Korea's independence from Japanese colonial rule in 1945 and the establishment of the Korean government in August 1948.

This chapter begins with a brief explanation of the history of Korea and the development of Korean law in order to help understand current features of the Korean legal system more easily. Part II provides an overview of the history of the development of Korean law, aiming at providing readers with relevant background information concerning Korean legal history. Part III presents a general overview of the legal system of Korean law and legal institutions of Korean government. Part IV explains the role of Korean law in the development of Korea's successful achievement of democracy and economic development. Part V explains the legislative process of Korean laws and regulations in the Legislative and the Executive. Part VI consists of a summary and conclusion of this chapter and prospect of Korean law in the future.

2 History of Korean Law

2.1 Overview

Korea is located in the Korean Peninsula between China and Japan in the East Asian region. It is divided into two parts since the independence from Japan in 1945, in the south with the Republic of Korea and in the north with the Democratic People's Republic of Korea. Korea has a long history more than 4,300 years since its first dynasty, Gojoseon (2333–108 BC) was established in 2333 BC in the northern part of the Korean Peninsula.

Legal tradition of Korea dates back to 4,300 years ago when the Gojoseon Dynasty enacted its own statutory law, Eight-Article Law (Pal-jo-geum-beob in Korean) which consisted of eight articles. The contents of three articles among them are known to the present. One of the articles stipulates that anyone who kills a person shall be killed. It reflects the old legal idea of lex talionis or eye for eye and ear for ear.

The development of Korean traditional law was greatly influenced by the introduction of the Confucianism and China's legal culture. But the Korean traditional and unique legal system and customary laws have existed throughout the long Korean history even though its legal system had been influenced from China. Korean society maintained its own traditional legal system until the modern judicial system was introduced to Korea at the end of the Joseon Dynasty in the nineteenth century. Korea adopted modern legal system at the end of the nineteenth century and in the beginning of the twentieth century when it introduced the concepts of Western legal system such as separation of judicial functions from the executive power by enacting the Court Organization Act which established an independent court in 1895.

2.2 Period of Three Kingdoms

In the Period of Three Kingdoms (BC 57–AD 668), there were three kingdoms, which were called Goguryeo, Baekje and Silla. The Goguryeo located in the Northern region in the Korean Peninsula, the Baekje in the South Western region and the Silla South Eastern region.

The judicial functions of the three kingdoms were in the hands of tribal councils or the chief of a clan, respectively. The Kingdom of Goguryeo, the biggest and the strongest among the three kingdoms, had a conference of tribal leaders serving as the top judicial organization. In the Kingdom of Baekje, it is known that one of the royal ministers assumed the judicial authority. The Kingdom of Silla assigned the judicial authority to local heads of administration.

2.3 Goryeo Dynasty

In the Goryeo Dynasty (AD 918–1392), King Wang Geon, the first king of the dynasty, set up a central government court (Ui-Hyeong-Dae) that handled legal issues and trials. Even though the legal system of the Goryeo Dynasty was much influenced from the Song Dynasty of China, it had its unique legal tradition in many aspects such as family relations and land ownership system.

At the end of its history, local administrators who ruled its own territories by armed forces, began taking up judicial functions. The mayor of the capital city Gaeseong, took charge of all civil cases arising within the city, while the head of each local administration handled the cases within his jurisdiction. The king's emissaries or provincial governors acted as the chief of the appeals court.

2.4 Joseon Dynasty

The Joseon Dynasty or Yi Dynasty, the last dynasty in Korean history, which existed from 1392 to 1910, completed comprehensive codification of then existing codes and published "The Great Code for Governing the Country" (Gyeong-guk-dae-jeon in Korean) in 1484. This Code functioned as the fundamental framework of the legal system throughout the Joseon Dynasty. It also was influenced from "The Code of Great Ming" (Ta-Ming-Liu in Chinese) which was enacted during the Ming

Dynasty of China. Although The Joseon Dynasty adopted "The Code of Great Ming" (Ta-Ming-Liu) of China in the field of criminal law, the traditional social order of Joseon Dynasty was ruled by ingenious and traditional customs and codes.[1]

The Joseon Dynasty had a sophisticated legal system, in which petty civil and criminal cases were handled by local chiefs of administration, while the governor of each province took care of the appeals cases and the first instance trials of serious criminal cases. Royal secret investigators, called Am-haeng-eo-sa in Korean, who were appointed and ordered directly by the King, sometimes took charge of local trials, serving as a kind of special circuit court. They investigated and people's complaints on the corruption case of the local officials and punished them.

Citizens who lost an appellate case against a governor were able to appeal to the central government's Ministry of Justice (Hyeong-Jo). The ministry acted as the final appeals court. The ministry handled civil and criminal trials and general legal affairs of the country. In addition, various government agencies carried out judicial functions. Sa-heon-bu rectified false charges. The City of Seoul (Han-seong-bu), the capital city of the Joseon Dynasty, took charge of trials relating to family or real estate registration. Eui-geum-bu handled crimes of treason and crimes by the royal family members.

The Office of Screening of King's Decree (Geom-sang-jo-rye-sa) served the role as the present Ministry of Government Legislation during the Joseon Dynasty. The Office of Screening of King's Decree (Geom-sang-jo-rye-sa) was in charge of government legislative affairs. Before the decree of the king was presented to the State Council of the Joseon Dynasty (Eui-jeong-bu), the decree had to go under close examination by The Office of Screening of King's Decree (Geom-sang-jo-rye-sa). This system ensured that there would not be any inconsistencies or conflict during the execution of administrative affairs.

As we can tell from these historical facts, the concept of rule of law was by no means unfamiliar idea in Korean legal tradition. However, these laws differed from the Western laws in many ways. During the Joseon dynasty, the administration and the judiciary were not divided systematically. The organization that conducted trials also exercised prosecutorial power. The bureaucracy of the Joseon dynasty, which was controlled by the king, exercised all the powers: the legislative, the judicial and the executive power and there was no concept of separation of powers. Governmental bodies were in charge of judicial functions, including prosecution and punishment of criminals. Local officials exercised a certain limited judicial power over their respective jurisdictions.

2.5 Introduction and Development of Modern Legal System

The modern legal system of Korea began to take shape with the Reforms for Modernization (Gab-o-gyeong-jang) in 1894. The first modern written Constitution was

[1] Song (1996).

introduced in Korea in July 1894. The Office of Legal Affairs (Beob-mu-a-mun) was established in 1894 to administer legal affairs and to provide prosecution and court functions. The separation of judicial operations from the government administration was recognized as a major step towards the formulation of the modern legal system. In July 1894, the Office of National Affairs (Gun-guk-gi-mu-cheo), the key government agency during the Reforms for Modernization (Gab-o-gyeong-jang), proclaimed that punishment can be imposed only as a result of a trial by a specialist organ, and prohibited the arrest of suspects by government agencies except those who violated military laws. By this measure judicial affairs were separated from the administration. On December 12, 1894, King Gojong promulgated the 14 Articles of Legal norms (Hong-beom-sib-sa-jo) to declare the modern principle of the rule of law for the first time of Korean history.

The Court Organization Act was promulgated to set up courts and to grant complete separation of the Judiciary from the Executive on March 25, 1895. The modernized prosecutorial system and attorney system was established under the Public Prosecutor Organization Decree of the King. These two laws were made in the course of the modernization of the legal system of Joseon Dynasty and provided that public prosecutors should be members of a court but should exercise their duties independently. The authority and duties of public prosecutors were investigation of crimes, direction and supervision of the police, maintenance of prosecution, execution of sentence, supervision of the proper application of laws. Since the By the Eul-sa Treaty in 1905 betweeb Korea and Japan, Korean government was put under Japanese government's supervision. Japan dispatched Japanese judges, prosecutors and other government officials to Korea to intervene in judicial and administrative affairs of Korea.

In 1910, Korea became a colony of Japan. During the colonial times between 1910 and 1945, Japanese legal system was applied to the Korea. Japanese laws and regulations, which had been influenced by the Western legal tradition, functioned as the primary source of law during the colonial times. Under the Japanese colonial rule, there were no institutional and procedural devices for separation of powers. The Japanese governor-general (Joseon-chong-dok) had the absolute administrative and legislative powers. The imperial Japanese Government tried to transplant its ruling system, including its legal system, to Korea. There was no chance of realization of constitutionalism in Korea during the Japanese colonial times.

Japanese colonial rule ended as a result of the Japanese defeat to the Allied Forces in World War II. After Korea gained independence in 1945 from Japan, Korean Peninsula was divided into two different political entities: the Republic of Korea in the South and the Democratic People's Republic of Korea in the North.

After Korea was liberated on August 15, 1945, U.S. military rule began in the Southern part of Korean Peninsula and Northern part was ruled by the Soviet Union. The American military regime in the South temporarily maintained the old legal and judicial systems, only changing the names of courts.

The Republic of Korea was formally established on August 15, 1948 after 3 years of U.S. military rule. A modern legal system institutionalized. The Constitution of Korea was promulgated on July 17, 1948. The separation of powers was guaranteed by the Constitution. The Constitution was amended nine times to the present as of 2012, in response to political and social changes. The current Constitution is the outcome of the latest amendment in 1987 after the democratization movement. The present Constitution declares that the Republic of Korea is the only legitimate country in the Korean Peninsula and imposed a mission of reunification on State authorities and people of Korea. The Constitution declares that the constituent power lies in the people of Korea and describes the law making process in general. The form of government under the present Constitution is a presidential system which has been modified to incorporate some elements of a parliamentary system. Korea has adopted a presidential system since it made its first Constitution in 1948, except a brief period of parliamentary system in the early 1960s after the Student Revolution on April 19, 1960. The Constitution stipulates the separation of powers among branches: the National Assembly as the legislative, the Executive as the executive, the Courts as the ordinary judiciary and the Constitutional Court as a specialized adjudication authority on the Constitution. The President and the government are in charge of the administration, the National Assembly is responsible for the legislation, and the Courts interpret and apply laws by making decisions over legal disputes, the Constitutional Court deals and decides on the constitutionality of laws and constitutional petitions.

Korean legal system was deeply influenced by the tradition of continental law, thus resembling the modern European civil law or Japanese legal system at the beginning of its modernization. However, with the growing interchange and influence of other countries, especially of the U.S., various laws and regulations were made or revised modelling the Anglo-American laws. In addition, many Korean customary laws or legal tradition were reflected and codified in the Civil Law of Korea. In this regard, Korean modern legal system absorbed and modified the necessary features of the European civil law system, Anglo-American law system and Korean customary laws altogether.

3 Legal System and Institutions

3.1 Legal System of Korea[2]

3.1.1 Overview

Written laws and regulations are the primary sources of law in Korea. The Korean legislative system consists of the Constitution, Acts and subordinate statutes (Orders and Rules of Local Governments, etc.). According to the statistics of the

[2] This part of article is written and compiled on the basis of the material of "A Guide to the Legislative System and Procedure in the Republic of Korea" by the Ministry of Government Legislation in 2010.

Ministry of Government Legislation of Korea, about 1,329 acts, 1,750 Presidential Decree, 1,528 Ordinances of Prime Minister and Ministries are in effect as of March 31, 2012.

The Constitution is the paramount law in the hierarchy of the Korean legal system. Acts passed by the National Assembly are enacted or amended to realize the constitutional targets and ideals and to protect people's rights. Orders refer to administrative legislation issued by the President, Prime Minister and Ministers. Orders are enacted to implement the Acts properly and effectively. The categories of Orders are Presidential Decrees, Ordinances of the Prime Minister, Ministerial Ordinances and Administrative Rules. According to the Korean Constitution, Treaties duly concluded and promulgated under the Constitution and the generally recognized rules of international law have the same effect as the domestic laws of Korea. The Acts and subordinate statutes form a certain hierarchy in terms of their effects. Subordinate statutes enacted under powers delegated by Acts or enacted for the purpose of enforcing Acts are not permitted to contain provisions in conflict with the Acts. Lower subordinate statutes that are enacted by the delegation of higher subordinate statutes or are enacted for the purpose of enforcing higher subordinate statutes are not permitted to contain provisions in conflict with the higher subordinate statutes.

The Supreme Court and the Constitutional Court are mandated to make judgment on the question of whether lower Acts and subordinate statutes are in conflict with higher Acts and subordinate statutes, which is raised in the course of enforcing and implementing such lower Acts and subordinate statutes.

In cases where the question of whether any order, any rule or any disposition is in violation of the Constitution or Acts is brought to court, the Supreme Court has the authority to make a final review of the question. There is no principle of *stare decisis* or precedent in the Korean legal system. However, as the lower courts tend to follow the legal interpretations ascertained by the Supreme Court in actual practice, the Supreme Court decisions are regarded as the secondary source of law. The question of whether any Act is in violation of the Constitution is decided by the adjudication on the constitutionality system and the constitutional petition system of the Constitutional Court.

3.1.2 Constitution

The Constitution is the paramount and the highest law in the Korean legal system. It stipulates fundamental matters concerning the rights and obligations of the people, fundamental structures of the Government, economic order, management of elections and local autonomy. The Constitution is the standard for legislation and amendment of Acts and subordinate statutes of Korea.

The First Constitution of Korea was enacted on July 17, 1948. There were nine amendments of Constitution so far. The latest amendment was made on October 29, 1987. The 1987 Constitution is presently in force.

The Constitution prescribes its fundamental principles, stipulates a guide to the legislative system and procedure and ensures that the sovereignty of Korea resides in the people and all authority comes out from the people. The Constitution also declares that Korea tries to maintain international peace, renounces all aggressive wars and observes international law.

The Constitution stipulates fundamental rights and duties of the people, declares that all the people are assured of human dignity and have the right to pursue happiness as human beings. The Constitution declares that all the people are equal before the law and there is no discrimination in political, economic, social and cultural life on grounds of gender, religion or social status. The Constitution also stipulates personal liberty, the right of access to courts, the guarantee of property rights, etc., and the duties of tax payment, national defense, education and work as the four fundamental duties of all the people. The Constitution stipulates the principle of *nulla poena sine lege* (no punishment without law), the principle of legislated taxation, requirements for the acquisition of Korean nationality, the expropriation and indemnification of property rights. The Constitution declares separation of powers. It establishes the Legislature, the Executive and the Judiciary and checks and balances among them. The economic order of is based on the market economy that values the economic freedom and creativeness of individuals and enterprises.

If an Act, Presidential Decree or Ministerial Ordinance is in violation of the Constitution, the Constitutional Court makes a decision on unconstitutionality of the relevant Act, Presidential Decree or Ministerial Ordinance by referring to the provisions of the Constitution and interpreting basic constitutional notions. The Supreme Court has the power to make a final review of the constitutionality or legality of administrative decrees, regulations or actions, when their constitutionality or legality is at issue in a specific trial. The full text of the English translation of the Korean Constitution is provided at the KLRI website (http://elaw.klri.re.kr/).

3.1.3 Act

Acts are the forms of legal norms stipulated by the legislative principles of the National Assembly. Acts are voted on the National Assembly and promulgated by the President in accordance with the Constitution. Acts become the source of law next to the Constitution in its importance. Acts prescribe the principle of legality, principle of legislated taxation, requirements for the acquisition of Korean nationality, expropriation and indemnification of property rights, establishment of Ministries and categories of local governments and such.

Any of the rights and freedoms of the people may be restricted by Acts in cases where it is deemed necessary to do so for the purpose of safeguarding national security and maintaining public order or public welfare. Even if such rights and freedoms are restricted, essential elements of such rights and freedoms are protected from being infringed on.

For cases on whether a subordinate statute is in conflict with an Act, which are raised in the course of enforcing such Act, the Adjudication on the Constitutionality of Acts and the Constitutional Complaints of the Constitutional Court addresses on whether any Act is in violation of the Constitution. The Supreme Court holds the authority to make a final review as to whether any order, rule, or disposition is in violation of the Constitution or Acts.

3.1.4 International Treaties and Generally Recognized International Law

International treaties mean written agreements concluded among nations. Generally recognized International laws mean international agreements, the enforcement power of which is generally recognized by the international community even though Korea is not a signatory nation thereto (such as the UN Charter), and include international customary laws. The Constitution of Korea stipulates the observance of international law, and prescribes that treaties concluded and promulgated under the Constitution and international laws generally recognized have the same effect as those of domestic laws. "The same effect as those of domestic laws" refers to the fact that any treaties or international laws falling under any domestic Acts or subordinate statues have the same effect as those of the relevant domestic Acts or subordinate statutes, respectively. When the government concludes any treaty in conflict with a domestic Act, the government is required to seek consent from the National Assembly in order to prevent such treaty from conflicting with domestic Acts. Some treaties require legislative measures for the enactment of domestic Acts in order to be properly implemented. Treaties and rules of international law are incorporated into the domestic legal system to form a hierarchy with relevant domestic laws.

3.1.5 Emergency Executive Order

Emergency executive orders and emergency financial/economic executive orders are issued by the President in the event of any national emergency. They can have the same effect of Acts only when the President obtains approval from the National Assembly. In the event of any national emergency, the President is empowered to issue an emergency executive order and an emergency financial/economic executive order, which have the same effect of an Act. The President is empowered to take a necessary minimum financial/economic disposition or to issue an emergency executive order that carries the effect of an Act to support such necessary minimum financial/economic disposition only at a time when he/she finds it necessary to take emergency measures to safeguard national security and to maintain public peace and order and he/she has no time to wait for the National Assembly to convene its emergency session following any domestic trouble and external threat, any natural disaster or any serious financial or economic crisis. The President is also empowered to issue an executive order that carries the effect of an Act only at a time when the country is in a serious conflict with any other country that could put national security in jeopardy and he/she finds it necessary to take emergency measures to defend the country and it is impossible to call the National Assembly into an emergency session. When the President takes such disposition or issues such executive order, he/she is required to promptly report to the National Assembly in order to seek approval from the National Assembly. If he/she fails to obtain such approval from the National Assembly, the disposition or executive order shall immediately cease to have effect.

3.1.6 Order

Orders refer to all of subordinate statutes enacted and enforced by administrative power under the grant of statutes. They are also called as administrative legislation. Administrative affairs are complex and diverse and requires expertise and speedy legislative responses. The Constitution grants the Executive a certain scope of the rule-making power. Orders include Presidential Decrees, Ordinances of Prime Minister and Ministries, and administrative rules.

The Constitution provides that the President may issue Presidential Decrees concerning matters delegated to him/her by law with the scope specifically defined and also matters necessary to enforce laws. The Executive's rule-making powers are recognized in the Constitution. The Executive can make regulations according to directions and the scope of the statutes. The National Assembly can delegate rule-making power to the President with a specific scope.

In addition to the Presidential power to make Presidential Decrees in order to implement the statutes, the Prime Minister and other Ministers can also issue Ordinances to implement the statutes and Presidential Decrees. Presidential Decrees, Ordinances of the Prime Minister and Ministers prescribe matters mandated by Acts and other matters necessary to enforce Acts with the purpose of enforcing the Acts properly and effectively.

Presidential Decree

The President, the head of the Executive, is empowered to enact Presidential Decrees. Presidential Decrees consist of delegated orders and executive orders. Delegated orders deal with the matters that are delegated by Acts within the specific scope of such delegation. Executive orders deal with other matters necessary to enforce Acts. The jurisdiction of such orders extends over all administrative affairs under the jurisdiction of the Executive.

Ordinances of Prime Minister and Ministerial Ordinances

The Prime Minister and the heads of ministries of the Executive, *ex officio* or under the powers delegated by Acts or Presidential Decrees, are empowered to enact

Ordinances of the Prime Minister and Ministerial Ordinances with respect to administrative affairs under their jurisdiction. Ordinances of the Prime Minister are enacted with respect to matters under the jurisdiction of the administrative agencies under the direct supervision of the Prime Minister such as the Ministry of Government Legislation, the Ministry of Patriots and Veterans Affairs, the Financial Services Commission, the Anti-Corruption & Civil Rights Commission. Ordinances of the Prime Minister and Ministerial Ordinances are generally viewed to have the same power in their hierarchy.

Administrative Rules

The administrative rules may be laid down for the purpose of assigning duties to public officials working for administrative agencies and getting higher administrative agencies to direct and oversee duties performed by public officials of lower administrative agencies and to set standards for performance of duties for lower administrative agencies. The administrative rules can be laid down by the logical competence of the administrative power without resorting to the delegation of any special authority prescribed in Acts and subordinate statutes.

The administrative rules consist of directives, regulations, public notices, etc. In principle, the administrative rules do not have any binding force on the general public. The administrative rules are recognized as the rules supplementary to Acts and subordinate statutes in the case that the administrative rules are laid down in accordance with the explicit delegation given by Acts and subordinate statutes.

Internal Rules of Constitutional Institutions

The National Assembly, the Supreme Court, the Constitutional Court and the National Election Commission may lay down its internal rules to the extent these rules do not conflict with Acts. The National Assembly may establish the rules of its own legislative proceedings and internal regulations. The Supreme Court may issue rules and regulations, under its judicial rule-making powers, concerning judicial proceedings, discipline within the courts, or management of business. The rules of the Supreme Court regulate matters governing litigation procedures, the judicial system, including registration and deposit, etc. The Constitutional Court and the National Election Commission also have a similar power to make its own regulations.

3.1.7 Municipal Ordinances and Municipal Rules of Local Governments

The Constitution guarantees local autonomy. Local governments exercise their self-rule legislative power to enact their municipal ordinances and municipal rules. Municipal ordinances are laid down after going through deliberation by local councils. Municipal rules are promulgated by the heads of local governments. Municipal ordinances and rules by local governments with the autonomous legislative power stipulated by the Constitution in order to perform their administrative affairs, constitute the national legal system. Local governments may enact regional provisions relating to local autonomy, within the limits of laws and regulations. The Municipal ordinances and rules are laid down within the scope of Acts and subordinate statutes.

3.2 Codes of Korean Law

3.2.1 Current Statutes of the Republic of Korea

"The Current Statutes of the Republic of Korea", compiled by the Law Information Service (LIS), is the country's one and only complete and official collection of Acts and subordinate statutes. This compilation of the Korean Codes contains all the Acts and subordinate statutes of Korea in force and is classified into volumes and sections for systematically and coherently supplementing them according as they are enacted, amended and repealed. It is printed in paper and disseminated to many legal institutions and government agencies. Accurate, fast and free Information on the all current statutes of Korea are offered through online services (http://www.law.go.kr) in Korean by the Ministry of Government Legislation.

3.2.2 English Version of Acts and Subordinate Statutes of the Republic of Korea

As the statutes and roles of Korea are becoming acknowledged in the global community, Foreign governments, business entities, universities, and research institutes have shown greater interest in the Korean legal system and Acts and subordinate statutes. The Korea Legislation Research Institute (KLRI) has translated Acts and Presidential Decrees in English and has provided free online services (http://elaw.klri.re.kr) aiming to increase understanding of Korean Acts and subordinate statutes for the foreigners. Free online services relating to Acts and subordinate statutes in English contribute to the achievement of the purposes of the internationalization and globalization of Korea. KLRI provides the largest and the most comprehensive collection of Korean law in English, comprising about 1,600 statutes including the Constitution, major Presidential Decrees and regulations as of 1212. KLRI also published the English version of the Statutes into 20 volumes according to criteria for detailed classification in paper until 2010. It is no more published.

3.2.3 History of Enactments, Amendments and Repeals of Statutes

The process of amending Acts and subordinate statutes in Korea is not that of supplementing the amended matters while leaving the existing provisions intact, but that of deleting and altering the existing provisions or phrases in the proper place or inserting newly amended or enacted matters in the relevant place. Accordingly, "The Current Statutes of the Republic of Korea" is inconvenient for their users to comprehend what any particular Act or subordinate statute was at the specific time in the past. For this reason, the Korea Legislation Research Institute published and distributed "the History of the Enactment, Amendments and Repeals of Statutes". Presently, this service is provided online via the website (http://www.law.go.kr) of the Ministry of Government Legislation.

3.3 Legal Institutions of Korea

3.3.1 Overview

Understanding legal institutions is an essential element of understanding Korean law. Constitutional power is divided into three branches based on the principle of separation of powers: the Executive, the Legislature and the Judiciary. Separation of powers limits each other's power and provides for checks and balances among the executive, legislative and judicial branches of government. Legislative power is vested in the National Assembly. Executive power is vested in the Executive Branch, headed by the President. Judicial power is vested in the courts comprised of judges and the Constitutional Court. In addition to the separation of powers provisions, the Korean Constitution has provisions concerning delegation of legislative power.

3.3.2 The Legislature

The legislative power is vested in the National Assembly that is comprised of members elected by direct vote of the people. The National Assembly holds the authority to approve the budget Bill and to inspect and audit state affairs. The National Assembly enacts statutory law, a primary source of law in Korea. The most essential power of the National Assembly is to enact, amend, and abolish laws. The scope of possible subject matters of legislation is not listed in detail in the Constitution. The article 40 of the Constitution stipulates that the Legislative power is vested in the National Assembly. The Constitution contains one general provision permitting legislation to restrict the rights and freedoms of the people in Article 37 (2) and a number of separate provisions granting general legislative power in specific areas, such as the organization of public bodies and their execution of powers and the protection of rights of the people. The National Assembly has the sole power to determine a specific legislation in the form of an Act. The National Assembly is entitled to propose and decide on the Amendments to the Constitution, to enact and amend statutes, to deliberate on and approve national budgets, and to consent to the conclusion and ratification of the international treaties. Its website (http://korea.assembly.go.kr/index.jsp) contains a full-text database of the statutes, rules, decrees, and proposed Bills.

The National Assembly Research Service (NARS) was established in 2007 to assist legislative activities of members of the National Assembly by undertaking research on legislative and national policy issues. Major duties of NARS are providing Assembly Members with its research and analysis reports upon request and conducting proactive research on emerging critical issues in legislation and public policy and publishes the results thereof.

3.3.3 The Executive

The President is the head of the Executive as well as the head of State. He/she is elected by direct vote of the people for a single five-year term. The President represents the State as the Head of the State and exercises overall control of the Executive that is comprised of the Prime Minister and Ministries.

The President, as the head of the Executive, is empowered to have final authority in the decision-making process within the Executive. Unlike in the U.S. Constitution, the Executive of Korea has the constitutional power to introduce Bills for consideration to the National Assembly. The President has powers to implement Acts as well as other authority entrusted to him/her by the Constitution. The President may issue Presidential Decrees necessary to the execution of any authority delegated to him/her by Act. He/she has the authority to take the minimum necessary actions, to issue orders having the effect of an Act, or to proclaim martial law in certain extraordinary circumstances under the prior or subsequent control of the National Assembly.

The State Council has the authority to deliberate on important affairs of the State. It consists of the President, the Prime Minister, and State Councilors appointed by the President on the recommendation of the Prime Minister with a size of between 15 and 30 members. The Prime Minister has a dual entity both as an assistant to the President and as a central administrative agency. Each ministry has a power to make ordinances, rules and regulations in accordance with the statutes. There are some ministries concerning legal affairs.

Ministry of Government Legislation

The Ministry of Government Legislation (MOLEG) is responsible for the legislative affairs of the Executive of the government. The primary duties of MOLEG are comprehensive control and coordination of the government's legislative affairs, statutory examination, statutory interpretation, and statutory improvement. It is an exclusive institution that specializes in monitoring all government legislative affairs, introduces and promulgates the reviewed legislative Bills, and further introduces and promulgates legislative Bills to the State Council that are submitted from the National Assembly. MOLEG has developed and operated legal information services that enable the public to more easily find legal information relevant to their lives. MOLEG operates the Korea Law Service Center for prompt and accurate statutory information service. Present and past laws and regulations of Korea are provided on the website so that the public can gain prompt and accurate access to all statutory information. All the current and chronological statutes and regulations as well as the authoritative interpretation of laws are available via the MOLEG's website. People can easily search for relevant laws by using keywords in search engines. This service is available on the website of MOLEG (www.moleg.go.kr/). The Easy-to-Understand Statute Project modifies long and complex sentences of the statutes to simple and clear sentences.

Ministry of Justice

The Ministry of Justice (MOJ) is a part of the Executive branch, separate from the Judiciary. The Ministry of Justice serves the people of Korea by guarding and enforcing the Constitution and laws. MOJ renders legal advice to the President, Prime Minister, and other Ministers. MOJ also supervises the prosecution. It is in charge of correctional and rehabilitative administration, and immigration. Public Prosecutors' Offices are under the jurisdiction of the Ministry of Justice.

Ministry of Public Administration and Security

The Ministry of Public Administration and Security is responsible for publishing and distributing the Official Gazette (Kwan-bo). The Official Gazette includes official notices on all new statutes, treaties, decrees and regulations. It is served via on line (http://gwanbo.korea.go.kr/main.gz).

Korea Legislation Research Institute

The Korea Legislation Research Institute (KLRI) is government-funded national policy research institute and works for the purposes of supporting national legislative policies and investigating or researching juristic and legislative issues with extensive expertise. KLRI investigates and publishes research materials on important legal information and legislative policies, research materials on important foreign legislation, research materials on legal terminology, and history of the Korean legal systems. The most comprehensive collection of Korean legislation in English can be obtained on Korea Legislation Research Institute's website (http://elaw.klri.re.kr). It has the largest collection of Korean laws in English, comprising about 1,600 statutes.

3.3.4 The Judiciary

The Judiciary refers to the national authority that exercises judicial power separate from the Executive and the Legislative. Article 101 of the Korean Constitution stipulates that judicial power belongs to a court consisting of judges to promote the rule of law. Article 27 of the Constitution states that all citizens possess the right to have a fair and prompt trial by legitimate legal procedures. The mission of the Judiciary is to establish a stable and peaceful society by ensuring consistency and predictability through the implementation of the rule of law. The Judiciary is composed of six types of courts, which are the Supreme Court, High Court, District Court, Patent Court, Family Court, and Administrative Court. The courts are empowered to adjudicate civil, criminal and administrative cases as well as electoral review and other judicial cases. The Judiciary does not enact statutory laws, but interprets and applies them to a specific case. The Judiciary creates what is called case law. This is formed by decisions from multiple courts that are respectively positioned in a three-tier court system: the District Courts being at the lowest tier, the High Courts at the middle tier, and the Supreme Court at the highest tier. There is no principle of *stare decisis* as in common law. Unlike in common law jurisdictions, case law in Korea is not deemed a source of law. Yet, the decisions of a higher court, particularly those of the Supreme Court, are of *de facto* binding effect. Subordinate court judges have a strong tendency to follow the rules set forth by the Supreme Court.

The Supreme Court is comprised of the Chief Justice and 13 Justices, serving as the final and highest tribunal regarding civil, criminal, family, administrative and military cases. The Supreme Court's opinions are recognized as the most authoritative precedents providing standards for the interpretation of laws, while contributing to the development of legal theories and practices.

The independence of judges is one of the core elements of the separation of powers and the rule of law and is regarded as a crucial part of free and democratic order. For this purpose Article 103 of the Constitution ensures that judges shall render judgment independently according to their conscience and in conformity with the Constitution and laws.

3.3.5 Constitutional Court

Apart from the general courts, Korea has a European model Constitutional court. The present Constitutional Court was established in 1988 in accordance with the current Constitution. The Constitutional Court is committed to fully protecting the constitutional rights of the people and adjudicates on the constitutionality of laws, impeachment, dissolution of a political party, competence dispute, and constitutional petitions.

The Constitutional Court has the authority to review whether an Act at issue is unconstitutional. The power to determine the constitutionality of laws is vested in the Constitutional Court as a check and balance mechanism for the Legislative.[3] A decision made by the Constitutional Court is binding on the ordinary courts, state organizations, and local governments. If laws or provisions are declared unconstitutional by the Constitutional Court, they cease to have effect from the date of such declaration, with the exception of criminal penalties, for which the law will lose effect retroactively.

Constitutional petitions are constitutional litigation adopted when the Constitutional Court was established. Under the Constitutional Court Act, anyone who believes his/her fundamental rights guaranteed by the Constitution has been infringed through the exercise or non-exercise of governmental powers may petition the Constitutional Court for relief. If a legislative Act, Presidential Decree, Ordinance or other law directly infringes upon an individual's fundamental rights, the individual may file a constitutional petition against the law itself.

4 Role of Law in the Development of Democracy and Economy

4.1 Role of Law in the Development of Korean Democracy

The main purposes of law can be defined to protect fundamental human rights and to realize social justice and democracy. Protection of fundamental human rights and realization of social justice and democracy explicitly listed from the first Constitution of 1948 to the 9th constitutional amendments of present Constitution of Korea.

The protection of human rights was the main issue after President Park Jung Hee adopted the Revitalizing Reform (*Yushin*) in October 1972. President Park declared a state of national emergency and adopted a new *Yushin* Constitution that gave dictatorial powers to the President, eliminated limits of President's term and abolished direct presidential elections. Under the *Yushin* Constitution, President had the power to appoint one-third of the members of the National Assembly. Through a series of emergency decrees, President Park also banned discussions on the constitution. University students, intellectuals, and religious leaders who demonstrated against the *Yushin* system were arrested and imprisoned. Korea's growing middle class increasingly sided with pro-democracy activists against so called the *Yushin* system. Students, politicians, intellectuals and workers strongly demanded the abolition of the *Yushin* system. The *Yushin* system was finally abolished by the assassination of President Park Jung Hee in 1979. After President

[3] Constitutional Court (2008).

Park's assassination, the Military in power amended Constitution in 1980, which was still undemocratic. Under the 1980 Constitution, Korean people participated against the rule of President Chun Doo Hwan for the restoration of democracy. The purpose of this constant democratic movement was to revise the 1980 Constitution to restore the direct presidential election system, the protection of fundamental human rights and the principle of separation of powers in the Constitution.

Constitutional democracy that had been suspended since 1972 *Yushin* system resumed by the 9th constitutional amendment of the Constitution in 1987 when President Chun accepted people's demand for the restoration of the direct presidential election system and full democracy. The 1987 Constitution consolidated and guaranteed democracy and the protection of human rights. Various laws regulations were enacted to guarantee human rights and to realize social justice and democracy after democratization under the 1987 Constitution.

The Freedom Of Information Act was enacted in 1996 to ensure people's rights to know and to secure citizen's participation in state's affairs and the transparency of the operation of state's affairs.

The Administrative Procedure Act enacted in 1996 totally changed Korean administrative Process. The purpose of this Act is to attain fairness, transparency, and confidence in administration, and to protect citizens' rights and interests, encouraging citizens' participation regarding administrative procedure.[4] A public hearing requirement and oversight hearings shall be held when it is needed to gather consensus on a wide range of opinions. The administrative preannouncement legislation process for the Bills was introduced for the effective and fair legislation.

The Framework Act on Administrative Regulation was enacted to reduce the burdens imposed by regulations by arbitrary or overlapping administrative investigations. The Regulatory Reform Commission has the power to review existing and proposed regulations in accordance with the requirements of statutes.

The National Human Rights Commission Act was enacted in 2001. The purpose of this Act is to contribute to the embodiment of human dignity and worth as well as to the safeguard of the basic order of democracy to ensure that inviolable, fundamental human rights of all individuals are protected and the standards of human rights are improved. The National Human Rights Commission was established as a national advocacy institution for human rights protection.

For the democratization of the judicial process, and for the effective protection of people's rights in the judicial process, many laws were enacted or amended.

The Administrative Litigation Act and The Administrative Appeals Act were enacted or revised to provide an expanded framework for recourse by citizens. The Act on Citizen Participation in Criminal Trials was enacted in 2007 to establish a juror system. Lay jurors are vested with the power to deliver opinions about fact finding application of governing laws and sentencing in a very limited scope in criminal trials.

[4] Park (2011).

Even though Korean legal system has adopted and enforced numerous democratic legislations after the restoration of democracy under the 1987 Constitution, Korean legal system still needs to improve to protect human rights more perfectly and to guarantee effectiveness of legislation. It is necessary for the Korean legal system to ensure more public participation, freedom of information, and improvement in judicial review to promote full-fledged democracy and sustain economic competitiveness in the global society.

4.2 Role of Law in the Development of Korean Economy

The development prospects of Korea after Independence from Japan in 1945 was pessimistic because of the division of the Korean Peninsula and the destruction brought by the Korean War. At the end of the 1950s, Korea was an aid-dependent country whose per capita income was one of the lowest in the world.

The Student Revolution on April 19, 1960 and the military coup on May 16, 1961 changed the environment of policy making totally. In the changed political atmosphere, whoever came to power had to present a strategic vision for the nation. The military coup, led by President Park Chung Hee sought to achieve industrialization.

Starting in the early 1960s, Korea adopted export-oriented industrialization policies. Korea's export-oriented industrialization was a strategy to secure economic independence.[5] Korea used international trade as an essential component of its development policy. The Korean Government drafted Five-Year Economic Development Plans. The government channeled all national energy into economic modernization. Korea lacked the domestic resources to carry out its economic development program. A critical development challenge for Korea in the early 1960s was to find financing sources from foreign countries. Korea had to rely heavily on foreign loans due to its low domestic capital accumulation at the time. Trade with foreign countries helped Korea to discover its comparative advantage and identify productive uses for capital. Export-oriented industries were given tax and financial incentives by the government.[6] Korea was able to exploit its latent comparative advantage in labor-intensive manufacturing by correcting for government and market failures of the past. International trade helped Korea to discover its comparative advantage, overcome the limits of its small domestic market and exploit scale economies, and upgrade its economy. For nearly two decades, President Park pushed ahead with such policies. Korea's coordinated and broad-based program of trade, industrial, and human resource development generated rapid growth.

While relying on global markets, Korea made conscious and concerted efforts for industrial upgrading, to climb up the value chain into higher value-added areas by making complementary investments in infrastructure and human capital.

[5] Won-chol (2009).

[6] Kim (2011).

Exports helped Korea to overcome the limits of its small domestic market and exploit scale economies. Trade allowed Korea to devise a powerful feedback mechanism by reinforcing successful experiments through rewards based on performance in competitive global markets. Trade also offered great learning opportunities and market tests for government policies and corporate strategies.

With a view toward securing economic and political independence, Korea introduced a number of export promotion measures in the 1960s. To provide institutional support in the area of foreign marketing and technology imports, the government established the Korea Trade Promotion Corporation (KOTRA) in 1962. The Economic Planning Board (EPB) was established in 1961 and formulated the Five-Year Economic Development Plans with powers to draft the budget and coordinate economic policies. Korea introduced safety nets with a view toward strengthening social cohesion. Korea established a national healthcare system in 1977. As for unemployment insurance, strong job security in exchange for weak labor rights was an integral part of the imposed social bargain under the authoritarian regime through 1960s–1980s in Korea. It made its remarkable transition from one of the poorest countries in the world to arrive at the doorstep of advanced countries.

Numerous laws and regulations were enacted to support Korea's economic progress during these several decades. Many laws were newly enacted to promote export and induce foreign capital such as Foreign Trade Act, Foreign Exchange Transactions Act, Act on Designation and Management of Free Trade Zones, Special Act on Designation and Management of Free Economic Zones, Foreign Investment Promotion Act, Korea Development Bank Act, Export and Import Bank of Korea Act, Credit Guarantee Fund Act. Laws and regulations on tax exemption such as Restriction of Special Taxation Act were enacted to support export-oriented industries and labor regulations. Laws to strengthen the competitiveness of small business were enacted like Small and Medium Enterprises Promotion Act, Industrial Bank of Korea Act.

While a regime that facilitates resource mobilization can be effective in the catch-up phase of development, an institutional platform that fosters autonomy, diversity, and experiment is critical to sustained productivity-led growth. Democracy has provided such a platform for Korea since 1987. After Korea was democratized in 1987, workers demanded wage increases as well as full-fledged rights to organize and take collective action. The economic crisis of 1997–1998 for Korea to introduce credible market-based discipline and reach a grand social bargain exchanging enhanced labor rights and social security for labor market flexibility. These social protection measures helped Korea to maintain social cohesion as it made its transition from an authoritarian developmental state to a democratic market economy.

Various laws and regulations were enacted to ensure social safety, health and social justice. such as National Health Insurance Act, Environment Conservation Act, Labor Standards Act, Minimum Wage Act, Occupational Safety and Health Act, Fair competition Act, Consumer Protection Act, Monopoly Regulation and Fair Trade Act, Act on the Structural Improvement of the Financial Industry, Framework Act on Consumers. These various laws and regulations contributed greatly to the continuous economic development and to ensure social safety and social welfare of Korea. One of the poorest countries in the world at the beginning of the 1960s, Korea joined the ranks of industrial democracies, becoming a member of the OECD (Organization for Economic Co-operation and Development) in 1996 and a member of G20 summit meeting in 2008.

5 Legislative Process of Korean Law[7]

5.1 Overview

Legislative process means a series of procedures ranging from the drafting of Bills to the promulgation. The legislative process is essential for law-governed countries to go through in order to ensure the justification of their legislation. Legislative processes are formal requirements for the enactment of Acts and subordinate statutes. Legislative processes of Acts, Orders and Ordinances are different from each other.

The Constitution grants the National Assembly the legislative power and permits the Executive and other agencies to exercise the law-making power in the form of subordinate statutes, such as Presidential Decrees, Ordinances. The legislative power of Acts is vested in the National Assembly and the legislative power of subordinate statutes is vested in the Executive and the Judiciary is vested to the matters delegated by Acts and other matters necessary to enforce Acts. Since subordinate statutes are required to be in confirmity with Acts, the National Assembly stands at the top of legislation institution in the law-making process.

The observance of the legislative process guarantees the procedural justification necessary to ensure the democratic features of Acts and subordinate statutes. The legislative process performs the function of controlling legislation necessary to ensure the appropriateness of legislative contents. The legislative process also serves to check and balance the power under the separation of powers while functioning as a system by which major national policies are determined in order to coordinate interests involving a large number of parties and interests among administrative agencies and to realize the principle that sovereignty rests with the people and the principle of the representative system. The Executive exercises autonomy in the field of administrative legislation.

Korea adopts the presidential system. But, unlike the U.S., the Korean Executive has the right to submit bills. The Constitution stipulates that bills may be introduced by members of the National Assembly or by the Executive. As the initiation of law-making process, Bills are submitted either by at least ten legislators or by the Executive. Whoever initiates legislation, the National Assembly, as the sole law-making body of the country, decides with a majority vote whether to pass the bill or not. Once the National Assembly passes a bill and the President promulgates it, it qualifies as statutory law and takes effect as indicated in the law itself.

[7] This part of article is summarized on the basis of "Laws on Green Growth and Economic Development in Korea" by the Ministry of Legislation in 2011.

Since statutory law is a primary source of law, customary law is to be applied only when there are no statutes available in the case being adjudicated. Customary law can be a useful means for a society to bridge the gap between reality and an existing norm that codification cannot promptly address. However, customary law seldom finds room for its functions due to the presence of a wide and comprehensive volume of statutory law in the Korean legal system.

5.2 *Legislative Process in the National Assembly*

5.2.1 Introduction of Bills

Members of the National Assembly may introduce any Bill to the National Assembly with the consent of not less than ten members of the National Assembly. With respect to any Bill that requires measures on budgets or funds, the legislators shall introduce such Bill accompanied by a written Cost Estimates for the Bill for the execution of the Bill. The National Assembly Act also prescribes that any Committees of the National Assembly may introduce any Bill on matters under its jurisdiction and in such cases, the chairperson of the relevant Committee shall introduce the Bill. Each of the Standing Committees may draft a Bill under its jurisdiction for itself and introduce the draft Bill. When any Committee intends to introduce any Bill, the Committee may set up a subcommittee mandated to draft such Bill.

The Constitution allows the Executive to introduce Bills. Bills proposed by the Executive are introduced to the National Assembly in the name of the President after undergoing deliberation by the State Council and the Prime Minister and the relevant members of the State Council are required to countersign the Bills.

The Supreme Court, the National Election Commission and the Board of Inspection and Audit have no constitutional rights to introduce Bills to the National Assembly. But they may present their opinions in writing to the National Assembly if it is deemed necessary to enact or amend related Acts.

The Legislative Counsel Office is established in the National Assembly Secretariat as an official parliamentary organization in charge of assisting legislators in drafting Bills. Legislators, floor leaders of negotiation groups, representatives of legislators' research organizations, the chairpersons and special counsels of Standing Committees and Special Committees of the National Assembly are entitled to ask the Legislative Counsel Office to draft Bills. A person who intends to ask the Legislative Counsel Office to draft any Bill, shall attach a summary of legislation that they intend to enact and data related to such Bill. Upon receiving a request from legislators for drafting any Bill, the Legislative Counsel Office organizes a team and the team works to grasp intentions of legislators who have asked for drafting the Bill and to examine problems involving the Bill. The team completes the drafting of the Bill after revising and supplementing the grounds of introducing the Bill and key points of the Bill. When the drafting of the Bill is complete, legislative researchers in charge of the work, the head of the Legislative Counsel Office and legislative counselors hold a meeting to examine the draft Bill and they, if necessary, supplement the draft Bill after hearing opinions of relevant institutions, experts or interested persons.

5.2.2 Examinations of Committees

When any Bill is introduced, the Speaker distributes the bill to the members of the National Assembly, reports it to the plenary session and refers it to the competent Standing Committee. The Speaker decides on which Standing Committee takes charge of a bill and in cases where the competent Standing Committee is unclear, he/she makes the decision after consulting with the Steering Committee. With respect to any bill that is deemed especially necessary, the Speaker may refer it to a Special Committee after consulting with the Steering Committee of the National Assembly after obtaining a resolution by the plenary session of the National Assembly.

Each Committee votes on any bill through the following process: the explanation of purposes by its introducer, a report on the outcome of examination by special counsels of the committee, general debate, public hearings, a report on the examination by the sub-committee, article-by-article examination. Each Committee, if necessary, may set up a sub-committee mandated to examine any specific bill and then makes a final examination of such specific bill at its plenary session according to the outcome of the examination by the sub-committee.

5.2.3 Examination by the Legislation and Judiciary Committee

When the competent Committee completes the examination of any bill, the bill is referred to the Legislation and Judiciary Committee in order for it to undergo the examination of its system, forms and wordings. The enactment or amendment of any Act results in changing the current system. The objectives of law-making must be attained while keeping them in balance with other Acts and in conformity with the provisions of the Constitution. The Legislation and Judiciary Committee examines whether the contents of any bill are unconstitutional, whether the bill is in conflict with relevant Acts, whether its balance is maintained and whether its provisions are contradictory to each other, and examines the correctness of the relevant Act and the suitability and uniformity of legal terms used in various Acts.

5.2.4 Deliberation at Plenary Session

After examination by the Legislation and Judiciary Committee, bills are sent to the plenary session. The chairperson whose Committee has examined and passed the bills reports the bills to the plenary session. The Introducer of the bill has to explain the purposes of the bill in the plenary session. The plenary session may vote after the process of question and debate is finished.

5.3 *Legislative Process in the Executive*

Bills of Acts and subordinate statutes introduced by the competent Ministries need to go through legislative process in the Executive. Legislative Process in the Executive includes complicated process.

5.3.1 Drafting of Acts and Subordinate Statutes

The ministries and agencies that are in charge of planning policies draft bills on matters under their respective jurisdictions. In cases where the contents of any bill are concerned with administrative affairs under the jurisdiction of more than two ministries, such ministries may jointly draft the bill.

In the case of any draft Ordinance of a ministry that overlaps in contents with that of any other ministry, the ministries concerned jointly prepare the draft Ordinance as their joint Ordinance.

The drafting of Acts and subordinate statutes is a series of processes in which the policy objectives of administrative agencies are explicitly expressed in clear and explicit words. The offices in charge of drafting Acts and subordinate statutes are required to analyze and forecast contents of policy goals, effects of the legislation, financial needs, optional alternatives, their impact on the current legal system.

5.3.2 Consultation with Relevant Ministries

After the drafting of any bill is complete, consultations on the details of the bill with relevant ministries are required. When any ministry completes the drafting of a bill, the ministry is required to consult with other relevant ministries about the contents of the bill and to coordinate contents of it. The ministry in charge of drafting Acts and subordinate is required to consult with the Ministry of Strategy and Finance about matters concerning budgetary needs, with the Ministry of Public Administration and Security about matters concerning the government organization and the local self-rule and with other relevant ministries about the inherent administrative affairs of such other ministries that are prescribed by the Government Organization Act. It is customary that all of the relevant ministries hold prior consultations. The prior consultations are necessary to ensure smooth cooperation among ministries in the course of enforcing Acts and subordinate statutes.

5.3.3 Consultation Between Government and Political Parties

Consultations between the government and the ruling party or cooperation with opposition parties are to be held when it is necessary. The government may hold consultations with the ruling party when it drafts major Acts that greatly affect key policy matters of the country and also may seek cooperation from opposition parties. This process is expected to raise the effectiveness of policies by harmonizing the position of the Executive with that of the political parties and facilitating smooth legislation in the National Assembly.

5.3.4 Administrative Preannouncement of Legislation

The Administrative Procedure Act requires administrative agencies to give administrative preannouncement of legislation that affects the rights and duties of citizens or the daily lives of citizens. A period for the administrative preannouncement of legislation is not less than 40 days. Anyone who holds his/her opinion on any bill may put forth his/her opinion. The administrative preannouncement of legislation of any bill is designed to make its contents related directly to the daily life of the people known in advance to them, to reflect various opinions of the people in its legislation, to expand the people's participation in the legislative process, to democratize the contents of legislation and to implement efficiently national policies through increased effectiveness of Acts and subordinate statutes. The administrative preannouncement of legislation may be omitted in cases where such legislation is urgently needed, prior publication is not necessary or difficult on the grounds of the nature of its contents or on other grounds, such legislation is designed simply to enforce any higher Act and subordinate statute, and the administrative preannouncement of legislation is expected to little affect the public interest.

5.3.5 Examination of Regulation by the Regulatory Reform Committee

When any draft Act and subordinate statute containing matters concerning regulations includes matters restricting the rights of the people or imposing obligations upon the people in order to achieve specific administrative objectives, the Regulatory Reform Committee must examine the bill. When every ministry intends to initiate any draft Act and subordinate statute containing matters concerning regulations, which includes matters laid down by public notices, ordinances and rules by the delegation of Acts, Presidential Decrees, Ordinances of the Prime Minister and Ministerial Ordinances and results in restricting the people's rights and imposing duties on the people, such ministry is required to file an application, accompanied by a statement on the regulatory impact analysis, a statement on the opinion following its own deliberation and a written summary of opinions put forth by administrative agencies and persons interested. The Regulatory Reform Committee must examine the draft Act and subordinate statute after undergoing the self examination by each administrative agency concerned of the regulatory impact analysis, the objectives and scopes of the regulations and methods of the regulations and opinions of persons interested and experts in accordance with the Framework Act on Administrative Regulations.

5.3.6 Examination of Bills by the Ministry of Government Legislation

The Ministry of Government Legislation establishes and executes the Government Legislation Planning System for the effective processing of annual government legislation. The Government Legislation Planning System controls the order of priority, opportunity and contents of government legislative Bills across the entire government spectrum. The Ministry of Government Legislation examines the bills proposed by the Ministries, not only the formal aspects of the relevant legislative details, such as legal terms and system of legal wording, but also practical aspects, such as their appropriateness, their level of conformity with the objectives of state affairs, their level of compliance with higher Acts and subordinate statutes. Any ministry that has initiated a draft Act and subordinate statute asks the Ministry of Government Legislation for examining the draft Act and subordinate statute after going through agreement with other relevant ministries and the examination of regulations by the Regulatory Reform Committee. In a bid to ensure the faithfulness and fairness of the examination, the Ministry of Government Legislation holds a joint bill examination meeting attended by government legislative officers and senior staff to examine all of draft Acts and major draft subordinate statutes. The examination of Acts and subordinate statutes is an act that performs a prior right relief function and serves a prior normative control role, which is aimed at preventing any Act and subordinate statute that carries illegal and unjust provisions in violation of the Constitution and other higher Acts and subordinate statutes from being enacted to infringe on the people's freedom and rights. Draft Acts, draft Presidential Decrees, draft Ordinances of the Prime Minister, draft Ministerial Ordinances, draft treaties, draft presidential directives, and draft directives of the Prime Minister are all subject to the examination of the Ministry of Government Legislation. In addition, all administrative rules, such as ministry directives, regulations, public notice are required to undergo the ex post examination of the Ministry of Government Legislation in order to ensure their legality.

5.3.7 Deliberation at State Council

When the Ministry of Government Legislation completes its examination of any draft Act and any draft Presidential Decree, such draft Act and draft Presidential Decree are put on the agenda of the State Council after undergoing examination by the vice-ministerial meeting. The vice-ministerial meeting deliberates on key matters of Bills in advance to be put on the agenda of the State Council and in the case of emergency, any bill may be put on the agenda of the State Council without undergoing the deliberation at the vice-ministerial meeting. The State Council is a top policy deliberation organ mandated to deliberate on important policies and holds the status of a constitutional institution. The State Council hears proposal explanations of Bills from the ministers of competent ministries and resolves, if requested, after undergoing debates.

5.3.8 Signature of President

Bills and Presidential Decrees passed in the State Council require the signature of the President. The President is required to sign and the Prime Minister and the ministers of competent ministries are required to countersign every draft Act and Presidential Decree. When a draft Act or a draft Presidential Decree is countersigned by the Prime Minister and the ministers of competent ministries after the State Council votes for it, the Ministry of Government Legislation submits it to the Office of the President for the President to sign it.

5.3.9 Submission of Bills to National Assembly

Draft Acts, after obtaining the signature of the President, are promptly submitted to the National Assembly. After the President signs Bills, the Minister of Government Legislation submits the bills to the National Assembly. When any bill is proposed or submitted to the National Assembly, the Speaker reports it to the plenary session, refers it to the competent standing committee. After completing examinations of bills by the competent standing committee, the bills are referred to the Legislation and Judiciary Committee for the examination of terms and system of legal wording. Then, the bills are to be deliberated upon and resolved at the plenary session of the National Assembly.

5.3.10 Promulgation

When a bill is transferred to the Government from the National Assembly, the Ministry of Government Legislation prepares a draft promulgation of the bill and submits it on the agenda of the State Council. The State Council determines whether the bill is promulgated. If any objection is raised to the bill, the President may exercise the veto power. The President is required to return the Bill accompanied by an objection statement to the National Assembly within 15 days from the date on which the bill is transferred to the Government and the President may ask the National Assembly to deliberate again on the bill. In cases where the State Council resolves to promulgate the bill as it is, the Prime Minister and ministers of competent ministries countersign the bill and then the President signs it. After finishing these processes, the bill is promulgated by being published in the Official Gazette. The Korean Government offers an online version of the Official Gazette.

In the case of any draft Presidential Decree, it is published in the Official Gazette after the Prime Minister and ministers of competent ministries countersign it and then the President signs it after undergoing deliberation thereon by the State Council. Ordinances of the Prime Minister and Ministerial Ordinances are published by competent ministries in the Official Gazette after the completion of their examination by the Ministry of Government Legislation.

6 Prospect of Korean Law

Laws and regulations are important methods for implementing national policies and democratizing societies. After the introduction of the modern legal system at the end of the twentieth century, the legal system of Korea has developed and accomplished a lot by accepting democratic and effective systems. Responding to increasing social demand for the democratization of the legal system, Korea has established legal infrastructure that fosters transparency, public participation, freedom of information, and judicial review to promote democracy and sustain economic development.

Many laws have been enacted to guarantee more free and democratic society. The efforts to reform judicial process for fair trials have been done. These achievements are substantial for the Korean legal system for more effective law and democratic legal process.

Korean law and procedure still have a long way to go beyond these accomplishments. Due to the growing demand of legislation in the modern and welfare nations, the number of laws and regulations has been rapidly increased in Korea. As a consequence of the surplus of laws and regulations, the effectiveness and efficiency of laws and regulations have been weakened. As a result, the purpose of legislation has not been achieved, and the side effects that legislators did not expect at Bill drafting stage have occurred, which lead to the crisis of legislation or the failure of legislation. The Korean legal system will be facing a drastic procedural and substantive change in the near future. Korea needs to establish a more open, responsive legal system. The legal system has to facilitate greater access to legal services and courts, and to make judges more responsive to citizens' requests. Exchanges and cooperation among individuals, enterprises and countries are increased due to the expansion of open networks and the development of communications technologies. More legal websites of the Korean law in English should be produced to enable access to free and uncountable information on the Korean legal system through the Internet.

In order to make better laws and less regulation, it is necessary to introduce a system of evaluating legislative impact in the Korean legal system, which analyzes the comprehensive impact of legislation scientifically and objectively through the whole process of legislation. By developing the Korean legal system constantly, the protection of civil rights and national competitiveness will be firmly enhanced.

References

Constitutional Court (2008) The twenty years of the Constitutional Court of Korea, Seoul, p 149

Kim C-y (2011) From despair to hope: economic policymaking in Korea, 1945–1979. KDI, Seoul, pp 127–128

Park K-s (2011) Public Administration Law (in Korean), 8th edn. Bakyoungsa, Seoul, pp 430–431

Song S-h (ed) (1996) Korean law in the global economy. Bakyoungsa, Seoul, pp 3–5

Won-chol O (2009) The Korea story: President Park Jung-hee's Leadership and the Korean Industrial Revolution. Wisdom Tree, Seoul, p 25

Websites

The National Assembly of Korea (http://korea.assembly.go.kr/index.jsp)
The Supreme Court of Korea (http://eng.scourt.go.kr/eng/main/Main.work)
The Constitutional Court of Korea (http://www.ccourt.go.kr/home/english/index.jsp)
The Ministry of Government Legislation of Korea (http://www.moleg.go.kr/english/)
The Ministry of Justice of Korea (http://www.moj.go.kr/HP/ENG/index.do)
The National Assembly Research Service of Korea (http://www.nars.go.kr/english/index)
Korea Legislation Research Institute (http://elaw.klri.re.kr)

Constitutional Law

Jongcheol Kim

1 Introduction

This chapter aims to introduce an outline and the main features of the Constitution of the Republic of Korea (hereinafter the "ROK") and to examine recent developments of constitutional democracy in the ROK. I will begin with a brief sketch of the history of constitutionalism in modern Korea. Next comes a section explaining the structure of the Constitution in terms of the two pillars of constitutionalism: democracy and the protection of basic human rights. Before jumping into the conclusion, I will look into the unique part of the Korean Constitution on the relationship between the State and the economy. The concluding part consists of features of Korean constitutionalism in the present context.

1.1 A Brief History of Constitutionalism in Modern Korea

1.1.1 Unique Constitutional Reality: Divided Polity

The ROK, internationally known as South Korea, is located in the Korean Peninsula between China and Japan in the East Asian region. After liberated from Japanese colonial rule between 1910 and 1945, the Peninsula was politically divided into two different polities in the course of military occupations, respectively, by the USA in the South and the Soviet Union in the North until 1948. The Korean War, which lasted from 1950 to 1953, consolidated this division of territory and then the two Koreas have been so far regarded as separate independent countries at least at an international level. However, since 1948 when the first effective constitutional

J. Kim (✉)
Yonsei Law School, Seoul, Republic of Korea
e-mail: jkim386@yonsei.ac.kr

Korea Legislation Research Institute, *Introduction to Korean Law*,
DOI 10.1007/978-3-642-31689-0_2, © Springer-Verlag Berlin Heidelberg 2013

government within the territory was launched, the ROK Constitution has explicitly declared that the ROK is the only legitimate country in the Korean Peninsula while imposing a mission of reunification on State authorities as a whole (current Article 3 and Article 4). Given that, the ROK courts recognize the Democratic Peoples' Republic of Korea (hereinafter the "DPRK"), internationally known as North Korea, as a unique political organization having double legal entities; on the one hand, the counterpart of the ROK in the political negotiations on reunification; and, on the other hand, a subversive organization of which political activities as well as other individuals' or organizations' activities supporting them can be prohibited and sanctioned according to the procedures prescribed by law.[1]

A fundamental difference between the two Koreas lies in their nature of constitutional systems. The ROK is based on constitutional democracy while the DPRK has developed a totalitarian political system based upon a combined ideology of both Marxism–Leninism and the "Juche Idea", a nationalistic ideology formulated by Kim Il-sung, emphasizing on the Korean People's spirit of self-reliance and independence. Now I will focus here on the development of constitutionalism of the ROK.

1.1.2 The Features and Legacy of the First Constitution of 1948

As soon as it became clear that the political deadlock in the negotiation process towards a unified new nation between the Soviet-occupied Northern territory and the US-occupied Southern half could not be solved in a short period, the US military government decided to allow the Korean People to establish a new nation within the Southern territory. On May 10, 1948, the first general election took place to establish the National Assembly as the legislative branch with the special competence of constitution-making.

The first constitution of 1948 was known to be influenced by the German Weimar Constitution 1919 at least in terms of the latters characteristic propensity for social justice as a basic norm governing the relationship between the State and society in general (economy in particular). It not only explicitly listed social rights such as the right to education, the right to work and the right to membership in trade unions along with civil and political rights, but also chartered social justice or public welfare as a basic standard to regulate economic freedom and the exercise of the right to hold property.[2] Although this inclination to social justice was not effectively realized in reality, its legacy was so strong that the ensuing constitutions have continued to keep this value as a governing norm on social and economic

[1] Constitutional Court Decision 92Hun-Ba48, July 29, 1993, *Decisions of the Korean Constitutional Court*, Vol. 5, No. 2, 65; Supreme Court Decision 2007Do10121 (Kong2011Sang, 148).

[2] The radical feature of the First Constitution can be identified by two representative provisions. First, workers are constitutionally entitled to the equal allotment of profits earned by private companies (Article 18). Second, it declared that economic order is based upon the accomplishment of social justice guaranteeing basic needs in normal life of every citizen and the well-balanced development of the national economy (Article 84).

relationships between individuals and the state. For example, what survived 9 revisions of the first constitution over 60 years was the format of the Constitution in that a separate chapter is given to the subject of national economy allowing a regulatory or facilitative role of the State over the economy to enhance public welfare, although there have been changes in its tone and the scope of the state's involvement in economy.

The "nominal" feature of the first constitution can also be found in the gap between the form of government envisaged in constitutional arrangements and its actual operation in reality. It adopted a modified presidential system incorporating a variety of institutional elements peculiar to a parliamentary system. The President was elected by the National Assembly rather than by the direct vote of the people. The State Council consisting of the President, the Prime Minister and State Councilors was envisaged to be the highest deliberative authority within the Executive, so that it should pass a resolution on major constitutional agenda referred to the President as the head of the Executive. However, contrary to the literal institutional arrangements in the Constitution, the First President Syng-man Rhee and his supporters tried to make the State Council and other constitutional authorities within the executive "nominal" institutions by yielding President's power as if the executive power was, like the USA, vested in the President alone. What is worse than the distorted operation of the executive power was President Rhee's relationship with the opposition and the National Assembly. President Rhee, who had been respected as a national hero due to his consistent commitment to the independence movement in the colonial period, had a tendency to ignore the principle of checks and balances and misuse political and executive power to oppress political opposition from the National Assembly and opposition parties. This gap between constitutional ideals and reality caused continuous political conflicts between the ruling class and the opposition during the Rhee government.[3] Not surprisingly, the first and second amendments of the First Constitution made, respectively, in 1952 and 1954 were the result of a wave of political strife caused mainly by the different views among political groups on how to reconcile the President's power with that of other administrative agencies and the National Assembly.

1.1.3 The Sagas of the Constitutional Amendments in 1952 and 1954

The 1952 constitutional amendment was motivated by President Rhee's supporters to introduce the direct presidential election to get rid of the power to elect the President from the National Assembly. Although this constitutional change was made in the course of severe political oppressions accompanied by the illegal abuse of law-enforcement power and was intended in bad faith to strengthen political influence of President Rhee whose chance of reelection was seemingly very dim

[3] Kwon Y-s (2006), pp. 142–143, 149–151.

because of his confrontations with the majority of the National Assembly, its long-term impact on the Korean constitutional history is not all negative, because the experience of direct election of the President became a legacy in the long process of democratization in following periods.

This ambivalent evaluation can be applicable to the 1954 constitutional amendment, too. It was unarguably initiated by President Rhee's faction to make a detour for him to be eligible for a third term, prohibited by the old constitution. President Rhee's faction conspired to make an exception for the incumbent President Rhee to serve for two more terms by making constitutional changes for, among others, the introduction of a referendum with the propaganda of strengthening democracy. Although this change was marred by not only its hidden conspiracy but also its procedural error in implementing a two-third quorum in the National Assembly for constitutional amendment, the propaganda for direct democracy contributed to the democratic education of the people.

1.1.4 The Civil Revolutionary Constitution of 1960

Dissatisfaction with the authoritarian rule of President Rhee for more than a decade in general, and the rigged presidential election in 1960 in particular, prompted the Korean people to overthrow the Rhee government in order to enhance constitutional democracy. With this first civil revolution in 1960, the new constitution went into effect. It adopted a parliamentary system to wipe out the authoritarian image of the presidential system. In a reaction to the nightmare of a rigged election, the Electoral Commission was constitutionalized as an independent agency with a nationalized organization. The constitutional entity of the Electoral Commission has so far been kept as one of the institutional features of Korean constitutional arrangements. Aside from a change in the form of government, the 1960 Constitution tried to strengthen the safeguards of fundamental rights. For example, it set a limitation on legislative power to regulate basic human rights by making the essential elements of each basic right unrestricted under any circumstances. In addition, reflecting the previous government's political oppression on the opponent, it absolutely prohibited censorship and prior restraints on assembly and association of the people. Moreover, the 1960 Constitution introduced, for the first time, the constitutional court as the final arbiter of the Constitution with the power of constitutional review.[4] However, it was not able to take a full opportunity to put these institutions into practice due to the military coup in 1961.

The collapse of the constitutional government set up as a result of a civil revolution had a significant impact on the development of Korean constitutionalism from then on. For example, by the short-lived experience of a parliamentary system,

[4] In the previous constitutions, the Constitutional Commission as a special agency has the competence of constitutional adjudication. However, the composition of the Constitutional Court could not be completed as the constitution was ceased by the military coup.

bad memory on this form of government was inscribed in the constitutional history of Korea and thus several attempts to switch to a parliamentary system once more have failed to obtain significant popular support. However, the spirit of self-determination and eagerness to the protection of basic human rights, which blossomed in the course of the civil revolution, remained at the heart and mind of the Korean people and became the driving force of unstopped movements for constitutional democracy challenging the longstanding authoritarian regimes that followed the military coup in 1961.

1.1.5 Military Junta, Party State and Pseudo-Constitutionalist Autocracy Between 1961 and 1979

After around two years' rule of the military junta, constitutional democracy was restored by the 1962 Constitution.[5] This Constitution returned to the presidential system in which the President was to be elected for a term of four years by direct public ballot and was barred from re-election for a third term. Aside from this change in the form of government, there are four main features of the 1962 Constitution that are worth mentioning. First, it constitutionalized the idea of the "party system" in which political parties were constitutionally recognized and every candidate for public office like the President as the head of the Executive and the members of the National Assembly was required to be nominated by any constitutionally recognized political parties. The legacy of the party system remained in the following constitutions until now, although the mandatory party nomination for elected public offices was abolished. Second, it gave for the first time to the Supreme Court the jurisdiction of constitutional review on the constitutionality of laws, which had been granted to a specialized commission or independent court since the First Constitution of 1948. The system of judicial review lasted until the Constitution 1972, and returned to the specialized commission system partly because the then authoritarian leader Chung-hee Park was dissatisfied with the Supreme Court's decision striking down the State Compensation Act in 1971. Third, it introduced a referendum for the process of constitutional amendment which has survived ensuing constitutional revisions to date. Fourth, it extended the power of the audit board which had been constitutionalized since 1948 by giving it the general power of inspection over the performance of the executive agencies and public servants of which a legislatively-created inspection agency had taken charge. The newly created Board of Audit and Inspection as a presidential commission continues to exist without significant changes until now and becomes another unique feature of Korean constitutional arrangements.

The constitutional democracy based upon the 1962 Constitution which had once been marred by the controversial amendment for extending the maximum number of terms of the President from two to three terms in 1969 came finally to the end by

---

[5] The Constitution of 1962 was enacted in 1962 but came into effect in December 1963.

a kind of self-inflicted palace coup organized by the then President Chung-hee Park in 1971. With the successful enactment of the 1972 Constitution, later known as the notorious "*Yushin* Constitution", President Park institutionalized an autocratic rule under the slogan "Korean-style democracy," which could not be compatible with the ideals and principles of constitutionalism, such as the separation of powers and the rule of law. The sovereign power of the people was constitutionally delegated to the National Convention for Self-Dependent Reunification, the chairperson of which was the President selected by itself rather than the direct public ballot. The President was intended to overpower other governmental branches and partisan-oriented political order in that he was entitled, among others, to select a third of members of the National Assembly and place an emergency order with the effect of restraining individual's basic rights.

1.1.6 Transition to the Flourishing Constitutional Democracy After 1980

The pseudo-constitutional regime collapsed thanks to the assassination of President Park by his right-hand man in the course of increasing challenges and resistance of the people calling for the restoration of constitutional democracy in 1979. However, despite the fall of President Park, the swift restoration of verified constitutional democracy did not occur since a group of military officers led by General Doo-whan Chun, the then head of the Military Security Force, successfully took over political power through a series of military coups in 1979 and 1980.[6] The new constitution of 1980 enacted by a referendum under martial order adopted a hyper-presidentialist governmental system where the President elected by the electoral college was envisaged to have ultimate executive authority overpowering other government branches. One symbolic camouflage of this autocratic system was the fact that the elected President was prohibited from rerunning after his or her first 7-year term, but such change could not be applied to the incumbent President. This institutional limitation to prevent long-term autocratic rule received strong support from the people, which made it survive the constitutional amendment in the wake of the People's uprising in 1987, although the term was reduced from seven years to five years. Although the 1980 Constitution had a fine list of fundamental rights and adopted, like previous constitutions, a constitutional review system, it has never been activated so that no cases were delivered partly because the Supreme Court with the power of initial review was very reluctant to refer those cases worth being reviewed to the constitutional adjudication process.

The rule with an iron fist under the 1980 Constitution led people to participate in the consistent movement for democratization. The aim of this longstanding movement was to revise the Constitution to restore the direct presidential election system and the checks and balances mechanism in constitutional arrangements which had been mostly disappeared since 1972. The people's determination to change the

[6] Supreme Court (en banc) Decision 96Do3376 (Jip45(1)Hyung, 1; Gong1997.5.1.(33), 1303).

authoritarian status quo expressed in the general election of 1985, which returned a victory to the opposition even in the oppressed political atmosphere. Stimulated by the victorious outcome of the election, the opposition started its campaign for constitutional amendment with an emphasis on the reform of presidential election to a direct ballot system. However, on April 23, 1987 President Chun refused to accept this request, and declared the next presidential election would take place through the electoral college system under the old constitution, mimicked as a "gymnasium election." As dissatisfaction with President Chun increased, the people poured out into the streets to demonstrate against his plan and, finally, the then presidential candidate Tae-woo Roh and the ruling Democratic Justice Party agreed with the constitutional amendment. The new constitution was drafted by a joint committee consisting of four equal number of representatives from the ruling Democratic Justice Party and the first opposition New Korea Democratic Party. By this constitutional amendment triggered by the People's Uprising 1987, constitutional democracy that had been collapsed or suspended since 1972 finally resumed in Korea. The 1987 Constitution, the ninth from the First Constitution of 1948, consolidated democracy and the rule of law to the level and extent that modern Koreans had never experienced until that time. It has successfully managed five consecutive peaceful transfers of government and is developing a stable system of human rights protection.

1.2 Characteristics of Korean Constitutional History from 1948 to 1987

Since the enactment of the First Constitution of 1948, nine constitutional amendments have been made. Although there were differences among these amendments, it is worthy to point out that only one amendment was nothing to do with change in governmental structure. The fifth amendment in November 29, 1962 was intended to provide interim measures in the addendum of the Constitution to sanction in retrospect those involved in illegal and corrupt activities under the Rhee Administration. It implied that lack of democratic tradition and relatively less consciousness of constitutionalism in society, as a whole, in the nation-building process tends to make the political system instable. However, Korean constitutionalism, even before 1987, developed a number of significant characteristics in the course of longstanding democratization.

First, as far as the form of government is concerned, representative democracy has always been guaranteed and such means as to allow direct involvement of the people in the governance have been exceptional. Referendum has been stipulated to be called upon under particular conditions while popular initiatives or recall has never been reflected in constitutional arrangements. Moreover, the presidential system has been preferred to the parliamentary system. Despite of this preference, however, it should be borne in mind that the presidential system implemented in modern Korea has been, in large part, adapted by some elements inherent in the parliamentary system. For example, in most Constitutions, the executive powers were not granted to the President alone, but a collective entity of administrative agencies and committees as a whole. As a corollary, it is not difficult to see that the Prime Minister, the State Council and State Councilors have been parts of the executive branch in most Constitutions. This feature remains in the present Constitution.

Second, most Constitutions, except the Constitutions of 1952, 1954 and 1960, have not adopted a bicameral system. It means that the period for which the Korean legislature consisted of two chambers was less than 10 years out of more than 60 years of the total constitutional history.

Third, all the Constitutions with no exception tended to empower the Legislature to exercise broad discretion in law-making, so that it has enjoyed great authority to elaborate on and/or supplement what the Constitutions explicitly delegated to the Legislature or left in abeyance. Unlike the Constitution of the United States where Congress can act only as prescribed by the Constitution, the legislative body was vested with the general regulatory power to guarantee national security and public order, or even to promote public welfare.

Fourth, there has always been a system of constitutional adjudication expressly entrenched in the provisions of the Constitutions, whether or not separate from the ordinary judiciary, although their performance can scarcely be said active. The present Constitution also has the Constitutional Court with the competence of five constitutional adjudicative powers.

Fifth, from the beginning, all Constitutions had a Bill of Rights ranged from civil and political rights to social, economical and cultural rights though such guarantees could hardly have reached its full-fledged level in practice.

1.3 An Outline of the Constitution

The present Constitution of 1987 features full-fledged constitutionalism by making both democracy and the protection of human rights entrenched. The Constitution, starting with the preamble, consists of 130 articles categorized into 10 chapters and addenda of 6 articles.

The preamble declares that the constituent power lies in the people of Korea "with the pride of a resplendent history and traditions dating from time immemorial", and describes the constitution-making process since 1948. It is worth noting that the preamble makes clear that the legitimacy of the Constitution stems from the Provisional Government established in the wake of the March First Independence Movement of 1919. It also elaborates on the visions and goals that the ROK has pursued through its constitutional history, for example, the enhancement of basic free and democratic order, contribution to lasting world peace and the common prosperity of mankind, and the safeguards of security, liberty and happiness for the people of Korea.

The first chapter, consisting of nine articles, sets forth general provisions. It includes three basic elements of the national state (sovereignty, nation, territory), a sacred mission for reunification imposed upon the constitutional polity as a whole, and general principles and basic institutions essential to constitutional democracy, such as the renunciation of all armed aggressions, respect for international law and principles, the political neutrality of the Armed Forces, the political impartiality of public officials, and the protection of political parties.

The second chapter is the Bill of Rights and Duties of the Nationals. The ensuing four chapters grant powers to the four branches of government: the National Assembly as the legislature, the Executive as the executive branch, the Courts as the ordinary judiciary and the Constitutional Court as a specialized adjudication authority.

The seventh chapter stipulates an electoral management mechanism on top of which hierarchy is the National Election Commission. The eighth chapter consists of two short articles devoted to brief principles of local autonomy.

One chapter showing a unique characteristic of Korean constitutionalism is the ninth chapter, which provides basic principles of national economic order and the relationship between the State and the economy.

The last chapter provides constitutional amendment procedures consisting of two stages: a concurrent vote of the National Assembly and a national referendum on the amendment proposal.

2 Fundamental Principles of the Constitution

2.1 The Principles of Popular Sovereignty and Democracy

The polity that the Constitution of the ROK has intended to establish and maintain is a democratic republic. Korea had a monarch before Japan's colonization, but became one of the few countries that the restoration of a monarch has never been seriously debated in the course of liberation after World War II. It has always been taken for granted since at least 1948 that the Korean people shall have the sovereign authority and all the powers of the government branches and agencies established by the Constitution shall be emanated from the people. What the present Constitution establishes to accomplish the ideal of democratic republic is a representative form of government rather than that of direct democracy. Although the people have the basic right to vote in elections to select members of the National Assembly and the President as the head of the State and the Executive, it is the representative branches that are constitutionally vested with the power of deciding the direction of policies and the ways of implementing them.

Only on two occasions are the people exceptionally empowered to take part in the decision-making process within the Constitution. First, the people are entitled to have a final say on whether a proposal to amend or revise the Constitution initiated by either the President or the majority of the total members of the National Assembly and then concurred by two thirds or more of the total members of the National Assembly [Article 130(2)]. Second, the people may have an opportunity to decide upon important policies relating to diplomacy, national defense, unification and other matters relating to the fate of the nation in a national referendum proposed by the President (Article 72). However, even in those cases where the people have a constitutional power or the right to take part in a referendum, the power to call a referendum on both occasions is granted to the President or the National Assembly.[7]

This system of representative government poses a critical danger of relegating the principle of popular sovereignty to a nominal justification for oligarchy or elitist democracy unless the people's right to vote is so entrenched to afford a real voice in elections of representatives. To make the right to vote be realized to the fullest extent possible, Article 24 safeguards the right to vote as a basic right as prescribed by the Act of the National Assembly, while Articles 41(1) and 66(1) provide the principles of universal, equal, direct and secret ballot by the people in presidential and National Assembly elections. It is well established in Korean constitutional jurisprudence that political rights, including the right to vote, are considered to hold a "supreme status over other fundamental rights in order to realize the principle of popular sovereignty" so that restrictions on such rights can be justified only when an extraordinary and compelling reason exists.[8] In 2007, the Constitutional Court invalidated an electoral law denying the right of Korean nationals residing abroad to vote in presidential and National Assembly elections on the grounds that the requirement of residence registration as a determinative factor to deny the eligibility of vote is of no rational legislative purpose and therefore violates the right to vote, the right to the equal treatment of Korean nationals abroad, and the principle of universal suffrage.[9] Changing its previous stance in the case with the same merit,[10] the Court unanimously held that reasons, such as obscure and intangible risks with regard to fairness of election or misuse of voting rights, financial difficulties or technical obstacles which can be overcome through efforts by the government, are not justifiable grounds for restricting such a supreme right pertaining to the principle of popular sovereignty.

[7] In the impeachment case against President Moo-hyun Roh, the Constitutional Court ruled that the President has discretion to decide whether a referendum is deemed necessary (Constitutional Court Decision 2004Hun-Na1, May 14, 2004, *Decisions of the Korean Constitutional Court*, Vol. 16, No. 1, 609).

[8] The Right to Vote of Nationals Residing Abroad Case (Constitutional Court Decision 2004Hun-Ma644, 2005Hun-Ma360 (Consolidated), June 28, 2007, *Decisions of the Korean Constitutional Court*, Vol. 19, No. 1, 859).

[9] Ibid., 859.

[10] Constitutional Court Decision 97Hun-Ma253·270 (Consolidated), January 28, 1999, *Decisions of the Korean Constitutional Court*, Vol. 11, No. 1, 54.

2.2 The Separation of Powers

The government envisaged in the present Constitution is a limited one. This is so, not only because one assumption underlying modern constitutionalism is a distrust in the government in general, but also because the Korean people had so far suffered from grave misuses and abuses of governmental power, especially by authoritarian Presidents.

One major tenet pertaining to limited government is the principle of separation of powers. It is designed to set structural limitations on constitutional arrangements to avoid the risk of official oppression by distributing governmental powers among different state branches and by allowing one branch to check and balance misguided or illegal actions of another.[11]

As outlined above, the Constitution distributes governmental powers to the National Assembly, the Executive, the Courts, the Constitutional Court and the National Election Commission. One feature the Constitution contains in this regard is that there are express provisions to guarantee autonomy and self-regulation of each branch. For example, each branch has the power to make rules of proceedings and internal regulations within the statutory boundaries in Article 64(1), Articles 75 and 95, Article 108, Article 113(2), and Article 114(6), respectively.

Aside from this formal distribution of powers, a subtle functional mechanism designed to impede the possible abuse of power is provided for in the Constitution. A number of provisions vest consenting or approving power in the National Assembly. This ranges from consent to the appointment of certain public office holders like the Prime Minister, the Chairperson of the Board of Audit and Inspection, the Chief and panel of Justices of the Supreme Court and the President of the Constitutional Court, consent to the conclusion and ratification of treaties listed in the Constitution like one pertaining to mutual assistance or mutual security, to approvals for emergency orders having the effect of Act. The President is empowered to veto legislation if it deems necessary and the vetoed bill can be an Act only when re-passed with a concurrent vote of two thirds or more of the members of the Legislature present. Even effective Acts can be subject to constitutional review by the Constitutional Court. Ordinary courts have jurisdiction over unreasonable or illegal governmental activities while the Constitutional Court is granted the power to determine whether activities or omission of legislative and executive branches infringes basic rights of the people.

It is sometimes very difficult, however, to draw a clear line between functions of different branches partly because even original functions of each branch can

[11] In some countries, like the USA, the structural principle of checks and balances developed as a safeguard against the possible abuse of governmental power is regarded as an independent one, separate from that of the separation of powers (Currie D 2000). However, in Korean constitutional jurisprudence, the latter is often understood as incorporating the former (Huh Y 2010; Constitutional Court Decision 90Hun-Ba24, April 28, 1992, *Decisions of the Korean Constitutional Court*, Vol. 4, 225).

intervene in that of another or the relationship between them. If the Legislature makes an obscure or overly broad law, it may result in the arbitrary use of power by the Executive or the Judiciary. This may be incompatible not only with the rule of law, but also with the separation of powers.[12] A number of laws enacted in the authoritarian period to restrict judicial discretion in examination of evidence and sentencing by allowing too much power to the prosecutors or setting out mandatory sentencing clauses were declared unconstitutional on those grounds.[13] However, in a 7-2 decision, the Constitutional Court ruled that the law granting to the Chief Justice of the Supreme Court the power to recommend a special prosecutor is not a violation of the principle of separation of powers.[14]

In sum, it is notable that the present Constitution breaks with the old legacy of authoritarian presidency outclassing other branches, at least in constitutional arrangements, although there are still some criticisms challenging misguided or unreasonable practices deeply rooted in actual politics.[15]

2.3 The Rule of Law or the Principle of Rechtsstaat

Although there are a variety of understandings of the rule of law or *Rechtsstaat*,[16] no one can seriously deny that it is another tenet pertaining to a limited government in the sense that governmental activities intended to restrict the rights and freedoms of the people should be based on the law enacted by their representatives.[17] More

[12] Constitutional Court Decision 89Hun-Ga8, January 28, 1992, *Decisions of the Korean Constitutional Court*, Vol. 4, 4, 18; Constitutional Court Decision 90Hun-Ba23, April 14, 1992, *Decisions of the Korean Constitutional Court*, Vol. 4, 162, 171.

[13] Constitutional Court Decision 92Hun-Ga8, December 24, 1992, *Decisions of the Korean Constitutional Court*, Vol. 4, 853, 882–883; Constitutional Court Decision 95Hun-Ga5, January 25, 1996, *Decisions of the Korean Constitutional Court*, Vol. 1, 1, 18–19.

[14] Constitutional Court Decision 2007Hun-Ma1468, January 10, 2008, *Decisions of the Korean Constitutional Court*, Vol. 20, No. 1 Part 1, 1, 33–34.

[15] Above all, one remaining task in the democratization process is the reform of institutions and practices in relation to law-enforcement authorities, like the police, prosecutors, and national intelligence officials, which have arguably been major means of socio-political control by the authoritarian Presidents. See Kim J (2010c), p. 147.

[16] The doctrine of the rule of law may be discerned from that of *Rechtsstaat* at least in terms of its diverse ideological origins and different paths of development. However, considering the purpose and scope of this chapter, it would be safe to assume that both are the same at least in the constitutional implications and functions in constitutional democracies. In fact, the Constitutional Court and the ordinary courts have used these two ideas as similar principles in their constitutional meanings by often citing together in the same context (e.g., "The system of impeachment against the President intends to realize the rule of law or the principle of *Rechtsstaat* that every citizen is governed by law and even a man of national power does not stand above the law[Emphasis added.]." Constitutional Court Decision 2004Hun-Na1, May 14, 2004, *Decisions of the Korean Constitutional Court*, Vol. 16, No. 1, 632–632).

[17] Kwon Y (2010).

specifically, the rule of law requires executive power to be implemented according to law and any governmental wrongs should be redressed in the judicial process. It also requires that cases and controversies relating to individuals' rights, whether private or public, are to be effectively resolved according to law by independent authorities.

As the idea of constitutionalism evolved, the emphasis in the idea of the rule of law moved from the formal conception to the substantive one. Therefore, that law as a norm of government made in due process of legislation is not enough to fulfill the rule of law; the substance of law itself should be due or just. One implication of this change is that even the legislative power should be subject to constitutional review in terms of substantive standards of due law. Not surprisingly, with the development of constitutionalism across the globe since the middle of the twentieth century, constitutional adjudication has blossomed in new democracies as well as old democracies.

The ROK is not an exception to this trend. The 1987 Constitution adopts a constitutional adjudication system, including constitutional review of the law and constitutional complaints. It also entrenches not only the due process of law in Article 12(1) and 12(3), but also the requirement in restricting basic rights and freedoms, and the prohibition of law infringing essential elements of basic rights and freedoms in Article 37(2). Elaborating on such open-ended clauses, the Constitutional Court has established a couple of substantive standards pertaining to the idea of the rule of law, such as the rule of clarity of law, the principle of proportionality and the principle of legal expectation or protection of trust.

The rule of clarity or the Korean equivalent of the doctrine of "void-for-vagueness" in American constitutional law requires that law should be as clear as possible to guarantee predictability of the people whose lives are affected by it. Generally speaking, although the rule of clarity should be implemented in all areas of law, criminal law requires its strictest application under the principle of nulla poena sine lege. For example, the Constitutional Court annulled the Family Ritual Standards Act on the ground that the concept of "reasonable scope in light of the true meaning of family etiquette and rituals" used as an element of criminal punishment was not sufficiently predictable in overall content to be used as a guide for one's action and thus violated the rule of clarity.[18]

The principle of proportionality, usually called the prohibition of excessive restriction in Korea, is also well established in Korean constitutional case law. The Constitutional Court derived this principle, not only from the idea of the rule of law or the principle of *Rechtsstaat* inherent in the Constitution, but also from the requirement expressed in Article 37(2).[19] In a number of cases, it developed a four-tier test in reviewing state's restrictions on the basic rights and freedoms of individual citizens. The four substantive standards of this test are (1) legitimacy or rationality of the objective, (2) appropriateness of the means, (3) the least restrictive

---

[18] Constitutional Court Decision 98Hun-Ma168, October 15, 1998, *Decisions of the Korean Constitutional Court*, Vol. 10, No. 2, 586.

[19] Kim J (2010a), p. 130.

means, and (4) balance between the importance of public interest and the degree of infringement of freedoms or rights. Legislation intended to limit fundamental rights must meet these four requirements to pass the test and to be declared constitutional.[20] One feature of the Constitutional Court's reasoning in this regard is that such strict criteria are, in principle, expected to apply regardless of the nature of the rights and freedoms at stake. This is quite different from the jurisprudence of its American counterpart, such as the "doctrine of double standards" in which the nature and emphasis of rights in terms of the relationship between the rights and State interests tend to be considered in deciding the level of requirements for constitutional review. For example, the Constitutional Court has sometimes been criticized that it applied the strict standard, such as the least restrictive means test, not only when fundamental values or interests of democratic society are at stake, but also when general economic or social regulatory issues requiring less strict review, like the "rational basis test," are taken on board.[21]

The principle of legitimate expectation or the protection of trust is another infra-principle derived from the idea of the rule of law according to the Constitutional Court. It is dedicated to the protection of expectations or trust on the part of the people, formulated from the law existing at the time of their actions so that no new law to the detriment of the people whose actions completed before its promulgation should be applied to them.[22] One typical example of this principle is the prohibition of *ex post facto* criminal punishment stipulated in Article 13(1) of the Constitution. The Constitutional Court recognized the need for the protection of legitimate expectations beyond cases related to criminal punishment and annulled a provision of the Regulation of Tax Reduction and Exemption Act on the ground that the amendment of tax law to the disadvantage of taxpayers during the applicable period of taxation, without any transitional clauses, infringed their legitimate expectation in having relied upon the existing law.[23]

3 Basic Structure of Government

3.1 Form of Government

The form of government under the present Constitution is a presidential system which, like the previous Constitutions, has been modified to incorporate some

[20] Constitutional Court Decision 89Hun-Ga95, September 3, 1990, *Decisions of the Korean Constitutional Court*, Vol. 2, 245.

[21] Kim J (2005a).

[22] Constitutional Court Decision 96Hun-Ga2, 96Hun-Ba7·13 (Consolidated), February 16, 1996, *Decisions of the Korean Constitutional Court*, Vol. 8, No. 1, 51.

[23] Constitutional Court Decision 94Hun-Ba12, October 26, 1995, *Decisions of the Korean Constitutional Court*, Vol. 7, No. 2, 447.

elements of a parliamentary system. First, although the President is the head of the Executive as well as the head of the State, the executive power is vested in the executive branch as a whole, rather than in the President alone. The collective layout of the executive power, however, is not a significant erosion of the presidential form of government, because it is generally accepted that the President, as the head of the Executive, is empowered to have a final authority in the decision-making process within the Executive. That is, other executive organs are considered assistants to the President so that their constitutional powers are apt to perform the function of procedural checks and balances within the decision-making process of the executive branch.[24] For example, the State Council is the highest deliberative authority within the Executive, but it is arguably construed that the President may not be bound by a resolution of the State Council. In fact, no such occasions have taken place, partly because deliberation at the State Council tends to be coordinated at the preparation stage by the President's secretarial aids and it is almost unthinkable in Korean political culture for the Council to decide against the explicit intention of the President. If some Councilors have different opinions from the President's, they would resign rather than defy the President's unequivocal opinion.

Second, the Prime Minister who is designed to be appointed by the President with the consent of the National Assembly is next down from the President in the hierarchy of the Executive and in the position to direct the Executive Ministries under the order of the President. He (or she) also takes the positions of Vice-Chairperson of the State Council and the first possible acting President when the office of the presidency is vacant or the President is unable to perform his/her duties. Given this constitutional status, the Prime Minister is understood to be accountable to the National Assembly so that he (or she) be subject to the no-confidence recommendation of the Assembly, although the President is not legally bound to that motion.[25]

Third, unlike the US Constitution, the Executive has the constitutional power to introduce bills for consideration at the National Assembly.

Fourth, the heads of executive ministries, like countries with a parliamentary system, shall be appointed by the President among State Councilors on the recommendation of the Prime Minister, and a State Councilor or Minister can be appointed among members of the National Assembly.[26]

---

[24] Constitutional Court Decision 89Hun-Ma221, April 28, 1994, *Decisions of the Korean Constitutional Court*, Vol. 6, No. 1, 239. In this 8-1 decision where the Government Organization Act together with the National Security Planning Agency Act, the Constitutional Court held that the President is the final decision-maker within the executive branch while others including the Prime Minster are assistants to the President.

[25] In the presidential impeachment case of 2004, the Constitutional Court made clear that the resolution for the removal of the Prime Minister or State Councilors from office cannot be construed to have binding force on the President because the nature of the resolution is literally a recommendation rather than a self-executing final decision.

[26] Article 43 of the Constitution prohibits members of the National Assembly from concurrently holding any other office prescribed by law, but the office of a State Councilor or Minister does not fall into the category of statutory prohibited offices.

3.2 *The Legislative Branch: The National Assembly*

3.2.1 Composition of the National Assembly

The third chapter of the Constitution confers legislative authority on the National Assembly whose members are elected directly by the people for a four-year term. The National Assembly has the sole power to determine in the form of an Act, what kind of electoral systems, including proportional representation, can be adopted and how many members are elected, being no less than 200 (Article 41 of the Constitution).[27]

At present, the electoral system for the National Assembly is a modified relative majority system in which a total of 243 constituency representatives are chosen at a single-member district under the majority rule and the remaining 56 members are elected by the party list system in one national constituency. The present electoral system is the result of an electoral reform responding to a decision of the Constitutional Court in 2001. In this landmark election law case, it struck down the element of proportional representation of the old election law, which was designed to distribute seats according to the number of votes cast in favor of candidates of political parties in constituencies instead of allowing the voters to cast a separate ballot to party list of their own choice.[28]

The Constitution has several provisions about the status of the members of the National Assembly. They are entitled to two notable constitutional privileges. First, they are exempted from being arrested or detained during the sessions without the consent of the National Assembly, except in cases of flagrante delicto. When a member is in a state of detention or arrest prior to the opening of a session, he or she shall be released during the session upon the request of the National Assembly, except in cases of *flagrante delicto* (Article 44 of the Constitution). Second, they shall not be held responsible outside the National Assembly for opinions officially expressed or votes cast during the session (Article 45 of the Constitution).

3.2.2 Powers of National Assembly

The possible subject matters of legislation are, unlike the federal Constitution of the US, not listed in detail in the Constitution. Rather, there is one general provision permitting legislation to restrict the rights and freedoms of the people in Article 37(2) and a number of separate provisions across the Constitution granting general

---

[27] The number of members of the National Assembly is the only constitutional regulation except electoral principles of universal, equal, direct, and secret ballot. Therefore, minimal age, citizenship, and residence requirements for the members of the National Assembly, and restrictions on the right to vote are provided in the Election Act.

[28] Constitutional Court Decision 2000Hun-Ma91·112·134 (Consolidated), July 19, 2001, *Decisions of the Korean Constitutional Court*, Vol. 13, No. 2, 77. See also Kim J (2002b).

legislative power in specific areas which cover not only the organization of public bodies and their execution of powers, but also the protection of rights of the people. Therefore, generally speaking, the scope of legislation is open to interpretation and thus, like other constitutional democracies, judicial decisions regarding legislation and political practices, in practice, may have a role in setting the limits of legislation. The constitutional principles such as the rule of law as outlined above together with the express provisions concerning the scope of legislation play a certain guiding role in this regard.[29]

Aside from the basic power of legislation, the Constitution grants a variety of powers to the National Assembly mostly in order to fulfill the objectives of democracy, the separation of powers and the rule of law. First, there are several clauses granting consenting or approving powers to the National Assembly to enhance checks and balances on the other Branches. These powers can be divided into two categories, depending on the nature of subject matters at issue. The first category is concerned with the composition of the other Branches. It has consenting powers in the appointment of the Prime Minister, the Chairperson of the Board of Audit and Inspection, the Chief and Associate Justices of the Supreme Court, and the President of the Constitutional Court. It also has the power to select three out of nine Constitutional Justices and three out of nine members of the National Election Commission. The second category of consent or approval powers of the National Assembly is apt to control powers of the other Branches, in particular that of the President. What require the consent or approval of the National Assembly are those powers which pose a danger of eroding constitutional principles by overriding essential powers of the other Branches. The President's emergency powers, such as the promulgation of orders having the effect of Act or the proclamation of martial law, may affect respectively the legislative power and the judicial power so that they are subject to the consent or approval of the National Assembly as the representatives of the sovereign people. The President's powers in relation to the accession and ratification of treaties of certain subject matters, which may have significant influence on the powers of the other Branches or public security and order of the country, should also be consented by the National Assembly before they come into force. Such subject matters include the declaration of war, the dispatch of armed forces to foreign states, the stationing of alien forces in the territory of ROK, treaties pertaining to any restriction on sovereignty, treaties that will burden the State or people with an important financial obligation and so on.

Other important powers granted to the National Assembly are related to the national budget. In the process of formulation and approval of the national budget, another dimension of the separation of powers is installed. The formulation of the national budget bill belongs to the Executive while the deliberation and determination of the money bill is under the jurisdiction of the National Assembly. The power to audit and inspect the closing of accounts of revenues and expenditures is given to the Board of Audit and Inspection (BAI). The BAI is institutionally located under

[29] Kwon Y-s (2006), pp. 409–421.

the direct jurisdiction of the President, but its constitutional functions are to be carried out independently of the President under Article 2 of the Board of Audit and Inspection Act.

The last, but not least, category of power in the hands of the National Assembly is one that, assuming the representatives of the sovereign people, is apt to control the other Branches. It has the power to inspect general affairs of the other Branches and investigate specific matters of their affairs (Article 61). It may also request the attendance and responses to the raised questions of the Prime Minister, State Councilors and other government delegates at any meeting of the National Assembly (Article 62). Moreover, the National Assembly may pass a recommendation for removal from office of the Prime Minister or State Councilors (Article 63). Finally, it is authorized to pass the motion for impeachment of high-level public officials designated under Article 65(1) and other Acts. One constitutional effect of the passage of the impeachment motion is the suspension of the impeached public officials from exercising their powers until the Constitutional Court's decision on that matter is delivered [Article 65(3)]. In the first impeachment trial against the then President Moo-hyun Roh in 2004, the Constitutional Court held that even if the minimum requirements of impeachment are met, it may decide whether an impeached official's violation of the Constitution or Act amounts to a sufficient level of gravity to remove him (or her) from public office. As far as President Roh was concerned, the Constitutional Court ruled that, although the violations of the Constitution or Act on three accounts were recognized, they were not sufficiently serious to remove him from office.[30]

3.3 *The Executive Branch*

The fourth chapter of the Constitution is divided into two sections, each of which is allocated to the President and the Administrative Branch, respectively. This formation can be evidence of the semi-dualist character of the executive branch, although different from that of the parliamentary system or the cabinet system.

3.3.1 The President

The Status of the President

The President is elected by the direct ballot of the people for a single five-year term. If the direct election results in two or more candidates receiving an equal largest

[30] Constitutional Court Decision 2004Hun-Na1, May 14, 2004, *Decisions of the Korean Constitutional Court*, Vol. 16, No. 1, 609. In this case, the Constitutional Court discerned the President from other officials in determining whether the required violation amounts to the required level of gravity because, being the head of the State as well as the head of the Executive elected directly by the people, the dismissal of the President can cause much greater change in the working of constitutional arrangements and political conflicts.

number of votes, the National Assembly selects the President in an open session [Article 67(2)]. Unlike in America, there is no vice-presidency.

The President, unlike his (or her) assistants like the Prime Minister or State Councilors, is not directly accountable to the National Assembly. The only way to remove the President from office is through the difficult process of impeachment. The impeachment trial can be formed only by the impeachment resolution supported by two thirds or more of the total members of the National Assembly and the decision of dismissal must be upheld by the concurrence of six out of nine Constitutional Justices. The President, like other public officials, may not be impeached for political reasons,[31] but only for "violations of the Constitution or other Acts in the performance of official duties."

Only one President has actually undergone an impeachment trial since 1948. In 2004, President Moo-hyun Roh was impeached for, among others, violations of the Election Act, corruption stemming from abuse of power and the unfaithful performance of presidential duties. The Constitutional Court found, first, that his open support for a political party at a press conference prior to the scheduled general election violated Article 9(1) of the Public Official Election Act requiring public officials' neutrality in elections; second, that his seemingly defiant comments on the warning of the National Election Commission which prohibits him from making political speeches in relation to general election was in violation of the presidential duty to uphold and protect the Constitution; and third, that his proposal of a national referendum on the people's confidence in his presidency was not compatible with Article 72(1) allowing referendum only on specific policies, and thus, breached his duty to uphold and protect the Constitution.[32] Despite these findings, however, as mentioned above, it refused to dismiss him from the presidency on the ground that they did not amount to the gravity enough to do so. The protection of the President from outside interference is reinforced by the provision of Article 84 vesting him with the privilege exempted from criminal charges except for insurrection or treason during his term.

Another case relating to the constitutional status of the President was also involved with President Moo-hyun Roh. In 2007, he filed a constitutional complaint to the Constitutional Court alleging that his freedom of political speech was breached by the warnings of the National Election Commission which relied upon an unconstitutional provision of election law. His political speeches at, among others, a political meeting organized by his supporters and an awarding convocation for his honorary doctoral degree around election periods caused fierce political controversies in particular from the Grand National Party, which finally denounced him to the Election Commission. It confirmed at the separate sessions for the two denouncements that his speeches were against the general neutrality

[31] Constitutional Court Decision 2004Hun-Na1, May 14, 2004, *Decisions of the Korean Constitutional Court*, Vol. 16, No. 1, 609.

[32] Constitutional Court Decision 2004Hun-Na1, May 14, 2004, *Decisions of the Korean Constitutional Court*, Vol. 16, No. 1, 609.

principle stipulated in Article 9 of Public Official Election Act and requested him to restrain himself from making speeches similar to those at issue.

In this complaint case, the Constitutional Court was divided on one substantive issue and on two procedural matters. Seven Justices agreed that President Roh's filing of complaint met the procedural requirements prescribed by the Constitutional Court Act while two remaining Justices disagreed with the majority, either because the warning at stake was merely a request for cooperation rather than a governmental activity restricting President Roh's right or because the President was unable to file a constitutional complaint in relation to his activities in the performance of presidential duties, and President Roh's speeches at issue had something to do with such duties. So far as the substantive merit is concerned, five Justices had the opinion that the election law provision is constitutional, while two Justices held of unconstitutional. The reasoning of the majority was, among others, that although the President has a constitutional status of politician or political institution, his freedom of political speech can be restrained for the sake of the prevailing interest of maintaining fairness in election management, because his status as the head of the Executive has a real danger of rigged election. The dissenting opinion of two Justices argued that the President, being by nature a political official, could not be subordinate to the public officials' general obligation of neutrality in election provided by Article 9 of the Public Official Election Act, so that the measure by the Election Commission was not grounded on justifiable law and thereby infringed upon President Roh's political right.[33]

The Powers of the President

The President's powers enumerated mostly in Sect. 1 of Chapter "Civil Law and Civil Procedural Law" by and large can be divided into four categories. First, he (or she) has authority to initiate proposals of national importance, such as constitutional revision or amendment and referendum on important policies. Second, with the consent or cooperation of the other Branches, he (or she) is empowered to get involved in the formation of the other Branches by appointing the Chief and Associate Justices, the Constitutional Justices and three members of the National Election Commission. He (or she) also appoints the Prime Minister, State Councilors, the heads of the Executive Ministries, the Chairperson and Commissioners of the Board of Audit and Inspection as well as public officials as prescribed by the Constitution and other Acts. Third, he (or she) has a variety of powers to implement Acts of the National Assembly as well as the authority entrusted to him/her by the Constitution. He (or she) is in the highest position in the hierarchical system of the Executive branch so that his/her directive and supervisory power may control the heads of the central administrative agencies,

[33] Constitutional Court Decision 2007Hun-Ma700, January 17, 2008, *Decisions of the Korean Constitutional Court*, Vol. 20, No. 1, Part 1, 139.

including the Executive Ministries, and may suspend or cancel any order or disposition by them when deemed unlawful or unjust.[34] He (or she) may issue Presidential Decrees necessary to the execution of any authority delegated to him/her by Act. He (or she) has authority to take the minimum necessary actions, to issue orders having the effect of an Act, or to proclaim martial law in certain extraordinary circumstances under the prior or subsequent control of the National Assembly. He (or she) may conclude and ratify treaties, receive or dispatch envoys, and declare war and conclude peace. He (or she) has authority to award decorations and other honors. He (or she) is commander-in-chief of the Armed Forces, the organization and formation of which shall be determined by Act. Fourth, the President is envisaged to play an important role in checking and balancing other branches as prescribed by the Constitution or other Acts. He (or she) may pardon crimes. He (or she) is entitled to attend and address the National Assembly or express his/her views by written addresses, although he (or she) has no obligation to be requested to attend and address it. He (or she) may promulgate the bill passed by the National Assembly or veto it.

Article 82 requires the President to exercise or carry out his/her powers and duties in writing with the countersignatures of the Prime Minister and the State Councilors concerned. What has yet to be decided authoritatively is the question of whether the acts of the President without the required countersignatures can be valid or what would happen if there exist neither the Prime Minister nor the State Councilors concerned.

3.3.2 The Administrative Branch

Section 2 of chapter "Civil Law and Civil Procedural Law" consists of four sub-sections. The first sub-section deals with the Prime Minister and the State Councilors. The second covers the State Council and other presidential advisory councils. The third sub-section consists of three Articles regarding the Executive Ministries, while the fourth concerns the Board of Audit and Inspection. By and large, the administrative branch consists of deliberative and advisory institutions and administrative agencies.

Deliberative and Advisory Institutions

The State Council consists of the President, the Prime Minister, and State Councilors appointed by the President upon the recommendation of the Prime Minister within a size between 15 and 30 members. It has the authority to deliberate on important affairs of the State enumerated in Article 89, ranging from basic plans for state affairs and general policies of the Executive, declaring war, draft

[34] Article 11 of the Government Organization Act.

amendments to the Constitution, proposals for national referendums, budgets, emergency orders, important military affairs, granting of pardons, demarcation of jurisdiction between the Executive Ministries, action for the dissolution of political parties, examination of petitions pertaining to executive policies to other matters presented by its members.

There are four presidential councils to be established by the authorization of the Constitution, but their establishment is not mandatory except the National Security Council, the advisory body for foreign, military and domestic national security policies prior to the deliberation of the State Council. In fact, the Advisory Council of Senior Statesmen, the chairperson of which is the immediate former President unless there is no such person, has never been established since 1988 when the first government under the present constitution inaugurated.

Administrative Agencies

The establishment of administrative agencies depends upon the will of the National Assembly because the Constitution delegated that authority to it, except for two rules regarding the status and order-making power of the heads of the Executive Ministries. Article 94 requires that heads of Executive Ministries be appointed among the State Councilors on the recommendation of the Prime Minister, while Article 95 confers order-making authority to them and the Prime Minister. At present, Article 2(2) of the Government Organization Act provides that central administrative agencies be basically categorized to Bu, Cheo, and Cheong unless differently provided by Act.[35]

The Prime Minister has a dual entity both as an assistant to the President and as a central administrative agency.[36] No active member of the military shall be appointed as either the Prime Minister or a State Councilor (concurrently the heads of Executive Ministries).[37]

One unique administrative agency established by the authorization of the Constitution itself is the BAI. It is the highest audit agency as well as inspection authority established under the direct jurisdiction of the President. The BAI is a rare case, in comparison with other democracies, that the highest audit agency is vested with additional general power by the Constitution to inspect the job performances of the executive agencies and public officials beyond the boundary of the settlement of the revenues and expenditures of the State and the accounts of public bodies. Following the evolution of constitutional democracy in the twenty-first century, which requires the independence and impartiality of the highest audit institution, the BAI's independence in carrying out its duties is guaranteed by

[35] As of February 2011, there are 15 *Bus*, 2 *Cheos*, and 18 *Cheongs*, as well as 4 basic executive commissions.

[36] Article 18(1) of the Government Organization Act.

[37] See Articles 86(3) and 87(4) of the Constitution.

Article 2(1) of the Board of Audit and Inspection Act, although there are still criticisms challenging the possible danger of indirect control by the President through his/her sweeping power to appoint high-level officials, and to formulate the budget, of the BAI. Recently, some politicians, including promising presidential candidates, have put forward a strong argument for the transfer of the BAI from the President's jurisdiction to that of the National Assembly or a newly established independent agency.[38]

One constitutional issue having drawn public attention is the constitutional or legal status of what is called "independent commission" established by Act. At the center of debates in this regard is the National Human Rights Commission (NHRC) set up for the first time in 2001. The legislative history of NHRCA shows unprecedentedly fierce debates about the desirable legal status and scope of powers between human rights activists who prefer the independent human rights commission with significant executive powers and the Ministry of Justice seeking to have one as its' affiliated institution with limited advisory powers.

The key issue in such debates is as to whether the establishment of an independent administrative agency institutionally separated from the executive branch is compatible with the Constitution. The advocates of an independent human rights agency argued that the Constitution would not prohibit the creation of a statutory independent agency for the completion of its basic goals, such as the protection of basic rights. The opponents argued that whatever good causes it pursues, such an administrative agency should be installed within the executive branch to which the executive power is entrusted. The compromised outcome of such debates was the obscure provisions about the legal status of the NHRC. The National Human Rights Commission Act provides no explicit provision to mention where the NHRC should be located in constitutional arrangements, but declares the purpose of the establishment and the principle of independence of the NHRC in dealing with the designated affairs in Article 3. As recently as in 2009, this obscurity finally backfired when the Ministry of Administration and Security attempted to curtail the number of public officials allotted to the NHRC by 21.2% through the revision of the relevant ordinance governing the organization of the NHRC.

The NHRC brought a competence dispute before the Constitutional Court, alleging that such revision constitutes a breach of its competence and thereby should be declared invalid. In a 6-3 decision in 2010,[39] the majority ruled that the NHRC is not entitled to file a competence dispute because it is a mere statutory agency so that it cannot be recognized as a constitutional institution having a constitutional basis for its establishment and thereby granted standing for a competence dispute. The dissenting opinions of three Justices opined that even those statutory institutions which have no explicit constitutional basis for its existence can be granted standing for a competence dispute if they are regarded as a

---

[38] See generally, Kim J (2002a).

[39] Constitutional Court Decision 2009Hun-Ra6, October 10, 2010, Official Gazette No. 169, 1821 (jurisdiction dispute between the NHRC and the President).

constitutional institution because their existence and authorities, like in the case of the NHRC, are derived from the Constitution and if there would be no way to redress the breach of their competence as such independent bodies.

3.3.3 Special Constitutional Agency: The Election Commissions

The seventh chapter of the Constitution covers a special administration of election management in that a specialized politically-neutral agency performs the constitutionally designated duties independently of the President and the other Branches.

In particular, it entrusts the authority of electoral management to the National Election Commission and subordinate Election Commissions.[40] This constitutionalization of the election commissions has its origin in the Constitution of 1960 that established the National Election Commission in the hope that it would contribute to the prevention of rigged and corrupt elections which had finally resulted in the April 29 Democratic Revolution ousting President Syng-man Rhee. Originally, the constitutional ambit of this independent agency was the fair management of elections, but it has been extended to cover the fair management of referendum and administrative affairs of political parties since the Constitution of 1972.

The National Election Commission, the highest in the administrative hierarchy of the election commissions, consists of nine members, three of whom are appointed by the President, three selected by the National Assembly, and the remaining three designated by the Chief Justice of the Supreme Court. The Chairperson of this politically neutral institution shall be elected by its members, but in reality there has been a long established practice that a Justice of the Supreme Court designated as a member of the Commission by the Chief Justice has taken the post. The origin of this practice that seems to be in contradiction to constitutional provisions can be traced back to the original provision of the 1960 Constitution in that the Chairperson should be elected among three Justices of the Supreme Court designated as members of the National Commission by the Chief Justice [Article 75-2(2) of the 1960 Constitution].

This practice has been criticized to have some practical and institutional problems. Practically, the Chairperson's term has been less than 2 years on average since it depends upon the term of the Justiceship. Institutionally, it would be problematic that the head of a constitutionally independent agency holds another principal position belonging to another branch. As recently as in 2005 in the 17th term of the National Assembly, an amendment bill for the Election Commission Act (Bill No. 173475) was proposed to change this practice by making the

[40] There are four prongs of subordinate election commission: 16 *Si* (special metropolitan city, metropolitan city)/*Do* (Provincial) Election Commissions, 249 *Gu* (ward)/*Si* (municipal)/*Gun* (country) Election Commissions and 3,479 voting District Election Commissions in each *Eup*/*Myun*/*Dong* to guarantee more convenient voting. See the English version of homepage of the National Election Commission (http://www.nec.go.kr/engvote/about/organization.jsp).

Chairperson of the National Election Commission permanent, but it failed to be passed before the end of the term.

Members of the Commission have a duty of political neutrality and, at the same time during the six-year term, are guaranteed strong protection like judges so that a difficult process of impeachment or a sentence of imprisonment without labor or a heavier punishment can remove them from office. Moreover, the National Election Commission may enjoy the self-regulatory rule-making power like other branches. In comparison with its counterparts in other democracies, what is unique in the Korean election management system is that the election commissions are constitutionally granted the power to issue necessary instructions to officials concerning the election and referendum affairs [Article 115(1)].

3.4 The Judicial Branch

Chapters "Criminal Law and Procedure" and "Commercial Act", respectively, have provisions for the courts and the Constitutional Court. From this outset, it is easily recognized that the Constitution takes a dualist path in distributing judicial power; on the one hand, ordinary judicial powers covering civil, criminal and administrative cases or controversies are entrusted to the Supreme Court and subordinate courts that the National Assembly chooses to establish[41] and, on the other, the Constitutional Court is established as the specialized tribunal having five designated jurisdictions of constitutional adjudication.[42]

3.4.1 The Supreme Court and the Independence of Judges

Composition of Courts

Article 101 entrusts judicial authority to the courts composed of judges whose qualifications are determined by the National Assembly in the form of Acts. The highest court is the Supreme Court consisting of the Chief Justice and Associate Justices appointed by the President with the consent of the National Assembly. The Chief Justice has the right to recommend Associate Justices and also the power to appoint ordinary judges with the consent of the Conference of Supreme Court

[41] As Article 101(2) and Article 102(3) delegate to the legislature the power to establish subordinate courts and their organization, Article 3(1), Part II and Part III of the Court Organization Act classify six categories of court: the Supreme Court, High Court, Patent Court, District Court, Family Court, and Administrative Court.

[42] There have been debates among constitutional law scholars on the nature of constitutional adjudication in Korean constitutional arrangements, but it would be safe to say that the Constitutional Court is constituted and performs its duties in a mostly similar manner to the judicial process. See Kim J (2005b), pp. 14–17, Jeong J-h (1994) and Huh Y (2009).

Justices. He also has authority to take part in the composition of the Constitutional Court and the National Election Commission by nominating three out of nine Justices or members of the Commission, respectively.[43]

There is no lay judge system in Korea as only those who are qualified as attorneys can be appointed as judges according to Article 42(2) of the Court Organization Act. Moreover, they are not elected by the people. This democratic deficit in the judicial process has been attacked in the course of democratization and was partially corrected by the introduction of what is called "participatory trial" in 2007.[44] Responding to increasing social demand for the democratization of the judicial process, the Act on Citizen Participation in Criminal Trials in 2007 was enacted to establish a juror system in which lay jurors are vested with the power to deliver opinions about fact-finding application of governing laws and sentencing in a very limited scope of criminal cases enumerated in Article 5 of this Act. However, the effect of the jurors' opinions is very limited because they have no binding force on judges according to Article 46 of the Act above. Furthermore, judges may decide whether or not to refer the case to the participatory trial in certain circumstances [Article 9(1)], despite the accused's express intention to take advantage of that trial. In a unanimous opinion in a constitutional complaint challenging the constitutionality of such provisions as allowing mere advisory effect to the jurors' opinions and limiting the scope of eligible cases,[45] it is ruled that they are constitutional because the people's right to participate in trials is not guaranteed by the Constitution as the right of access to the court.

The only special court recognized by the Constitution is a court-martial. Despite its special status, decisions of a court-martial should be subject to appellate review by the Supreme Court, unless the Constitution allows it in express terms. Article 110(4) recognizes that military trials under extraordinary martial law may not be appealed in cases of crimes of soldiers and employees of the military, military espionage, crimes as defined by law in regard to sentinels, sentry posts, supply of harmful foods and beverages, and prisoners of war, except when sentenced to the death penalty.

The Independence of Judges

The independence of judges is one of the core elements of the separation of powers and the rule of law and thus is regarded as a crucial part of free and democratic

---

[43] This is under criticism among public commentators and constitutional scholars on the ground that the Chief Justice with less democratic legitimacy in comparison with the President and the National Assembly is granted the same authority as the latter two. See Kim J (2010b).

[44] For a theoretical account for people's participation in the judicial process from the perspective of participatory democracy, see Kwon Y-s (2006), pp. 563–566.

[45] Constitutional Court Decision 2008Hun-Ba12, November 26, 2009, *Decisions of the Korean Constitutional Court*, Vol. 21, No. 2, Part 2, 493.

order.[46] Article 103 of the Constitution ensures that "judges shall render judgment independently according to their conscience and in conformity with the Constitution and laws". This principle can be put into practice to the fullest extent by providing realistic institutional safeguards for judicial independence so that judges can carry out their sacred duty without fear of reprisals by other branches. Article 106 assures that only the limited possibility of impeachment or a sentence of imprisonment without prison labor or heavier punishment can remove judges from office, and that only disciplinary action can suspend them from office, have their salary reduced or inflict on them any other unfavorable treatment. However, this assurance can be materialized only when they are guaranteed to hold office, like the assurance of life tenure for federal judges in the USA Constitution,[47] for long enough to eliminate any possible outside influence on them. The term of office of the Chief Justice of the highest court is 6 years without the possibility of reappointment, while that of the Associate Justices 6 years with that possibility. Ordinary judges other than such Justices may hold office for 10 years and be reappointed as prescribed by law. The relatively short term of office and the possibility of reappointment have been criticized for equipping the President and political parties with dangerous tools to have influence on judicial decisions.

As far as the independence of judges is concerned, it is notable that a number of laws that are intended to limit discretion of judges in sentencing in criminal or administrative proceedings have been reviewed in terms of whether they amount to violation of the independence of the Judiciary. For example, an early Constitutional Court struck down a law which made a hit-and-run driver who intentionally abandoned the victim to death be sentenced to such aggravated punishments as imprisonment of 10 years or more, life imprisonment, and death penalty on the ground that such a law deprived judges of the discretion to consider the nature of the committed crime and the situation of the accused in criminal proceedings.[48]

3.4.2 Constitutional Court[49]

Jurisdiction

Although only three articles, from Article 111 to Article 113, are allotted in the Constitution for the Constitutional Court, its five jurisdictions have no less, and

[46] The ROK Constitutional Court unequivocally confirmed this in a case reviewing the constitutionality of the controversial provisions of the National Security Act. See Constitutional Court Decision 89Hun-Ga113, April 2, 1990, *Decisions of the Korean Constitutional Court*, Vol. 2, 49 (Adjudication on unconstitutionality of Article 7 of the National Security Act).

[47] Article III, Section 1 of the Constitution of the USA.

[48] Constitutional Court Decision 90Hun-Ba24, April 28, 1992, *Decisions of the Korean Constitutional Court*, Vol. 4, 225 (Constitutional petition concerning Article 5-3(2) 1 of the Act on the Aggravated Punishment, etc. of Specific Crimes).

[49] For a brief introduction to the constitutional adjudication system of the ROK, see Kim J (2010a), ch. 6. The author takes advantage of some relevant parts of that essay in this section without specific citations.

even more, importance than any other branch because all of them have a vital influence on their workings in constitutional arrangements so that they be fundamental to constitutional democracy in the ROK. In the first, and the most important, jurisdiction, the Constitutional Court has the authority to review whether or not an Act at issue is unconstitutional. Its second jurisdiction concerns the removal of high-level public officials, including the President, while the third is to determine the fate of political parties under the ideal of "militant democracy (*streitbare Demokratie*)".[50] It may also involve the proper working of the separation of powers by taking in charge of competence disputes between State agencies, between State agencies and local governments, and between local governments. The last, but not least, authority goes with the protection of basic human rights and freedoms, and thus, it may have a final say in constitutional complaints where private individuals may challenge governmental activities and omission to redress their basic rights.

Since such fundamental authority is entrusted to the Constitutional Court by express provisions, unlike in the USA, there has been no serious doubt about the justification of constitutional adjudication itself. However, as soon as the constitutional influence of such authority represented in crucial constitutional conflicts, there have been public debates on whether it has a political role or judicial role in constitutional arrangements, or what kind of limitations on the abuse of power by the Constitutional Court can be introduced. In particular, since 2004 when two landmark decisions, the presidential impeachment trial and the annulment of the Relocation of Capital Act, were made, the Court impressed conflicting images either as a bastion of democracy and basic human rights or as usurper of legislative power in the people's mind.[51]

At any rate, the Constitutional Court has become a vital constitutional coordinator, since in the increasing number of cases[52] it has been requested to decide even on matters that used to be decided in the political process.[53]

---

[50] The origin of this ideal can be traced in Article 21(2) of the Basic Law of the Federal Republic of Germany. Article 8(4) of the ROK Constitution prohibits a political party from having a purpose and acting contrary to the basic democratic order. It implies that a totalitarian or autocratic regime denying constitutional democracy, for example, the rule of institutionally dominant one political party as in a communist state cannot be allowed even if an absolute majority of the people wishes to adopt.

[51] Park J (2008).

[52] As of January 31, 2011, 22 years after its establishment, the Court has invalidated or partially repudiated legislative acts in 526 cases, of which 273 cases were referred by the ordinary courts for rulings on the constitutionality of laws and 253 cases were heard in the form of constitutional complaints. The latter number is exclusive of 106 cases in which statutory provisions were struck down in the course of constitutional complaints directly challenging governmental powers under Article 68(1) of the CCA. See the official statistics of the Constitutional Court on its website http://english.ccourt.go.kr/.

[53] In this sense, the ROK is not an exception to the global trend of "judicialization of politics" or "Juristocracy". See Kim J (2008) and Hirschl R (2006).

Composition of Constitutional Court

The Constitutional Court consists of nine Justices appointed by the President. The President's power of appointment in this regard is constitutionally limited because he (or she) may only appoint a maximum of three out of nine Justices him/herself while he (or she) should appoint three selected by the National Assembly and three designated by the Chief Justice of the Supreme Court, respectively (Article 111(2) of the Constitution). To be appointed as Justices, all candidates should be "qualified as judges," be more than 40 years of age, and have more than 15 years of career experience as a judge, prosecutor, or attorney [Article 111(2) of the Constitution and Article 5 of the Constitutional Court Act (CCA)].

The term of office and retirement age of Constitutional Justices are the same as those of Justices of the Supreme Court. Until their retirement age, no Justices are forced out of office against their will unless they are impeached or are criminally sanctioned with a sentence of imprisonment without prison labor or more severe. Justices are subject to constitutional obligations not to join a political party or participate in politics (Article 112(2) of the Constitution and Article 9 of the CCA).

The Chief Justice of the Court is appointed by the President with the consent of the National Assembly. He (or she) represents the Court, takes charge of the affairs of the Court, and directs and supervises public officials under his (or her) her authority.

Some problems with the process of appointing Constitutional Justices and the status of Constitutional Justices have been noted.[54] First, the power of nomination of three Justices by the Chief Justice of the Supreme Court has been criticized because of its lack of democratic legitimacy.[55] Second, strong criticism has been raised against the Constitutional requirement that only those qualified as judges be chosen as Justices. Given the homogeneous culture of the legal profession due to a highly selective judicial examination process combined with a simplified training course, such a requirement inhibits the diversity of Court Justices. Third, it has been pointed out, as in the case of the Supreme Court, that the relatively short term of Justices with their reappointment scheme may hinder the independence of the Court by making Justices sensitive to the opinions of those with appointive power.[56]

Major Institutional Features[57]

Intensified Quorum in Major Forms of Decision

In general, the Court rules on a majority basis. However, Article 113(1) of the Constitution and Article 23(2) of the CCA require a special quorum of six Justices

[54] Kim J (2005b), pp. 9–48.

[55] Yang K et al. (1999).

[56] Kim J (2005b), pp. 27–28.

[57] Another noteworthy problem is the required mandatory representation by attorney in the constitutional adjudication procedure according to Article 25 of the CCA. This means that without

when the Court repeals a law, impeaches certain public office holders, decides to dissolve a political party, or makes a decision to uphold a constitutional complaint. Such an intensified quorum is also required to overrule a precedent on the interpretation and application of the Constitution or of law made by the Court [Article 23(2) of the CCA]. The underlying justification of the special quorum is to make it much more difficult that other independent branches' decisions are made void or rejected.[58]

Dualism in Constitutional Review of Norms

Only legislation made by the National Assembly and others with the same entity can be reviewed by the Constitutional Court. According to Article 107(2) of the Constitution, constitutionality of subordinate legislation, such as administrative orders, regulations, rules, and measures, is subject to the Supreme Court's judgment. This dualism causes serious problems: "the Constitution has no express provision concerning whose opinion would be final if there is a difference in constitutional interpretation between the two institutions. This incomplete dualism not only sows the seeds of conflict between the two institutions, but also poses a danger of undermining the consistency and uniformity of constitutional order. Moreover, the Supreme Court's power to review administrative legislation can seriously undermine the function of constitutional complaints by excluding almost all administrative actions, which have the highest possibility of violating human rights."[59]

Exclusion of Judicial Judgments from Constitutional Complaints

Article 68(1) of the CCA excludes judicial judgments from the Court's jurisdiction over constitutional complaints. At first glance, this exclusion may not raise any serious objections, especially because ordinary courts, including the Supreme Court, like the Constitutional Court, consist of judges and are envisaged to be guardians of constitutional rights just as much as the Constitutional Court. From this viewpoint, one could consider such review as one more and final instance for the Constitutional Court to review judicial decisions. However, it is argued that the judicial branch itself is a public authority which has a danger of abusing power,

an attorney, ordinary citizens cannot bring their cases before the Court as they are forced by law to hire an attorney. The problem of this requirement is that it may prevent those with limited financial resources from having recourse to the Court. For this reason, Article 25(3) of the CCA was challenged in 1990. The Court upheld the constitutionality of this provision, however, on the ground that "mandatory representation by attorney would be advantageous to the petitioners by guaranteeing professional and skillful representation and thus preventing reckless and negligent pursuit of complaints." Constitutional Court Decision 89Hun-Ma120·212 (Consolidated), September 3, 1990, *Decisions of the Korean Constitutional Court*, Vol. 2, 296.

[58] However, giving state institutions a much higher priority may not be compatible with the ideal of constitutional adjudication cherishing the protection of constitutional rights and the rule of law. For other problems with this special quorum, see Kim J (2001).

[59] Ibid., p. 28.

although this danger is comparably less than legislative and administrative counterparts, and therefore it is justifiable to establish another mechanism to control judicial power in order to intensify the protection of individual constitutional rights.

The Court upheld the exclusion clause itself in a constitutional complaint case by saying that it is within the discretion of the Legislature to decide as to what extent the Constitutional Court has jurisdiction over constitutional complaints. However, at the same time, the Court made clear that the exclusion clause should not be interpreted as allowing courts to apply the laws made unconstitutional by the Court in ongoing ordinary cases. Thus, in exceptional cases where the courts infringe the peoples' constitutional rights by applying unconstitutional laws, even judicial judgments can be subject to the Court's review.[60]

3.5 Local Autonomy

The ROK is a unitary State and thus, the vertical distribution of governmental powers is implemented in the relationship between the central government and local autonomous governments. Unlike most countries having a federal system, central authority appears to be very extensive so that the powers delegated to local autonomous bodies are few and defined by Acts of the National Assembly. To avoid any misunderstanding, Article 117(1) expressly provides that the powers of local governments are confined to the administrative matters pertaining to the welfare of local residents, management of relevant properties and rule-making within the delegated ambit of Acts and accompanying subordinate regulations in relation to local autonomy.[61] Moreover, Articles 117(2) and 118(2) of the Constitution delegate to the National Assembly a wide discretion in determining the types of local governments and all the required matters in relation to the organization and operation of local councils. The only constitutional requirement in the organization of a local government is that the local government shall have a local council [Article 118(1)].

However, it is construed that the wide nature of central legislative authority does not amount to the infringement of the essential element of local autonomy. In a competence dispute brought by a group of local governments against the BAI, the Constitutional Court recognized such a constitutional limitation on legislative discretion, although the majority opinion refused to find in that case that the statutory provision that BAI's right to audit and inspection can be extended to

---

[60] See Constitutional Court Decision 96Hun-Ma172·173 (Consolidated), October 31, 2002, *Decisions of the Korean Constitutional Court*, Vol. 9, No. 2, 842.

[61] Constitutional Court Decision 2001Hun-Ra1, October 31, 2002, *Decisions of the Korean Constitutional Court*, Vol. 14, No. 2, 362, 370; Constitutional Court Decision 2002Hun-Ra2, October 31, 2002, *Decisions of the Korean Constitutional Court*, Vol. 14, No. 2, 378, 386.

"autonomous affairs" of local governments is in violation of such limitation and thereby infringes on local governments' rights to autonomy.[62] It stressed, among other things, that the independence of the BAI in its function is statutorily guaranteed as opposed to the normal central agencies, and that the relationship between the central government and local governments is a sort of conciliation in pursuit of the common objectives of enhancing welfare of nationals as well as residents by way of harmonizing the efficiency of central administration and autonomy of local administration while distributing administrative functions and responsibilities among them.[63] This does not mean that the Court is reluctant to recognize self-governing power of local governments because, in another competence dispute case between Seoul Metropolitan City and the Executive Branch in re a group of central executive agencies including the Minister of Public Administration and Security, the Court ruled that if the head of a central administrative agency conducted a sort of comprehensive and blanket inspection on the autonomous affairs of a local government without any proof of specific violations of relevant statutes, it infringed on the self-governing authority of the local government guaranteed by the Constitution and the Local Autonomy Act.[64]

4 Basic Constitutional Rights and Duties

After providing the elements of the statehood and some basic orders of the State in the first chapter, the present Constitution embodies the Bill of Rights in the second chapter. It enumerates a variety of basic rights ranging from civil liberties, equality, political rights to economic, cultural and social rights in 27 Articles. Unlike the Bill of Rights in the USA, the Constitution of the ROK has not only a list of freedoms and rights, but also a couple of open-ended clauses which can be used to recognize unenumerated basic rights. Furthermore, it contains a general limitation clause which allows the legislative branch to enact law to regulate those rights and at the same time imposes the limit on such regulation. In addition, two basic duties of the people, that is, the duty to provide national defense and to pay taxes are also provided.

[62] Constitutional Court Decision 2005Hun-Ra3, May 29, 2008, *Decisions of the Korean Constitutional Court*, Vol. 20, No. 1, Part 2, 41.

[63] Constitutional Court Decision 2005Hun-Ra3, May 29, 2008, *Decisions of the Korean Constitutional Court*, Vol. 20, No. 1, Part 2, 41.

[64] See Competence Dispute over Inspection of Autonomous Affairs of Local Government Case (Constitutional Court Decision 2006Hun-Ra6, May 28, 2009, *Decisions of the Korean Constitutional Court*, Vol. 21, No. 1, Part 2, 418).

4.1 *Structure of Constitutional Rights Protection*

4.1.1 The Idea or Prototype of Basic Rights

Article 10 of the Constitution declares that every individual shall have human dignity and worth and the right to the pursuit of happiness and the State shall have a constitutional obligation to recognize and protect such unalterable basic human rights of individuals. The ensuing Articles enumerate specific basic human rights such as equality, civil liberties, political, social, economic and cultural rights from Article 11 to Article 36. However, this list of rights and freedoms is not construed to be exhaustive because Article 37(1) states that "freedoms and rights of citizens shall not be neglected or denied on the grounds that they are not enumerated in the Constitution." This open-ended provision is a constitutional basis of unenumerated rights, together with Article 10 construed to be a prototype or basic idea of all constitutional rights.[65]

4.1.2 The Subject of the Basic Rights

On the surface, the Constitution seems to presume that the basic constitutional rights are guaranteed to nationals because the title of the Korean Bill of Rights has been the Rights and Duties of the Nationals since the First Constitution of 1948 and all the provisions in this chapter have used nationals as the subject of the rights and freedoms.

However, the Constitutional Court recognized that not only foreigners but also legal persons are able to enjoy constitutional rights as much as nationals unless the nature of a particular right and freedom, itself, is interpreted to be inapplicable thereto.[66] Those rights which, by nature, require additional conditions to be qualified as their subject are political rights, in particular the right to vote in national elections and the right to hold public office, which basically presume the citizenship of the polity, and social rights which are prone to be dependent upon the national economy connected to citizenship in the polity.

As far as the legal person is concerned, there is no point for any artificial entity to claim those civil liberties derived from the direct nature of natural persons having human dignity and worth. Furthermore, public authorities including the State[67] and

---

[65] Constitutional Court Decision 89Hun-Ma82, September 10, 1990, *Decisions of the Korean Constitutional Court*, Vol. 2, 306, 310.

[66] Constitutional Court Decision 93Hun-Ma120, December 29, 1994, *Decisions of the Korean Constitutional Court*, Vol. 6, No. 2, 477, 480; Constitutional Court Decision 90Hun-Ma56, June 3, 1991, *Decisions of the Korean Constitutional Court*, Vol. 3, 289, 295–296.

[67] Constitutional Court Decision 93Hun-Ma120, December 29, 1994, *Decisions of the Korean Constitutional Court*, Vol. 6, No. 2, 477, 480.

local governments[68] are construed to have no standing to claim the basic rights unless the purpose of their establishment is to enhance the protection of the basic rights concerned, and thus, there is no reasonable reason why they should be excluded from the protection of such rights. For example, State universities may claim basic rights because the objective of their establishment to educate the people is the same as that of private universities.[69]

4.1.3 General Restriction on Basic Rights and Its Limit

What is unique in the basic rights protection system in the Korean Constitution is the general restriction provision of Article 37(2) whereby rights and freedoms may be restricted, although this is possible only when four constitutional conditions are all met.

The first condition is the so-called "rule of statutory reservation" in that every regulation of basic rights needs a statutory basis. According to the Constitutional Court's case law, to meet the requirement of this principle, it is necessary but not sufficient that specific restraints on a certain basic right have a formal basis under the law made by the National Assembly. Rather, it is required that the essential elements of such restraints be decided not by the executive agency, but by the Legislature itself as the representatives of the people.[70] By this reason, Article 36(1) of the Korean Broadcasting System Act that allowed the board of the Korean Broadcasting System to set the amount of the broadcasting fee without any resolution or intervention of the National Assembly, but merely by obtaining the approval of the Minister of Public Information, was declared nonconforming to the Constitution.[71]

The second is the requirement of constitutional objectives divided into three categories like national security, public order and public welfare. Since these objectives use such highly abstract concepts, this condition can be regarded as declaratory. Not surprisingly, there is no case where the violation of this condition was found.

The third limit requires that the restraint be deemed necessary to meet the legislatively prescribed ends. This condition is regarded as the basis of the proportionality principle in Korean constitutional jurisprudence. As introduced

[68] Constitutional Court Decision 2004Hun-Ba50, February 23, 2006, *Decisions of the Korean Constitutional Court*, Vol. 18, No. 1, Part 1, 170, 179.

[69] Constitutional Court Decision 92Hun-Ma68, October 1, 1992, *Decisions of the Korean Constitutional Court*, Vol. 4, 659.

[70] The Court calls this rule as "parliamentary reservation". See Constitutional Court Decision 98Hun-Ba70, May 27, 1999, *Decisions of the Korean Constitutional Court*, Vol. 11, No. 1, 633, 643–644.

[71] Television Broadcasting Fee Case (Constitutional Court Decision 98Hun-Ba70, May 27, 1999 *Decisions of the Korean Constitutional Court*, Vol. 11, No. 1, 633).

above in II. C., the Korean Constitutional Court has used this requirement elaborated in the four-tiered test more frequently than any other requirement.

The final condition requires that the regulation shall not amount to the infringement of core elements of basic rights and freedoms. For example, Article 186(1) of the Patent Act, which entrusted to the Patent Office the exclusive power of fact finding in patent disputes, was struck down because it contravened the essential element of the right to a fair trial by depriving the courts of having an opportunity to decide on matters of fact.[72]

4.2 *Categories of Basic Rights*

By and large, the basic rights that the Constitution safeguards can be divided into six categories: civil liberties, the right to equality, the right to hold property, the right to political participation, procedural rights, and social rights.

4.2.1 Civil Liberties

Civil liberties are primary rights and freedoms among modern human rights and thus their protection constitutes the fundamental element of constitutional democracy. The Korean Bill of Rights enumerates most civil liberties recognized by most constitutional democracies and, as mentioned above, it is well acknowledged that even unenumerated liberties, like the right to life, must be guaranteed.[73]

Human Dignity and Worth, Right to Pursue Happiness

It is well established in Article 10 of the Constitution that human dignity and worth and the right to the pursuit of happiness are not only the ultimate objective (or idea) of all basic rights, but also the constitutional basis of specific civil rights to personality and to the pursuit of happiness.[74] The Constitutional Court views these rights, in particular the right to the pursuit of happiness, as comprehensive rights often overlapping with a variety of civil rights and freedoms, enumerated or

---

[72] Constitutional Court Decision 92Hun-Ga11, 93Hun-Ga8·9·10 (Consolidated), September 28, 1995, *Decisions of the Korean Constitutional Court*, Vol. 7, Vol. 2, 264, 278.

[73] Constitutional Court Decision 95Hun-Ba1, November 28, 1996, *Decisions of the Korean Constitutional Court*, Vol. 8, No. 2, 537, 545.

[74] Constitutional Court Decision 89Hun-Ma82, September 10, 1990, *Decisions of the Korean Constitutional Court*, Vol. 2, 306, 310; Constitutional Court Decision 98Hun-Ma216, June 1, 2000, *Decisions of the Korean Constitutional Court*, Vol. 12, No. 1, 622, 648.

unenumerated.[75] Construing these rights more broadly, the Court has elaborated the right to personality and the right to the pursuit of happiness so that a number of unenumerated rights have been recognized. They include the right to personal autonomy, like the right to choose one's partner in marriage or sexual life or the right to personal information,[76] the right to rest,[77] the right to smoke or the right to be free from smoking,[78] and the like.

Civil Rights and Freedoms

Specific civil rights and freedoms, other than the right to personality and the right to the pursuit of happiness, are enumerated from Article 12 to Article 22 of the Constitution.

Article 12 guarantees personal liberty. In response to the dreadful abuse of law enforcement powers during autocratic regimes, this clause articulates, in detail, specific rights and principles in relation to criminal proceedings. They range from important principles for criminal procedures like the principle of *nulla poea sine lege*, prohibition of self-incrimination, due process of law, the exclusionary rule, to procedural rights, like the right to prompt access to legal counsel, the right to be informed of the reason of arrest or detention and the right to access to legal counsel, and the right to request the court to review the legality of the arrest or detention. In addition, Article 13(1) and (2) provides the prohibition of *ex post facto* law and protection from double jeopardy, while Article 13(3) forbids the State from treating people unfavorably not because of their own conducts but because of their relatives' activities.

Article 14 safeguards freedoms to choose one's residence and of free movement, while Article 16 protects against the intrusion of residence without a warrant.

Article 15 guarantees the freedom to choose one's occupation, but it is generally construed that this freedom covers not only the freedom to select one's job in the narrow sense, but also the freedom to maintain and conduct one's occupation in

---

[75] Constitutional Court Decision 2006Hun-Ba35, October 30, 2008, *Decisions of the Korean Constitutional Court*, Vol. 20, No. 2, Part 1, 793, 804–805.

[76] For cases on the right to choose one's partner in marriage or sexual life, see Constitutional Court Decision 89Hun-Ma82, September 10, 1990, *Decisions of the Korean Constitutional Court*, Vol. 2, 306, 310; Constitutional Court Decision 2000Hun-Ba60, October 25, 2001, *Decisions of the Korean Constitutional Court*, Vol. 13, No. 2, 480, 485; Constitutional Court Decision 99Hun-Ba40, 2002Hun-Ba50 (Consolidated), May 26, 2005, *Decisions of the Korean Constitutional Court*, Vol. 14, No. 2, 390, 397. Regarding the right to personal information based upon human dignity and worth, the right to the pursuit of happiness, see Constitutional Court Decision 99Hun-Ma513, 2004Hun-Ma190 (Consolidated), May 26, 2005, *Decisions of the Korean Constitutional Court*, Vol. 17, No. 1, 668, 683.

[77] Constitutional Court Decision 2000Hun-Ma159, September 27, 2001, *Decisions of the Korean Constitutional Court*, Vol. 13, No. 2, 353, 362.

[78] Constitutional Court Decision 2003Hun-Ma457, August 26, 2004, *Decisions of the Korean Constitutional Court*, Vol. 16, No. 2 Part 1, 355–363.

specific manners. The Constitutional Court discerns these freedoms in reviewing specific cases in a way of applying more stringent standard of review to those cases involved in the freedom to choose one's occupation than freedom to engage in occupation.[79]

Article 17 protects against the intrusion of private life and secrecy that are usually conceived as "privacy". The importance of this freedom has been growing due to the development of communications technology. It is often invoked together with the right to personality based on Article 10 by persons whose personal information is collected and/or used by public bodies, in particular public officials subject to the disclosure of personal information including military records, criminal records, medical data and wealth reports.[80]

Article 18 protects against the intrusion of the secrecy of correspondence. Correspondence is a specialized form of privacy. Thus, it would be natural to assume that it is included to stress the importance of this form of privacy. This assumption can be reinforced by a historical explanation that it would have been difficult to replace a specialized freedom used to exist since the first Constitution of 1948 (i.e. protection of correspondence secrecy) with a more general one (i.e. that of private life and secrecy) under the circumstances in which invasion of correspondence has never been unusual under authoritarian regimes

Article 19 guarantees freedom of conscience. It has been one of the hot potatoes producing hard cases especially for the judiciary in the period of transition from authoritarian regimes to democracy in Korea, because autocratic governments tended to control political dissidents by suppressing diverse moral and political ideas and dissemination thereof among the public. One fundamental issue this clause has often given rise to is the meaning of conscience, including the question of whether it covers thought or ideas. The jurisprudence of the Constitutional Court on this matter is unclear and confusing. In some cases, the Court viewed conscience in a broad sense in that it includes "a world view, a life view, an ideology, a belief and also, even if not rising to the level of such thinking, those values or ethical judgments in inner thoughts pertaining to one's formation of personality".[81] In other cases, it is viewed in a narrow sense in that a "strong and sincere voice of one's mind without acting according to which one's existential value would

[79] Constitutional Court Decision 99Hun-Ba76, October 31, 2002, *Decisions of the Korean Constitutional Court*, Vol. 14, No. 2, 410.

[80] Constitutional Court Decision 2005Hun-Ma1139, May 31, 2007, *Decisions of the Korean Constitutional Court*, Vol. 19, No. 1, 711, 724–727 (disclosure of medical records of public officials above 4th grade); Constitutional Court Decision 2006Hun-Ma402·531 (Consolidated), April 24, 2008, *Decisions of the Korean Constitutional Court*, Vol. 20, No. 1, Part 1, 674, 681–684 (disclosure of criminal records of election candidates).

[81] Constitutional Court Decision 89Hun-Ma160, April 1, 1991, *Decisions of the Korean Constitutional Court*, Vol. 3, 149, 153; Constitutional Court Decision 96Hun-Ga11, March 27, 1997, *Decisions of the Korean Constitutional Court*, Vol. 9, No. 1, 245, 263; Constitutional Court Decision 92Hun-Ba28, November 27, 1997, *Decisions of the Korean Constitutional Court*, Vol. 9, No. 2, 548, 571.

collapse."[82] A greater concern has been given to the latter concept because, if this concept were taken by the Court, the scope of the protection of freedom of conscience would become significantly narrow. For example, in a law-abidance oath case, the majority of the Court ruled that the requirement of an oath to abide by law in the parole review process only to those inmates convicted of the violation of two major political criminal laws, such as the National Security Act and the Assembly and Demonstration Act, did not fall under the scope of protection guaranteed by freedom of conscience, because the exclusion of parole could not constitute the deprivation of a right but a privilege and thus the original legal status of such inmates has not been changed.[83] The dissenting opinion presented by two justices argued that the requirement of an oath to abide by law to applicants for parole can amount to the deprivation of "expected" liberty and thereby have a direct impact on their conscience.[84]

The issue of "conscientious objection" is another example showing the narrow stance taken by the Court in terms of the scope of freedom of conscience. In 2004, the Court held that the Military Service Act which criminalizes those who, upon the receipt of a conscription notice, fail to enlist or report for duty without justifiable causes, are constitutional because freedom of conscience is not envisaged to safeguard an individual's right to deny the duty to provide national defense and to request the State to introduce an alternative service system for them. The dissenting opinion is that lack of minimum legislative efforts to provide an alternative service system by forcing only active military service fails to conform to freedom of conscience.[85]

Article 20 safeguards freedom of religion and at the same time forbids the establishment of religion as well as blurring the boundary between religion and the State. Freedom of religion has been interpreted to have three sub-categories, that is, freedom of religious belief, freedom of religious activities, and freedom of religious assembly or association.[86] While the first freedom is absolute because it is

[82] Constitutional Court Decision 2002Hun-Ma518, October 30, 2003, *Decisions of the Korean Constitutional Court*, Vol. 15, No. 2 Part 2, 185, 208; Constitutional Court Decision 98Hun-Ma425, April 25, 2002, *Decisions of the Korean Constitutional Court*, Vol. 14, No. 1, 351, 364–366.

[83] Constitutional Court Decision 98Hun-Ma425, 99Hun-Ma170·498 (Consolidated), April 25, 2002, *Decisions of the Korean Constitutional Court*, Vol. 14, No. 1, 351, 364–366. For a sketch of this case in English, see also, Constitutional Court (2008), pp. 238–240.

[84] Constitutional Court Decision 98Hun-Ma425, April 25, 2002, *Decisions of the Korean Constitutional Court*, Vol. 14, No. 1, 351, 353–354.

[85] Constitutional Court Decision 2002Hun-Ga1, August 26, 2004, *Decisions of the Korean Constitutional Court*, Vol. 16, No. 2, Part 1, 141.

[86] Constitutional Court Decision 2000Hun-Ma159, September 27, 2001, *Decisions of the Korean Constitutional Court*, Vol. 13, No. 2, 353, 360.

connected to the inner state of mind, the other two freedoms must be subject to governmental restrictions.[87]

Article 21 guarantees freedom of speech and of the press, along with freedom of assembly and association. These freedoms are the backbones of a democratic republic so that they shall be treated as having preferred positions,[88] and thus, any regulation on them must pass the stringent review recognized by the Constitutional Court. The reinforced position of these freedoms can be found in the express prohibition on licensing or censorship of speech and the press, and on licensing of assembly and association in Article 21(2).

Like its counterparts in most liberal democracies, the Constitutional Court developed a couple of criteria by which the constitutionality of any legislation limiting freedom of expression can be evaluated. They include the rule of clarity (equivalent to "void as vagueness" in American constitutional law jurisprudence) and the rule against overbreadth. In addition, the Court has been very anxious to control censorship by the executive agencies to the extent that a number of laws introducing various content-based review systems have been struck down.[89] Moreover, the Court has derived the constitutional right to know from freedom of expression.[90]

Despite all these positive features, there are also some negative aspects in regard to freedom of expression. First, Article 21(3) enables the Legislature to assert its wide latitude in determining the standards of news service and broadcast facilities. Second, Article 21(4) expressly sets forth the limit of freedom of speech and the press by providing that, "neither speech nor the press shall violate the honor of other persons nor undermine public morals or social ethics."

Article 22(1) sets forth the protection of freedom of learning and arts while Article 22(2) gives special attention to the rights of authors, inventors, scientists, engineers and artists.

---

[87] Constitutional Court Decision 2000Hun-Ma159, September 27, 2001, *Decisions of the Korean Constitutional Court*, Vol. 13, No. 2, 353, 361.

[88] Constitutional Court Decision 89Hun-Ma163, September 16, 1991, *Decisions of the Korean Constitutional Court*, Vol. 3, 518, 524; Constitutional Court Decision 95Hun-Ga16, April 30, 1998, *Decisions of the Korean Constitutional Court*, Vol. 10, No.1, 327, 338.

[89] E.g. Constitutional Court Decision 93Hun-Ga13, 91Hun-Ba10 (Consolidated), October 4, 1996, *Decisions of the Korean Constitutional Court*, Vol. 8, No. 2, 212, 225 (concerning the Korea Public Performance Ethics Committee); Constitutional Court Decision 2000Hun-Ga9, August 30, 2001, *Decisions of the Korean Constitutional Court*, Vol. 13, No. 2, 134, 150–151 (concerning the Korea Media Rating Board); Constitutional Court Decision 99Hun-Ga1, September 16, 1999, *Decisions of the Korean Constitutional Court*, Vol. 11, No. 2, 245, 253–258 (concerning the Korea Performance Arts Promotion Council, specifically for video works).

[90] Constitutional Court Decision 92Hun-Ma177,199 (Consolidated), July 21, 1995, *Decisions of the Korean Constitutional Court*, Vol. 7, No. 2, 112, 125.

4.2.2 Right to Equality and Principle of Equality Before Law

Article 11(1) of the present Constitution provides the principle of equality before the law. It is generally accepted that although this clause does not mention the right to equality, but it is inherent in the principle itself.[91] To avoid any misunderstanding, the latter paragraph of this provision sets forth that "there shall be no discrimination in political, economic, social, and cultural life on account of sex, religion or social status." The classification of discrimination in this paragraph has been construed not exhaustive so that discrimination on any ground other than sex, religion or social status is prohibited as well.

By equality, it is not meant that everyone must be treated equally under all conditions, but that those in similar circumstances must be treated equally while those in different circumstances treated differently.[92]

In reviewing whether a law or State action is in breach of the right to equality, the Constitutional Court has developed a basic two-tier test. The first test is called the "arbitrariness test" in that the standard of review is highly deferential because most distinctions will be declared constitutional if they are based upon a "reasonable basis." The second standard, called the "proportionality test," is applied to cases which fall under two categories requiring a stricter scrutiny in that all the classifications under these categories must be justified by sufficient proportionality between the purpose of discrimination and the means employed to achieve that purpose. These two categories belong to either cases connected to certain areas of interest which the Constitution expressly order the State to provide extra protection, such as women's entitlement to equal employment under Article 32(4) of the Constitution, or other cases in which unequal treatment may cause substantial restraints on the basic rights involved in such treatment.[93] This second standard of review is further elaborated into a two-pronged strict test: relaxed strict scrutiny and strict scrutiny in the narrow sense. Whilst the latter maintains a stringent posture, the former is developed to diminish the degree of scrutiny when the Constitution specifically recognizes privileged treatment, even though such treatment may cause a danger of severe infringement of other persons' interests.[94]

---

[91] Constitutional Court Decision 88Hun-Ga7, January 25, 1989, *Decisions of the Korean Constitutional Court*, Vol. 1, 1, 2.

[92] Constitutional Court Decision 89Hun-Ga 37·96 (Consolidated), May 24, 1989, *Decisions of the Korean Constitutional Court*, Vol. 1, 48, 54; Constitutional Court Decision 90Hun-Ba27through34, 36through42, 44through46, 92Hun-Ba15(Consolidated), April 28, 1992, *Decisions of the Korean Constitutional Court*, Vol. 4, 255, 271; Constitutional Court Decision 91Hun-Ga3, February 24, 1994, *Decisions of the Korean Constitutional Court*, Vol. 6, No. 1, 21, 33.

[93] Constitutional Court Decision 98Hun-Ma363, December 23, 1999, *Decisions of the Korean Constitutional Court*, Vol. 11, No. 2, 770. See also Kim J (2010a), p.131.

[94] Constitutional Court Decision 2000Hun-Ma25, February 22, 2001, *Decisions of the Korean Constitutional Court*, Vol. 13, No. 1, 386, 404–405; Kim J (2010a), p.131.

4.2.3 Right to Hold Property

Article 23(1) of the Constitution recognizes a general right to hold property. This clause is interpreted to have further significance so that it has been viewed, not only as a constitutional safeguard through which individuals' civil liberties become realistic, but also as constitutional evidence that the ROK pursues a capitalist free market economy.[95]

Although the right to hold property was originally recognized as a sort of civil liberty in modern constitutionalism, it is notable that the constitutional recognition of property rights in Korea has been made in a different form and substance from that of other civil liberties in the field of economy, like freedom of occupation. While the latter liberties are guaranteed without separate conditions attached to their contents and limitations, the former right is subject to the Legislature's wide latitude in determining its contents and limitations as prescribed by the second paragraph of Article 23(1).[96] The Constitutional Court confirms this interpretation by differentiating the nature of legislature's role in specifying the open-ended contents of property rights from that in restricting the given contents of other freedoms, although it stresses that this very difference cannot be used to defy private property rights *per se*.[97]

Moreover, Article 23(2) imposes an additional obligation, which is not found in provisions for other constitutional rights, on property right holders by providing that the "exercise of property rights shall conform to public welfare." Generally speaking, this provision succeeds Article 15(2) of the 1948 Constitution which in turn benchmarked Article 153(3) of the Weimar Constitution 1919. The Constitutional Court ruled that this constitutional requirement of conformity to public welfare may allow legislature to restrict owner's use of property even without just compensation, unless the restriction forces the owner to endure unreasonable sacrifice.[98]

[95] Constitutional Court Decision 88Hun-Ga13, December 22, 1989, *Decisions of the Korean Constitutional Court*, Vol. 1, 367.

[96] Article 23(1) of the Constitution provides that "The property rights of all citizens shall be guaranteed. *The contents and limitations thereof shall be determined by Act.*" (Emphasis added).

[97] Constitutional Court Decision 92Hun-Ba20, July 29, 1993, *Decisions of the Korean Constitutional Court*, Vol. 5, No. 2, 44

[98] Constitutional Court Decision 89Hun-Ma214, 90Hun-Ba16, 97Hun-Ba78 (Consolidated), *Decisions of the Korean Constitutional Court*, Vol. 10, No. 2, 927. Where any unreasonable restriction on private property causes unusual burden on the owner thereof, compensation must be accompanied to it on the ground of the prohibition of excessive restriction or proportionality principle based upon Article 37(2) of the Constitution as well as the rule of law. According to the KCC, the nature of compensation in this regard is different from just compensation required for expropriation or takings for public necessity by Article 23(3). While the latter requires a full, pecuniary compensation, the former does not. In the jurisprudence of the Court, compensation based upon Article 23(1) and (2) should not be confined to pecuniary compensation so that legislature may wield wide discretion in determining in what form of compensation is desirable.

Article 23(3) provides for the conditions of takings. It requires that expropriation or takings of private property for public use should be accompanied by just compensation as provided for by law made by the National Assembly. The jurisprudence of the Court in this regard is that just compensation means the full value of loss, which is not determined purely by market value, but by objective economic value. Therefore, incidentally increased market value such as development value driven by speculation in the real estate market cannot be regarded as a standard against which just compensation is evaluated.[99]

In addition, Chapter "Private International Law" of the Constitution titled "Economy" contains principles and specific regulations which affect the possession and exercise of property rights.

4.2.4 Right to Political Participation

The right to political participation is the right envisaged to safeguard people's participation in certain political processes, like elections. Although it is connected to civil liberties in the political sphere, in Korean constitutional law, it is usually distinguished from them partly because the subject matter of this right is basically confined to the nationals rather than all human beings including foreigners and thereby its actualization is more dependent upon implementation of laws than other civil freedoms.[100] This right in the Korean context can be divided into three prongs: the right to vote in elections, the right to hold public office, and the right to vote in referenda.

Article 24 guarantees the right to vote in elections. The Constitutional Court regards this right as having a preferred position because it constitutes the basis of a democratic republic.[101] Thus, any restraint on this right must pass the highest level of scrutiny.[102] However, it seems open to the question as to whether the Court has applied this principle to the relevant cases in a strict manner, because it tends to be reluctant to abolish certain legislative requirements for voters who wish to participate in constitutionally guaranteed elections. It declared constitutional the law suspending the right to vote, of those sentenced to imprisonment without prison

[99] E.g., Constitutional Court Decision 89Hun-Ma214, 90Hun-Ba16, 97Hun-Ba78 (Consolidated), December 24, 1998, *Decisions of the Korean Constitutional Court*, Vol. 10, No. 2, 927, 956–957.

[100] Thus, the right to political participation here needs to be differentiated from a political liberty in the sense that although it can be exercised in relation to political process like elections, it's focus is not directly given to the conduct of voting or holding public office but to a form of expressive conduct, for example, the freedom of political speech guaranteed as a sort of civil liberty.

[101] Constitutional Court Decision 88Hun-Ga6, September 8, 1989, *Decisions of the Korean Constitutional Court*, Vol. 1, 199, 208.

[102] Constitutional Court Decision 2004Hun-Ma644, 2005Hun-Ma360 (Consolidated), June 28, 2007, *Decisions of the Korean Constitutional Court*, Vol. 19, No. 1, 859, 873–874.

labor or heavier punishment until the expiration of that sentence.[103] The dissenting opinion of one Justice in this case rebutted the majority opinion by arguing that this fundamental political right in a preferred position must be protected to the fullest extent so that any legislative restraint on this right without direct delegation of the constitutional text must be subject to the strictest scrutiny under the rule against excessive restriction, and that, to use the suspension of the right to vote as a sanction for crimes not related to an election or political process cannot be regarded as a legitimate legislative purpose.[104] It also ruled that the law setting the age of 20 years as the minimum age of voters constitutional while the minimum age in various fields of law, private or public, in particular for the compulsory military service is far lower than that age.[105] One exceptional decision the Court withdrew its previous deferential tendency in the same election law cases can be found in the Overseas Koreans' Voting Rights Case in 2007.[106] In this case, Article 37(1) of the Public Officials Election Act was nullified on the ground that the requirement of residency in Korea as the only factor to deprive overseas Koreans of their right to vote in national elections cannot meet the required rule against excessive restriction, and thereby encroached on overseas Koreans' right to vote, right to equality and the principle of universal suffrage.

There are two elections the Constitution expressly grants to nationals the right to cast their ballots: elections for the members of the National Assembly and presidential elections. Local elections for the members of local councils are also guaranteed by the Constitution, but since the authority to choose procedures for these elections is delegated to the Legislature, who can take part and how they may take part in the local elections, in principle, depends upon the will of the legislative branch. In particular, how to select the head of a local government depends basically upon the Legislature's choice. Also, the Legislature may introduce elections for other public officials when deemed proper or necessary.[107]

Apart from the nationals' right to vote at elections, the right to vote on referendum is another constitutional right that falls under the category of the right to political participation, although on only two occasions can such right be guaranteed by the Constitution: national referenda on important policies initiated by the President under Article 72 of the Constitution and national referenda on

[103] Constitutional Court Decision 2002Hun-Ma411, March 25, 2004, *Decisions of the Korean Constitutional Court*, Vol. 16, No. 1, 468, 479–482.

[104] Constitutional Court Decision 2002Hun-Ma411, March 25, 2004, *Decisions of the Korean Constitutional Court*, Vol. 16, No. 1, 468, 483–490.

[105] Constitutional Court Decision 96Hun-Ma89, June 26, 1997, *Decisions of the Korean Constitutional Court*, Vol. 9, No. 1, 674, 678–683; Constitutional Court Decision 2000Hun-Ma111, June 28, 2001, *Decisions of the Korean Constitutional Court*, Vol. 13, No. 1, 1418, 1426–1429.

[106] Constitutional Court Decision 2004Hun-Ma644, 2005Hun-Ma360 (Consolidated), June 28, 2007, *Decisions of the Korean Constitutional Court*, Vol. 19, No. 1, 859, 875–879. For an English summary of this case, see the Constitutional Court (2008), pp. 332–335.

[107] Constitutional Court Decision 2000Hun-Ma283·778 (Consolidated), March 28, 2002, *Decisions of the Korean Constitutional Court*, Vol. 14, No. 1, 211, 223.

constitutional amendments or revisions under Article 130(2). However, the right to participate in a local referendum introduced by Article 13-2 of the Local Autonomy Act cannot be regarded as a constitutional right protected by Article 24 of the Constitution.[108]

Article 25 safeguards the right to hold public office, including the right to stand for elections.[109] This right, as opposed to freedom of occupation, is a particular safeguard to those holding public office, so that the former right can be applied instead of the latter if the two rights are alleged to be simultaneously infringed by the same cause of action.[110]

4.2.5 Procedural Rights

The basic rights per se are not self-executing. If there is no redress when they are infringed, they are merely political declarations or rights on paper. In order to make the rights have more significance and provide a protective environment, there must be some mechanism through which personal grievances and opinions for better governance are to be delivered to the public authorities. If there is wrongdoing on the part of the State whose main duties of which are to do their best to protect the basic rights, some material compensation should be secured, not only to redress the loss but also revive public's confidence in the State. Procedural rights are the very rights that are envisaged to make it possible for people whose rights are infringed to redress the violation and thereby materialize such substantive rights. The Constitution guarantees these procedural rights from Articles 26 to 30.

Article 26 provides the right to petition in writing to any governmental agency and thereby imposes on such agencies the duty to examine such petition. Article 28 safeguards the entitlement to claim just compensation from the State when an arrest or detention is made, but there is no indictment in that case. Article 29 guarantees a claim for just compensation from the State or other public authorities involved when there are wrongful activities of such public authorities. One controversial exception of such liabilities of the State is stipulated in Article 29(2) of the Constitution in that a group of public officials designated by that clause are denied the right to claim damages against the relevant public authorities. This clause is the constitutionalized version of an actual provision of the State Compensation Act, which was acknowledged to be in breach of equality principle by the Supreme

[108] Constitutional Court Decision 2000Hun-Ma735, June 28, 2001, *Decisions of the Korean Constitutional Court*, Vol. 13, No. 1, 1431, 1439.

[109] Constitutional Court Decision 88Hun-Ga6, September 8, 1989, *Decisions of the Korean Constitutional Court*, Vol. 1, 199, 214; Constitutional Court Decision 99Hun-Ma112·137 (Consolidated), December 14, 2000, *Decisions of the Korean Constitutional Court*, Vol. 12, No. 2, 399, 409; Constitutional Court Decision 2000Hun-Ma25, February 22, 2001, *Decisions of the Korean Constitutional Court*, Vol. 13, No. 1, 386, 413.

[110] Constitutional Court Decision 99Hun-Ma135, December 23, 1999, *Decisions of the Korean Constitutional Court*, Vol. 11, No.2, 800, 811.

Court in 1971. The Constitutional Court repeatedly dismissed constitutional complaints challenging this clause only because it does not have the authority to review provisions of the Constitution.[111]

The most important procedural right safeguarded by the Constitution is the right to trial by judges. Without this right, the judicial power is mostly unthinkable in constitutional arrangements. Article 27(1) provides that "all nationals shall have the right to be tried in conformity with the laws by judges qualified under the Constitution and the laws." Article 27(3) also guarantees the right to a speedy trial, while Article 27(4) and (5), respectively, declares a presumption of innocence and protects a victim's entitlement to make a statement during the proceedings of a trial of the case involved.

It has been construed that if qualified judges' authoritative involvement is not attained at least once in both the finding of facts and the application of law, respectively, it shall amount to the infringement of the core elements of the right to trial by judges.[112]

4.2.6 Social Rights

Social rights are those rights which guarantee an individual to request the State to provide certain entitlements necessary to maintain a humane livelihood and sustain a life worthy of a human being. Traditionally, these rights are differentiated from civil and political liberties in that the latter has a negative character while the former has a positive feature. Although the dichotomy of positive and negative has become blurred due to the growing complexity of the protection mechanism of basic rights, the separate recognition of this category of rights still has great significance partly because their fulfillment is much more dependent upon the national economy or budget and thereby requires additional qualifications like citizenship to enjoy them. In the area of international human rights law, this category is categorized as "Economic, Social and Cultural Rights" as opposed to "Civil and Political Freedoms."

Since the First Constitution of 1948, Korean constitutionalism has featured social state characteristics at least in the explicit recognition of social rights in the constitutional text. In the present Constitution, well-ranged rights are guaranteed from the right to education, the right to work, the right to trade unions, the right to a healthy and pleasant environment to the right to respect for family life.

Article 31(1) guarantees the right to receive equal education according to one's abilities. To materialize this basic right, the State must actively carry out an

[111] Constitutional Court Decision 95Hun-Ba3, December 28, 1995, *Decisions of the Korean Constitutional Court*, Vol. 7, No. 2, 841; Constitutional Court Decision 94Hun-Ma118, June 13, 1996, *Decisions of the Korean Constitutional Court*, Vol. 8, No. 1, 500; Constitutional Court Decision 2005Hun-Ba28, May 26, 2005.

[112] Constitutional Court Decision 2001Hun-Ga18, February 28, 2002, *Decisions of the Korean Constitutional Court*, Vol. 14, No. 1, 98, 103.

effective public education system. The Constitution expressly articulates some specific institutions to which the State must provide special contribution to promote the right to education. They include free compulsory education, access to lifelong education, and the autonomy of institutions of higher learning [Articles 31(2), 31(3), 31(4), 31(5)]. The Constitution protects certain substantive values, such as independence, professionalism and political impartiality of education, to promote the right to education so that any legislative attempt to significantly undermine these values can be declared unconstitutional and become ineffective, although the National Assembly is constitutionally given a wide latitude to formulate educational policy in relation to basic matters pertaining to the education system [Article 31(4) and (6)].

Article 32 guarantees the right to work and secures the duty of the State to provide a variety of special protection for minorities. The areas of concern in this regard range from the employment opportunities and optimum wages of workers, standards of working conditions, the discrimination of working women and working children, and privileges for those who have given distinguished service to the State, wounded veterans and policemen, and members of the bereaved families of military servicemen and policemen killed in action [Article 32(2) to (6)].

Article 33(1) provides the right to trade unions. However, the fact that Article 31(2) allows too wide a legislative latitude in determining the scope of public officials who are entitled to exercise the right to association, collective bargaining and collective action for enhancing working conditions has been under attack for a danger of being misused to deny all of these rights to the considerable extent of public officials. This concern became reinforced by the Constitutional Court's interpretation that the principle of proportionality or the rule against excessive restraints cannot be applied to the cases of the public officials whose right to trade unions is denied by the Act on the Establishment and Operation of Public Officials' Unions, because the Constitution delegates to the Legislature the authority to deny such rights.[113] One dissenting opinion in this case had a view that despite the formal constitutional delegation of the power to set up the scope of public officials regarding the right to trade unions, the legislative latitude cannot be absolute so that the law denying overall union rights of a wide range of public officials must be subject to the rule against excessive restraint.

Article 34(1) provides the entitlement of a life worthy of a human being. In the ensuing clauses, the Constitution orders the State endeavor to promote a variety of social protection in relation to humane livelihoods and life styles. They include social security and welfare in general, the welfare and rights of women, senior citizens, the young, the disabled and the poor in particular. The nature of these entitlements and the State's duty has been the topic of public and professional

[113] Constitutional Court Decision 2005Hun-Ma971, December 26, 2008, *Decisions of the Korean Constitutional Court*, Vol. 20, No. 2, Part 2, 666.

debates since this clause was first inserted into the Constitution's text in 1962. However, although the actualization of this clause is heavily dependent upon legislative efforts, it is generally accepted that those entitlements cannot be regarded mere directives or guidance for the State but they are to be "abstract" basic rights from which more materialistic statutory rights can be derived.[114]

In Article 35 and Article 36, more social rights with abstract characteristics are listed: the right to a healthy and pleasant environment, the entitlement of assured comfortable housing, the entitlement to protective motherhood, and the protection of the heath of the people.

What has drawn more focused attention from the Constitutional Court in recent days is the right and freedom of marriage and family life guaranteed by Article 36(1) of the Constitution. For one thing, although this clause makes clear that marriage and family life shall be sustained on the basis of individual dignity and gender equality, longstanding social practice has prevented this idea from being fulfilled to the maximum extent. There have been a number of discriminatory clauses in civil codes as well as criminal codes subject to constitutional review. Some representative cases[115] include the law banning same-surname-same-origin marriages,[116] patrilineality as the basis for nationality law,[117] the male-centric householder system,[118] and the compulsory patrilineal family name system.[119]

4.2.7 Constitutional Duties

There are two basic constitutional duties recognized by the Constitution. First, Article 38 imposes on the people the duty to pay taxes as prescribed by law. The authority to determine the types and rates of taxes is expressly entrusted to the National Assembly under Article 59 of the Constitution. This mechanism is construed to embody the modern democratic idea of "no taxation without representation". The Constitutional Court has made clear that the legislative power to levy

[114] Constitutional Court Decision 93Hun-Ga14, July 21, 1995, *Decisions of the Korean Constitutional Court*, Vol. 7, No. 2, 1, 30–31; Constitutional Court Decision 97Hun-Ga10, 97Hun-Ba42, 97Hun-Ma354 (Consolidated), February 27, 1998, *Decisions of the Korean Constitutional Court*, Vol. 10, No. 1, 15, 30; Constitutional Court Decision 98Hun-Ma216, *Decisions of the Korean Constitutional Court*, Vol. 12, No. 1, 622, 647.

[115] For the summaries of these cases in English, see the Constitutional Court (2008), pp. 414–438.

[116] Constitutional Court Decision 95Hun-Ga6 through 13 (Consolidated), July 16, 1997, *Decisions of the Korean Constitutional Court*, Vol. 9, No. 2, 1–2, 11–18.

[117] Constitutional Court Decision 97Hun-Ga12, August 31, 2000, *Decisions of the Korean Constitutional Court*, Vol. 12, No. 2, 167, 182–183.

[118] Constitutional Court Decision 2001Hun-Ga9·10·11·12·13·14·15, 2004Hun-Ga5 (Consolidated), February 3, 2005, *Decisions of the Korean Constitutional Court*, Vol. 17, No. 1, 1, 18–25.

[119] Constitutional Court Decision 2003Hun-Ga5, December 22, 2005, *Decisions of the Korean Constitutional Court*, Vol. 17, No. 2, 544.

taxes must abide by the principle of proportionality and thus, for example, the imposition of surtaxes on those who failed to carry out the duty to pay taxes must conform to the required proportionality between the gravity of violation and the level of sanction.[120]

The second duty the Constitution imposes on the people is the duty to provide national defense. Article 39(1) stipulates that "All citizens shall have the duty to provide national defense as prescribed by law." The Constitutional Court interpreted this duty in a broad sense that includes not only a direct contribution to the military service, like military conscription, but also the duty to provide indirect cooperation to a military order.[121] The ensuing clause in Article 39(2) forbids any unfavorable treatment on account of the fulfillment of one's obligation of military service. The meaning of "unfavorable treatment" in this clause has often been discussed when the Court had opportunities to consider the question of whether this clause can be interpreted to request the State to provide appropriate compensation for serving in the military. Its answer was negative on the ground that the duty to provide national defense, such as military conscription, cannot be regarded as a special sacrifice deserving proper returns.[122] For example, the Court ruled that the extra-point system given to veterans in civil service examinations cannot be justified by the "unfavorable treatment" clause.[123]

It needs to be mentioned here that in addition to these general duties of the people, the Constitution have two more clauses to impose certain duties on the people. First, Article 31(2) of the Constitution obligates a group of people with children to provide their children with at least elementary schooling and other compulsory education as provided by law. Second, Article 32(2) provides for the people's duty to work while making clear that the extent and conditions of such duty must be prescribed by law in conformity with democratic principles. These specific duties can be differentiated from the above general duties in relation to tax payment and national defense because, unlike the latter duties, the former obligations are directly connected to the enhancement of basic rights of the duty holders themselves or their special relations.

---

[120] Constitutional Court Decision 2004Hun-Ba26, February 24, 2005, *Decisions of the Korean Constitutional Court*, Vol. 17, No. 1, 242, 250.

[121] Constitutional Court Decision 91Hun-Ma80, December 28, 1995, *Decisions of the Korean Constitutional Court*, Vol. 7, No. 2, 851, 868; Constitutional Court Decision 2002Hun-Ba45, November 28, 2002, *Decisions of the Korean Constitutional Court*, Vol. 14, No. 2, 704, 710.

[122] Constitutional Court Decision 98Hun-Ba33, December 23, 1999, *Decisions of the Korean Constitutional Court*, Vol. 11, No. 2, 732, 746; Constitutional Court Decision 2002Hun-Ma484, June 26, 2003, *Decisions of the Korean Constitutional Court*, Vol. 15, No. 1, 802, 807–808.

[123] Constitutional Court Decision 98Hun-Ba33, December 23, 1999, *Decisions of the Korean Constitutional Court*, Vol. 11, No. 2, 732, 746.

5 Constitution and The Economy[124]

One feature of the Constitution of the ROK is that there is a separate chapter entitled "The Economy" designated for the relationship between the State and the economy. Chapter 9, consisting of seven Articles, sets force basic principles governing the national economy and basic institutions the constitution-makers think important to pursue and implement those principles.

5.1 Basic Principles of Economic Order

Article 119(1) of the Constitution states that "the economic order of the Republic of Korea shall be based on respect for the freedom and creative initiatives of enterprises and individuals in economic affairs." Together with the recognition of property as a basic constitutional right, this provision is construed to make clear that the Korean economic order is a capitalist economy.

However, it might be too hasty to anticipate that the Korean Economy is a purely laissez-faire economic order, because a competing principle, i.e., the principle of democratization of the economy allowing the State's wide intervention in the economy is ensued in Article 119(2) providing that "the State may regulate and coordinate economic affairs in order to maintain the balanced growth and stability of the national economy, to ensure the proper distribution of incomes, to prevent the domination of the market and the abuse of economic power and to democratize the economy through harmony among the economic agents." The Constitutional Court has put forward a compromised interpretation of these seemingly competing ideas of economic order that, although the basis of economic order is free-market centered order respecting private property rights and free competition, the State may intervene in the economy to eliminate social problems stemming from free market and to pursue social welfare and justice.[125]

As a consequence, the Korean economy can be regarded as a kind of mixed-economy or a "social market economy" in the sense that market can be regulated to promote social welfare. However, it is not meant that the State can intervene in the economy whenever it wishes because of the principle of subsidiarity in that the State's intervention in private economy should be implemented only when it is necessary to complement self-determination on the part of individuals and enterprises.[126] It is also reiterated in a number of cases that even when the State's

---

[124] This section is based upon the author's previous paper. See Kim J (2005a).

[125] E.g., Constitutional Court Decision 96Hun-Ga4, 97Hun-Ga6·7, 95Hun-Ba58 (Consolidated), May 28, 1998, *Decisions of the Korean Constitutional Court*, Vol. 10, No. 1, 533, 534.

[126] E.g., Constitutional Court Decision 88Hun-Ga13, December 22, 1989, *Decisions of the Korean Constitutional Court*, Vol. 1, 377.

intervention is required, it should be limited to the degree and level restricted by the proportionality rule stemming from the rule of law principle.[127]

5.2 Democratization of the Economy: Pluralist Economic Order

As mentioned above, democratization of the economy is declared as a counter-balancing principle to the free-market economy in the Constitution.[128] To implement this principle, the Constitution of the ROK is construed as arranging a pluralist economic order by promoting the organization and management of socio-economic self-help groups, such as cooperative societies for farmers and fishermen, federation of small and medium businesses, and consumers' cooperative association [Article 123(5) and Article 124].[129] The organization and activities of trade unions, the most important interest groups in a capitalist economy, are not mentioned in this part of the Constitution, but more strongly protected by workers' constitutional rights of association, collective bargaining and collective action safeguarded in Article 33 of the Constitution.

Furthermore, the Constitution mandates that the State shall establish and implement plans to comprehensively develop and support agriculture and fisheries, and small and medium enterprises [Article 123(1) and (3)]. In particular, the State is obliged to endeavor to stabilize the prices of agricultural and fishery products by maintaining an equilibrium between the demand and supply of such products and improving their marketing and distribution systems [Article 123(4)].

Balanced development of the national economy is not confined to the dimension of functional industrial division but also required in the dimension of regional division. Therefore, the Constitution imposes constitutional duty on the State to foster regional economies to ensure the balanced development of all regions [Article 123(2)].[130]

---

[127] E.g., Constitutional Court Decision 94Hun-Ga2, November 30, 1995, *Decisions of the Korean Constitutional Court*, Vol. 7, No. 2, 544.

[128] Cf. Kwon Y-s (2006), pp. 897–898.

[129] See Kim J (2006).

[130] The Constitutional Court confirmed this in the Local Soju Compulsory Purchase System case. The Court ruled that, while the primary aim of regional economic development stated in Article 123 is the reduction of economic disparity among regions, there is no concrete regional disparity calling for such adjustment under the Liquor Tax Act seeking to maintain one soju maker in every province (Constitutional Court Decision 96Hun-Ga18, December 26, 1996, Decisions of the Korean Constitutional Court, Vol. 8, No. 2, 680).

5.3 State's Preemption of Natural Resources and Energies

Article 120 of the Constitution represents the principle of socialization of natural resources and energies. The State secures preemptive power to grant licenses to exploit, develop or utilize minerals and all other important underground resources, marine resources, water power, and natural energies available for economic use for a limited period, as prescribed by the National Assembly Act [Article 120(1)]. In this regard, the State should establish a plan for the balanced development and utilization of natural resources and land [Article 120(2)].

5.4 Land Regulation

Land is very important in the economy and welfare of the people because it is the basis for their daily lives, in particular economic activities. The efficient and balanced utilization of land is more crucial in the ROK than other countries because of its high population density, traditional preference for land ownership and, as a corollary, severe land speculation.

Article 122 states that the State may impose, as prescribed by Act, restrictions or obligations necessary for the efficient and balanced utilization, development and preservation of State-owned land. Together with the State's duty to make a plan for land use, this provision confers a wide discretion to regulate land use on the State. There are a number of statues for regulating land use. They include the Framework Act on the National Land, the National Land Planning and Use Act, and the Restitution of Development Gains Act.

5.5 Nationalization of Private Enterprises

Under the Constitution, in principle, private enterprises shall not be nationalized nor transferred to local government ownership. However, under special conditions stated in the Constitution, there is an exception to this principle. Article 126 provides that urgent necessities of national defense or the national economy confirmed by the National Assembly Act may justify nationalization of, or similar State intervention in, private enterprises.

5.6 Other Economic Arrangements

The ROK is a developing country based upon the export-driven economy in which foreign trade is crucial to the national economy. Reflecting this circumstance, the

Constitution expresses the State's power to regulate foreign trade and its obligation to promote it (Article 125). However, this constitutional power becomes practically nominal as far as the WTO system is concerned.

Another interesting provision is Article 121(1), which declares that tenant farming shall be prohibited and the State is obliged to promote the agricultural land-to-the-tillers principle. However, the leasing of agricultural land and the consignment management of agricultural land to increase agricultural productivity and to ensure the rational utilization of agricultural land or due to unavoidable circumstances, shall be recognized under the conditions prescribed by Act. This reflects the historical need for the eradication of feudal legacy in the past.

In addition, the State is supposed to strive to provide social and institutional infrastructure necessary for stable economic development, for example, the implementation of policies to develop science and technology, information and human resources, the encouragement of innovation, and the establishment of a system for national standards and relevant national advisory organizations.

6 Concluding Remarks: Recent Challenges and Responses in Korean Constitutionalism

Since the Moo-hyun Roh Administration, when constitutional strife has become routine in normal politics, the movement for the amendment or revision of the present Constitution has recurred. This movement, initiated not only by politicians but also civil society across the political spectrum, pointed out a number of problems arguably inherent in the Constitution of 1987.

First, it was made too hasty under a strong influence of major political forces led by Young-sam Kim, Dae-jung Kim, Tae-woo Roh, and Jong-pil Kim to reflect Korean people's genuine will and ideal of democracy and the rule of law, although some important progresses, such as people's direct presidential elections and the introduction of the Constitutional Court system, were accomplished through it.

Second, the form of government which the present Constitution envisaged to establish is a "balanced" system in which systematic cooperation between the National Assembly and the President is a pre-condition of well-functioning of the system, by giving them a room for intervention in each other's power. However, this system is very unstable because, according to political situation changes, it can result in either imperial presidency or a divided government leading to ungovernable presidency. The President's lack of accountability originated from one-term limitation is another source of criticism.

Third, the ROK Constitution needs to reflect a changed atmosphere within and outside the Korean Peninsula. The confrontation between South and North Koreas has caused a couple of fundamental constitutional issues repeatedly. Globalization and the creation of economic blocs have transformed the relationship between domestic constitutional issues and international issues into a highly intermingled complex system, so that the independence of a sovereign nation has become vulnerable at least in the level of national economy. In response, the status of the people in this changing environment needs to be readjusted to the new development.

In the course of public movements, the Final Report of the Advisory Commission on Constitutional Amendment for the Speaker of the National Assembly was published on August 2008. There were three points in this Report. First, the Bill of Rights should be reorganized in a manner that is supplemented by new freedoms and rights, such as the right to life and security and the basic right to access to information. Second, the constitutional structure of the government should be reformed in the direction of lessening President's power, for example, by changing the form of government from the current five-single term presidency to the semi-presidential or premier-presidential system. Third, the judicial system should be democratized and rationalized by adopting new institutions and changing the formation of the Judiciary, including the Constitutional Court. Proposed judicial reforms include the repeal of recommendation power of the Chief Justice of the Supreme Court for Associate Justices when there is vacancy, the introduction of abstract norm control,[131] the transfer of jurisdiction of election suits from the ordinary courts to the Constitutional Court.

Despite the plausibility of the arguments for constitutional reform, however, it is also true that some problems with current constitutional politics can be solved, not only by way of constitutional amendment, but also legislative reform or changes in political culture which play a substantial role in the working of constitutional arrangements. Given the above considerations, the premise to the specific arguments for constitutional amendment may be such that they are envisaged to respond to the cause of problems imbedded in the target constitutional institutions and the alternatives to the present system are more effective than other means like legislative solutions. Without such practical implication, arguments for constitutional amendment cannot easily attract public support.[132] From this point of view, what should be given more attention would be how to enhance independence and effectiveness of non-political branches such as the Judiciary, the Constitutional Court, the Election Commission, and the Board of Audit and Inspection rather than the relationship between the Legislature and the Executive partly because the latter factor requires more constitutional flexibility than the former.

Furthermore, irrespective of the persuasiveness of constitutional reform, it is the will of the sovereign people that decides whether or not a new Constitution is necessary. If they prefer practical agenda like economic and social policies to the institutional or constitutional change, this choice should be respected in the real politics.

---

[131] "Abstract norm control" is a system of constitutional review as opposed to "concrete norm control" in that even if there is no specific cases or controversies in the judicial proceedings, the Constitutional Court may review whether laws governing such hypothetical cases are compatible with the Constitution upon the request of designated applicants such as the President or members of the National Assembly.

[132] For the rough examination of the Final Report above from this point of view, see Kim J (2010c), pp. 125–157.

References

Constitutional Court (2008) The Twenty Years of the Constitutional Court of Korea. Constitutional Court, Seoul.

Currie D (2000) The constitution of the United States: a primer for the people, 2nd edn. University of Chicago Press, Chicago.

Hirschl R (2006) The new constitutionalism and the judicialization of pure politics worldwide. Fordham Law Rev 75:721 ff

Huh Y (2009) Constitutional theory and constitutional law, New 3rd Edition. Pakyoungsa, Seoul, pp 1179–1180

Huh Y (2010) Theory of the Korean constitution. Pakyoungsa, Seoul, pp 717–719

Jeong J-h (1994) Issues regarding the constitution of the Constitutional Court and constitutional judicial proceedings. Public Law 22(2):39–40

Kim J (2001) Some problems with the Korean constitutional adjudication system. J Korean Law 1(2):26–28

Kim J (2002a) A critical analysis of the constitutional status and function of the board of audit and inspection. Public Law 31(2):195–223

Kim J (2002b) Critical review of the decision of unconstitutionality on the method of voting and distribution of seats in the system of nationwide proportional seats – Constitutional Court Decision 2000Hun-Ma91.112.134 (Consolidated), July 19, 2001. Study Const Pract 3:321–366

Kim J (2005a) Property rights and economic order under the constitution of the Republic of Korea. In: Proceedings of the 1st Asian Forum for Constitutional Law 2005 – Constitutionalism and Constitutional Adjudication in Asia, September 24, 2005. Seoul National University, Seoul

Kim J (2005b) A proposal for reform in the composition of the constitutional court. Const Law Rev 11(2)

Kim J (2006) Social polarization and the Korean Constitutional Law. Korean J Law Soc 31:9–32

Kim J (2008) Government reform, judicialization, the development of public law in the Republic of Korea. In: Ginsburg T, Chen A (eds) Administrative law and governance in Asia: comparative perspectives. Routledge, New York, pp 101–126, Ch. 6

Kim J (2010a) The structure and basic principles of constitutional adjudication in the Republic of Korea. In: Cho K (ed) Litigation in Korea. Edward Elgar Publishing, London, Ch. 6.

Kim J (2010b) Constitutional revision and judicial reform. Const Law Rev 16(3):120–123

Kim J (2010c) Does Korean democracy really need another constitutional revision?: a critical review on proposals of the Advisory Commission for constitutional revision for the speaker of the national assembly. Korean J Law Soc 38:125–157

Kwon Y-s (2006) The Relevance of Constitutional Law: Theories and Discourses. Bobmunsa, Seoul

Kwon Y (2010) Constitutional law. Bobmunsa, Paju Bookcity, p 146

Park J (2008) The judicialization of politics in Korea. Asian-Pac Law Policy J 10:67–83

Yang K, Kim M-h, Nam B-h (1999) Report of Research on How to Amend the Constitutional Court Act, Series for Studies on Constitutional Adjudication, the Constitutional Court, No. 10, pp 14–16

The Role of Administrative Law in Economic Development and Democracy in Korea

Hamyoung Jeong

1 The Birth of Korean Administrative Law

1.1 Historical Background

Korea won its independence from Japan in 1945. Korea has experimented with its own democracy since it established the Democratic Constitution and its Government in 1948. In 1948, the U.S military government, led by General John R. Hodge, departed from the Korean peninsula after their 3-year governance. Korea has adapted a presidential system with a brief period of parliamentary cabinet system in the early 1960s, since Korea made its own Constitution in 1948.[1] U.S. law and legal practice have not only influenced Korea, but also left their mark on international transaction law and many other laws.[2]

Some aspects of Western democratic political and legal systems were introduced into Korea during the Japanese colonial period. Under the Japanese colonial government, there were no institutional and procedural devices for separation of powers. The Japanese governor-general had unrestrained executive and legislative power. He could issue decrees in the Korean peninsula and was a de-facto king of Korea. The local courts were just subordinate administrative organizations of the governor-general's authoritarian government. The imperial Japan tried to transplant its government, including its court structure, directly to Korea. There was no chance of realization of constitutionalism in the Korean peninsula during the days of Japanese colony.[3]

[1] Lee (2005).

[2] Wilson (2010).

[3] Ahn (1997).

H. Jeong (✉)
KyungPook National University Law School, Daegu, Republic of Korea

Korea Legislation Research Institute, *Introduction to Korean Law*,
DOI 10.1007/978-3-642-31689-0_3, © Springer-Verlag Berlin Heidelberg 2013

Syngman Rhee was the first President of the newly-formed Republic of Korea and held strong anti-Japanese and anti-communist views. He maintained fierce authoritarian control over the government even though his political ideology was based upon the American democratic model. The North Korean army invaded South Korea in June, 1950 and the Korean War continued for 3 years. The Korean War led, not only to the deaths of millions of people, but also to the total destruction of its industrial facilities. President Rhee's administration became increasingly unpopular in the late 1950s. He resigned soon after a large-scale student demonstration on April 19, 1960. The prevalent corruption led to the overthrow of President Rhee in a sense.

After President Rhee's resignation, the South Korean National Assembly adopted a new constitution that created a bicameral parliamentary system. Prime Minister Chang Myon was elected under this new system in 1960. Chang's administration was plagued with political and economic scandals. The replaced Second Republic fell to a coup d'etat by General Park Chung Hee in 1961.[4]

President Park Chung Hee initiated a period of centralized bureaucratic control over the economy and the financial system. He formed an Economic Planning Board to coordinate economic policies, with a mandate to promote exports and, later, heavy industrialization. President Park launched anti-corruption drives, got rid of thousands of bureaucrats, and promoted meritocratic policies. These measures were successful and the economy took off. President Park consolidated his power in the early 1960s and South Korea was following a state-lead capitalist development path.[5]

President Park grew an obviously authoritarian regime after his launching of the Fourth Republic in 1972. General Chun Doo Hwan established the Fifth Republic in 1981. Following massive protests in 1987, Chun's designated successor, Roh Tae Woo, launched a democratization program that led to significant constitutional reforms, including direct presidential elections and the creation of the Constitutional Court. A major administrative overhaul was begun under President Kim Young Sam in 1993, and reforms accelerated after the election of his successor, Kim Dae-Jung in 1997.[6]

Korean administrative law originated in the era of Japanese colonial days and modeled after the Japanese adaptation of the Western European model; there were no separate administrative courts, however. During the days of colonial rule, all court proceedings were usually conducted before Japanese judges. There was an aversion to judicial procedures among Koreans during the days of Japanese colonial rule. Korea's own series of authoritarian governments also provided little incentive to litigate administrative acts for a long time. Although the Administrative Litigation Act was passed in 1951, there was actually little recourse to sue against administrative acts. The bureaucrats enjoyed great discretionary power. To be

[4] Choi (2006).

[5] Ohnesorge (1996).

[6] Ginsburg (2001), 590–91.

reviewable by the court, administrative acts had to constitute an exercise of public authority that restricted a plaintiff's legal right, and had additionally to constitute the final and conclusive stage of the administrative process with immediate legal effect. Even if one was successful in overcoming these hurdles, remedial provisions were minimal. Thus, there was little incentive to litigate.[7]

Korea revised its Administrative Litigation Act in 1984 and it was applicable to only a very narrow range of concrete administrative acts by State actors. The act discouraged litigation through strict standing requirements, by placing the burden of proof on plaintiffs with few means to access government documents and by limiting remedies to the quashing of particular administrative acts. The act also lacked a mechanism through which a court could issue an injunction against agency's actions and restricted standing so that collective interests could not be easily vindicated through it. Furthermore, the act required plaintiffs to exhaust administrative remedies before filing suit under it and the courts carved out only few exceptions.[8]

1.2 History of Administrative Law Reform

Things began to change after the creation of the Fifth Republic in 1981. President Chun Doo Hwan turned increasingly to rule-of-law discourse. The Administrative Appeals Act of 1984, which provided for an expanded framework for recourse by citizens, was revised. A complaint could bring an administrative appeal against an administrative action on the ground that it was not only an illegal act, but also an abusive exercise of discretionary power.[9]

This act essentially provided for appeals of administrative actions to a superior administrative agency and gave superior agencies the power to revise or cancel illegal measures adopted by subordinate administrative authorities. All public authorities were required to establish their own administrative appeals commission to hear particular appeals against them. Each administrative appeals commission was comprised of 15 members and chaired by the head of the public authority. This meant that each Ministry would be responsible for hearing complaints against it. The Administrative Appeals Act provided a means for superior bureaucrats to control subordinate bodies, but did not provide for a truly independent constraint by the courts. Korean administrative law sought to minimize judicial oversight.[10] However, administrative litigation began to increase after 1990, reflecting the evolving procedural framework.

[7] Ibid. 596–97.

[8] Ohnesorge (2006), 115–117.

[9] Korean Statute No. 9968. Section 5. revised on Jan. 25, 2010.

[10] Ginsburg (2001), 598.

In 1992, President Kim Young Sam became the first civilian to be elected President since 1960, and took several steps to control prevalent corruption. Such measures included establishing a public official wealth registration system to identify discrepancies in individual wealth before and after careers in public service.[11] He also established the Presidential Commission on Administrative Reform in April of 1993. This Commission recommended the passage of an Administrative Procedure Law[12] as well as a number of deregulatory steps and government reorganization. Further support came from the academic community, which had long pressed for an administrative procedural regime as an essential element of legal modernization in Korea.[13]

The judiciary also emphasized the importance of procedural constraints on administrative actions. Korean Constitution provides that all citizens should enjoy personal liberty under Article 12 (1) "No person can be arrested, detained, searched, seized or interrogated except as provided by law. No person shall be punished, placed under preventive restrictions or subject to involuntary labor except as provided by law and through lawful procedures." The Korean Constitutional Court also ruled that the lawful procedure clause must be applied to administrative actions even though the clause was originally intended to apply criminal punishments.[14]

With respect to specific administrative acts, the Administrative Procedure Act legalizes agency decision-making with respect to applications by requiring agencies to promulgate decision criteria in advance, including time periods within which the agency must act. It also requires notice and an opportunity for at least an informal hearing prior to administrative action affecting private rights. It requires that agencies should provide grounds and reasons for their decisions.[15]

Toward the end of the twentieth century, Korea transitioned from a dictatorship to a vibrant and developing democracy, one that has flourished in recent decades. There was dramatic economic growth during that period, something that became known as the Asian Tiger phenomenon.[16]

1.3 The Rule of Law in Korea

The rule of law defines that the system in which all public authority is governed by law and the law is viewed as a product of the legislative body. Additionally, public administrative agencies should be stood by law.[17] In Germany, the Rechtsstaat

[11] The Public Officer Ethics Act, revised on June 11, 1993. Kor. Stat. No. 4566.

[12] Issued on Dec. 31, 1996. Enforced on Jan. 1, 1998. Kor. Stat. No. 5241.

[13] Kim (2009).

[14] Korean Constitutional Court 92HunGa8 Dec. 24, 1992.

[15] Ohnesorge (2006), 126–127.

[16] Bingham et al. (2007), 389.

[17] Park (2010), 14–23.

concept is similar to the rule of law but is translated as state rule through law. The Rechtstaat concept also has been developed into the Verfassungsstaat after the World War II.[18] The Korean concept of the rule of law is closer to the German notion of Rechtstaat.[19]

Germany's Rechtstaat concept was introduced as the rule of law doctrine in Korea like many other public law doctrines. Under the Rechtstaat concept, the State is based on the supremacy of a national constitution by exercising coercion. It guarantees the safety and constitutional rights of its citizens. Additionally, civil society is an equal partner to the state. Separation of powers, between the executive, legislative and judicative branches of government limits each other's power and provides for checks and balances. The judiciary and the executive are each bound by law (no acting against the law), and the legislature is bound by constitutional principles.

There are very important principles of the Rechtsstaat: transparency of state acts and the requirement of providing reasoning for all state acts, judicial review of state decisions and state acts, reliability of state actions, prohibition of retroactivity, and the principle of the proportionality of state actions. In the Rechtsstaat, statute constituted the highest source of law, binding administrators. The statute is the main source of legally binding power, and state acts should be based thereon. Individuals would be able to have access to the courts and to secure a remedy against wrongful encroachments on their legally protected interests.[20]

1.4 The Overly-Recognition of Executive Rule-Making Power and Policy-Making Powers

The Korean Constitution has separation of powers provisions. Legislative power is vested in the National Assembly [21] Executive power is vested in the Executive Branch, headed by the President.[22] Judicial power is vested in courts composed of judges.[23] In addition to the separation of powers provisions, the Korean Constitution has provisions concerning delegation of legislative power. The Korean Constitution provides that the President may issue presidential decrees concerning matters delegated to him by law with the scope specifically defined and also matters necessary to enforce laws.[24] It means that the Executive's rule-making powers are overly recognized in the Korean Constitution.

[18] Rosenfeld (2001), 1307, 1328.

[19] Park (2010), 14–23.

[20] Barber (2003).

[21] Korean Constitution Chapter III. Article 40.

[22] Korean Constitution Chapter IV. Article 66.(4).

[23] Korean Constitution Chapter V. Article 101.(1).

[24] Korean Constitution Chapter IV. Article 75.

The Executive can make regulations according to directions and the scope of the statute. This means that the National Assembly can delegate rule-making power to the President with a specific scope. This provision can be interpreted as the delegation provision. In addition to the President's power to make presidential decrees in order to implement the statute, the Prime Minister and other Ministers can also issue ordinances to implement the statutes and presidential decrees.[25] The Local Government may also enact regional provisions relating to local autonomy, within the limits of laws and regulations.[26]

The Judiciary may also issue regulations to implement the statutes. The Supreme Court may make regulations to expedite and implement the statutes.[27] The Constitutional Court also has the similar power to make regulations.[28]

There are two different types of administrative regulations. The first kind of regulation has legally binding power, and the other does not. There are great deals of bureaucratic controls over the process of drafting legislation and policy implementation in Korea.[29]

2 Rapid Economic Development

Shortly after the Republic of Korea was born, the Korean War broke out in 1950, dividing the country into the Democratic South and the Communist North. Japanese colonization and the Korean War made Korea one of the poorest countries in the world. From the 1960s to the 1980s, South Korea's economy made extraordinary progress, which, in turn, drastically changed the cultural and social landscape of the country. During the three decades preceding the 1997 financial crisis, the Korean economy grew from that of a poor developing country to one of the world's leading economies. In 1996, Korea joined the prestigious OECD club of wealthy nations, after taking several measures to liberalize its capital markets. Korean economic transformation was built upon the education and entrepreneurial energy of the Korean people, the maintenance of a generally stable macro-economic environment, and high levels of public and private savings and investments. One of the major sources of Korean economic development was government policies. They encouraged industrialization, heavy industry development, a strong export orientation, active promotion of foreign investment, and technology transfer.[30]

[25] Korean Constitution Chapter IV. Article 95.

[26] Korean Constitution Chapter VII. Article 117 (1).

[27] Korean Constitution Chapter V Article 108.

[28] Korean Constitution Chapter VI. Article 113(2).

[29] Ginsburg (2001), 593.

[30] Final Report and Legal Reform Recommendations to the Ministry of Justice of the Republic of Korea (2001), 550–553.

The Korean Government financially relied on foreign loans guaranteed by state-owned banks. It used a variety of measures to prefer certain firms over others and direct them to specific industries. Korean policymakers used administrative guidance to ensure that Chaebols received policy loans for government-led projects.[31] Under the Korean model, bureaucrats usually operated with substantial administrative discretion, and used informal administrative guidance to induce voluntary compliance by the regulated community under implicit threats of retaliation.[32]

There are several statutes which are labeled as promotion laws in Korea, such as the Science Education Promotion Act,[33] the Vocational Education and Training Promotion Act,[34] the Culture and Arts Promotion Act,[35] the Game Industry Promotion Act,[36] the Aerospace Industry Development Promotion Act,[37] and the Alternative Energy Development Promotion Act.[38] They do not have regulatory frame works and provide policy directions. With these promotion laws, the Korean Government can provide information, subsidies and tax deductions to industries. The Government presents a clear government policy direction. The industries can also allocate scarce resources to specific areas. This policy can prevent waste of resources and promote rapid social development to catch up with high technology in a short term. A government initiative presents a model of social development.[39]

In January 2000, Korea enacted the Software Industry Promotion Act to apply a modern framework to the software industry.[40] The Act aimed to re-enforce the competitiveness of the Korean software industry and to contribute to sound national economic development.[41] According to the Act, the government can provide tax deductions, financial support, and information services to the software industry.[42] The software industry has developed incredibly during the last decade and the Korean Government predicted that the total amount of export of software-related products will be more than 10 billion dollars in 2011.[43]

Most large publicly held Korean corporations are affiliated with a business group, the so-called Chaebol.[44] There is no statutory provision defining Chaebol in Korea. It is defined as a group of formally independent firms under single

[31] Kim (2008).

[32] Bingham et al. (2007).

[33] Korean Statute No. 10083, March 3, 2010 partly revised.

[34] Korean Statute No. 10339, June 4, 2010 partly revised.

[35] Korean Statute No. 10108, March 17, 2010 partly revised.

[36] Korean Statute No. 10219, March 31, 2010 revised.

[37] Korean Statute No. 9589, April 1, 2009 partly revised.

[38] Korean Statute No. 9931, Jan. 13, 2010 partly revised.

[39] Woon (2003).

[40] Korean Statute No. 10220, March 31, 2010 partly revised.

[41] Id. Section 1.

[42] Id. Section 18, 25, etc.

[43] www.mke.go.kr, last visited on Feb. 22, 2011.

[44] Seo (2006).

common administrative and financial control, owned and controlled by certain families. Korea's economic development was spearheaded by the family-dominated Chaebol, and the Korean Government's industrial policies were carried out through the Executive's policy preference. It was much more important than competition law in shaping Korea's industrial structure.[45]

The rapid industrialization and the strong ties between the Government and Chaebols resulted into serious corruption. There have been decade-long tension between the economic benefits of Chaebol-led growth and the political influence of the business groups. The rapid growth of Chaebols is actually considered to be the result of political decisions by the government—the result of governmental favoritism through interlocking relations among politicians or government policy-makers and entrepreneurs.

This regime of informal administration seems to correspond closely to the notion of the official perspective. The official perspective reserves wide areas of discretion, justified by special expertise. It also shields authority from challenge and criticism. The regimes of informal practices, which had been developed in the Korean legal system, are representing a living one in a sense. It is based on the principle of voluntary consent given by the party who receives the guidance.

There were prevalent uses of administrative guidance, which provided information, suggestions, and public goal settings. The problem with administrative guidance is that it can easily become a means of coercive control, especially when it is conducted informally and hidden from outside review. Normally administrative guidance is not practiced in open violation of the law and is based on some supporting legal arguments. Closed relationships behind closed doors between the Government and Chaebols might easily indulge into corruption because of its lack of outside control or oversight. Chaebols do indeed possess considerable power vis-a-vis the State and have been linked to a long series of political scandals. It was notorious that bribery, influence peddling, and extortion by officials have not been eradicated from politics, business and everyday life in Korea.[46]

3 Administrative Law Reform in Korea

3.1 Administrative Procedural Law

Academics had been discussing the need for an administrative procedural law for many years before its eventual enactment in 1996 in Korea. Such law is necessary because individuals and interest groups should be provided with opportunities to both observe and contribute to policy-making. Therefore, a public hearing requirement for proposed public policies should be considered as a means

[45] Ohnesorge (2010).

[46] Gilson and Milhaupt (2011).

to promote many elements of good governance. Oversight hearings on existing policies and programs are another useful tool, particularly as a means to maintain accountability.[47]

It is critical for decision-makers to be aware of the concerns, views, and circumstances of the public. Officials must explain their policies in open forums as well as at oversight hearings in advance of final determinations. Thus, their incentives to give earnest consideration to the choices and the interests they are advancing are sharpened. The Administrative Procedure Act radically changed Korean administrative law.[48]

Korean law requires agencies to establish processing periods and publicly announce standards for issuing dispositions.[49] Korean law requires formal hearings, but only when required by statute or deemed necessary by the agencies involved.[50]

The Korean Supreme Court ruled that an infringing administrative disposition was unlawful. The disposition was made without having undergone the process of a hearing on the grounds that notice of the hearing had been returned or on the grounds that the party concerned with the administrative disposition had been absent on the date of the hearing.[51] Article 14 (4) 3 of the Administrative Procedure Act stipulates that it is possible to omit the hearing process when reasonably deemed that the hearing of opinions is impractical or the hearing is clearly unnecessary considering the nature of the relevant dispositions.

According to a prior case, the Supreme Court ruled that whether the hearing of opinions is impractical or the hearing is clearly unnecessary must be determined by the nature of the administrative disposition concerned, and not by whether the hearing notice had been returned nor by the method of notification of the hearing, etc. The Supreme Court ruled the fact that the party concerned with the administrative disposition had been absent on the date of the hearing notified as such, alone did not justify the administrative agency's infringing administrative disposition conducted without having opened the hearing required by the Administrative Procedure Act or subordinate statutes in the same case.

It is laid down in the Administrative Procedure Act that a public hearing shall be held when it is needed to gather consensus on a wide range of opinions considering the potentially extensive influence of the relevant dispositions.[52]

This provides a mechanism for group participation in the administrative process. The Act also requires agencies to give reasons for adverse dispositions unless considered insignificant, and, upon request, to give reasons for favorable dispositions.[53]

---

[47] Esty (2006).

[48] Ginsburg (2001), 606.

[49] The Korean Administrative Procedure Act, Articles 19 and 20.

[50] The Korean Administrative Procedure Act, Articles 22.

[51] Korean Supreme Court Decision 2000Du3337 (April 13, 2001).

[52] The Korean Administrative Procedure Act, Article 27.

[53] The Korean Administrative Procedure Act, Article 23.

Administrative guidance is another case of informal practice. The Administrative Procedure Act of 1996 explicitly devotes a chapter to administrative guidance.[54] This section begins by setting the principle that administrative guidance should be minimal and only when it is necessary to achieve its purpose and should not be exercised against the will of the affected party.[55] This establishes a presumption against excessive guidance, although it is unlikely to have much impact as it is the bureaucrats who define the purpose of any particular exercise of guidance. Non-compliance with administrative guidance must not result in negative treatment by the agency.[56]

It would ensure that administrative guidance will be based on proper authority and that its acceptance will be strictly voluntary. Any use of sanctions for non-compliance will be prohibited. The Korean statute requires the agency to provide written guidance if so requested, except in cases of "extraordinary administrative inconvenience."[57]

Korean law requires administrative agencies to give prior notice of the proposed legislation that affects the rights and duties of citizens or the daily lives of citizens, and to allow public comment.[58] The procedures for this are to be prescribed by Presidential Decree. There is a similar chapter requiring prior notice of administrative action for four categories of policies, namely those that are "of great influence to the livelihood of citizens," that involve conflicts of interests among many citizens, that impose burdens on many citizens, and other matters that require wide accumulation of opinions from citizens.[59]

Together, these provisions are even more open than American notice-and-comment requirements for rulemaking, for they extend notice requirements to proposed legislation. This reflects the Korean practice that most statutes are, in fact, drafted by the bureaucracy. By providing an additional forum for comments on legislative proposals, Korean law opens up the policy process to those parties that lose in the Legislature. Public access to rulemaking through notice-and-comment-type procedures helps to inform interest groups when the Administration is seeking to overturn previous statutory decisions through subordinate lawmaking, allowing them to mobilize against change. The Korean legal system takes this one step further by extending notice requirements to proposed legislation itself.[60]

The fact that these provisions of the Administrative Procedure Act were enacted, reflects an important shift in Korean politics away from the executive dominance associated with developmental-state authoritarianism. These provisions become not only a reflection of a changed political dynamic, but also represent a new

[54] Ohnesorge (2006), 127.

[55] The Korean Administrative Procedure Act, Article 48 (1).

[56] The Korean Administrative Procedure Act, Article 48 (2).

[57] The Korean Administrative Procedure Act, Article 49.

[58] The Korean Administrative Procedure Act, Chapter 4. Articles 41, 42, 43, and 45.

[59] The Korean Administrative Procedure Act, Chapter 5. Article 46 and 47.

[60] Ginsburg (2001), 618.

mechanism through which politics may be further reformed. If these provisions of the Administrative Procedure Act are implemented aggressively, they will contribute to the further shift of power away from the executive branch and the State, toward the private sector.[61]

3.2 Administrative ADA

Korea had never employed the mechanism of the administrative court in spite of that the German origins of its administrative law system. The ordinary courts of appeals were the courts of first instance of litigation under the Administrative Litigation Act. Korea took the step of creating a specialized court as a division of the Seoul District Court, as well as administrative divisions in each of local courts.[62]

The 1994 amendments to the Administrative Litigation Act established the very first specialist administrative court at district level. The amendments also eliminated the requirement that a plaintiff exhausts administrative remedies, significantly expanding justiciability. In 1995, the Administrative Appeals Act of 1984 underwent a drastic revision. Instead of vertically segmented administrative adjudication in individual ministries, a new Administrative Appeals Commission under the Prime Minister was set up to handle virtually all administrative appeals against the central government. The members are senior public officials and the chair is the Minister of Legislation. This Commission is empowered to revoke or alter administrative dispositions as necessary. Its rulings are binding. If the agency concerned fails to abide by them, by not issuing an appropriate disposition, the ruling authority may directly issue the disposition. While Korea was expanding access to courts for administrative litigation, it was centralizing administrative appeals into a powerful new body.[63] The administrative appeals system is a mechanism allowing people whose legal rights have been violated, or who have experienced any form of injustice, by administrative agencies to appeal free of charge. Compared to going to court, this free-of-charge scheme provides quicker and simpler service to the people.[64]

South Korea is installing these new processes in a variety of its government institutions and creating both an opportunity and a need for participation by its citizens in the policy process. This is changing both the nature of information available to the Government in making public policy choices and the likely range of outcomes in conflict resolution. In addition to the above changes to the administrative law framework, Korea passed the Civil Petitions Treatment Act in 1997.[65]

---

[61] Ohnesorge (2006), 127.

[62] Ibid, 128.

[63] Ginsburg (2001), 606–7.

[64] Administrative Appeals Act, Korean Stat. No. 8852, revised Feb. 29, 2008.

[65] Enacted on Aug. 22, 1997, Korean Stat. No. 5369.

The Act supplements the administrative law regime by allowing petitions to be brought by any individual who alleges that an administrative act infringed his or her rights, or caused inconvenience and burden to citizens.[66] It extends not only to unlawful acts but also to "unreasonable" acts. It established a National Grievance Settlement Committee under the Prime Minister to receive, investigate and settle civil petitions. The Committee moved into the Anti-Corruption and Civil Rights Commission of Korea in 2008. To ensure consistency, the jurisdiction of the Committee extends only to acts for which another appeal has not been made. This was part of the effort to reinvent the Korean Government by ensuring responsiveness in public administration.[67]

Another element of reinventing the Korean Government was the Framework Act on Administrative Regulation.[68] Its aim is to reduce procedural burdens imposed by regulations, as exemplified by arbitrary or overlapping administrative investigations. The introduction of the Program for Reduction of Administrative Burden on Businesses was designed to reduce the workload of business incurred by information provision requirements, such as reporting, filing, and testing. It established the general principle of cost-benefit analysis and accordance with statutory purposes for all regulations, required agencies to conduct regulatory impact analysis. It established the Regulatory Reform Commission, co-chaired by the Prime Minister to review existing and proposed regulations in accordance with the requirements of statutes.[69]

The Regulatory Reform Commission has abolished numerous regulations that had not been based on adequate statutory authority and has facilitated the National Assembly's amendment to hundreds of statutes. Some 58 percent of Korea's regulations were abolished or amended throughout 2000.[70]

As part of this process of both democratization and administrative law reform in the early 1990s, Korea implemented new mechanisms for voicing, participation, and dispute settlement in the executive branch. Specifically, it adopted notice-and-comment processes not only for rule-making, but also for legislative proposals, the great majority of which are drafted by government ministries. It created an Ombudsman to receive complaints about administrative bureaucracy from members of the public.[71]

Ombudsman, Administrative Appeals, and National Grievance Settlement Committee are merged into the Anti-Corruption & Civil Rights Commission (ACRC) in 2008. This new-born committee's missions are to resolve people's grievances by protecting their rights and fighting corruption.[72] To achieve these goals, ACRC

---

[66] Ibid. Section 2.

[67] http://www.acrc.go.kr/eng_index.html last visited on May 10, 2011.

[68] Korean Stat. No. 5368. Enacted on Aug. 22, 1997.

[69] Ibid. Chapter 4, Section 22.

[70] Ginsburg (2001), 609.

[71] Bingham et al. (2007), 390.

[72] Act on Anti-Corruption and the Foundation of the Anti-Corruption & Civil Rights Commission Section 11.

places the greatest priority on the protection of people's rights and interests. Individuals may personally file complaints or designate another person to act on his or her behalf, via direct visit, mail, the Internet, fax, etc.[73]

People's grievances are about illegal and unfair practices of administrative agencies.[74] An investigator in ACRC may demand explanations on complaints, filed with submission of relevant materials and documents to the administrative agency concerned, and attendance and testimony of complainants, stake-holders, witnesses and relevant staff members.[75]

The investigator conducts an on-site investigation at the agency concerned and seeks advice from specialists. Upon the completion of investigation, the Commission deliberates opinions on evidences submitted. Based on the deliberation results, it recommends corrective measures or issues official opinions on the complaints or the relevant laws, institutions, and policies.[76]

The Commission immediately notifies matters for judgment to the parties concerned. The related administrative agencies should report how they implement these results within 30 days after receiving notification of the judgment from the Commission.[77]

ACRC is dedicated to identifying ineffective administrative systems and fixing them.[78] ACRC fulfills one of its missions, which is to root out the cause of people's grievances by uncovering systems that burden people and subsequently recommending institutional reform or voicing its own opinions.[79] To this end, it is devoted to discovering systems to be improved through a variety of channels like investigation of civil complaints, analysis of repeatedly filed complaints, review of suggestions made by citizens and civic groups, media monitoring, etc.

ACRC is dedicated to enhancing the quality of related systems by selecting the tasks that have a great impact on the everyday life of ordinary people. ACRC takes appropriate follow-up measures to ensure that recommendations are immediately incorporated into the present system.[80]

ACRC formulates national anti-corruption policies to be implemented at each level of the government. ACRC discusses and coordinates government-wide measures designed to prevent corruption in a short or long term.[81]

ACRC annually assesses the levels of integrity of public sector organizations by surveying citizens who have had firsthand experience with public service.

[73] Ibid. Section 39.

[74] Ibid. Section 2, 5.

[75] Ibid. Section 29.

[76] Ibid. Section 42.

[77] Ibid. Section 50.

[78] Ibid. Section 1.

[79] Ibid. Section 12.

[80] http://www.acrc.go.kr/eng_index.html last visited on May 10, 2011.

[81] Act on Anti-Corruption and the Foundation of the Anti-Corruption & Civil Rights Commission Section 27.

The Commission also evaluates the anti-corruption initiatives taken by public organizations on a regular basis. The fundamental objective of these assessments is to encourage public organizations to make voluntary efforts to tackle corruption. ACRC makes recommendations to help government agencies to amend ambiguous, corruption-prone laws and institutions, and regularly confirm the implementation of ACRC's recommendations.[82]

Corruption impact assessment is an analytical mechanism designed to identify and remove corruption-causing factors in laws and regulations. Under this system, every proposed enactment and amendment as well as existing legislation are examined for any factor that could contribute to the occurrence of corrupt practices.[83]

3.3 Korean Freedom of Information Act

Information law reflects the same political rationale as administrative procedure. There had been a lot of discussion to introduce an American-style Freedom of Information Act in Korea. The Korean Constitutional Court confirmed that the public has the basic right to access to public information on the basis of Article 21 of the Korean Constitution, regardless of statutory provisions.[84]

Korean administrative law should encourage, not just transparency, but also access to information in order to ensure that those who are interested in an issue have adequate data and analysis to assess the decisions that are being advanced. To make participation in the policy process meaningful, basic information on what and how it is being decided needs to be made available to all. Thus, a core element of administrative law requires that public information needs to be accessible.

This commitment might involve a variation of the concept of the Freedom of Information Act (FOIA). Korea has had local ordinances requiring information disclosure at the local-government level.[85] Local ordinances requiring information disclosure made sense to help citizens monitor governmental performance. In Korea, shifting coalitions provided incentives to encourage the release of government information. More open information law allows interest groups, the public, and opposition politicians to check if the bureaucracy has failed to carry out its statutory obligations. In 1994, the central government made and enforced "administrative information disclosure operation guidance."[86] The Korean Government

[82] Act on Anti-Corruption and the Foundation of the Anti-Corruption & Civil Rights Commission Section 27.

[83] http://www.acrc.go.kr/eng_index.html last visited on May 10, 2011.

[84] The Korean Constitutional Court, 90HunMa133 (May 31, 1991).

[85] In 1991, CheongJu City Local Government promulgated regional regulation, relating to public information disclosure.

[86] Korean Prime Minister Regulation No. 288.

enacted the Act on Disclosure of Information by Public Agency ("Korean FOIA") on December 31, 1996.[87]

Korean FOIA was enforced in 1998. The Government made a major amendment in 2004. The 2004 amendment, known as the Korean Electronic FOIA amendment, effectively took Korean FOIA to the Internet, requiring each public entity to post guides for making FOIA requests on its website. Further, this amendment encouraged online public access to public information by requiring public authorities to make certain information available in electronic form. In April 2006, the government opened the comprehensive public information disclosure system named as www.open.go.kr. In 2009, 1,288 public entities, including the National Government, regional governments, educational entities and other public entities provided information disclosure service, such as information index searching, requesting, copy, fee payment and so forth. As a result, government websites thrived on the Internet. A further statutory change was the passage of Korean FOIA, which established the principle of freedom of information and provides for the right to apply for information, with narrow exceptions to protect privacy.

Korean FOIA provides public access to public records by two methods: affirmative agency disclosure and public requests for disclosure. Affirmative public record disclosure takes place through the publication of public information and the availability of certain records for public inspection and copying. Government research project information is provided at the IP address: www.prism.go.kr. Public enterprise management information is provided at www.alio.go.kr. Regional government administrative information is provided at the IP address: www.laiis.go.kr. Local public enterprise management information is provided at the IP address: www.cleaneye.go.kr. Education-related information is provided at the IP address: www.academyinfo.go.kr and www.schoolinfo.go.kr.[88]

Public requests for disclosure, Korean FOIA's most well-known component, allows any member of the public to request access to information held by Korean public entities without showing a need or reason for seeking the information.[89]

Although the public has a statutory right to request government records, agencies are not always required to comply with Korean FOIA requests. Through the eight exceptions, Korean FOIA balances the value of public disclosure against other important considerations, including national security, individual privacy, sensitive business information, speculation in real estate and so forth.[90]

Rather than requiring agencies to withhold information subject to an exception, public entities are granted discretion to determine whether to safeguard or disclose that information. Korean FOIA does provide access to records held by Korean

---

[87] Korean Stat. No. 5242.

[88] https://www.open.go.kr/pa/html/eng_main.htm, last visited on Jan. 25. 2011.

[89] https://www.open.go.kr/pa/html/eng_RetrieveInfoDisclosureGuide02M.htm, last visited on Jan. 25. 2011.

[90] The Act on Disclosure of Information by Public Agency, Article 9.

public entities, such as regional governments, public enterprises, or public schools. According to Korean Supreme Court ruling, private universities are also subject to Korean FOIA[91] since private universities are a private entity, but their education service is an aspect of public service. The Government budget is also provided to private universities as a subsidy.

The Korea Securities Dealers Association (established in 1953, merged into the Korea Financial Investment Association in 2009) was not subject to Korean FOIA, however.[92] The Association's service is not public in nature and its members are limited as only private securities firms.

[The number of requests for public information][93]

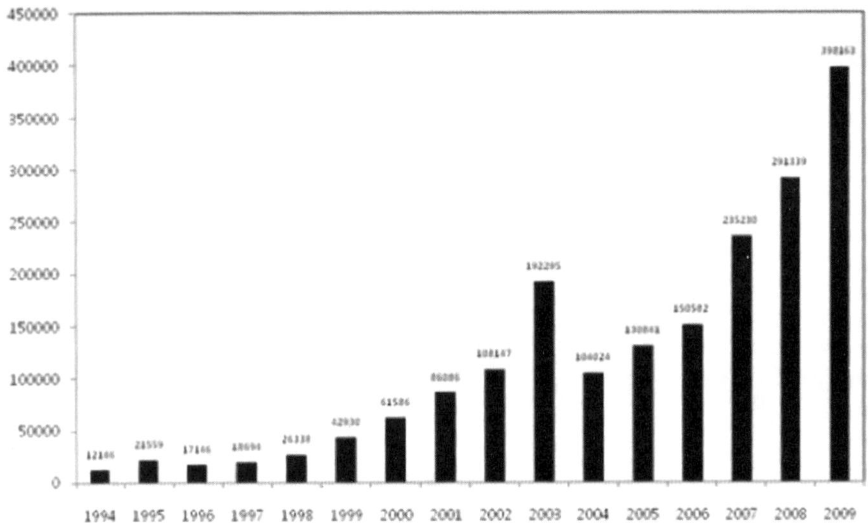

Administrative insulation from the public and judicial scrutiny has been dramatically reduced by the passage of Korean FOIA. The transparency of administrative decision making has apparently been enhanced. The public has the opportunity to access the information held by Government agencies. After the 2004 Korean Electronic FOIA amendment, the number of information request dramatically increased and the main way to request is via the Internet and the main formation of disclosure is via e-mail.

[91] Korean Supreme Court, 2004Du2783 (Aug. 24, 2006).

[92] Korean Supreme Court, 2008Du5643 (Apr. 29, 2010).

[93] The annual report of public information disclosure in 2009 (in Korean) 10.

[The number of information disclosure requests in 2009][94]

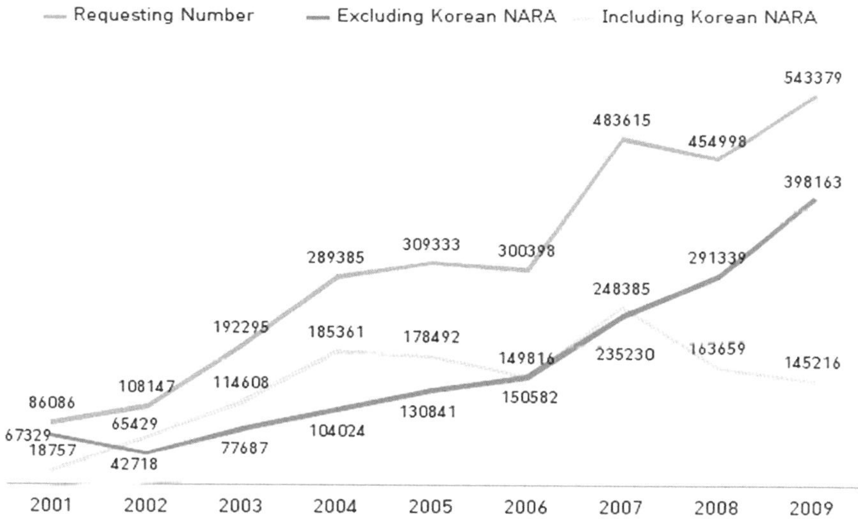

According to a Supreme Court decision, Articles 1, 3 and 6 of the Act prescribe that, in principle, public institutions shall publicly disclose information in their possession and management in order to ensure people's rights to know and secure their participation in state affairs and the transparency of the operation of state affairs. Public institutions must disclose information unless grounds for non-disclosure are expressly provided under the Article 7(1) of the Act. Public institutions must provide permissible reasons, set forth under the Article 7(1) of the Act, when they decline to disclose information upon request. This is because non-disclosure conflicts with certain legal interests or basic rights upon specific confirmation and examination of information requested to be disclosed. Thus, it cannot be justified to reject a request for disclosure merely upon a general ground. Accordingly, the whole purport of alleging Items 4 and 6 of the Article 7(1) of the Act cannot be viewed that the defendant cited them merely as exemplary grounds for not disclosing the information of this case under the presumption that the information of this case constituted information non-disclosable under the Article 7(1) of the Act.[95]

The Supreme Court also ruled that the information disclosure system under Korean FOIA is a system disclosing information held and managed by public agencies in its original condition. A public agency can search and redact basic material to meet disclosure requests when information is held and managed in electronic form and such work does not cause particular obstacles to computer systems operated by the public agency concerned.[96]

[94] The annual report on public information disclosure in 2009 (in Korean) 46.

[95] Korean Supreme Court, 2001Du8827 (Dec. 11, 2003).

[96] Korean Supreme Court, 2009Du6001 (Feb. 11, 2010).

4 Extended Scope of Remedies Relating to Government Liability

The Korean Constitution provides that the people have a fundamental right to compensation for injury caused by the State.[97] The purpose of the Article 29 of the Korean Constitution is to allow an injured person—a person who has suffered damage through an illegal act of any public official—to sue the Government or public officials for monetary compensation. Sovereign immunity is denied by the Korean Constitution, itself. Since the government is involved in so many daily activities, it is inevitable that mistakes will sometimes be made and people will sometimes be injured in various ways. The State Compensation Act proscribes the specific condition of government liability. There are two different kinds of liability: personal liability and public organization liability. The Article 2 of the State Compensation Act prescribes personal liability.[98] The Article 5 of the State Compensation Act prescribes public organization liability.[99]

4.1 *Liability of Public Officials*

The Supreme Court ruled that the Government was liable when a police officer's use of a gun passed beyond the limits permissible under ordinary social norms, in consideration of all the relevant circumstances.[100] A police officer may use a weapon within limits reasonably necessary for the situation when there are reasonable grounds for using a weapon.[101]

In determining whether a police officer's use of a weapon satisfies these requirements, the court should conduct the relevant inquiry as to whether a police officer's use of a weapon is reasonable in light of ordinary social norms. The court should take into account the category and nature of the crime at issue, the severity of legal interests encroached on, the immediate threat of serious physical harm, the number of police officers involved, the offender at the scene, the kind of weapon, the manners of using a weapon, and other surrounding circumstances.

When the police officer fired a gun, aiming at the tires of a motorcycle in order to stop the suspects who were riding a 50 cc small motorcycle and then the passenger was seriously injured in the stomach by the mistake, the Supreme Court ruled that "the police car could have pursued them within a short distance, they would have

[97] Korean Constitution, Article 29.

[98] The State Compensation Act, Article 2.

[99] The State Compensation Act, Article 5.

[100] Korean Supreme Court, 2003Da57956 (May 13, 2004).

[101] Article 11 of the former Act on the Performance of Duties by the Police Officers (amended by Act No. 5988 of May 24, 1999).

been suppressed by the continued pursuit or captured by other police officers in the area who could have been radioed with a request to do so."[102]

The State Compensation Act covers not only executive officers' misconduct, but also that of judicial officers and legislative officers. The Supreme Court ruled that "the State is liable for damage for a breach of duty where the Constitutional Court dismisses in error a complaint for review (as a result of misinterpretation of the filing requirements) and where separate proceedings to bring appeals and motions for correction of errors are not provided."[103]

According to separation of powers, the judiciary obtained some independence.[104] Litigants suffering disadvantages or loss at the end of a trial are expected to seek remedies to recover their rights and legal interests by means provided by law where separate proceedings for appeals and motions for correction of errors are provided. The judiciary decision that violates rules of judicial proceedings does not warrant the State's liability for damage under the Article 2(1) of the State Compensation Act unless extraordinary circumstances exist where a judge clearly failed to conduct himself or herself as a judge in accordance with the purpose of adjudicatory process.

4.2 *Defects of Public Facilities*

What is the meaning of defective construction or management of public facilities specified in the Article 5 (1) of the State Compensation Act? It refers to the circumstance where public facilities, which are built for the public purposes, fail to provide a customarily required safe condition. It is difficult to deem it as a defect in construction or management of public facilities even though a perfect state of the construction or management of public facilities cannot always be maintained.

The level of responsibility to take protective measures imposed on the constructor or manager of public facilities is what is customarily requested by society in proportion to the level of danger posed by the public facilities. Defective construction or management of a road should be determined in accordance with the social customs by comprehensively considering various matters, such as the road usage conditions including location and structure of the road, traffic volume and traffic condition at the time of the accident, the original usage, location, and shape of the physical defects.[105]

[102] Korean Supreme Court, 2003Da57956 (May 13, 2004).

[103] Korean Supreme Court, 99Da24218 (July 11, 2003).

[104] Article 103 of Korean Constitution. Judges rule independently, according to their conscience and in conformity with the Constitution and the law.

[105] Cheong (2011), 562.

The Supreme Court has ruled that defects in road management could not be found merely on the facts that the ice on the road located in a mountain area was left unattended and that there was no warning or danger sign on the road considering the characteristics of snow, meteorological and geographical features, and consequent relative safety of the road.[106]

5 Judicial Review of Executive Action Has Been Re-Enforced

5.1 Standing

Article 35 of the Administrative Litigation Act provides standing requirements to sue for litigation for affirmative nullification, etc.[107] "The legal interests to seek" is interpreted as "legally protected interests." The Supreme Court ruled that the legally protected interests refer to the case where individual, direct and specific interests are protected by laws and regulations that such administrative disposition bases itself upon and by relevant laws and regulations and in the case where general, indirect and abstract interests that the general public commonly has are generated as a result of the protection of public interests, it shall not be deemed that legally protected interests exist.[108]

The residents living outside of the areas evaluated for environmental impact assessment thereupon shall not be deemed to be qualified to be plaintiffs who shall fight over the disposition of public waters reclamation license and the disposition of the approval for the implementation of the farmland reclamation project in accordance with the environmental right stipulated in the Korean Constitution[109] or the Article 6 of the Framework Act on Environmental Policy.[110]

The residents living inside areas evaluated for environment impact assessment are qualified to seek revocation of disposition of public water reclamation license and disposition of the approval for the implementation of the farmland reclamation project, however. The people, living outside of the areas, got some influence from a public project but their interests were indirect and abstract. Therefore, they did not have standing to sue to nullify the government's approval for the public project.

---

[106] Korean Supreme Court, 99Da54998 (April 25, 2000).

[107] The Administrative Litigation Act, Article 35.

[108] Korean Supreme Court, 2006Du330 (March 26, 2006).

[109] The Constitution, Article 35.

[110] Article 6 of the former Framework Act on Environmental Policy (revised by Act No. 6846 of December 30, 2002).

5.2 *Mainly Administrative Dispositions*

The Korean administrative procedure regime encourages judicial oversight. In the past, the exhaustion of administrative remedies was a requirement for filing an administrative lawsuit with the court. However, an administrative lawsuit may be filed without first resorting to administrative remedies, unless otherwise provided for by law with the establishment of the Administrative Court. The Administrative Court was established on district court level, on March 1, 1998. Korea's only Administrative Court is located in Seoul. The respective district court's three-judge panel performs the function of the administrative court until a separate administrative court is established in that respective region. The Administrative Court has jurisdiction over tax, eminent domain, labor, and other administrative cases. Administrative lawsuits are governed by the Administrative Litigation Act.[111] Administrative cases are legal disputes relating to mainly administrative dispositions. The term "disposition, etc." means the exercise of, or refusal to exercise a public power by an administrative agency as a function of law enforcement in relation to a specific fact, other similar administrative actions and an adjudication on the administrative appeal according to the Administrative Litigation Act.[112]

The term expiration notice from a public university to its faculty member is an example of an administrative disposition in Korea. According to relevant statutes, assistant professors of national or public universities who are employed as term-based faculty can be considered as having rights under the law or as a matters of fair reasoning to request a fair evaluation process for their reappointment, based on reasonable criteria, and they may reasonably expect to be reappointed upon successful fulfillment of the evaluation criteria concerning their abilities and qualities. The Supreme Court ruled that a term expiration notice sent by the university hiring authorities for the purpose of rejecting the renewal of the appointment affects the afore-said legal relations of university faculty members. Therefore, such notice constitutes a disposition subject to an administrative litigation.[113]

Even the administrative dispositions relating to an agency's discretionary power is subject to administrative litigation when it is exercised beyond the limits of its discretion or the discretion is abused.[114] The Korean Supreme Court ruled the head of the subordinate local autonomous entity's promotion of its public official in spite of a superior local autonomous entity's discipline demand constituted an unlawful disposition as it went significantly beyond the permissible scope of exercising a discretionary power.[115]

---

[111] The Administrative Litigation Act, Article 1.

[112] Cheong (2011), 708.

[113] Korean Supreme Court, 2000Du7735 (April 22, 2004).

[114] The Administrative Litigation Act, Article 27. The court may revoke even the discretionary disposition by an administrative agency when such a disposition is exercised beyond the limit of its discretion or the discretion is abused.

[115] Korean Supreme Court, 2005Chu62 (March 22, 2007).

Under the Local Public Officials Act, a local autonomous entity employee has a legal duty not to conduct collective acts and the violation of such duty is subject to disciplinary action.[116] The public official belonging to the Northern District Office of Ulsan Metropolitan City participated in an unlawful strike by the National Public Officials Union and the head of the superior local autonomous entity has demanded a series of orders to take disciplinary action. Ignoring the Ulsan Metropolitan City Mayor's demand to take disciplinary action, the head of the Northern District Office promoted the very official who took part in the unlawful strike. The promotion disposition by the head of the subordinate local autonomous entity shall be deemed as an illegal disposition as detracting from the permissible scope of a discretionary power. Thus, for the head of the superior local autonomous entity to cancel the promotion disposition by the head of the subordinate local autonomous entity shall be deemed as legitimate as it is based upon the Article 157 (1) of the Local Autonomy Act,[117] and it shall not be deemed to have violated the law.

5.3 *Administrative Regulations*

Administrative regulations are normally not subject to administrative litigation. They were not considered as a final position of a public agency, rather only provided general standards to act for the public and public entities themselves. An administrative regulation is general and abstract, and it is not characterized as an administrative disposition. However, the regulation itself sets the final position of a public agency, and then the regulation is not subject to administrative litigation.[118]

The notice has the same nature. The notice may be deemed a regulatory order or an administrative regulation; however, if it has a characteristic of regulating citizens' specific rights and duties or affecting their legal relations by itself without any further intermediate executory action, it constitutes an administrative disposition. The Supreme Court held that a notice of the medical care benefit guidelines regarding psychotropic drugs issued by the Ministry of Health and Welfare is an administrative disposition in nature because it has by itself a characteristic of regulating legal relations among pharmaceutical companies, medical care institutions, patients, and the National Health Insurance Corporation. Other intermediate executory action is not necessary for the notice. A company supplying

[116] Article 69 of the Local Public Officials Act (Disciplinary Causes) (1) If a public official falls under any of the following subparagraphs, a resolution on discipline shall be requested, and a disciplinary action shall be taken according to the result of such disciplinary resolution: (1) When he violates this Act and any order issued under this Act, and the Municipal Ordinance or Municipal Rule of a local autonomous entity; (2) When he does not fulfill his duties (including that imposed by other Acts and subordinate statutes on him due to his status as a public official), or he neglects his duties; and (3) When he commits an act detrimental to his prestige or dignity.

[117] The Local Autonomy Act, Article 157.

[118] The Korean Supreme Court. 95NU7994 (Sept. 20. 1996).

psychotropic drugs has legal standing to dispute the effectiveness of a notice of the medical care benefit guidelines issued by the Ministry of Health and Welfare because the company possesses direct and specific legal interests protected by law relating to national health insurance.[119]

In some cases, an administrative regulation would be subject to constitutional complaints. The specific provision sets forth the conditions for restriction on fundamental rights, which results in a subordinate regulation designating matters not mandated by its primary law. Thus, the specific provision restricts the fundamental rights without legal grounds and violates the principle of statutory reservation It also infringes the complainant's freedom of occupation for this reason. The person may raise a constitutional complaint against this specific provision of the administrative regulation to the Constitutional Court.[120]

An administrative regulation is not considered an administrative disposition, but it would be considered as an exercise of governmental power. The Licensed Administrative Agent Act provides for the conditions to be a licensed administrative agent and the Enforcement Decree of the Licensed Administrative Agent Act sets the implementation standards. A portion of the Article 4 in Section 3 of the Enforcement Decree of it which states, "check the supply level of licensed administrative agents and, in case the qualifying examination thereof is deemed necessary, set plans for holding the examination."

The complainant, who had been preparing for the qualifying examination for licensed administrative agents, inquired about the examination with the relevant ministry, which replied, "the license for administrative agents has been given to experienced public officials, and qualifying examinations have not been, and will not be conducted in the future." In response, the complainant filed a constitutional complaint challenging the constitutionality of the provision, arguing that the Article 4 in Section 3 of the Enforcement Decree of the Licensed Administrative Agent Act, which limits the condition for conducting the qualifying examination until there is a need in consideration of the level of supply of licensed administrative agents, in fact blocks the route to become a licensed administrative agent by passing the qualifying examination and thus infringes on the complainant's occupational freedom.

The Constitutional Court ruled that a portion of Article 4 in Section 3 of the Enforcement Decree of the Licensed Administrative Agent Act violates the Constitution as it contradicts the principle of statutory reservation and therefore violates the freedom of occupation of the complainant, who aspires to be a licensed administrative agent through a qualifying examination.[121]

An omission to engage in administrative rule-making is also subject to the constitutional complaint.[122] The Industrial Accident Compensation Insurance Act

---

[119] The Korean Supreme Court. 2003Mu23 (October 9, 2003).

[120] The Korean Constitutional Court Act, Article 68-1.

[121] Korean Constitutional Court, 2007Hun-Ma910 (April 29, 2010).

[122] Park (2010), 874.

provided that the compensation was paid to the surviving families when workers died or were missing from industrial accidents. The basis for calculation of the compensation to be paid to the surviving families was victims' average wages (the amount calculated by dividing the total amount of wages paid to a relevant worker during the three calendar months immediately before the day on which grounds for calculating his average wages arose by the total number of calendar days during those three months) and the labor law delegates to the Minister of Labor the duty to determine and publicly announce the average wage in order to provide a detailed criterion appropriate for a specific case when it is impossible to determine the average wage. The Minister of Labor omitted to provide administrative rule-making about average income in spite of delegation of legislation.

Sailors disappeared when the ship, in which they were aboard, sank in a storm on their first day of work. Since there was no record of salary for the missing people after they were hired by the ship owner, it was impossible to calculate their average wages. When the surviving spouses filed for the compensation, the Korea Labor Welfare Corporation only paid compensations using the minimum standard of compensation. The complainants instituted an administrative litigation for compensation, and filed the instant constitutional complaint, arguing that an omission to provide administrative rule-making by the Minister of Labor infringed on the basic rights of the complainants. The Constitutional Court adjudicated that omission of administrative rule-making by the Minister of Labor about average income in spite of delegation of legislation by a statute violated the Constitution.[123]

5.4 Administrative Guidance

The Korean Supreme Court ruled that the State did not need to compensate the damage suffered by the entities on the basis that the lawful administrative guidance did not have a coercive power.[124] However, the unlawful administrative guidance, which was an actual order from the financial minister by the direction of the President, was declared as unconstitutional by the Korean Supreme Court.[125]

5.5 Administrative Planning

The Government formulates an administrative plan to set future governmental goals and provides some information to the public. The plan is not fixed and final one. According to circumstances, it can be changeable. The agencies have broad

[123] Korean Constitutional Court, 2000Hun-Ma707(Jul. 18, 2002).

[124] Korean Supreme Court, 2006Da18228(Sept. 25, 2008).

[125] Korean Supreme Court, 96Da21706(Jul. 23, 1999).

discretion to set an administrative plan. Plans do not prescribe present obligations and duties to the person. Administrative planning is not usually subject to judicial review. The administrative plan is subject to judicial review when it sets administrative duties to the residents.[126]

5.6 *Administrative Surcharge*

There are two traditional methods to secure performance of administrative law duties in Korea. One method is administrative compulsory execution against the non-performer of administrative obligation imposed by law, and the other is administrative punishment against the violator of an obligation. The compulsory execution and immediate compulsion would be in the category of administrative compulsion. Mandatory enforcement, indirect enforcement, and compulsory collection originate from compulsory execution. Administrative punishment is the punishment directed at the person who has violated an administrative legal obligation. The purpose of administrative punishment is to prevent future violation. Administrative criminal punishment and administrative disciplinary penalties are categories of administrative punishment. Administrative dispositions to secure performance of administrative law duties are subject to judicial review by the court.[127]

There are several fairly new methods to secure the performance of administrative law duties in Korea. There are public notifications of a violator's name, administrative surcharge, and termination of electric service and water service.[128] The administrative surcharge is to confiscate unlawful profits from disobedience to administrative orders. It has become a major administrative enforcement measure since the 1990s. According to a survey, there were about 80 positive laws, which had administrative surcharge clauses even in July of 2002.[129] The Korean Constitutional Court has adjudicated that an administrative surcharge is constitutional and is not contrary to the double jeopardy clause of the Korean Constitution.[130] The administrative surcharge had mainly a deterrent and retributive purpose but also a remedial purpose for breach of administrative duties. The disposition relating to the administrative surcharge is also subject to judicial review.[131]

The next table shows that the administrative cases have recently and steadily increased in Korea. It means that the scope of judicial review of administrative activities has been extended and the judiciary has actively exercised it. The

[126] Korean Supreme Court, 96NU10096(Sept. 26, 1997).

[127] Park (2010), 385–400.

[128] Id. 421–431.

[129] Park and Kim (2002).

[130] The Korean Constitutional Court, 2001HunKa25, (2003. 07. 24).

[131] Korean Supreme Court 2001Du10387 (Jan. 10, 2003).

extended judicial review has checked abusive exercises of government authorities and re-enforced their fairness and objectivity.[132]

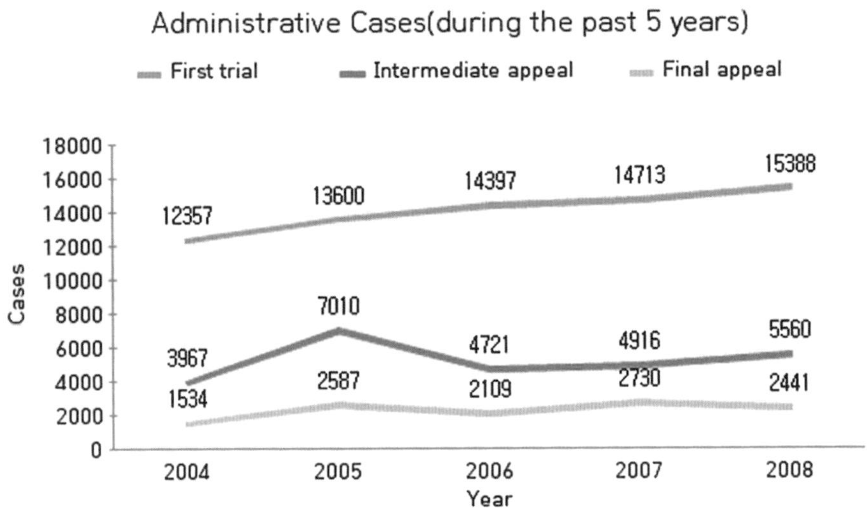

6 Conclusion

In Korea, administrative law reforms seek to negate the official perspective and to establish a more open, responsive legal system. Their aims are usually to make official decision-making processes more visible to the public and more clearly grounded in formal rules. They aim to form citizens into more independent and autonomous agents under the regime of more explicit rules, not only at the point of the enforcement or application of law, but also in the more proactive arena of enactment of law, by promoting their participation in policy making. The reforms also seek to facilitate greater access to legal services and courts, and to make judges more responsive to citizens' demands.

Under the current statutory framework, citizens have the arrays of choices in challenging administrative action. They no longer need to exhaust administrative remedies before going to court. The Information Disclosure Act allows citizens more access to public information on which to base their complaints. These rules reinforce each other to open up policymaking and expand control of administration.

Korea adopted administrative procedure regimes. Korea formalizes the process of issuing administrative dispositions and takes on the puzzling task of legalizing administrative guidance. The 1996 Administrative Procedure Act expanded the

[132] http://eng.scourt.go.kr/ 2009 Introductory Book of the Supreme Court of Korea.pdf. 58.

formal records required for agencies to make rules and to issue dispositions, established a presumption against administrative guidance, and set up extensive notice-and-comment rule making procedures. The Korean statute includes provisions opening up the policy making process through public comment and hearings on drafting legislation. The new Korean system provides external control of bureaucrats for the first time, along with public participation in policymaking. It combines open policymaking with greater control of policy implementation. Korea re-codified a system where administrative action is subject to review by ordinary courts, established a designated court. Revisions to the Korean Administrative Appeals Act and the new Civil Petitions Act provide for enhanced review of external authorities.

Korean administrative law has a role to play in providing solutions to problems of non-transparency and corruption, which were legacies of tradition and rapid state-lead economic developments. It makes sense for proponents of transparency to advocate the reform of administrative law regimes toward broader standing rules, more flexible approaches to judicial review, and greater public involvement in administrative rulemaking. Korea diverged in both law and practice from this common base, and now reflects administrative legal infrastructure that fosters transparency, public participation, freedom of information, and meaningful judicial review to promote full-fledged democracy and sustain economic development.

References

Ahn KW (1997) The influence of American Constitutionalism on South Korea. South Ill Univ Law J 22:72–73

Barber NW (2003) The Rechtsstaat and the Rule of Law. Univ Toronto Law J 53:446–447

Bingham LB, Lee SW, Chang WK (2007) Judicial independence and legal infrastructure: essential partners for economic development: participatory governance in South Korea: legal infrastructure, economic development, and dispute resolution. Pac McGeorge Glob Bus Dev Law J 19

Cheong H-J (2011) Administrative Law (in Korean)

Choi C (2006) Military conscription and human rights in the Republic Of Korea: the right of conscientious objection. Temple Int Comp Law J 20:136–137

Esty DC (2006) Good governance at the supranational scale: globalizing administrative law. Yale Law J 115:1531

Final Report and Legal Reform Recommendations to the Ministry of Justice of the Republic of Korea, University of Iowa. J Corp Law 26:550–553

Gilson RJ, Milhaupt CJ (2011) Economically benevolent dictators: lessons for developing democracies. Am J Comp Law 59:285–286

Ginsburg T (2001) Japanese law symposium: dismantling the "Developmental State"? administrative procedure reform in Japan and Korea. Am J Comp Law 49

Kim J (2008) A forensic study of Daewoo's corporate governance: does responsibility for the Meltdown Solely Lie with the Chaebol and Korea? Northwest J Int Law Bus 28: 273, 309

Kim C-Y (2009) Administrative Law (in Korean), pp 372–374

Lee I (2005) The law and culture of the apology in Korean dispute settlement. Mich J Int Law 27:19–20

Ohnesorge J (1996) State, Industrial Policies & Antidumping Enforcement in Japan, South Korea and Taiwan. Buffalo J Int Law 3:334

Ohnesorge J (2006) Chinese administrative law in the northeast mirror. Trans Law Contemp Probl 16

Ohnesorge J (2010) The future of law and development, part V: "Beijing Consensus" anyone? Northwest Univ Law Rev Colloq 104: 257, 258

Park K-S (2010) Public Administration Law (in Korean)

Park Y-D, Kim H-J (2002) Actual Operation Conditions and Improvements of Penalty Surcharge System (Korea Legislation Research Institute, in Korean) 29

Rosenfeld M (2001) The Rule of Law and The Legitimacy of Constitutional Democracy. Southern California Law Review 74: 1307, 1328

Seo J (2006) Who will control Frankenstein? The Korean Chaebol's corporate governance. Cardozo J Int Comp Law 14: 21, 23

Wilson MJ (2010) U.S. legal education methods and ideals: application to the Japanese and Korean systems. Cardozo J Int Comp Law 18:334

Woon LK (2003) The problem and suggestion with the software industry promotion act. Korean Administrative Law Study (in Korean) 124–125

Civil Law and Civil Procedural Law

Youngjoon Kwon

1 Introduction

The purpose of this chapter is to give readers a general reference and information on Korean civil law and civil procedural law. These two areas of law cover a wide range of subjects. Thus, they are highly comprehensive in their scope. In particular, the Korean Civil Code is the lengthiest of all the statutory laws in Korea. Therefore, it is nearly impossible to give detailed accounts on every aspect of these two areas of law here in this chapter. Rather, this chapter aims to give an overall picture of these areas of law and to highlight some essential features thereof. Furthermore, this chapter also intends to give some insight on dynamic aspects of these areas of law. This dynamism mainly comes from interaction between Western form and Korean substance, as I will later explain in more detail. Against this backdrop, this chapter is structured as follows: Part II is the preliminary part of this chapter, aimed at providing readers with relevant background information concerning Korean legal history and institutions; Parts III and IV present a general overview of Korean civil law and civil procedure law, respectively; Finally, Part V gives a brief summary and conclusion of the chapter.

2 Background Information

2.1 *Historical Background*

Korea has been developing its own unique tradition of the rule of law throughout its history. The first dynasty, *Kojoseon* (2333–108 B.C), already established its own

YJ. Kwon (✉)
Seoul National University, Seoul, Republic of Korea

Korea Legislation Research Institute, *Introduction to Korean Law*,
DOI 10.1007/978-3-642-31689-0_4,

statutory law, consisting of eight articles.[1] The last dynasty, *Joseon* (1392–1910) completed comprehensive codification of existing codes and published "The Great Code for Governing the Country" (*Kyeongguk Taejon*) in 1484. This functioned as the core framework of the legal system in the dynasty.[2] As one can tell from this, the rule of law was by no means a foreign concept in Korean legal tradition. However, these laws significantly differed from Western laws. Although introduction of Western ideas of laws began as early as the seventeenth century, it initially faced some opposition and criticism. However, Korea finally geared up for the proactive reform of its legal system patterned after the Western model at the turn of the twentieth century. This came to an abrupt halt in 1910, when Japan forcefully annexed Korea to colonize it.

From then until the end of the World War II in 1945, Japanese law functioned as the primary source of law in Korean territory. Since Japanese law had already been heavily influenced by the Western legal tradition, Korea was somewhat involuntarily exposed to a full-scale and indirect influx of Western laws. In 1912, the colonial government promulgated a decree entitled "Decree on Civil Matters on *Joseon*" (조선민사령) in which enforcement of Japanese law concerning civil matters in the colony was declared. By virtue of this decree, the Japanese Civil Code and Civil Procedural Code became the governing norms in Korea in the area of private legal relationships and litigation arising therefrom. Of note was that private legal matters not covered by the laws were to be handled under Korean customary law, according to the decree. The difficulty for colonial judges was the complexity of defining the existence and contents of Korean customary law. Therefore, the colonial government and judges had to undergo a thorough investigation of Korean customs and ascertain their contents in each case they encountered.[3] This implies that what they considered to be the identification of Korean customary law might possibly have been the part-creation of Korean customary law through the window of Western (or in some cases, Japanese) legal concepts.[4]

Japanese colonial rule ceased with the end of the World War II, and the Republic of Korea was formally established on August 15, 1948. A modern legal system began to be built up. The process of making drafts for the Civil Code and the Civil Procedural Code took considerable time and effort. The outbreak of the Korean War (1950–1953) made this task even more challenging. Despite all the difficulties, drafts of these codes were prepared and finally enacted. They all took effect as of 1 January 1960. On the whole, they were deeply influenced by the tradition of continental law, thus resembling German or Japanese law. However, there were some major changes from Japanese law that were enforced in the past, along with codification of Korean customary laws or legal tradition.

[1] Only three of them remain known. They stipulate capital punishment for murder, compensation with grains for personal injury, and the enslavements of thieves.

[2] Chun et al. (1980), Legal Attitude of the Late Yi Dynasty, in B.D. Chun, W. Shaw and D. Choi, p. 8.

[3] Kim (2009).

[4] Id. p. 247.

2.2 Institutional Background

Understanding legal institutions is an essential element of understanding Korean law. Key institutions in this regard are the National Assembly and the judiciary.

The National Assembly enacts statutory law, a primary source of law in Korea. As the initiation of law-making process, Bills are submitted either by ten or more legislators or by the Government, meaning an administrative branch. In the 17th National Assembly (2004–2008), a total of 7,489 Bills were submitted.[5] Of these, 6,387 Bills were from legislators, whereas 1,102 were from the Government.[6] However, the Civil Code and the Civil Procedural Code are generally handled by the Government. For example, the ongoing project for the amendment of the Civil Code, which I will elaborate on later, was initiated by the Ministry of Justice. Whoever initiates legislation, the National Assembly, as the sole law-making body of the State, decides with a majority vote whether to pass the Bill. Once the National Assembly passes the bill and the President promulgates it, it qualifies as statutory law and takes effect as indicated in the law itself. Since statutory law is a primary source of law, customary law is to be applied only when there are no statutes available in the case being adjudicated. Theoretically speaking, customary law is a useful means for a society to bridge the gap between reality and an existing norm that codification cannot promptly address. In reality, however, customary law seldom finds room for its functions due to the presence of a wide and comprehensive volume of statutory law. Therefore, most disputes regarding civil law and civil procedural law are governed by statutory law.

The judiciary does not enact statutory law, but interprets and applies it to a specific case. By so doing, the judiciary creates what is called 'case law'. This is formed by decisions from multiple courts that are respectively positioned in a three-tier court system; the District Courts being at the lowest tier, the High Courts at the middle tier, and the Supreme Court at the highest tier. Unlike in common law jurisdictions, case law in Korea is not deemed a source of law. Therefore, there is no principle of stare decisis as in common law. Yet, the decisions of a higher court, particularly those of the Supreme Court, do have a *de facto* binding effect. Subordinate court judges have a strong tendency to follow the rules set forth by the Supreme Court.

[5] http://likms.assembly.go.kr/law/jsp/main.jsp.

[6] Id.

3 Overview of Korean Civil Law

3.1 *Overall Structure*

Korean civil law is primarily governed by the Korean Civil Code (민법, hereinafter, 'KCC'). The KCC is a comprehensive and fundamental body of norms covering the entire area of private law. It bears much resemblance to the overall structure of the Bürgerliches Gesetzbuch (BGB), the Civil Code of Germany, in that it follows a Pandekten system. The hallmark of this system is to place the general principles at the fore front, then to subsequently provide concrete doctrines concerning particular areas of the subject matter.

After this manner, the KCC is divided into five Books—General provisions (Book 1), the law of rights in *rem* (Book 2), the law of obligations (Book 3), the law of family (Book 4), and the law of inheritance (Book 5). The law of contracts, torts, and unjust enrichment are governed by the law of obligations (Book 3) along with some part of general provisions (Book 1), whereas the law of property and the law of security rights are governed by the law of rights in *rem* (Book 2) along with some other part of general provisions (Book 1).

3.2 *Law of Obligations*

3.2.1 The Law of Contracts

Contract and Concept of Juridical Act

Provisions governing the law of contracts are primarily contained in Chapter 2 (contract) of Book 3 (the law of obligations). Furthermore, Chapter 5 (juridical act) and Chapter 7 (prescription) of Book 1 (general provisions) contain a large number of provisions applicable to contracts. Concerning the relationship between Book 1 and Book 3, one might need to understand the notion of juridical act (*bubryulhangwi*). This concept has its origin in the concept of 'Rechtsgeschäfts' in German law. A juridical act is a single or combined indication of will that is intended to have legal consequences. A juridical act composed of a single indication of will is a unilateral act. Whereas, a juridical act with combined indication of will is a contract. Book 1 governs a juridical act, automatically extending its scope of application to a contract, which is a typical form of a juridical act. On the other hand, Chapter 2 of Book 3 governs matters specifically pertaining to a contract.

The law of contracts is the area of law where world-wide harmonization has vigorously continued. Numerous model contract laws, such as the Principles of European Contract Law (PECL) and the Principles of International Commercial Contract (PICC), or international conventions, such as the United Nations Convention on Contracts for the International Sales of Goods (CISG), are some examples of this effort. This implies that contract law in separate jurisdictions is in fact already mutually similar to make harmonization more feasible. In this regard, Korean contract law also contains features and elements of contract laws common with other jurisdictions.

Formation and Validity of Contracts

Formation

The sole requirement for the formation of a contract in Korea is a legal agreement between contracting parties. Consideration, as is recognized in common law jurisdictions, is not a precondition to the enforcement of a contract. A legal agreement is comprised of an offer and an acceptance. An offer becomes effective when it reaches the offeree, and cannot be withdrawn unless the withdrawal reaches the offeree before or at the same time as the offer (§527). As for an acceptance, the KCC employs the mirror image rule. Consequently, a reply to an offer which purports to be an acceptance, but contains additions, limitations or other modifications, is a rejection of the offer and constitutes a counter-offer (§534). Conceptually, a mere invitation to treat is distinguished from an offer, since it contains no demonstration of present and definite intent to form a contractual relationship. Generally, words exchanged in the course of preliminary negotiations or advertisements are not deemed offers. Therefore, no contractual liability accrues from these expressions.

In line with this, parties are free to negotiate and are not liable for failure to reach agreement. However, there are some exceptional cases where a party incurs liability for breaking off negotiations in breach of good faith and fair dealing.[7] Additionally, misrepresentation in the course of negotiation may lead to liability, as well. However, these are all deemed tort liability rather than contractual liability. In Korea, a series of decisions concerning pre-contractual liability were handed down recently concerning false or exaggerated commercial advertisements. A majority of them concerned condominium advertisements.[8] Buyers of condominiums in reliance upon the advertisement later brought lawsuits against sellers on the ground of either contractual or tort liability, claiming that the advertisement was false or unduly overstated. In cases where claims have been accepted, the court either recognized some advertisements as constituting an offer,[9] or perceived some false advertisement as constituting a tortious act even when it was deemed a mere invitation to treat.[10]

---

[7] Supreme Court Decision 99Da40418 Decided on June. 15. 2011; Supreme Court Decision 2001Da53059 Decided on April. 11. 2003.

[8] Supreme Court Decision 2005Da5812,5829,5836 Decided on June. 1. 2007; Supreme Court Decision 2009Da1313 Decided on April. 23. 2009; Supreme Court Decision 2007Da59066 Decided on July. 22. 2010.

[9] Supreme Court Decision 2005Da5812,5829,5836 Decided on June. 1. 2007.

[10] Supreme Court Decision 2009Da1313 Decided on April. 23. 2009; Supreme Court Decision 2007Da59066 Decided on July. 22. 2010.

Validity

When there is a legal agreement between parties, the contract becomes valid in principle. However, there are some factors rendering the contract either void or voidable. These factors fall into either of two categories: ① the contract does not comply with the form or the content that law specifically designates, or ② the expressions of intent that constitute the contract are defective. Generally, a contract does not require any form to gain validity. There are no provisions or statutes comparable to the Statute of Frauds in common law. However, there are some exceptions. For example, when one of the contracting parties is a governmental agency, the written form of a contract is legally required (Act on Contracts to which the State is a Party, §11). In terms of contents, a contract is made void when its content is in breach of good morals and social order (§103) or mandatory law. A contract is also held void when one party takes advantage of weaker party and makes excessively unfair contract (§104). Finally, a contract is also made void or voidable when there is a defective expression of intent. A false declaration (§107) and a sham transaction (§108) are typical grounds for the nullity of the contract. A mistake (§109), fraud and duress (§110), or lack of the capacity to perform a juridical act (§5,10,13) are grounds for avoidance of the contract.

Although a contract is rendered null in its entirety, Article 137 allows partial nullity if the contract would have been made even without the invalid part. The same principle is applied to partial voidance. This is often used by the courts in modifying a contract to ensure a fairer outcome. In cases where excessiveness of attorney's fee was at issue, the Supreme Court used this device to render the excessive portion of the fee as uncollectable while leaving an appropriate portion applicable, based on the assumption that the attorney and client might have made a contract at that fee level.[11] This somewhat overstretches the doctrine in order to judicially modify the contents of a contract for the purposes of an equitable conclusion.

Parties to the Contract

Legal Capacity

A contractual relationship is the nexus of contractual rights and duties. Only natural or legal persons are capable of bearing such rights and duties (§3). Natural persons refer to all human beings, while legal persons refer to certain associations of persons or independently organized capital that has been registered as legal persons in the public registry. Animals and unincorporated associations that are not legal persons do not possess general legal capacity. Another issue is the capacity to perform juridical acts. In contract law, this refers to the capacity to make contracts. Legal persons always possess this capacity, since they can make contracts through

[11] Supreme Court Decision 91Da8722 Decided on December. 13. 1991; Supreme Court Decision 91Da29804 Decided on March. 31. 1992.

their organs, such as their representatives. Natural persons have this capacity unless they are either minors (under 20), quasi-incompetent or incompetent persons. They can only make a contract with the help of their legal representatives. Otherwise, contracts are in principle voidable.

Recently, a draft civil code amendment on this issue has been submitted to the National Assembly. According to this draft which is set to become effective as of 1 July 2013, the legal adult age will be lowered from the current 20 to 19 in order to reflect rapid social changes and global trends. It also contains some changes to the terminology and the scope of 'quasi incompent' and 'incompent' persons while adding more flexibility to the system.

Agency

Agency are laid down in the general provisions of the KCC (§114–135). Declarations made by the agent in the name of the principal have immediate legal effect for and against the principal. The agent is under no liability and acquires no rights except where he has acted without authority. In cases of lack of authority, the third party still has the option, either to bind the principal to the contract when he ratifies the declaration by the unauthorized agent (§133), or to pursue an unauthorized agent for liability in cases of non-ratification (§135). If the representation by the agent qualifies the requirements of apparent representation (§125,126,129), the principal is responsible for the act of the agent.

Contract Interpretation

Interpretation of a contract is the most contested issue in contract-related litigation. Although there are no rules of interpretation stipulated in the KCC, the following rules are generally observed.

The starting point is to identify what the contracting parties intended at the time of the agreement. Where each party attaches the same meaning to the terms used in their agreement, the interpretation should be in accordance with that meaning, even if a third party might interpret the language differently.[12] However, most disputes arise when the contracting parties attach different meanings to the same term. In this case, what a reasonable observer might think of the terms becomes the criteria by which the term is interpreted.[13] The other possibility is when both contracting parties have failed to agree on possible contingencies that materialize afterward. To fill this unexpected gap, the court is allowed to supplement the contract according to the hypothetical and reasonable intentions of contracting parties.[14]

---

[12] Supreme Court Decision 93Da2629, 2636 Decided on October. 26. 1993.

[13] Supreme Court Decision 2001Da32120 Decided on September. 5. 2003.

[14] Supreme Court Decision 2005Da13288 Decided on November. 23. 2006.

There is no parol evidence rule in the KCC in the sense that contracting parties are still allowed to submit evidence of prior or contemporaneous negotiations, even with the existence of the final written form agreement. Yet, the final written form agreement is likely to have stronger probative force in actual litigation.

Performance

When a valid contract is made and its substance is confirmed, the parties have contractual duties to perform their obligations. The performance of an obligation may also be effected by a third person unless the nature of an obligation does not so permit or the parties have declared a contrary intention (§469②). Time and place for performance are to be determined by the parties. If not, the KCC provides supplementary rules. The time for performance, if not agreed upon in the contract, is when the oblige actually demands the performance of the obligation (§387②). Regarding the place for performance in the absence of any agreement, delivery of specific goods shall be made at the place where the goods were situated at the time of the contract, whereas other performance shall be made at the obligor's present domicile (§467). A tender of performance relieves the obligor from liability for non-performance (§461).

Non-performance and Remedies

When a party does not perform its contractual obligation, the aggrieved party is entitled to demand specific performance in accordance with the contract, unless enforcing such performance is impossible or inappropriate due to its nature. Specific performance in the case of non-performance does not require intention or fault by the defaulting party. In fact, it is merely enforcing the agreement that the defaulting party has already consented to.

A more common remedy for non-performance is to claim for damages. In this case, either intention or fault in non-performance is required. Parties are free to contract for liquidated damages in advance (§398). In the absence of such agreement, the general rules for assessment of the damages for breach of the contract are to be applied (§393). According to a general rule, the defaulting party should compensate the aggrieved party such damages as would ordinarily arise from that breach. Special damages outside the scope of ordinary damages can only be recovered when the defaulting party foresaw or could have foreseen the special circumstances giving rise to such damages. This 'foreseeability' requirement has stemmed from a common law doctrine evolved from Hadley v. Boxendale.[15] As for the relevant date for the assessment of damages, Korean courts have construed that

[15] 156 Eng. Rep. 145 (Ex. 1854).

the date of default should be the criteria.[16] However, in the case where the value of the goods in question was subject to substantial fluctuation after the damages had occurred and such fluctuation could have been foreseen, Korean court has stated that such fluctuation should be taken into consideration when assessing damages.[17] Punitive damages are not allowed under Korean law.

Another way of dealing with non-performance is to rescind the contract and claim restitution if the aggrieved party has already performed its duty (§543–548). The breach has to be significant enough to frustrate the purposes of the contract and justify the termination of the contractual relationship. Non performance due to hardships or change of circumstances can also be grounds for rescission of the contract.[18] Although there is no general statutory provision on this, a general doctrine akin to frustration and force majeure based on good faith principle leads to this conclusion. However, in practice a defense arising from this doctrine is rarely accepted by the court.

Finally, there is also warranty liability for defective goods in sales contracts (§549–584). Here, the absence of fault by the defaulter does not count as any excuse for his non-performance. The buyer may claim reduction of the contract price, claim for the damages and/or rescind the contract. Warrant liability and general liability for the breach of contract can stand together, and the aggrieved party may claim on both or either of these grounds.

Assignment

In principle, any right of a contractual party is assignable unless it is prohibited by agreement, law, or by its nature. Under Korean Supreme Court precedents, a future obligatory right may also be assigned if: (1) such right is specifiable; and, (2) it is reasonably expected that such right will arise in the near future.[19] Notice of assignment by an assignor to the obligor of a right, or consent by the obligor to such assignment is required for the assignee to enforce the assigned right against the obligor (§450①). Furthermore, in order to set up the assigned right against a third party, the deed of the assignment has to be in writing along with the certified date on it (§450②). This is meaningful when there is more than one assignment of a single right. Should this occur, then the assignment with the earlier certified date prevails over another.

Assignment of the contractual right, or receivable, is widely used as a financing tool. "Asset-backed Securitization Act" (자산유동화에 관한 법률) is noteworthy in this respect. Under this law, the pool of receivables is transferred to a special-purpose

[16] Supreme Court Decision 84Daka1532 Decided on September. 10. 1985.

[17] Supreme Court Decision 94Da61359,61366 Decided on June. 14. 1996.

[18] Supreme Court Decision 2004Da31302 Decided on March. 29. 2007.

[19] Supreme Court Decision 88Daka6358 Decided on June. 25. 1991; Supreme Court Decision 95Da7932 Decided on July. 30. 1996; Supreme Court Decision 2002Da7527 Decided on November. 8. 2002.

company ("SPC") or a trustee for the purpose of financing with a simpler and convenient perfection process as set forth in the law.

Prescription

A right to performance of an obligation is subject to prescription in accordance with relevant provisions in the KCC. There are a number of differentiated periods according to the nature of rights. The general period is set forth as 10 years, starting from the time the right becomes exercisable (§162,166). Figuring out the starting point is not always simple or clear. According to a series of Supreme Court decisions, factual obstacles, such as ignorance of the existence of rights, do not bar right-holders from exercising their rights.[20] However, there are a few cases where the Supreme Court has held that the prescription period does not run when it is unreasonable to expect the right-holders to exercise their rights.[21] However, on the whole, Korean courts have been reluctant to widely apply prescription in difficult cases. Perhaps this is due to the tendency of Korean courts to pursue fair and just outcomes in each case. Sometimes a defense based on prescription is barred by the good faith principle.[22]

Currently, the Korean Civil Code Amendment Committee has come up with a draft, to keep pace with the global trend toward shorter periods and simpler prescription regimes, with a shortened period of prescription (3 years commencing from the time the obligee knows the exercisability of the right and identity of the obligor, but limited by a maximum of 10 years from the time creditor was able to exercise the right) and abolition of shorter prescription periods that were blamed for making the prescription regime unnecessarily complicated.

Representative Types of Contract

The KCC, from §554 to §733, offers provisions on 14 typical types of contract. Based on the notion of the freedom of contract, contracting parties can choose the form and substance of the contract. It does not have to fit into one of the 14 types of contract already provided for in the KCC. In this sense, these types of contract stipulated in the KCC are merely model forms of the frequently used contracts. However, these provisions on prototype contracts are not insignificant. They provide a basic doctrinal platform on which various contracts can be built. Of course, most of them are default provisions that parties can opt out of by an agreement. However, these provisions apply to legal relationships between contracting parties if there is no such agreement, which is usually the case. It should also be noted that

---

[20] Supreme Court en banc Decision 84Nu572 Decided on December. 26. 1984; Supreme Court Decision 2003Du10763 Decided on April. 27. 2004.

[21] Supreme Court Decision 99Da66427 Decided on February. 11. 2003; Supreme Court Decision 2002Da64957 Decided on April. 8. 2003.

[22] Supreme Court Decision 95Da29895 Decided on December. 12. 1997.

there are some mandatory provisions that are enforced to the contracting parties regardless of their intention. Most of these provisions are contained in the special statutes, with the exception of lease as will be explained below in the relevant part. With the rise of the necessity for more paternalistic intervention by the State to ensure the fairness of the contract, these provisions play an enhanced role in modern society.

Given the purpose and the length of this chapter, it would suffice to take a glance at sale and lease, the two most frequently used contract forms.

Sale

A sale is a form of contract in which a seller transfers the title of the object in exchange for money offered by a buyer. It is perhaps the most common type of contract found in daily transactions. The law of sale has been subject to intense harmonization efforts due to its universality, as can be witnessed in the CISG (United Nations Convention on Contracts for the International Sale of Goods) or the PICC (Principles of International Commercial Contract). For this reason, provisions on sale in the KCC do not look so different from those in other major countries. However, there are some distinctive features on the law of sale in Korea worth noting.

Firstly, international sale of goods is governed by the CISG, which has become effective in Korea as of Mar. 1, 2005. Considering that major trading partners, such as the U.S., China and Japan, have all signed and ratified the CISG, a large portion of the international trade in goods are expected to be governed by this Convention unless agreed otherwise. Although there are still few cases in which the CISG has actually been applied, more and more scholarly attention is being given to this norm.

Secondly, the law of sale in Korea is distinct in terms of its unique remedy—warranty liability for defective goods (§570–584)—as described, above, in the remedies section. This remedy is provided by virtue of law. Therefore, there need be no warranty contract or express or implied representation by the seller. So long as there is no agreement between the seller and the buyer to opt out of the warranty liability provisions in the KCC, this liability is automatically imposed on the seller. Here, the absence of fault on the seller does not amount to an excuse for the defect. Apart from the liability of non-performance, the buyer may claim reduction of the contract price, claim for the damages and/or rescind the contract within the prescribed time set forth by the law.

Thirdly, there are various statutes that regulate sales that involve consumers as one of the contracting parties. This is mainly in order to prevent businesses from engaging in fraud or unfair practices by taking advantage of their superior information resources and bargaining position. Among them are "Regulation of Standardized Contracts Act" (약관의 규제에 관한 법률) that regulates standard form contract, "Installment Transactions Act" (할부거래에 관한법률) that regulates installment contract, "Door to Door Sales Act" (방문판매 등에 관한 법률) that regulates door-to-door sales, phone-soliciting sales, and multi-stage sales. These laws share a common goal- to ensure fairness of the contract in order to protect consumers.

Lease

A lease entails a form of contract in which the lessor allows the lessee to use and profit from the subject matter in return for rent. The KCC provides a number of general provisions governing the law of lease (§618–654).

A notable feature of the law of lease is that the relevant legislations, including the KCC as well as other special statutes specifically designed to regulate lease, contain some mandatory provisions that cannot be modified or excluded by agreement of the contracting parties. This is especially true in the realm of a real estate lease. In the country where real estate, such as land or a building, is scarce in its number in comparison with exceedingly high population, a lessee tends to be disadvantaged in the lease contract and therefore requires stronger protection. Therefore, protection of the lessee has been at the heart of the law of lease in Korea.

The "Housing Lease Protection Act" (주택임대차보호법) is noteworthy in this respect. Since a lessee's position is generally deemed inferior to that of a lessor in terms of bargaining position as well as economic status, he is vigorously protected by the above Act. The protection is offered in three aspects; the protection for the continuity of the lease term, the protection for the stability of the rent, and the protection for the refundability of the security deposit.

As for the continuity of the lease term, the law sets 2 years as the minimum period [§4(1)]. This means that the term is deemed 2 years in the absence of an agreed term or even when the parties have agreed to a term of less than 2 years. However, this restriction exists to protect the lessee, not to restrict their freedom of contract. Hence, the lessee can still rightfully assert that an agreed lease term of less than 2 years has expired and call for the return of the security deposit. Another aspect of this protection is regarding the renewal of the lease. If the lessor fails to notify the lessee of a refusal of the renewal or of the change on the terms and condition of the lease contract, 6 months to 1 month before the term of the lease expires, the lease is deemed to have been renewed under the same terms and conditions [§6(1)].

As for the stability of the rent, there is no specific provision that restricts the amount of rent. Hence, this is fully left to the freely negotiated contract. However, there is a provision in the Act that either the lessor or the lessee can request an increase or decrease of rent if the stipulated rent or deposit becomes unreasonable due to the change of economic circumstances (§7). However, in cases of an increase, it shall not exceed the ratio set in accordance with the criteria prescribed by Presidential Decree, which is currently 5 %.

The final type of protection concerning security deposit is perhaps the most important in its significance. There are generally two forms of housing lease in terms of security deposit. One is *Chonse* with refundable deposit with no monthly rents, and another is *Wolse* with refundable deposit, with monthly rents. Some *Wolse* arrangements provide that the lessee does not pay a deposit, but pays the rent for the entire tenancy at the beginning. In *Chonse*, the amount of the deposit is much higher than in Wolse, since the lessor takes the interest accruing from the deposit as a form of rent. This functions as a private financing mechanism, in which a landlord receives a lump sum of money by providing his real estate for a period of time instead of paying interest. At the end of the tenancy, usually determined on a 2-year basis, the lessor returns security deposit to the lessee. Deductions can be made by the landlord for repairs and damages. If the lessor does not return the security deposit, the lessee has the right to retain the property until the deposit is returned. All the more, the Housing Lease Protection Act provides the legal ground for a statutory lien that can be easily created by simple administrative procedures. According to the Act, if the tenant has moved into the house and completes the resident registration which can be easily done in the nearby administrative bureaus, the lessee is endowed with a statutory lien on the security deposit [§3(1)]. In the country where the amount of security deposit is substantial as to account for the large portion of the lessee's assets, this sort of protection reduces the legal risk of being defaulted on the security deposit.

3.2.2 The Law of Torts and Unjust Enrichment

The Law of Torts in General

The law of torts in Korea is based on the provisions from the KCC §750–766. Torts, according to this part of the Code, are categorized into either general or special form.

As for the general form of torts, Article 750 encompasses the whole field of traditional fault liability cases. According to this provision, the liability for torts requires four elements: unlawfulness, willfulness or fault, damage and a causal connection between the act and the damage.[23] The useful, yet tricky feature of this provision lies in the flexibility of these requirements. For example, the notion of 'unlawfulness' is a flexible term by which embracing a wide variety of torts in a single framework is made feasible. Though this notion presupposes the existence of law, it is widely accepted that it may result from 'unwritten law', as well as 'written law'. The breadth and flexibility of the notion comes at the sacrifice of predictability. The same can be said of 'fault'. It presupposes a general duty of care, which cannot always be exhaustively specified in a written law. Therefore, the duty has been recognized in a seemingly infinite variety of situations. Although the notion of 'damage' is more clear and graspable than other requirements, it still gives rise to some sophisticated problems. For example, in the case where compensation was sought based on the wrongful birth of a child, whether or not the requirement of

[23] Besides these requirements set forth in Article 750, Article 753 and 754 presupposes the requirement of liability capacity.

damage is satisfied has been fiercely debated.[24] Finally, the causal connection between the act and the damage is tricky as well. It is not simply a factual issue. Rather, it is infused with value judgments in order to filter out any event not considered responsible for the damage.

Some other provisions provide grounds for special forms of tort. Article 756 governs the employer's liability for damage caused by the employee. If the employer can prove that he has exercised due care in the appointment and the supervision of the employee, the employer can be exempted from liability. However, in practice this allegation is almost always rejected. Another important form is liability of the possessor or owner of a structure. According to Article 758, the possessor bears liability for damage caused to another person by reason of any defect in the construction or maintenance of a structure he possesses unless he proves that he has exercised reasonable duty of care. In the event the possessor gets off the hook, the owner bears strict liability. In addition, there are also provisions for liability of possessors of animals (§759) and joint tortfeasors (§760).

As for remedies, monetary compensation is the means of recovery stated in the Code (§751). There is no statutory restriction to the recovery for pure economic loss or non-economic damage. In this regard, the scope for compensation in Korea seems wider than some countries, i.e. Germany, where compensation for pure economic loss and emotional loss are restricted. The prevailing opinion and the precedents have shown negative positions toward the availability of injunctions as a secondary remedy for torts, based on the fact that the KCC remains silent on the feasibility of injunctions against tortious acts. Injunction was only allowed under a claim due to the infringement of an 'absolute right', such as a right in *rem* or personality right.[25] However, a recent Supreme Court decision paved the way for the injunction as a general remedy for torts.[26] According to this decision, an injunction against a tortious act may be granted if monetary compensation alone is not deemed an adequate remedy for damage and the balance of harms weighs in favor of the party seeking the injunction.

The Law of Torts in Specific Areas

A wide variety of disputes are adjudicated under the law of torts. Therefore, this area of law has not only developed in its entirety, but also in specific areas, respectively. Below are some major areas that comprise a substantial part of the law of tort.

Automobile accidents are the most common cause for tort litigation. The Guarantee of Automobile Accident Compensation Act (자동차손해배상보장법) mainly regulates these disputes. According to this Act, any person who operates an

[24] Supreme Court Decision 98Da22857 Decided on June. 11. 1999. In this case, the claim was rejected.

[25] Supreme Court Decision 93Da40614,40621 Decided on April. 12. 1996.

[26] Supreme Court Decision 2008Ma1541 Decided on August. 25. 2010.

automobile shall be liable to compensate any damage caused by the automobile in the process of driving such vehicle (§3). Automobile owners are required to purchase a liability insurance policy in accordance with the Act (§5①), and the victim of the accident may file a claim for an insurance payout with the insurer (§10①). Therefore, most lawsuits in these fields are filed against insurers rather than against vehicle owners.

Defamation is also another typical tort. Commonly, lawsuits are brought by an individual against a media entity, such as a newspaper company, claiming that the individual has been defamed by the defendant. Defamation lawsuits raise the challenging issue of balancing free speech and personal dignity. According to Article 21 of the Constitution of Korea, all citizens shall enjoy freedom of speech and the press, yet neither speech nor the press shall violate the honor or rights of other persons nor undermine public morals or social ethics. This constitutional limitation, quite different from the first amendment of the USA Constitution, implies that Korea is prone to grant relatively broader protection of personal dignity than the USA, by considering personal reputation or other public values to be as important as free speech. Preliminary injunctive relief, so long as it is granted under strict requirements, does not constitute prior restraint.[27] However, there is growing tendency toward broader protection of free speech, as evidenced in recent cases based on "actual malice" doctrine on public figures.[28] According to Article 310 of the Criminal Code, a defamatory expression shall not be punishable if the facts alleged are true and solely in the public interest. This logic also applies to civil cases. Courts have leniently construed that reasonably believing the facts to be true also satisfies the requirements for the exemption from liability.[29]

Product liability has also become the major issue in the law of tort. In the past, claims over bodily injury or economic loss due to a defective product were based on general tort law of the Civil Code. As of 7 July, 2002, the Product Liability Act (제조물책임법) was put into effect. Under this Act, defects are categorized into three types—manufacturing defect, design defect, and inadequate instructions or warning—after the manner of the third restatement of torts in the USA, although the Act still allows different types of defect as long as they meet the general standard for a defect. The manufacturer bears primary liability. When the manufacturer is not known, the supplier of the defective products may also be liable under the Act. Korea has seen a recent surge in product liability cases. Among a number of product liability litigation that has taken place, tobacco litigation has drawn attention of the public. In a controversial lawsuit brought by a number of smokers and/or their heirs, the plaintiffs vainly claimed that the once state-run company and the Government

[27] Supreme Court Decision 2003Ma1477 Decided on January. 17. 2005.

[28] Supreme Court Decision 2000Da37524,37531 Decided on January. 22. 2002; Supreme Court Decision 2002Da64384 Decided on July. 8. 2003; Supreme Court Decision 2001Da53387 Decided on February. 27. 2004.

[29] Supreme Court Decision 85Daka29 Decided on October. 11. 1988.

should take responsibility for producing and selling hazardous tobacco without adequate warning.[30]

The Law of Unjust Enrichment

A person who has obtained unjust enrichment is obliged to relinquish it to the person at whose disadvantage the enrichment was obtained (§741). This single general norm is an expression of the general equitable principle that no person should be allowed to profit at another's expense without making restitution for unfair benefits. This provision embraces all kinds of cases where unjust enrichment is at issue. For example, this provision covers a case where performance was done according to a contract which later turned out to be null and void. It also applies to a case where A's flock of sheep wanders onto B's land and feeds on the grass. The former case has more to do with the law of contracts, whereas the latter has more to do with the law of torts. For these reasons, the law of unjust enrichment is considered a supplementary norm for both the law of contract and the law of tort.

The requirements for unjust enrichment are fourfold; benefit by one person (enrichment), loss by another person (detriment), causal link between the benefit and the loss (causation), and a lack of legal grounds (non-justification). In most cases, the fourth factor—a lack of legal grounds—becomes a core issue. If the alleged legal ground is a contract, the issue is whether or not the contract is valid. This leads us to the above mentioned question of contract validity concerning the law of contracts. Even when the contract is invalid, the law sometimes provides legal grounds for the enrichment. For instance, a *bona fide* purchaser who purchased property, other than real estate, from a non-owner acquires it without being liable for restitution to a real owner (§249). If the alleged legal ground is other than contract, then the issue is as to whether that ground is legally justified. For instance, if the person acquires a benefit by way of judicial enforcement, it is not deemed unjust enrichment unless the judicial decision on which the enforcement was based is declared invalid.[31]

When each of those requirements is met, a person who has been enriched is obliged to return what he has gained. In principle, one is supposed to return whatever object she has gained. If one is not able to do so, one is to pay the amount representing the reasonable value of the benefit. There are some exceptional cases in which a claim for the reversal of unjust enrichment is barred. One representative case is the prohibition of reversal of enrichment based on an illegal cause (§746). If the legal ground under which the enrichment is obtained constitutes an infringement of good morals and social order, a claim for the reversal of unjust enrichment is prohibited. As a result, the enriched person legally acquires what benefits he has obtained. A typical example of this is a case where A subsidizes B for gambling in

[30] Seoul District Court Decision 99Gahab104973 Decided on January. 25. 2007; Seoul High Court Decision 2007Na18883 Decided on February. 15. 2011.

[31] Supreme Court Decision 94Da41430 Decided on June. 29. 1995.

the form of a loan. Although a loan contract between A and B is deemed null and void due to its violation of public policy, B can raise a defense arguing that A cannot claim for the reversal. However, where the illegality of an enriched person is significantly greater than that of a disadvantaged person, reversal can be allowed.[32]

3.3 *Law of Rights In* Rem

3.3.1 Definition of "Right In *Rem*"

Book 2 of the KCC (§185–372) along with some part of Book 1 (§98–102), governs the law of rights in *rem*. The right in *rem* is a concept that stems from continental law. It is the right directly exercised over a thing, and has absolute effect against anybody. The absolute and monopolistic aspect of this right makes it distinct from a right in *personam* that is primarily governed by Book 3 of the KCC. Due to the absolute effect of a right in *rem* imposing a duty on the general public to respect the right holder, defining and publicizing the type and contents of the right in rem in advance becomes imperative. In this regard, the numerus clausus principle is provided (§185). The KCC enumerates eight types of right in *rem*: possessory right, ownership, superficies, servitude, *Chonsegwon*, right of retention, pledge, and mortgage.

3.3.2 Subject of Rights In *Rem*

The subject of the right in *rem* is a thing—any corporal object and manageable natural power (§98). It is subsequently categorized into either an immovable or a movable. An immovable is the land, and other independent things—representatively a building—that are attached to the land (§99①). Land and buildings are considered to be separate and independent real properties. This is a peculiar feature of Korean law as opposed to Western legal traditions. Therefore, ownership of land and the building which stands on such land can belong to different persons. Accordingly, if A owns land and B owns a building on that land, it is necessary that B lease the land or obtain the superficies in order to secure the ownership of the building. Everything, other than an immovable, is deemed a movable (§99②). This distinction is relevant with respect to the modes of acquisition and the types of right in *rem* available. Most importantly, the acquisition, transfer and extinction of rights in rem over immovables are subject to registration (§186).

---

[32] Supreme Court Decision 93Da12947 Decided on December. 10. 1993.

3.3.3 Registration System

All transfers of rights in *rem* over immovables, unless they are done pursuant to law, take effect upon their registrations (§186). During the colonial period when the Japanese Civil Code was in effect, this was not the case. The transfer took effect when both parties agreed upon the transfer of right in *rem*, and the registration was only a requirement for its effect over third parties. Therefore, making registration a constitutive element of the transfer of rights in *rem* was a huge shift from the past paradigm. There is no state guarantee of title. In other words, there is no protection for the *bona fide* purchaser of immovables, unlike in movables. However, any rights which are registered are deemed to exist as registered. Consequently, the burden of proof rests on the party who argues that the registered rights are null and void.

The bulk of registration-related rules are provided for in the Real Estate Registration Act (부동산등기법). Korean real estate registration is part of the non-contentious jurisdiction of the courts. Registry offices are maintained in each district court. The registries are staffed by registrars who have received years of specialized legal training and who work under the overall supervision of the court. They review each application for real estate registration only for formalities. They do not verify the identities or legal capacity of parties or determine compliance with any sales conditions or payment. Korea has been turning a paper-based registry into an electronic one to promote cost effectiveness and swiftness of the registration system. As of now, the public registries in Korea are entirely digitalized. They are publicly accessible via the Internet.

3.3.4 Ownership

Ownership is considered the most complete right among all types of right in *rem*. It includes the right to use, enjoy, and dispose of things in the most absolute way, unless prohibited or restrained by relevant laws or regulations. Consequently, ownership includes relevant power to exclude others from the use, enjoyment or disposal of one's thing without one's consent (§211). The concept of ownership is roughly comparable, though not exactly identical, to 'freehold title' in common law countries.

In reality, however, ownership can be regulated by a significant number of laws. Due to scarcity of real estate and its importance to the national economy, ownership over real estate is more widely subject to regulation. In this context, the absoluteness of the ownership was called into question in favor of various social interests, such as city planning, environmental protection and the economy in general. There are no legal restrictions on the ownership of real estate by particular classes of persons. However, it should be noted that under the Foreigner's Land Acquisition Act (외국인토지법), foreigners and foreign entities are required to report to the relevant governmental entity after a land purchase contract has been closed (§4).

Ownership can be held by several persons. The KCC stipulates three forms of joint-ownership: co-ownership, partnership-ownership, and collective ownership.

Co-ownership is the loosest form of joint-ownership, where joint-owners can freely dispose of their shares (§263). Partnership-ownership is the form of ownership of a partner in partnership relations (§271). This is more restricted than co-ownership in that each partner should obtain the consent of each other partner when disposing of the share or altering the property (§272). Collective-ownership is a distinctive form of joint-ownership when a piece of property is owned collectively by the members of the association which is not a juristic person (§275). Each member of the association is entitled to make use of the property and take the profits from it, but the administration and disposition of property is determined by resolutions from a general meeting of the members (§276). Another important legislation in this regard is the Act on the Ownership and Management of Aggregate Buildings (집합건물의 소유 및 관리에 관한 법률) in which sectional ownership of the building is addressed.

3.3.5 Rights In Rem to Use Real Estate

Superficies

Superficies is a right in *rem* to use another person's land for the purpose of owning the buildings or other structures thereon (§279). Superficies can also be created for using the underground part of the land or the space above the land (§289 2). This right is created by agreement between relevant parties. Yet, it is very rarely seen since most land owners do not want to be burdened by this right due to its relative perpetuity. The duration of a superficies should not be less than 15 or 30 years if the superficies is for owning buildings (§280,281), while there is no such provision for a lease. Rather, this right is sometimes used for a mortgagee over the land to prevent the land owner from constructing a building which will eventually lower the value of the mortgaged land. Another form of superficies frequently used is a superficies by virtue of customary law. This form of superficies is created when the ownership of the land and the building which belonged to the same person are transferred, respectively, to different persons. Unless there is agreement to demolish the building, the owner of the building automatically acquires superficies by virtue of customary law.

Servitude

Servitude is defined as a right in *rem* to use the land of another person for the convenience and benefit of one's own land (§291). In most cases, servitude concerns a right of way, a right to have a cable or a pipeline, or water rights. Unlike Germany or Japan, the KCC does not recognize "personal servitude"—servitude in favor of specific persons.

Chonsegwon (Right to a Registered Lease on Deposit Basis)

Chonsegwon is a peculiar right in rem that entitles a right-holder to use the real estate owned by another person by paying deposit money (§303). Although the amount of deposit money is settled between parties, it generally hovers between 30 % and 70 % of the value of the real estate. Unlike a lease, no rent is paid on a regular basis. The settlor of *Chonsegwon* receives deposit money in full and benefits from the interest accruing therefrom during the duration of this right. The right-holder enjoys absolute and monopolistic effects, has the right to request an auction when the settlor of *Chonsegwon* delays the return of the deposit money, and has priority over deposit money when the real estate is subject to forced sale. This is, in principle, clearly differentiated from lease which only confers a right in *personam* to the lessee. However, the line has become blurred due to several special pieces of legislation protecting a certain group of lessees of the house or commercial buildings [the Housing Lease Protection Act (주택임대차보호법) and the Commercial Building Lease Protection Act (상가건물임대차 보호법)] by extending strong protection for the lessee as is shown in *Chonsegwon*.

3.3.6 Security Rights In *Rem*

Right of Retention

If the possessor of property or a negotiable instrument belonging to another person has any claim arising from such property or instrument, and if payment of the claim is due, one may retain possession of the property or the instrument until the claim is satisfied, unless the possession has originated in an unlawful act (§320). In practice, this right is widely used in securing a claim arising from a construction project against the owner of the building, by retaining possession of the building until the payment is made in full. This may be a powerful tool for the creditor since it can be claimed against anybody including a new purchaser or a mortgagee of the building. However, there is also strong concern that it is creating legal uncertainty since this right is not registered in the public registry. Therefore, the third party has trouble ascertaining the existence and scope of the right. Consequently, the abolition of this right over immovables, while leaving it available merely for the sake of movables, is currently under in-depth discussion in the Civil Code Amendment Committee.

Pledge

A pledge under the KCC requires the delivery of possession or control over the pledged movables or rights to the secured creditor until payment (§329,345). In practice, a pledge over movables is rarely used in commercial contexts. Since pledged movables need to be physically delivered to the pledgee, it creates problems for the pledgor who might need them to carry out his business or daily life, and often to the pledgee as well who takes the risk of liability from possessing them. A pledge over certain rights is used relatively frequently in commercial contexts. In this pledge, control over pledged rights is transferred to the pledgee. The means of transferring the control differs based on what kind of right it is.

A pledgee who has either possession or control over pledged assets can satisfy his claim by selling the assets by auction (§338) or exercising the pledged right directly (§353). However, a pledge is incomplete in terms of publicity. Although the transfer of possession or control over the pledged assets may serve some degree of publicity function, it is not always clear from the third party's standpoint whether a pledge has been created.

Mortgage

A mortgage is the most frequently used security right. It is a non-possessory right-in *rem* against immovables (§356). Unlike a right of retention or a pledge, a mortgage is perfected upon its registration in principle. Thus, this is highly recognizable, satisfying the demand for publicity. A mortgage is established and transferred in accordance with the general rules on rights in immovables. Therefore, it is created by agreement and corresponding registration, subject to some exceptions (§649).

A mortgagee does not possess or control the immovable, but only secures equity in its value for the purpose of securing the underlying claim. On account of its absolute effects, a mortgagee can assert this right against anybody. Therefore, the new owner of the mortgaged immovable is subject to the right of the mortgagee. In the case of default, a mortgagee may sell the mortgaged property by auction to satisfy his claim (§363).

A mortgage cannot be assigned separately from its secured claim (§361). This indicates that the mortgage is inseparably connected with the underlying claim. As a result of this principle, the total or partial absence of a secured claim results in total or partial nullification of the mortgage. As an exception to this principle, a fluctuating obligation can be secured by a mortgage in the form of a floating sum mortgage (§357). Here, a mortgage can be created by settling only the maximum amount of the debt to be secured and reserving the determination of the debt in the future. In such cases, the extinction or transfer of any debt which occurred before the debt is determined does not render a mortgage null and void. In practice, this form of mortgage is much more frequently used than the general form.

The Factory and Mining Estate Mortgage Act (공장 및 광업재단저당법) also provides for the special forms of mortgage, which allows a mortgage over the entire estate of a factory or mining business, including land, buildings, equipment and intangible property. The Act on Mortgage on Automobiles and Other Special Movables (자동차등특정동산저당법) provides for the creation of security interests in the form of mortgage on registrable movables, such as automobiles, heavy construction equipment, vessels and aircraft.

Other Security Rights

An effective secured transaction regime is a fundamental component in any financial system. It provides a legal regime through which secured creditors can reduce risks relating to the granting of loans or other forms of credit to business enterprises and consumers. In that sense, the KCC alone is not sufficient in serving this purpose. Hence, there are other forms of security rights that have been created either by customary or statutory laws. The typical example of a security right under customary law is a "Yangdo-dambo", a form of non-possessory security right outside the scope of the KCC. A debtor transfers title to his property while the possession of the property is retained by the debtor. The title comes back to the debtor upon the full payment of the secured debt. This right covers both immovables and movables, yet is widely used in movables due to the convenience of not having to deliver the possession of the property to the creditor. In terms of corporate financing, asset-backed securitization is broadly used. The "Asset-Backed Securitization Act"(자산유동화에 관한 법률) governs this procedure. The originator obtains financing by selling the pool of assets to a SPC (Special Purpose Company), which in turn issues asset-backed securities to investors. The pool of assets being securitized typically consists of small and illiquid assets that are unable to be sold individually, such as payments from credit cards, auto loans, and mortgage loans. In particular, this has been a fruitful source of financing for large companies in Korea.

Another noteworthy change that will take place is the new security right regime over movables and receivables. On 10 June 2010, Korea promulgated the Act on Security Rights in Movables and Receivables (동산·채권 등의 담보에 관한 법률). This Act will take effect as of 11 June 2012. This provides for the framework for the registration system for security rights in movables and receivables. However, it does not completely replace the current security right system in this field. Rather, this is intended to leave it untouched, while providing people with another option that is more secure and predictable.

3.4 Family Law and Inheritance Law

3.4.1 Family Law

Book 4 of the KCC governs family law. It regulates familial matters, such as marriage, divorce, parents and children, parental authority, and guardianship. Confucian perspectives inspired some elements of Korean family law. Concepts, such as *Chinjok* (relatives), *chon* (a unit for assessing the distance between relatives), and *hoju* (head of the family—this concept was abolished as a result of the amendment) were introduced in the KCC. Unlike previous Books, this part of the Code has gone through frequent amendments to date, in the midst of tension between Korean tradition and modern legal ideas.

Marriage and Divorce

Marriage

The minimum age for marriage is 18 years old (§807). Still, a minor, who is under 20 years old (§4), or an incompetent person needs to obtain the consent of parents or guardians in order to marry (§808). A marriage takes effect upon reporting it in accordance with the provisions of the Act on the Registration etc. of Family Relationship (가족관계의 등록등에 관한 법률) (§812). If not reported, the marriage is not legally binding. Same-sex marriage is not allowed under Korean law.

Once marriage takes effect, husband and wife bear duties to live together and to support and aid each other (§826). They also have a right to represent each other for home affairs (§827) as well as joint liability for obligations with respect to home affairs (§832). Unless otherwise stated in a contract, matrimonial property is held in co-ownership (§829).

An interesting feature of Korean marriage law is that it prohibits marriage between a certain scope of close relatives. In the past, Article 809 codified a traditional rule prohibiting marriage between *dongseong dongbon* (men and women who have the same surname and ancestral origin). This has been much criticized on the ground that it infringes on the freedom of choice in marriage while reinforcing excessive paternalism. This Article was declared unconstitutional by the Constitutional Court in July 1997, for the reason that it broadly restricts sexual self-determination which originates from the right to pursue happiness and especially the right to choose the spouse in marriage, and is contrary to the Constitution.[33] The National Assembly passed an amendment to Article 809 in March 2002, which came into force on 31 March 2005 as Article 809-1. It only prohibits marriage between men and women who are closely related.

Divorce

Husband and wife may obtain a divorce by agreement (§834). However, they need to undergo a certain procedure to ensure their sincere intention for a divorce (§836-2). First, they should undergo a deliberation process. Couples with children need to undergo a 3-month deliberation process while childless couples can end their marriage after a 1-month period. On-the-spot divorces are still granted in cases of physical or sexual abuse. If their intention for a divorce remains constant, the family court then confirms the agreement. A divorce by agreement takes effect upon reporting (§836).

Another method of obtaining a divorce, when no agreement is reached between husband and wife, is to obtain a judicial decision ordering a divorce. When the enumerated grounds for a judicial divorce are satisfied, a husband or a wife can file for a divorce (§840). Unlike in some Western jurisdictions, Korean law only

[33] Constitutional Court Decision 95Hun-Ga6 Decided on July. 16. 1997.

recognizes a fault-based divorce. As a result, the party who is responsible for the breakdown of a marriage cannot file for a divorce suit. In practice, however, Korean courts have been lenient toward this. When the breakdown of a marriage is so serious that it does not seem feasible to reinstate the relationship, courts tend to interpret leniently toward finding that one of the grounds for a judicial divorce has been met.

The legal process for a divorce usually involves issues of child custody and support, visitation rights, division of property and debts. Agreement, if any, prevails. If the divorcing spouses fail to reach agreement, the family court can decide on their behalf. Usually division of property is a controversial issue in the process. As a default rule, each spouse has a claim to property acquired during marriage through cooperation (§839-2). The court has a broad discretion to determine what property is divisible and to determine the method of its division, taking into consideration how the property was originally acquired. Korean law does not have the exact concept of alimony, which is based on an obligation to provide financial support to one's spouse after divorce. Yet, consolation money and the division of property fulfill a similar function of spousal support.

Parents and Children, Guardianship

Parents have the parental authority over their minor child. In case of an adopted child, the adoptive parents have this authority (§909①). This authority is comprised of rights and duties to protect and educate the child, to designate the place of residence, to take disciplinary action when necessary, to manage the child's property, and to represent the child in legal transactions (§913–920). It is jointly exercised by both parents during their marriage. If the parents fail to reach agreement, the Family Court makes a determination upon the request of the parties (§909②). When one parent is unable to exercise it, the other is entitled to exercise it alone (§909③).

If no parental authority over a minor survives or if a person of parental authority is unable to exercise the right of representation with respect to the juristic acts or the right to manage property of a minor, a guardian is appointed (§928). This also applies to an incompetent or quasi-incompetent person (§929). A guardian can be designated either upon the wishes of a parent (§931) or by the provision that sets the order among relatives whereby a guardian is appointed (§932–935). If there is no person to become a guardian in accordance with Articles 931 to 935, the court steps in and appoints a guardian *ex officio* (§936).

New Family Registration System

As of 1 January 2008, the Act on the Registration of Family Relationship (가족관계의 등록등에 관한 법률) has taken effect in Korea. This Act governs the registration of family relationship whereby legally significant events relevant to the family relationship including birth, marriage, divorce or death are registered. This regime totally replaces the former *hoju* system, a male-oriented family registry system. *Hoju* refers to the legal head of the family. It was at the center of controversy with respect to gender equality, since women were prohibited from being appointed as a hoju. Under this system, a deceased man is usually succeeded by his first son, not by his widow. This was criticized as being unconstitutional, and consequently the Constitutional Court declared in its landmark decision that it was incompatible with the Constitution, for it violated the right to gender equality and the dignity of individuals.[34] As a result, the Civil Code amendment for abolishing the *hoju* system passed the National Assembly in March 2005, and was totally replaced by a new family relation registration system described above.

3.4.2 Inheritance Law

Book 5 of the KCC is the final Book that governs inheritance law. Inheritance and wills are covered by this Book.

3.4.3 Inheritance

The inheritee's estate passes in its entirety immediately upon death to the inheritor (§997,1005). The term 'estate' not only covers rights, but also obligations, as long as they are not strictly personal to the inheritee. This transfer of estate takes place by virtue of law. This means that no legal transaction or transfer of possession or registration is required. No knowledge of the inheritor is necessary for succession either.

In the case of more than one inheritor, joint inheritance takes place (§1006). The estate becomes the joint inheritors' join property according to their shares in the inheritance (§1007). This joint-ownership exists only as a share in the estate as a whole, not in the individual assets of the estate. Consequently, co-inheritors can only dispose of their shares in the estate as a whole, and not of their shares in individual assets of the estate. The ratio of the share is identical among inheritors (§1009①). However, the spouse of the inheritee gets 50 % more than other inheritors. This joint-ownership among co-inheritors can be terminated by the division of the estate (§1012–1018). The manner in which division takes place can be determined by the will of the inheritee or by the third person designated in the will, if any, to determine the method of division (§1012). The deceased may also prohibit the division of the estate up to 5 years after succession takes place (§1012). Otherwise, every co-inheritor has the right to demand division at any time. When agreement among inheritors is not reached, the family court decides on who acquires what property and to which extent.

[34] Constitutional Court Decision 2001Hun-Ga9,10,11,12,13,14,15, 2004Hun-Ga5 (Consolidated) Decided on February. 3. 2005.

It is possible for an inheritor to repudiate the inheritance or limit the inherited liability to the scope of inherited assets. In the former case, the inheritor is deemed not to have inherited at all from the time of the commencement of the inheritance (§1042). In the latter case, the inheritor is obliged to perform the obligations and transmit testamentary gift of the inheritee only to the extent of the property to be acquired through the inheritance (§1028). In both cases, the inheritor needs to make such declaration to the Family Court within 3 months after the inheritor is informed of the commencement of an inheritance (§1019①,1028,1041).

3.4.4 Wills

A will or testament is a legal declaration by the testator that affects the specific relationship regarding family status or estate that takes effect upon the testator's death. Commonly, a will concerns whom the testator wishes to inherit the estate. This can also be done through means of an inheritance contract. While a will is a one-sided declaration of intent which, until death, is revocable, an inheritance contract is concluded between the testator and the inheritor, and cannot be revoked without a legal ground.

The testator has to be at least 17 years old in order to leave a valid will (§1061). Considering the significance of a will, strict compliance with formalities is required. These formalities are enumerated in the KCC (§1065–1072). If formalities are not satisfied, a will is deemed invalid. A will comes into effect at the time of the testator's death (§1073①). If a will is subject to a condition precedent, it becomes effective upon satisfaction of the condition (§1073②).

Though a testator has freedom to decide on who will acquire how much of the estate, this may conflict with legitimate interests of the inheritors. Therefore, the KCC sets forth the boundary line of the testator's freedom on behalf of the interests of the inheritors by securing them a certain share on their behalf. This legal reserve of inheritance for lineal descendants or the spouse of an inheritee, is secured at half of their statutory share, while it is one-third for lineal ascendants or siblings of an inheritee (§1112).

3.5 *Distinctive Features of Korean Civil Law*

3.5.1 Bridging the Gap Between Western Form and Korean Substance

The dynamism of delving into Korean law lies in its efforts to bridge the gap between Western form and Korean substance.[35] The legal framework of the nation in the modern context was first set up only half a century ago, while the history of the nation

[35] See generally, Kwon (2011).

exceeds 4,300 years. In the process of customizing long-standing Korean society into the new legal framework, some interactions between Western form and Korean substance have taken place. Korean civil law was no exception. It has constantly striven to harmonize the form of the law and the substance of society. The role of the courts in Korea has been significant in this regard. Without sufficient prior experience and precedents, courts had to creatively apply newly enacted legislation in a way that would meet the needs of society and its ever-changing circumstances.

For example, the registration of real estate was not a requirement for transfer of title under colonial law. The notion of registration itself was not deeply rooted in the legal consciousness of Koreans. As the newly established KCC required a registration for transfer of title, patterned after the German Civil Code, there was huge confusion. Although the KCC allowed 6 years of grace period for the registration, lay people were not fully complying with this new legal standard usually out of ignorance. The claim by a buyer against a seller to cooperate in the registration process became extinct with a prescription period of 10 years (§162). A great number of buyers who paid the full price and used the property during the extensive period were at risk of not being able to acquire legal ownership of the property due to the extinction of a claim. With this confusion arising from prevalent Korean legal consciousness that has not fully caught up with the new framework, the Supreme Court has come up with a creative solution by interpreting that the prescription period does not run when the purchaser has paid the full price and exercised one's right by occupying and using the property, thereby saving many people from losing the option to gain legal ownership.[36]

Another interesting legal case that reflects Korean reality deals with a *de facto* acquisition of private property without compensation. Beginning from the 1960s, a massive development plan was carried out throughout the nation. Numerous people voluntarily yielded a part of their property to be used as a new road within their communities. After decades, owners of these properties, mainly inheritors or purchasers of the land that was being used as a road, began to bring a claim for unjust enrichment against local governments which were allegedly occupying the road by maintaining and repairing it. Although in principle, the courts in Korea decided in favor of the plaintiff, the claims were sometimes denied under a specific theory created by the Supreme Court.[37] According to that theory, the owner cannot be compensated if she has abandoned the right to use and profit from the land at issue. This doctrine has frequently been applied to cases where the owner had voluntarily provided the land for a public road, for her own benefit. This doctrine has been criticized for not being consistent with doctrines of rights in *rem*, since one cannot abandon a right in *rem* only partially. Further, it was criticized for being used as a tool to justify a *de facto* acquisition without compensation. However, courts have employed this doctrine in order to reject the claim by owners who have not

[36] Supreme Court en banc Decision 76Da148 Decided on November. 6. 1976.

[37] Supreme Court Decision 97Da27114 Decided on December. 12. 1997; Supreme Court Decision 97Da52844 Decided on May. 8. 1998.

attended to their properties while their properties serve for a greater public purpose. Arising out of peculiar Korean circumstances in which compensation for acquisition was not yet firmly settled, Korean courts strived to get out of social turmoil by modifying legal dogmatics.

Confucian culture also influenced some part of the law in an intriguing way. For example, in a Supreme Court case in 1998,[38] it was held that the owner of an apartment unit could not evict the tenants for failure to pay rent, where the tenants were the owner's own elderly father and ailing brother who were unable to find employment due to their poor health. In this case, the moral obligation of filial piety was imposed, showing that Korean society still requires Confucianism principles in order to determine the outcome of some legal disputes. On the other hand, long-standing customary laws based on Confucianism have been done away with by the Supreme Court. The typical example is a *jong-joong* decision in 2005.[39] *Jong-joong* is a traditional patriarchal clan organization with the aim of performing ancestral rituals for a common ancestor as well as strengthening bonds among a clan's members. It has been solid customary law that only adult males were able to become members of this clan organization. This also meant that only males were entitled to the *jong-joong*'s assets. Because females were not able to become members of the jong-joong, it meant they were deprived of the chance to enjoy a share of the wealth. In this case, married daughters who were deprived of the chance to enjoy in a share of the wealth filed a statement of claim against their *jong-joong*. The Supreme Court finally acknowledged that the subordination of women deriving from Confucianism tradition was no longer acceptable in the current legal order based on the idea of gender equality. Consequently, the Supreme Court declared, contrary to the long-standing customary law, that married females are entitled to equal membership and property rights associated with *jong-joong*. This is a typical example of equality prevailing over traditional values.

3.5.2 Harmonizing Local Standard with Global Trends: Ongoing Amendment of the Korean Civil Code

Besides building coherent norms that work best for Korean society, another significant mission of Korean civil law is to constantly harmonize itself with global trends. The recent legislative movement to recodify the KCC is noteworthy in this respect. In early 2009, the Ministry of Justice announced its ambitious four-year plan to push for the comprehensive amendment of the KCC. This is a ground-breaking project in that it strives to amend entire areas of the Civil Code for the first time since its initial enactment. Family and inheritance law, which already has several stages of amendment, is outside the scope of this project. This is in line with the

---

[38] Supreme Court Decision 96Da52670 Decided on June. 12. 1998.

[39] Supreme Court Decision 2002Da1178 Decided on July. 21. 2005; Supreme Court Decision 2007Da27670 Decided on November. 20. 2008.

global trends of recodification of civil code throughout the world. The committee for the amendment of civil code was formed in February 2009. It consists of some thirty committee members from the academia, the judiciary and the bar association. The committee is divided into six sub-committees and is working on the draft in the respective fields of the code. The committee is striving to reflect extensive judge-made laws in Korea. It will also incorporate significant changes in the Korean society that have rendered some parts of the Civil Code obsolete. In line with international harmonization of private law, the committee is also referring to international conventions, such as the CISG (United Nations Convention on International Sale of Goods) or international model laws, such as the PECL (Principles of European Contract Law), the PICC (Principles of International Commercial Contracts) and the DCFR (Draft Common Frame of Reference). Meanwhile, recent amendments or efforts for the amendment in other countries, including Germany, France, China, and Japan will also be considered. It is too early to tell at this stage what this committee will bring forth. However, significant changes are definitely in store for us.

4 Overview of Korean Civil Procedural Law

4.1 Overall Structure

Civil procedure in Korea is governed by the Korean Civil Procedure Code (민사소송법, hereinafter 'KCPC').[40] In addition to this Code, the Rules of Civil Procedure (민사소송규칙, hereinafter 'RCP') was promulgated by the Supreme Court of Korea, and is serving as a supplemental norm to the KCPC. Besides these two main bodies of norms, there are adjacent statutory laws, such as the Civil Execution Act (민사집행법), the Family Litigation Act (가사소송법), and the Debtor Rehabilitation and Bankruptcy Act (채무자의 회생 및 파산에 관한 법률).

The KCPC is comprised of 7 chapters and 502 provisions. The first four chapters account for the most part of the KCPC. The first chapter sets forth general provisions on courts, parties, litigation costs, and litigation procedure in general. The second chapter provides various provisions concerning litigation procedure of the court of first instance. The third chapter is a chapter on appeals, while the fourth chapter deals with re-trials. Case law in the area of civil procedure also plays an important role. There are a relatively small number of scholars concentrating on the field of civil procedure, in comparison with the number of scholars in civil law. This may be partly ascribed to the prevalent, but inappropriate idea that civil procedural law is reserved rather for judges and practitioners than for scholars.

[40] See generally, Kwon (2007). Much of this article has been used in this chapter.

4.2 Guiding Principles

Article 1 of the KCPC declares that fairness, swiftness and efficiency stand as guiding principles of Korean civil procedure.

4.2.1 Fairness

Fairness can be understood from two different perspectives; substantive and procedural fairness. Substantive fairness pursues finding of the truth and drawing a just conclusion, while procedural fairness pursues the neutrality of the tribunal and equal treatment of the parties by giving them an equal and fair opportunity to present their cases. In general, they are mutually complementary. However, there is delicate tension between these two values, as well. Tipping toward procedural fairness might harm the goal of finding truth, especially when a party is not capable enough to perform procedural acts properly by oneself. Tipping toward substantial fairness might be helpful in drawing a just conclusion, but might endanger procedural fairness when the court excessively intervenes in the proceedings to reach what it considers a right conclusion. Article 136 of the KCP provides a basis for the intervention of the court to clarify pleadings by parties as well as setting forth its limitation, functions as an equilibrium balancing these two values. On the whole, the Korean judiciary has been tilting slightly toward the substantive fairness side, by actively making use of this clause as a vehicle to draw what it considers a just outcome, especially in cases where either or both of the parties are not represented by attorneys.

4.2.2 Swiftness

Swiftness is another value that has been pursued rigorously by the Korean judiciary. The idea of "Justice delayed is justice denied" is set forth in Article 27 of the Constitution of Korea in which the right of the citizens to a speedy trial is guaranteed. This idea is found throughout the KCPC. For instance, parties bear responsibility for timely presentation of pleadings (§146). Failure to make pleadings or appear on the date of pleadings may result in disadvantageous treatment (§146,150,268). The KCPC also prescribes a recommended period for the rendering of the judgment (§199), which is 5 months from the date of filing.

4.2.3 Efficiency

In terms of efficiency, the KCPC has adopted several features designed to focus more on contested disputes and spend less time on uncontested disputes. For example, if the defendant remains silent by failing to submit a written answer within 30 days from the receipt of the statement of claim, the court may deem that the defendant has admitted the facts described in the statement of claim and go on to render a judgment without holding a hearing. The Small Claims Trial Act (소액사건심판법) is also worth noting in that it provides for an expeditious and convenient process for small claims while alleviating the burden on the court system.[41] This process was first introduced in 1973, mainly in order to get rid of delay, complexity and costliness of the regular trial by providing people with an accessible, simple, speedy and inexpensive mechanism for minor dispute resolutions.[42]

4.3 *Jurisdiction and Parties to the Procedure*

4.3.1 Jurisdiction

Domestic Jurisdiction

A lawsuit should be filed in the court with competent jurisdiction.

As for subject matter jurisdiction, District Courts, including their branch courts, hold original jurisdiction over civil cases. A single judge presides over a case unless the amount in controversy exceeds 50 million Korean won.[43] A three-judge panel will take a case in which the amount exceeds the above limit and a case which has been transferred from a single judge due to its difficulty and complexities. There are some special types of cases that are handled by a single judge even when the amount in controversy exceeds the limit mentioned above. These matters are enumerated in the Regulation on the Subject Matter Jurisdiction in Civil and Family Litigations (민사 및 가사소송의 사물관할에 관한 규칙), one of the Supreme Court regulations.

Territorial jurisdiction is determined by the venue of the case. The general venue of the case is based upon the domicile of the defendant. The court that has authority over that geographic location has territorial jurisdiction (§2).[44] The KCPC also provides rules for special venues. Even in the absence of a general venue, the court still has territorial jurisdiction when one of these special venues are within its geographical boundary. Important among these special venues are workplace (§7), the place where an obligation is to be performed (§8), the location of the property (§10), the place where a tort was committed (§18), and the place for

[41] Small claims refer to the claims for the payment of money, fungibles or securities not exceeding 20 million Korean won (equivalent to approximately 27,800 U.S. Dollar as of 23 January 2011).

[42] See Kwon (1996), at 451.

[43] It is slightly more than 44,500 U.S. dollars, as of 23 January 2011.

[44] There are some special provisions for the general forums of an ambassador or a minister (§4): the place of the Supreme Court—Seoul, a juristic person (§5): the place of its principle office, or state (§6): the seat of the government agency representing the relevant litigation—the Ministry of Justice in Gwacheon, Gyunggi, or that of the Supreme Court—Seoul).

registration of real estate (§21). Jurisdiction can also be established by agreement between parties, or pleading as to the merits of a case in the court of first instance without filing any objection to jurisdiction (§30).

When multiple venues establish a jurisdiction, the plaintiff can bring a suit in any one of those venues. When several claims are joined in a single lawsuit, it may be brought to any one of the courts having jurisdiction over one of those claims (§25①). If the court finds that it lacks jurisdiction, it should rule to transfer the case to the competent court (§34①). Even when the case falls under its jurisdiction, the court may transfer the case to another competent court in order to avoid any significant damage or delay (§35).

International Jurisdiction

Though the KCPC provides for no explicit provision for international jurisdiction, the Private International Act (국제사법) states that a Korean court has international jurisdiction when a party or a case in dispute is substantially related to Korea (§2①). It also states that the court is to comply with reasonable principles in accordance with the idea of allocation of international jurisdiction, when deciding on the substantiality of the relationship of the case to Korea (§2②). In practice, Korean courts tend to look at the territorial jurisdiction clauses in the KCPC and, if necessary, attempt to apply or modify the domestic doctrines in light of legal reasoning.[45]

4.3.2 Parties to the Procedure

Standing

In principle, a prospective party's standing is determined by the KCC and other relevant laws. According to the KCC, natural persons and legal persons hold this standing (§2). Yet, Article 52 of the KCPC adds another type to this list. An unincorporated association or foundation may become a party to a lawsuit, as long as it has essential elements of a legal person. Among these elements are a decision-making body, a representative or an administrator of the association, and separate assets for the association, itself. Partnership, itself, is not qualified to be a party in the civil procedure unless it satisfies the requirements mentioned above. A minor, a quasi-incompetent person, or an incompetent person, as stipulated in the KCC, does possess standing. However, they do not possess capacity to engage directly in proceedings. This means that even when they become parties to a civil procedure, they are not eligible to represent themselves in the proceedings.

[45] Supreme Court Decision 2002Da59788 Decided on January. 22. 2005.

Consequently, they should be represented by their legal representatives as determined by the KCC or other relevant laws.

No Mandatory Representation by a Lawyer

Parties may have an attorney-at-law as a legal counsel in the proceedings. However, representation by a lawyer is not mandatory in Korea. This is so, regardless of the type of the court. Therefore, parties can still litigate in the Supreme Court without legal support of a lawyer. In reality, many of these parties are helped by para-legals with certain levels of legal knowledge and experience who offer fair legal services for typical types of cases with reasonable fees. However, these para-legals cannot represent their clients as a legal counsel. They only offer limited scope of legal support.

Once parties decide to appoint someone to advocate on their behalf, it should be a licensed lawyer admitted to the Korean Bar Association. Foreign lawyers, who are not members of the Korean Bar Association, are not permitted to act as a counsel for a litigating party in Korean civil proceedings. However, this is not without exception. In cases where the amount in controversy falls short of a specific amount (50 million Korean won), the court may permit certain persons other than lawyers to represent the party.[46]

A plaintiff or defendant who cannot afford the costs of the lawsuit is entitled to legal aid, unless it is evidently expected that the party in question will lose the case (§128). The court may grant legal aid upon application or *ex officio*. Such grant entails temporary or permanent exemption from legal costs, including fees arising out of proceedings or fees for a court-appointed lawyer (§129).

Plurality of a Party

The KCPC allows for joinder of parties as plaintiffs or defendants. In cases where the rights or liabilities forming the subject matter of a lawsuit are common to many persons, or are generated by the same factual or legal grounds, these persons may join in the lawsuit as co-litigants (§65). The same shall also apply in cases where the rights or liabilities forming the subject matter of a lawsuit are of the same sort, or are generated by the same sort of factual or legal grounds (§65). The KCPC also allows a third party to join existing proceedings. However, the joining party should possess sufficient connection between his claim and the existing proceedings.

[46] These persons are those who keep a close living relation with the party and are in a kinship within a specific scope, or those who are in a specific relationship under an employment contract, etc, with the party, such as the handling of, or assistance in, the regular affairs concerning such cases (§88①).

Addition of the new party is allowed at any stage in the proceedings before the closing of the hearing.

4.4 Commencing the Procedure

4.4.1 Filing Statements of Claim

Civil proceedings are initiated when the plaintiff files a statement of claim with the court (§248). A statement of claim is a written document in which the plaintiff states the parties, the legal representative or counsel, if any, the relief sought for which the action is instituted, and causes of action (§249). Filing a statement of claim sets a boundary on the subject matter for adjudication in accordance with the principle of party disposition. This principle is the procedural aspect of the general right of self-determination, meaning that the parties, rather than the court, determine the initiation, subject-matter, and termination of the proceedings. Evidence need not be included in or attached to the statement of claim. However, the plaintiffs tend to attach substantial evidence, such as a copy of the written contract in a contract-related dispute or a certificate of title in a property-related dispute. This is even recommended by the court since this facilitates and expedites the proceedings.

4.4.2 Review of Statements of Claim

Once a written statement of claim is submitted to the court, the case is assigned to a judge or judging panel. The presiding judge reviews if the statement of claim meets the necessary requirements. These requirements are as follows:

Firstly, the statement of claim should state all the elements required by Article 249, as mentioned above. Secondly, stamps as required under relevant rules and regulations should be affixed to the statement of claim.

If it turns out that any of these requirements is not satisfied, the presiding judge will order the plaintiff to correct it within a designated period (§254①). Failure to comply with the order might result in either a reiteration of this order by the presiding judge or in the dismissal of the statement of claim, at the discretion of the presiding judge (§254②). However, a dismissed statement of claim can be re-filed if the defects are subsequently cured.

4.4.3 Serving Statements of Claim

If a statement of claim has met the necessary requirements, the court serves the defendant with a duplicate (§255①). It must be served on the defendant in time for the person to take action in her own defense. Along with the copy of the statement of claim, other relevant documents, such as instructions on the civil procedure and the order for the submission of a written statement of defense, are enclosed and served together.

The service is regarded as an official act, which is to be effected *ex officio* by the court. It is usually delivered by registered mail. However, a designated court official or a marshal, upon the request of the court or the plaintiff, can also serve these documents. If the service turns out unsuccessful due to an incorrect address specified in the statement of claim, the presiding judge orders the plaintiff to correct it within a designated period. Failure to comply with this order may result in the dismissal of the statement of claim. If it becomes obvious that it is impossible for the plaintiff, acting without negligence, to specify the defendant's actual address, the presiding judge orders the giving of public notice as an alternative means of service (§194). This is done by posting the above documents on the designated court's bulletin board or in other manners as prescribed by the Supreme Court Regulations (§195). The successful service of a statement of claim has some substantive effects as well, such as interruption of the prescription period (§265).

The defendant, upon receiving a statement of claim, is required to file a written statement of defense within 30 days from receiving service of the statement of claim (§256①). If the defendant accepts the claim or admits all the facts, the court may proceed to a judgment without conducting a trial (§257). No express objection to the statement of claim leads to the same result. These mechanisms all serve the goal of a swift trial.

4.4.4 Voluntary Dismissal of Statements of Claim

The plaintiff may dismiss the case voluntarily after the statement of claim has been filed. However, the plaintiff needs to obtain approval from the defendant to do so if dismissal is to take place after the defendant has made her pleadings on the merits (§266②). If the defendant does not object to the dismissal by the plaintiff within 2 weeks, she is deemed to have consented to the dismissal (§266⑥). Voluntary dismissal is without prejudice unless it has been made after the rendition of judgment (§267).

4.5 *Pre-trial and Trial Proceedings*

4.5.1 Pre-trial Proceedings

The KCPC provides rules for pre-trial proceedings. However, the court is not obliged to conduct this process. The court can either undergo this process or proceed directly to the trial proceedings, based on which option better enables an efficient and prompt trial. When the court chooses to conduct pre-trial proceedings, it aims to clarify and narrow down the facts and the legal issues to be reviewed in the trial.

When the defendant submits a written statement of defense contesting the claim, the presiding judge may require parties to submit further briefs and evidence. After a series of exchanges, if the presiding judge feels that issues have been made clear and substantial documentary evidence has been submitted, a pre-trial is conducted. The presiding judge, or one of the judges within the same judicial panel commissioned by the presiding judge, holds a conference (§282①). Sometimes a personal appearance of the parties is ordered. During the conference, the judge discusses the issues of the case with the parties and their counsels. If necessary, they consider the simplification and sharpening of the issues. During this conference, the judge and the parties also develop a plan for the upcoming procedures. For instance, setting the date of hearings and a limitation on the number of witnesses may be discussed and planned. The possibility of reaching a settlement can also be deliberated upon. In practice, the presiding judge frequently makes an attempt to conciliate the case at this stage. Most of the time, this is the stage when issues have been clarified both to the court and the parties, misunderstanding has been mitigated, and the parties have become less combative. A separate settlement conference may be planned and conducted at the discretion of the presiding judge. In practice, a considerable number of cases are settled in the form of compromise or conciliation.

4.5.2 Trial Proceedings

Presenting Oral Submissions

Trial proceedings are governed by the principle of party presentation, meaning that the parties have the privilege and responsibility to present the facts and evidence to the court (§134①). In this sense, the KCPC is based on an adversarial system.

These proceedings are conducted in oral hearings. If a pre-trial conference was held beforehand, the parties state the outcome of the pre-trial pleadings on the first hearing date (§287②). If not, parties start stating what they have submitted in the form of claims, written defenses, or briefs. Each party has the opportunity to be appraised of the opponent's allegations and must be allowed to comment and to react accordingly. In the past, it was customary for parties or attorneys to add a few simple words on submitted documents without elaborating on their contents and backgrounds. This was due to the idea that the judge and the counter-party already had a chance to review the submitted documents, so it is time-consuming to go over them again in the courtroom. Heavy caseload and need for speedier case-handling justified this convention. Yet, it was criticized for being not in line with the principle of oral hearing. As of recently, Korean courts strongly emphasize oral communication in the courtroom. They tend to give sufficient time to the parties and attorneys so that they can clarify their allegations and evidence in more detail.

Presenting Evidence

Unless the facts are undisputed among parties or are so apparent that they do not require any proof, the facts alleged by the parties need to be proved by evidence. Parties are responsible for gathering and presenting relevant evidence. The court is not allowed to consider evidence that has not been presented by either of the parties. Even in an extreme case where the judge clearly knows the existence of the evidence based on personal knowledge, the judge has no choice, but to disregard it unless it is submitted by either of the parties.

According to the KCPC, there are six types of evidence: examination of witnesses, examination of parties, expert testimony, documentary evidence, inspection, and other evidence (drawings, photographs, recording tapes, video tapes, magnetic discs for computers and other articles created to store the information therein). Assessing the relevance and the materiality of the evidence is fully at the discretion of the court. Hence, there is no clear-cut rule concerning the probative values of each type of the evidence. In practice, there is a general tendency of placing more weight trust on documentary evidence than testimony by a witness. According to a Supreme Court decision, the document by which the juristic act has been performed presumes the existence and the content of that juristic act.[47] Therefore, these documents, such as written contracts or agreements, are usually considered the most powerful evidentiary sources.

There is no discovery procedure in Korea. No general obligation of one party to produce documents at the request of the other party is recognized. Instead, Korean law possesses an alternative procedure: an order by the court to submit a document. The court, upon the motion of the party, may order the holder of a document to submit it under certain circumstances (§344). The holder of a document shall not refuse the order issued by the court. In case of refusal by a party to the litigation (§349), the court may admit the claims of the other party in such document to be true. In addition, refusal of a third party is sanctioned by fine (§351,318,311①).

4.6 *Closing Procedures*

4.6.1 Closing Hearings

When all the necessary pleadings and evidence have been made or submitted, and the case has become ripe for the final adjudication, the court closes the oral proceedings and sets a date for rendering a judgment. In practice, a decision is rendered 2 or 3 weeks after the closing of the proceedings unless the nature of the case requires a longer interval.

[47] Supreme Court Decision 2010Da56616 Decided on November. 11. 2010.

4.6.2 Judgments

After the closing of the trial, the court deliberates on the case. If the case was tried by a panel of three judges, each of them has independent status as to deliberation and voting. The presiding judge does not have superior authority as far as the judicial decision is concerned. The judgment in this case is made by a majority. No record of the vote can be made open to the public, with the exception of the Supreme Court rulings.

Following deliberation, a decision is handed down. The KCPC recommends the court to render a decision within 5 months after the institution of the lawsuit (§199), and within 2 weeks (or 4 weeks if the case is sophisticated) after the hearing has been closed (§207①). Although such time-limits are deemed only guidelines, a considerable number of civil cases are handled within the designated period. In practice, decisions by the court of first instance in Korea usually take the following form. First, the court illustrates the facts of the case, and then proceeds to summarize the parties' claims and their legal basis. After spotting issues therefrom, the court then states the conclusion and its grounds. Decisions in Korea are generally brief.

4.6.3 Appeal and Final Appeal

When a decision is rendered, the losing party is entitled to appeal the judgment. The appellant must have a legitimate interest in taking recourse against the judgment, meaning that the appellant should have been aggrieved by the judgment. Therefore, only the losing party is entitled to appeal. An appeal must be lodged within 14 days from the date of the service of the judgment on the party in question (§396①). Cross appeals may also be lodged by the respondent to an appeal or by any other party (§403). If the losing party does not appeal against the judgment within the designated time, it becomes final and conclusive.

Appellate proceedings in Korea are not substantially different from the original proceedings of the first instance, in that parties are allowed to make arguments and submit evidence. New allegations or submission of new evidence is permitted so long as it does not infringe upon a time-bar. Therefore, the appellate proceedings have the characteristics of the continuation of the previous proceedings. When the appeal is found meritorious, the appellate court vacates the judgment and renders its own decision. The appellate court is not allowed to grant more than the party has requested. On the other hand, when the appeal is found groundless, the court dismisses the appeal.

The judgment of the appellate court may be appealed again to the Supreme Court of Korea. No separate decision by the Supreme Court to hear an appeal from a lower court, such as a writ of *certiorari* in the U.S. Supreme Court, is required. Although the possible causes for appeal is are to matters of law, the Supreme Court of Korea sometimes shows leniency to accept appeals based on factual issues. This was possible under the unique doctrine of "the violation of the rule regarding taking of evidence", justifying the dispute of the facts at the highest level in the form of the matter of law. The Supreme Court either dismisses the final appeal when it is groundless, or remands the case when it is found to have due grounds. The final decision of the Supreme Court has binding effect on lower courts with respect to the specific case in issue. Unlike in common law jurisdictions, the decision does not have binding force on later cases of a similar nature. However, Supreme Court decisions seem to influence lower courts to a great extent in subsequent cases. In this regard, Supreme Court decisions may be said to function as powerful precedents with *de facto* binding force.

4.7 Alternative Dispute Resolution

Civil litigations are often expensive and time-consuming. The social costs incurred from litigations can be saved by making better use of "Alternative Dispute Resolution (hereinafter 'ADR')". ADR encompasses a wide array of practices, the purpose of which are to manage and swiftly resolve disputes at a lower cost than formal litigation and with as little adverse impact as possible on business and personal relationships. Mediation and arbitration are two typical forms of ADR in Korea.

Mediation, sometimes referred to as conciliation, is perhaps the most common ADR technique widely used in Korea. Mediation is typically led by the court or a court-annexed mediation center. The more typical circumstance is that a judge suspends the litigation procedure tentatively and submits the case to mediation where a judge, himself, becomes the mediator. Although a great number of cases have been settled in this manner, this court-oriented mediation has also been a target of some criticism. While mediation requires a mediator to actively step in and assist negotiations of disputants in order to facilitate a voluntary and mutually acceptable settlement, judges, who are expected to keep a distance from either party to sustain their neutrality and integrity are usually not appropriate for this job. For this reason, the judiciary is striving to utilize court-annexed mediation centers, or non-judicial mediators to a higher extent.

The number of arbitrations in Korea is also rapidly increasing. Since arbitration is the product of an agreement to arbitrate, there should be an arbitration clause in order to proceed to this process. Once the arbitrator's decision is issued, it becomes enforceable. Due to its friendliness to the idea of private autonomy and efficiency in terms of costs and expertise, arbitration is favored by more and more companies these days as they frequently opt to incorporate an arbitration clause in their contracts. The Arbitration Act (중재법) in Korea provides legal grounds for this field of law.

4.8 Distinctive Features of Korean Civil Procedural Law

4.8.1 Responding to Flood of Litigation

Korea is by no means a non-litigious country, although some past authoritative accounts of Korean legal culture have portrayed Korean legal culture as litigation-averse.[48]

According to statistics as of 2009, the total number of litigious cases reached 6,345,439. Civil litigation accounted for 65.2 % of this total number, amounting 4,135,591 civil cases. Even more striking is the number of cases in the Supreme Court. The number of litigious cases filed with the Supreme Court reached a surprising 32,361 cases, of which 10,704 were civil cases. Considering there are only 14 Supreme Court Justices, this volume of cases is truly overwhelming. This is due to the lack of certiorari as in the U.S. court system and the tendency of Korean people to bring the case all the way up to the Supreme Court once they get involved with litigation. The caseload in Korea is much higher than its neighbor, Japan. As of 2008, the total number of cases filed in Korea was more than nine times higher than the number in Japan,[49] even though the population in Japan was three times higher than the population in Korea.

However, swiftness and efficiency of the trial process seems substantially unimpaired by the challenge of this enormous number. As at 2009, average duration between filing of the case and the rendering of the decision by the court of first instance is 129.9 days, a little longer than 4 months. In the same year, average duration for U.S. district courts was 8.9 months.[50] Speedy trial in Korea was made possible thanks to the fact that more than 70 % of the cases fall into the category of small claims. These cases are handled under special procedural rules provided by the Small Claims Trial Act (소액사건심판법), which is designed to provide an expeditious and convenient process for small claims. Furthermore, the hard-working attitude of Korean judges might be another reason. It is customary for relatively young and dedicated judges to stay until late at night struggling with cases. An average Korean judge handles approximately 1,000 cases a year.[51]

---

[48] Hahm (1986).

[49] The total number of the cases filed in Korea during the year 2008 totals 18,402,098 (6,345,561 of which are litigation cases, meaning that there are adversarial parties), whereas the number for Japan in the same period totals 2,252,438 (547,017 of which are litigation cases). Japanese judicial statistics are available at Supreme Court of Japan http://www.courts.go.jp/english/ and Korean judicial statistics are available at Supreme Court of Korea http://eng.scourt.go.kr/eng/main/Main.work.

[50] Judicial Business of the United States Courts, 2009 Annual Report of the Director, at, http://www.uscourts.gov/Statistics/JudicialBusiness/JudicialBusiness.aspx?doc=/uscourts/Statistics/JudicialBusiness/2009/JudicialBusiness2009.pdf.

[51] See http://news.hankooki.com/1page/opinion/200909/h2009090821262376070.htm.

4.8.2 Defining Role of Judge in Civil Litigation

Basically, parties are the main players in the field of civil litigation. However, it is the judge who conducts all the proceedings. A controversial point concerns as to how much the presiding judge can render guidance for the pleading. In connection with the role of the judge in the civil procedure, this has been a much debated issue. It is common in Korea to see parties with asymmetric capacities, i.e. between an individual with no lawyer against a huge company represented by a large law firm. The individual often calls for 'justice' by demanding the court to take an active role to intervene in the case and draw a just and fair conclusion. In this event, judges struggle to satisfy the notion of substantive fairness within the framework of the adversarial system. Article 136 of the KCPC provides that the presiding judge may ask the parties questions, and urge them to offer proof in order to clarify the legal relations on factual or legal matters. It further states that the court should give the parties an opportunity to state their opinions on legal matters which they are deemed to have evidently overlooked. Korean courts sometimes use this provision to strike a balance between their sense of justice and the impartiality of the judiciary. It is not always easy to draw a bright line between these two seemingly conflicting demands. The Supreme Court has proposed a guideline by using notions of passive and active elucidation.[52] Passive elucidation, intended to clarify what has been alleged, is allowed. However, active elucidation, intended to attract or suggest a new assertion, is prohibited. An exception to this would be the duty of the court to indicate a legal point which the party has evidently missed (§136④).

5 Conclusion

Within a relatively short period, Korean civil law and civil procedural law have undergone numerous changes, since their establishment until the recent amendment efforts. Different dimensions, including legal doctrines from Western jurisdictions, long-standing culture and tradition in Korean society, as well as constant efforts of legislators and jurists to harmonize these factors have interplayed in a dynamic way as to form the current law. Though this chapter is merely an outline on Korean civil law and civil procedural law, it is hoped that it serves as a useful reference point in grasping the whole picture of these intriguing fields of Korean law.

[52] Supreme Court Decision 97Da38442 Decided on February. 27. 1998.

References

Literatures

Chun BD et al (1980) Traditional legal attitudes. University of California, Berkeley

Hahm P (1986) Korean jurisprudence politics and cultures. Yonsei University Press, Seoul

Kim M (2009) Customary law and colonial jurisprudence in Korea. Am J Comp Law 57(1):214

Kwon O (1996) Small claims courts in Korea and the U.S.; a comparative analysis. In: Song S (ed) Korean law in the global economy. Bakyoungsa, Seoul

Kwon Y (2007) Litigating in Korea: a general overview of the Korean civil procedure. J Korean Law 7(1)

Kwon Y (2011) Bridging the gap between Korean substance and western form. In: Black A, Bell G (ed) Law and legal institutions of Asia. Cambridge University Press, Australia

Websites

The National Assembly of the Republic of Korea (http://likms.assembly.go.kr/law/jsp/main.jsp)

The Supreme Court of Korea (http://eng.scourt.go.kr/eng/main/Main.work)

Korean Legislation Research Institute (http://elaw.klri.re.kr)

Criminal Law and Procedure

Kwoncheol Lee

1 Introduction

Lay people may find the legal system difficult to comprehend. Moreover, it is more challenging for them to understand the overall concepts of foreign legal systems. However, the best way to fully understand and point out the problems of the laws in one country is to be familiar with other legal systems. Hopefully, this chapter will assist readers willing to become familiar with Korean criminal law and procedure and thus, to more fully understand the criminal justice systems of their own countries.

Certain crimes or offenses to be deterred by punishment, such as murder and robbery, do not vary considerably among societies, as if they are universal crimes needing suppression throughout all communities. However, in accordance with its circumstances, each society has its own way to define various crimes and to formulate appropriate punishments. Korea also has its own principles and rules in exercise of national penal authority and through time, has improved criminal sanctions suitable to each respective era.

The main purpose of this chapter is to understand noteworthy improvements in the criminal justice system. First of all, this chapter explores principles and practices particular to criminal law and procedure. In parts of criminal law, we will go through principles, special conditions for prosecution and punishment which differentiate Korea from common law traditions. In respect of criminal procedure, basic process relating to investigations and trials will be explored first. New efforts for improving appropriate punishments and new approaches for fair trial, guarantee of defendants and enhancement of victims' rights will be examined in their respective fields.

K. Lee (✉)
Baekseok University, Cheonan, Republic of Korea
e-mail: kwoncheol.lee@gmail.com

Korea Legislation Research Institute, *Introduction to Korean Law*,
DOI 10.1007/978-3-642-31689-0_5, © Springer-Verlag Berlin Heidelberg 2013

2 Criminal Law

2.1 Basic Structure of Criminal Code

2.1.1 Principles in Criminal Law

Principle of "Nullum Crimen, Nulla Poena Sine Lege," and Its Derivatives

In the Korean criminal justice system, the most important rule relating to the legislation and exercise of national penal power is the principle that there is neither a crime nor a punishment without law (nullum crimen, nulla poena sine lege). During the 1960s and 1970s, authoritarian military regimes after the Korean War utilized criminal law to oppress dissidents and control the public. In order to keep such illegitimate exercise of penal authority in check, this principle has played a significant role in overall criminal law. The main purpose of this principle, accordingly, is to protect citizens from the arbitrary exercise of governmental penal power by placing controls on that power. The Korean Constitution and criminal law present provisions to declare this principle. The Constitution provides that "no person shall be punished, placed under preventive detention or subject to involuntary labor, except as provided by Act and through lawful procedures."[1] In addition, it states that no citizen shall be prosecuted for any act which does not constitute a crime under the Act in force at the time it was committed.[2] Criminal law also provides that the criminality and punishability of an act shall be determined by the law in effect at the time of the commission of that act.[3]

A handful of rules derive from this principle. First, no law should be vague on the types of prohibited conduct and the punishments to be imposed. Moreover, it also requires that the length of criminal sanction should be provided for in detail. Thus, no sentence of indeterminate imprisonment or detention may be allowed. Second, the principle prohibits ex post facto law since retroactive criminal laws destroy the people's trust in law in force. However, ex post facto law is allowable if the application of ex post facto law is advantageous to the defendants.[4] Third, the principle prohibits courts from analogizing a provision to punish an offense when there is no specific criminality in such conduct. Use of analogy or interpretation of provisions beyond a reasonable degree may be considered legislative conduct of courts and thus, violates the principle of division of powers. Under this principle,

[1] Constitution, Art. 12(1).

[2] Constitution, Art. 13(1).

[3] Criminal Act, Art. 1(1).

[4] Criminal Act, Art. 1(2). When a law is amended after the commission of a crime so that the act thereby no longer constitutes a crime under the new law or the punishment therefor under the new law becomes less severe than under the previous law, the new law shall apply.

customary criminal law cannot be used to judge guilt and punishment, and courts should rely solely on laws enacted by the National Assembly.[5]

Scope of Application of Criminal Law

Temporal Limits

The scope of application of the Criminal Act is from the time of enactment to the time of abolishment thereof. Therefore, the Government may not retroactively punish a person who committed an act which is not a crime under the penal code, even though the law subsequently classified the act as a crime. However, the retroactive effect of the Criminal Act may be admitted in limited cases. A new law can be applied to an offender if the application of the new law would be more favorable to the offender. When a law is amended after the commission of a crime and such act thereby no longer constitutes a crime under the new law or the punishment under the new law becomes less severe than under the previous law, the new law is to apply.[6] For example, if a person committed larceny and the applicable punishment for the crime was imprisonment for 1 year at the time of the commission of the crime, but the punishment for the crime changed to imprisonment for 6 months at the time of trial, the court may apply the new law to the offender and thus, he/she can be sentenced to the lesser penalty.

Venue

The Criminal Act adopts the territorial principle in terms of venue for its application. Generally, the Act applies to both Korean nationals and foreigners who commit a crime in Korean territory. However, the Act also admits jurisdiction of Korean courts over foreigners who have committed certain crimes in foreign countries. A foreigner committing any of the following crimes in a foreign country may be brought to trial in Korea and sentenced: crimes concerning the Korean national flag, currency, securities, postage and revenue stamps, and crimes concerning insurrection or foreign aggression against Korea.[7] In addition, when the Republic of Korea or a Korean national is the victim of a crime committed in a foreign country, the Criminal Act may apply to the crime.[8]

---

[5] This is distinguished from the Civil Act in which customary law may be used when no Act applies. Civil Act, Art. 1. provides that "if no provisions applicable to certain civil affairs exist in any Act, customary law shall apply, and if no applicable customary law exists, sound reasoning shall apply."

[6] Criminal Act, Art. 1.

[7] Criminal Act. Art. 5.

[8] Id. 6.

Persons Under the Criminal Act

In principle, the Criminal Act applies to all persons in eligible temporal limits and venues for the application. However, the Korean Constitution provides exceptions to the principle. The President of the Republic of Korea, while in office, may not be prosecuted for any crime other than insurrection or treason.[9] Second, a member of the National Assembly has Parliamentary privilege. He/she is not to be held liable outside the Assembly for any of his/her opinions officially expressed nor for votes cast inside the Assembly. Therefore, even though a congressman makes a slanderous statement, he/she may not be prosecuted for such remark if it was expressed in connection with his/her job in the Assembly. He/she may be submitted to disciplinary measures inside the Assembly.

2.2 Constitution of Crime

2.2.1 Actus Reus and Mens Rea

In order to evaluate whether an action is a crime, an act should amount to an actual criminal act and comprise two elements: Actus Reus and Mens Rea. For example, the Criminal Act provides that "a person who inflicts bodily injury upon another shall be punished. . .."[10] The Act describes an assault causing bodily harm in the abstract. However, in order for the act to be a crime which is punishable, it should meet the requirements of Actus Reus and Mens Rea. The subdivided requirements for the assault, for an example, are as follows (Table 1):

2.2.2 Illegality of Acts

If an act meets all of the requirements of Actus Reus and Mens Rea, it constitutes a crime in that such behavior is against social norms. However, such behavior can be permitted and regarded as a lawful act when it falls under any of the following categories which justify the act.

Self-defense

When a person performs an act in order to prevent imminent infringement of his/her own or another person's rights, he/she is exempt from any punishment. If such act exceeds a degree reasonable for prevention, however, the person in question may be

[9] Constitution, Art. 84.

[10] Criminal Act. Art. 257.

Table 1 *Actus Reus* and *Mens Rea* of assault causing bodily harm

Actus Reus	Agent	A person
	Object	Body of another person
	Act	Assault
	Result	Body injury
	Causation	Between assault and injury
Mens Rea	Intent, negligence, or recklessness	Intent to cause injury by assault

punished. In such cases, the punishment should be reduced from the usual sentence. When he/she engages such excessive conduct in fear, surprise, excitement, or confusion, he/she should not be punished.[11]

Necessity

An act done in order to avoid imminent danger against his/her own or another person's rights is not punishable. The act should be reasonable in degree for the avoidance.[12] A defense is permitted only when the interest protected exceeds the interest sacrificed. If the two interests are equal, the act may not be permitted under the necessity rule. While self-defense requires the infringement to be unjust, the necessity rule does not require the danger to result from an unjust act or circumstance.

Acts According to Social Rules (a.k.a. Justifiable Acts)

When a person performs an act in accordance with any Act, or in pursuit of accepted business practices, or within socially accepted rules, the person may not be punished.[13] For example, when a public official performs his/her duties with proper authority, such as executing search warrants or the death penalty, he/she may not be punished although the act seems to infringe another person's rights.

Self-help

The last exception to criminality is self-help. According to this exception, an act performed to avoid impossibility of, or significant difficulty in, preserving a claim by legal procedure may be justified and thus, not punishable when reasonable grounds exist.[14] For example, when a hotel employee restrains a guest who has

[11] Criminal Act. Art. 21.

[12] Criminal Act. Art. 22.

[13] Criminal Act. Art. 20.

[14] Criminal Act. Art. 23.

attempted to flee without paying the charge, the act falls into the justifiable act category and is not punishable.

2.2.3 Liability

Liability means culpability for a wrongdoing when the wrongdoer both intended to do and actually did an illegal act even though he/she was competent to comply with legitimate rules. He/she is to blame because he/she was able to recognize right and wrong and he/she realized he/she was doing an illegal act when he/she did the act. On the other hand, if he/she cannot help doing the act under certain circumstances, he/she may be exempt from punishment or criminal sanctions can be imposed in a lesser degree. A person under the age of 14 is presumed "incompetent for liability," and thus, he/she may not be punished with any criminal sanctions under the Criminal Act.[15] Those under 14 may be sentenced with protective detention under the Juvenile Act.

A person who is unable to discriminate or to control his/her will due to a mental disorder is also exempt from punishment.[16] However, a punishment inflicted on a person who lacks capacity to discriminate or control his/her own will is to be mitigated not exempted.[17] In addition, the Criminal Act provides that "punishment shall be mitigated for an act by deaf-mutes." There are significant critiques of this provision in that even though culpability concerns psychological issues, the Act deems a physical handicap to be a psychological issue disregarding the fact that deaf-mutes also lead normal lives due to the improvement of scientific technology and education.

2.3 Requirements for Prosecution and Punishment

The Korean penal code has two special types of prerequisites for the exercise of national penal power of prosecution and punishment. These are not the universal requirements for all crimes, but applied to specific categories of crimes. In some cases, only the victim of a crime or another person holding the right to file a complaint under law may charge the offender. A prosecutor may not indict the offender unless the victim or an eligible person files a complaint. Even though an investigative authority may initiate an investigation into a case, the case is to be terminated if the victim or a person eligible to file a complaint withdraws such. For example, if a rape victim does not file a complaint against the offender, a prosecutor may not bring the offender to trial. Similarly, victims of insult and privacy

[15] Id. 9.

[16] Id. 10(1).

[17] Id. 10(2).

violations must file a complaint for the crime to be prosecuted. Recently, Korean society raised a tremendous outcry on these prerequisites, especially concerning rape, and the Korean criminal justice system is gradually eliminating these prerequisites. According to the law amended in 2010 for the protection of children and juveniles, a public prosecution may be initiated for a sexual offense committed against a child or juvenile even though no complaint is filed by the victim.[18]

In Korean criminal law, there are other concepts similar to the requisite for prosecution. First, if a crime of larceny or unlawful usage of an automobile was committed among family members, the Government may not exercise penal power over the offender. In such cases, the court would exempt the offender from punishment.[19] For example, if A and B (friend of A) stole a wallet in possession of A's father, A will be exempt from punishment under the relevant provision, while B will be punished for theft. Second, in criminal cases of battery,[20] bodily Injury due to negligence,[21] blackmail,[22] and defamation,[23] the State may not prosecute (though it may initiate an investigation) if the victim ensures that he/she does not desire the offender punished.

2.4 Inchoate Crimes

Criminal attempts refer to a situation in which an offender did not complete the intended crime or his/her intended effect has not been appeared. An attempted crime may be punished only if the punishment for the attempted crime is specifically provided for in each provision concerned. The punishment for an attempted crime may be lesser than that for a completed crime. There are three types of attempted crimes. If a person voluntarily ceases his/her criminal act that he/she initiated or prevents the result of the culmination thereof, the punishment is to be mitigated or exempted.[24] Unlike a voluntarily ceased crime, if an intended crime is not completed due to any external factor, the court may impose a punishment lesser than that for a completed crime.[25] When a person attempts a crime which is impossible to commit because of unsuitable means or mistakes about target objects, the court should impose punishment if there has been a resulting danger. However, in such cases the punishment may be mitigated or exempted.[26]

[18] Act on the Protection of Children and Juveniles from Sexual Abuse, Art. 16.
[19] Criminal Act, Art. 344.
[20] Id. 260(1).
[21] Id. 266(2).
[22] Id. 283(1).
[23] Id. 307.
[24] Id. 26.
[25] Id. 25.
[26] Id. 27.

2.5 Punishment

2.5.1 Types of Punishment

Criminal sanctions under the Korean penal code are of two types: punishment and security measures. The former means deprivation of legal rights (benefits and protection by law) from convicts for the cost of their crime in which punishment is based on the culpability of criminals and the commission of a crime. Security measures are based on the possibility of recidivism and may be imposed on convicts in order to prevent re-offenses.

According to the penal code, there are nine types of punishment: death penalty, imprisonment, imprisonment without prison labor, deprivation of qualifications, suspension of qualifications, fines, detention in a correctional facility, fines for negligence, and confiscation. These types can be categorized according to the similarity of the legal rights relinquished from convicts; punishment by taking life (death penalty), punishment by restricting physical freedom, punishment by depriving the offender of property, and disqualification.

Death Penalty

The Criminal Act stipulates felonies subject to the death penalty, including insurrection,[27] inducement of foreign aggression,[28] espionage,[29] acts benefiting the enemy,[30] murder,[31] murder after rape,[32] murder after robbery.[33] Generally, capital punishment is to be carried out in a prison by hanging, but the Military Criminal Act allows execution by a firing squad.[34] Although Korean criminal law has allowed capital sentences, there has been extreme ongoing controversy regarding the death penalty.

Abolitionists argue that the death penalty is unconstitutional because it is a cruel and uncivilized punishment as well as a deprivation of the ultimate source of human dignity and value. They argue that the deterrent effect of execution is less than the generally expected and that execution cannot be reversed if the conviction is found wrongful. With respect to the purpose of punishment, the death penalty can accomplish neither rehabilitation nor correction of criminals. On the other hand,

---

[27] Id. 87.

[28] Id. 92.

[29] Id. 98.

[30] This includes benefiting an enemy by conscripting troops for the enemy (Criminal Act, Art. 94), providing or destroying equipment (Criminal Act, Art. 95 and Criminal Act, Art. 96).

[31] Id. 250.

[32] Id. 301-2.

[33] Id. 338.

[34] Military Criminal Act, Art. 3.

supporters argue that the death penalty surely has a deterrent effect because life is the most valuable thing to humans and, in terms of retribution, it is necessary to impose the death penalty on a convict who committed such atrocious crime and cannot be rehabilitated with other programs in the justice system.[35] The Constitutional Court upheld the death penalty, stating that the punishment "can deter crimes" and that it helps to "protect innocent and ordinary citizens as well as significant public interests."[36]

The implementation of the penalty was, in no small measure, influenced by a political situation. During the fiery conflicts between the left and right wings after liberation from Japanese colonial rule, the death penalty was often used for political purposes. This tendency continued after the Korean War and under consequent military regimes. At present, there is a moratorium on the death penalty that has lasted about 15 years because President Dae-jung Kim himself was put on death row by the military regime oppressing democratic movements. No executions have been carried out since the last ones took place on December 31, 1997 when 23 people were put to death.

From the perspective law, the Supreme Court also plays a significant role in such situations by proposing strict requirements for capital punishment as follows: (1) the crime was very dangerous because it was committed by not less than two persons; (2) there are no mitigating factors in the motive; (3) it was committed premeditatedly; (4) committed in a cruel manner, resulting in serious harm; and (5) the defendant does not show any remorse during the trial.[37]

Punishment Restricting Physical Freedom

Korean criminal law provides for three types of punishment relating to physical freedom. First, imprisonment is the severest punishment among them. Inmates under prison sentence are required to labor in the facilities. Imprisonment can be sub-classified into life imprisonment and imprisonment for a fixed term. The term ranges from 1 month to 30 years and can be increased to 50 years.[38] Before the revision in 2010, the Act prescribed the range of imprisonment from 1 month to 15 years and increased its upper limit to 25 years. Imprisonment without prison labor is a less severe punishment than imprisonment per se, which is imposed on convicts who have committed negligence or a political crime. However, such convicts may petition to perform labor in a correctional facility. Detention in a correctional facility is applied to offenders who have committed minor offences. The term for the detention is limited to less than 30 days.[39]

[35] Kim et al. (2011).

[36] Constitutional Court Decision 95Hun-Ba1, November 28, 1996.

[37] Huh (2005).

[38] Criminal Act, Art. 42.

[39] Id. 46.

Punishment by Depriving the Offender of Property

A convict who is punished by a fine should pay the amount within 30 days from the date when the judgment has become final. If he/she does not pay the fine in full by the deadline, he/she shall be detained in a workhouse for a term of not less than 1 day and no more than 3 years, or in the case of a fine for negligence, from 1 day to 29 days.[40] A fine for negligence is similar to a fine, but it imposed for minor crimes. Fines are deemed appropriate for crimes relating to corporations and greed. In addition, a fine may avoid the disadvantages of incarceration, such as learning criminal skills from other inmates. However, some suggest that fairness issues might occur because the effect of a fine penalty depends on the amount of assets the convict has. Moreover, fines do not affect the criminal's personality and thus, do not contribute to rehabilitation and education of the offender.

Confiscation is imposed in addition to other punishments. Generally, a judgment for confiscation depends on the discretion of the judge. The following goods may be confiscated: (1) effects used or sought to be used in the commission of a crime; (2) goods produced by or acquired by means of criminal conduct; (3) goods received in exchange for those items mentioned in (1) and (2).[41] For example, the court may issue a confiscation order regarding pistols used for murder, deadly weapons prepared for robbery, money loaned for gambling, and ladders used for burglary. However, bribes,[42] opium, morphine and composite thereof, or paraphernalia for smoking opium[43] are to be mandatorily confiscated by law. In addition, even though the accused is not convicted, confiscation may be ordered when the requisites of confiscation are satisfied.[44]

Disqualification

Under the Korean Criminal Act, deprivation of qualifications and suspension of qualifications fall into this category. These punishments are in addition to other punishments. They are imposed concurrently with other sentences. Deprivation of qualifications means that the severest sentence deprives the convict of some qualifications relating to public affairs as a natural consequence of the sentence. No person who is sentenced to the death penalty or life imprisonment can become a public official. He/she is also disqualified to run for office and cannot vote.[45]

Similar to deprivation, suspension of qualifications may be imposed with imprisonment for a specific term. In such cases, the effect of suspension remains valid

[40] Id. 69.

[41] Id. 48.

[42] Id. 134.

[43] Id. 206.

[44] Id. 49.

[45] Id. 43(1).

until the execution of punishment is completed or exempted.[46] The term of suspension ranges from 1 to 15 years.[47]

2.5.2 Suspending Execution of Sentence

The Korean penal system allows courts to suspend the execution of a sentence under certain conditions. Even though a defendant is found guilty and the court may impose a sentence on him/her, the sentence may be postponed for a certain period. If the term elapses without any further offense on the part of the convict, the sentence is lifted and the convict will have no criminal record. This originates from the British and American probation systems. In order for a court to suspend a sentence, the following prerequisites must be met: First, the offender is subject to imprisonment for not more than 3 years. Thus, the suspension must not be imposed in cases of a violent crime or felony, the possible sentence of which exceeds 3 years or in cases of a fine; Second, there should be mitigating circumstances the court takes into consideration, such as: (1) the age, character and conduct, intelligence and environment of the offender; (2) offender's relation to the victim; (3) the motive for committing the crime, the means and the effect thereof; and (4) circumstances after committing the crime. The term of suspension may not exceed 5 years and the court may order probation, community service, or attendance in an appropriate lecture. This system was designed to help a minor offender to re-enter society by preventing him/her from being confined in a correctional facility and thus, stigmatized by the community.

2.5.3 Security Measures

Apart from criminal sanctions, Korean criminal law allows the Government to impose security measures on convicts in cases where a punishment is not likely to help him/her integrate into the community or accomplish the purpose of punishment, such as special deterrence, due to his/her special circumstances. It is a preventive measure to substitute or complement a punishment, and thus mainly focuses on the prevention of crime. Because of this characteristic relating to prevention, a court should take into account for a security measure the commission of a crime, predictability of the crime committed by the convict, possibility of recidivism, and so forth. The principle of proportionality and due process should be strictly applied when the court orders such measures. In addition, the prerequisites and procedure for the order and enforcement should be duly provided for in Acts. The Constitution also clearly states that no person shall be punished, placed under preventive restrictions or subject to involuntary labor, except as provided by law

[46] Id. 43(2).

[47] Id.

and through due process.[48] Criminal law provides for several types of security measures: community service, an order to take classes,[49] probation under a suspended sentence[50] and parole.[51]

Medical treatment under custody is one of the security measures which have been implemented in Korea. Prosecutors may request courts to order the treatment. The eligible candidates for this treatment are limited to those who have committed an offense in a state of mental disorder, addiction to narcotics, alcohol or other drugs, or psychosexual disorder. The treatment may be ordered when a court judges that such person is likely to recommit a crime and to require special education, betterment and medical treatment. In addition, there shall be reasonable assessment that the treatment is likely to facilitate their rehabilitation. If a convict is sentenced to this treatment, he/she shall be transferred to a medical facility and receive appropriate treatment. The term for custody may not exceed 15 years for a person with a mental disorder and 2 years for a person struggling with an addiction.[52]

2.6 *New Measures in Criminal Law*

2.6.1 Sentencing Reform

The Korean criminal justice system has been under strong criticism due to too lenient sentencing and inacceptable disparities among judges since the early 2000s. To tackle this issue, since 2007 the Korean National Assembly has established the Sentencing Commission and assigned it to enact sentencing guidelines, anticipating that the guidelines may guarantee fair and objective sentencing reflecting the common views of ordinary citizens about punishment.[53]

The sentencing guidelines include seven types of crime and each guideline respectively applies to a certain type of crime, each with its own sentencing range sheet. However, it does not provide any guidelines for death penalty or the imposition of capital punishment which is totally under the judge's discretion. The sentencing factors in each category of crime are divided into two groups, accordingly their gravity. The first group is called 'special sentencing factors,' encompassing 'special aggravating factors' and 'special mitigating factors.' 'General sentencing factors' also have two subcategories. More weight is placed on special sentencing factors than general sentencing factors. Unlike overseas

[48] Constitution, Art. 12(1).

[49] Criminal Act, 62-2.

[50] Id. 59-2.

[51] Id. 73-2(2).

[52] Mental Treatment and Custody Act, Art. 16.

[53] Court Organization Act. Art. 81-2.

practices, the existence of a criminal record is a mere factor neither more decisive nor influential than others.

In order to apply the guidelines, a judge should follow the following four steps: (1) decide the type within each category of crime, (2) apply the appropriate sentencing range, (3) determine the actual term of sentence, (4) decide whether to suspend the sentence or not. However, the guidelines do not have binding authority on judges. If a judge provides grounds for non-compliance with the guidelines in his/her decision, he/she may issue a sentence despite the guidelines.

2.6.2 Zero Tolerance for Sexual Crimes

Electronic Monitoring of Specific Criminal Offenders

The National Assembly passed a Bill relating to electronic monitoring of criminals, which allows attachment of electronic devices on criminals who committed a sexual crime, kidnapping, or murder.[54] A prosecutor may request the attachment if he/she judges that the applicable person shows a possibility of recidivism. The purpose of this Act is to protect citizens from specific crimes by taking additional measures against offenders by attaching to their bodies an electronic device that enables tracking of their locations and movements. In addition, it is expected that the enforcement thereof may help them to reenter the community by preventing them from repeating their crimes and by rectifying their character and conduct.

A probation officer is responsible for enforcing a GPS tracking order under the direction of the prosecutor and for supervising offenders' compliance with the conditions and facilitating the rehabilitation of offenders.[55] Tracking information, managed by the chief probation officer, is supposed to be kept and administered for 5 years after completion of the monitoring and supervision. Access to tracking data may be permitted only for the purpose of supervision, court trial and hearings for early discharge from the monitoring. In the case of using tracking data for criminal investigation, the investigative authority should proceed with warrants issued by the judge.[56]

Registration and Disclosure of Personal Information of Sex Offenders Against Children or Juveniles

Under the Act on the Protection of Children and Juveniles from Sexual Abuse which went into force in 2011, sex offenders must register their personal information and the court has the authority to order any disclosure of the identity of sexual

[54] Act on the Electronic Monitoring of Specific Criminal Offenders, Art. 2.

[55] Act on the Electronic Monitoring of Specific Criminal Offenders, Art. 12; Art. 15.

[56] Id. 16.

offenders to the public. A person who commits a sexual crime against a child or juvenile[57] may be subject to registration and, if he/she is issued an order from the court, he/she shall submit all of the following personal information to the head of the police office having jurisdiction over his/her place of residence: (1) name; (2) resident registration number (similar to social security number); (3) address and actual place of residence; (4) occupation and location of workplace; (5) body size (height and weight); (6) photo (taken within 6 months from the date of registration); (7) registration numbers of vehicles owned.[58] This information is to be preserved by the Minister of Gender Equality and Family for 20 years from the date on which it is initially registered.[59] The Minister may distribute registered information to prosecutors or the heads of police offices at all levels for the prevention and investigation of sex offenses against children or juveniles.[60]

The court is to render judgment in cases of a sexual offense against a child or juvenile in concurrence with an order to disclose information concerning a person who commits sexual assault against a child or juvenile under the age of 13, or a person who commits a sexual offense against a child or juvenile under the age of 13 and is deemed likely to repeat the offense.[61] This information is to be open to the public; however, it will not disclose all the information the offender has submitted. Of the information above, the address and actual place of residence is limited to an administrative district or town. In other words, the exact number of house or street is not to be public knowledge. In addition, the occupation and workplace information as well as resident registration number are not released to the public. In contrast, the summary of a sex offense against a child or juvenile is to be open to the public.[62]

Pharmacotherapy of Offenders of Sexual Crimes (Chemical Castration)

In 2010 the Korean National Assembly passed a Bill allowing pharmacotherapy of sexual deviants who commit sexual violence against persons under 16 years old. A sexual deviant is a person who has a psychosexual disorder showing a propensity for sexual activity, including pedophilia and sexual sadism.[63] With respect to drugs for such treatment, the Ministry of Justice established an advisory committee of fewer than 20 experts who specialize in drug treatment. The drugs will be determined after hearing from the committee, and the Ministry makes an official announcement on the drugs.

[57] Act on the Protection of Children and Juveniles from Sexual Abuse, Art. 33.

[58] Id. 34.

[59] Id. 38.

[60] Id. 37.

[61] Id. 38.

[62] Id. 34.

[63] Medical Treatment and Custody Act, Art. 2(1)3.

A prosecutor may request pharmacotherapy when he/she judges that the defendant shows a possibility of recidivism. However, the prosecutor should provide diagnosis of a psychiatrist on the mental state of the defendant before requesting pharmacotherapy.[64] The court should issue a treatment order for 15 years or less when it finds appropriate grounds and the defendant should be put into probation in due course.[65]

The order is implemented by probation officers, and the person subject to the treatment is transferred to a medical treatment facility.[66] The drug treatment starts from 2 months before the release of the person at issue, so that authorities may verify the effects and side effects of the treatment.[67] If a medical doctor demonstrates the opinion that the side effects will cause serious irrecoverable harm to his/her body, the injection of the drug should be temporarily paused and approval for ceasing injections must be given by the probation committee.

The pharmacological treatment should be provided along with psychotherapy.[68] A psychiatrist or specialist with over three years' experience of treating sexual offenders operates a psychotherapy program for correcting perceptual distortions and sexual disorders as well as reducing recidivism and understanding victims of sexual crime.

2.6.3 Decriminalization

Sexual intercourse under pretence of marriage was criminalized at the beginning of the enactment of the Korean criminal code in 1953. The code stipulated such behavior by males as a crime, following West Germany which prescribed such crime with the purpose of protecting women. It was amended two times, in 1975 and 1995. However, the provision had consistently been criticized as an old-fashioned provision disregarding women's capacity to make their own choices about sexual intercourse. Abolitionists submitted the provision for review before the Constitutional Court in 2002, but the Court upheld the provision, stating that it should be regulated for the maintenance of social order. Seven years later, in 2009, the Court overruled its precedent with a decision of six to three and provided the reason for overruling that the provision violates the constitutional duty of the Government to support and realize a gender-equal society, pointing out that it had been often abused or misused as a measure for blackmail to or compensation from a male partner.

---

[64] Act on Medical Treatment of Sexual Impulse of Sex Offenders, Art. 4.

[65] Id. 89(1).

[66] Id. 11(2).

[67] Id. 12.

[68] Enforcement Decree of the Act on Medical Treatment of Sexual Impulse of Sex Offenders, Art. 6.

3 Criminal Procedure

3.1 History of Criminal Procedure Legislation

In the early 1900s, Japan invaded and colonized Korea by usurping its sovereignty over foreign affairs and judicial power. In the aftermath, in 1909, the Korean Government handed its judiciary power over to the Japanese resident-general, and criminal trials on Korean nationals were brought in the courts under the resident-general. The most important purpose of enacting criminal procedure in this era was the reinforcement of ruling power by criminal trial and the enhancement of efficiency in the trials. Therefore, forceful power was conferred on the investigative authorities and at the same time, the trial process was simplified. For example, under the Joseon Criminal Code of 1912, enacted by the Japanese resident-general, the police (including military police) were able to punish by caning immediately after finding a suspect, if he/she was a Korean national. In this process, the police did not need to wait for prosecution or conviction. Moreover, investigative authorities were entitled to issue warrants for investigation, and prosecutors could detain a suspect for 20 days at his own discretion without any check or review. Accordingly, Korea came to have bitter experiences of distorted spirit and practice in criminal procedure. Along with liberation from Japanese occupation in 1945, Korea bore the heavy task to remedy the abuses that occurred during Japanese occupation.

Without any opportunity to reform the procedure, however, amendment to criminal procedure was performed under the initiative of the U.S. military administration after liberation from Japan. Having observed the persistent practice of infringing human rights by criminal procedure even after liberation from Japan, the U.S. military administration legislated and enacted Ordinance No. 176 which declared its purpose as reforming criminal procedure in order to fully guarantee citizens' right to freedom from illegal detention. To fulfill this purpose, the Ordinance adopted a handful of procedures. For example, it prohibited investigative authorities from detaining suspects without warrants issued by the court. Moreover, the Ordinance guaranteed defendant's right to communication with defense counsel and set forth a bail system as well as judiciary review of detention warrants. However, the fledging country did not have solid political and economic infrastructure and insufficient human resources to fully implement the new procedures. A series of reforms to the provisions related to habeas corpus pointed in desirable directions and contributed to the formulation of democratized criminal procedure.

In 1954, one year after the Armistice Agreement, the Korean National Assembly passed a Bill for criminal procedure, which is the first modern Korean code of criminal procedure made with Koreans' own hands. During the work of enactment, basic philosophies were considered and are still alive in Korean criminal procedure: protection of human rights (it can also be regarded as rights of defendants and suspects), efficiency, accuracy, and expedition in criminal investigation through trials. Among them, most important for the enactment is the guarantee of defendants' rights through the restriction on abusive exercise of investigative authority.[69] It fortifies guarantees of defendants' rights by setting forth such provisions as privilege of defendants and suspects against self-incrimination, rights to participate in criminal trial, reduction of detention duration, and restriction of emergent arrest. Since then, the four philosophies have held special places in Korean criminal procedure and played a significant role in the persistent amendment of procedure.

3.2 Basic Criminal Case Procedure

It is common practice around the world to bifurcate criminal procedure in accordance with the seriousness of the crime committed. When a heavy sentence is expected, the defendant will be tried under a relatively strict procedure. On the other hand, summary procedure may be applied in relation to a defendant who may receive a lesser sentence. Korea also has such characteristics in the procedure and established the former as a primary rule of criminal procedure.[70]

3.2.1 Process for General Crimes

Investigation

The initial process of criminal procedure is investigation. The code of criminal procedure describes a handful of factors to trigger an investigation: arrest of a flagrant offender,[71] inquest of a person who died unnaturally,[72] complaint by a victim of crime,[73] accusation by any person who believes that an offense has been committed,[74] and surrender of a suspect to the police.[75] If an investigative authority initiates the case, it files charges. In general practice, a police officer initiates the case and serves it to a prosecutor who has authority over the police for the investigation.

The code of criminal procedure provides for two types of investigation: investigation based on voluntariness and investigation under compulsory measures. The code declares that the former is the primary method of investigation. For example, in principle, an investigation into a suspect shall be conducted without placing

[69] Byun (2007).

[70] Shon (2010).

[71] Criminal Procedure Act, Art. 212.

[72] Id. 222.

[73] Id. 223.

[74] Id. 234.

[75] Id. 240.

him/her under detention.[76] On the other hand, for an effective investigation, the code also allows some compulsory measures under strict limitations. Accordingly, only measures prescribed in the code of criminal procedure may be used to the least extent necessary in order to achieve the objects of an investigation.[77] In specific practice, the code provides for detailed types of and procedures for the measures. Compulsory measures include arrest, detention, search, and seizure. When investigative authorities use such measures, they are required, in principle, to obtain a warrant from a judge. In an emergency, the authorities may carry out the measures first and request the issuance of the warrant ex post facto. For example, flagrant offenders and suspects meeting the emergency arrest requirements can be arrested without a warrant.[78] Along with strict limitations of compulsory measures, the code of criminal procedure sets methods to protect defendants' right to defense. An eligible defendant may exercise the right to retain defense counsel,[79] to communicate with counsel during detention,[80] to request judicial review of the legality of arrest and detention,[81] to request preservation of evidence,[82] and privilege against self-incrimination.[83] According to the results of the investigation, the prosecutor may terminate the case without filing charges or may indict him/her and bring the defendant to court. Only the prosecutor may exercise such discretion.

Trial Proceedings

The prosecutor's submission of a written indictment to court triggers trial proceedings. The defendant, defense counsel, and the prosecutor may request disclosure of documents or evidence.[84] Before commencement of a trial, the presiding judge may place the case under a preparatory hearing for an efficient and very careful examination. For these proceedings, the prosecutor and the defendant or defense counsel shall collect and organize evidence in good order in advance and cooperate with each other, so that preparatory proceedings prior to trial can progress smoothly.[85]

At trial, the following proceedings are taken in order: The presiding judge informs the defendant of his/her right to refuse to make a statement during the

[76] Id. 198(1).

[77] Id. 199.

[78] Id. 211; 200-3.

[79] Id. 30(1).

[80] Id. 243-2.

[81] Constitution, Art. 12(6); Criminal Procedure Act, Art. 214-2.

[82] Criminal Procedure Act, Art. 184.

[83] Id. 244-3.

[84] Criminal Procedure Act, Art. 266-3.

[85] Id. 266-5.

trial[86] and asks to provide his/her personal information, including name, age, domicile and occupation in order to verify identity.[87] After the public prosecutor recites facts of indictment, the criminal charges, and applicable provisions of law as described in the written indictment, the defendant states whether he/she admits the facts of indictment.[88] After questioning the defendant or defense counsel as necessary to organizing issues, of the evidence is examined.[89] During the examination, the public prosecutor or the defense counsel may successively examine the defendant with necessary questions concerning facts of indictment and circumstances after the examination of each piece of evidence is complete. When testimony and examination of evidence are complete, the prosecutor and the defendant or defense counsel in turn present their final submissions and pleas. First, the prosecutor makes his/her submissions on the case, including the facts and application of law.[90] Then, the defendant makes a final plea. As a final step in the case, a sentence is pronounced, in principle, on the date when pleadings and arguments are closed.

3.2.2 Process for Minor Offenses

If a crime is relatively minor, it is unnecessary to proceed with a full scale of criminal process, and the criminal may be sentenced without being put to trial. The Korean criminal justice system provides for two types of such procedures in order to guarantee efficiency of proceedings: summary judgment and summary order. First, the chief officer of a police station requests judgment for a marginal crime punishable with a fine not exceeding 200,000 won (approximately USD 200) or penal detention. In such cases, a competent judge for this proceeding may render summary judgment and impose an appropriate sentence without regular trial for the crime.[91] The summary order system is stipulated in the criminal procedure code and a prosecutor may request a court's order on the defendant, based on the dossier submitted by the prosecutor. Without public trial, the court may impose a fine or confiscation. While a summary judgment in general demands the presence of the defendant and the court has a verbal trial by interviewing the defendant, the court in the summary order system reviews a case based only on the documents submitted by the prosecutor. Accordingly, evidential procedure law is more strictly applied in a summary order. In both processes, if the judgment or order is confirmed without appeal by the defendant, the effect will be treated as that of a trial in court.

[86] Id. 283-2.

[87] Id. 284.

[88] Id. 286.

[89] Id. 290.

[90] Id. 291-2.

[91] Act on the Proceedings for Summary Judgment, Art. 2.

However, a protest by the defendant against the judgment or order becomes a request for a regular trial.[92]

3.3 *New Measures in Criminal Procedure*

During the past half century, practitioners and scholars have criticized the criminal justice system for not fully guaranteeing defendants' constitutional rights, undermining the transparency of investigations as well as citizens' trust in criminal trials. At the same time, however, no efforts have been made to reform it through full-scale and in-depth research into the system. Accordingly, Koreans have not had opportunities to revise criminal procedure in a way to fulfill citizens' eagerness for its effectiveness and transparency. Due to this kind of criticism and the desire to enhance the system to the degree of other developed countries, the Korean Government and the National Assembly provided meaningful mechanisms to fulfill the expectation by revising the procedure in 2007. Several significant aspects of the revision are discussed below.

3.3.1 Civil Participation in Criminal Trials

Case Subject

Unlike a jury trial in the United States, the right to jury trial is extended only to some, not all, defendants. There are two practical reasons for limiting jury trials to specific crimes. First, since the Korean legal system has followed the inquisitorial tradition for a long time, there needs to be a test for the appropriate operation of jury trials which is deeply rooted in the adversarial system. Second, because Korean criminal trials are based on the inquisitorial tradition, Korea does not have sufficient resources and infrastructure for a full-scale jury trial in all cases.

The Act on Citizen Participation in Criminal Trials describes the crimes subject to jury trial which are limited to violent crimes, including murder, felony murder, manslaughter, serious assault, serious battery, and rape. Some white-collar crimes, such as bribery and embezzlement are also subject to jury trial.[93] If a defendant is charged with a crime subject to jury trial, the court is to inform the defendant of the right to jury trial. If the defendant does not submit a written application for jury trial within 7 days, the court may presume that the defendant wishes a bench trial.[94] If the court receives such application from the defendant or defense counsel, the court notifies the prosecutor to prepare for a jury trial.

[92] Criminal Procedure Act, Art. 448.

[93] Act on Citizen Participation in Criminal Trials. Art. 5.

[94] Id. 8.

An application by the defendant is not a sole requirement for jury trial. The statute allows judges to choose bench or jury trial. The court can order a bench trial against a defendant's application in the following three situations: (1) if the court finds a possibility that jurors or their family members will be concerned about any infliction of harm on their lives, bodies, or property when participating in a jury trial; (2) when it is impractical to conduct the jury trial because a co-defendant does not desire a jury trial; (3) when the court determines that jury trial is not suitable for that case for any reason.[95] Before the court decides on a bench trial, however, it should confer with the prosecutor and the defendant/defense counsel. The parties can appeal the court's decision.

Pre-trial Conference

After accepting a defendant's request for jury trial, the court is to hold a pre-trial hearing, which Korean criminal courts generally have not required for bench trials. While the Korean Criminal Procedure Act stipulates such hearing merely as optional in a traditional bench trial under the court's discretion,[96] the hearing has been adopted as mandatory in participatory trials,[97] which means that the court should have a pre-trial conference in order to clarify, in advance, all the issues and organize the evidence which will be admitted in the trial. Deciding which evidence to exclude and in what order evidence is to be presented will prevent jurors from becoming prejudiced or biased. The court decides the admissibility of evidence, and the parties may not request additional evidence during the hearing after the court's determination unless it falls under the proviso.[98] The court and parties also outline disclosure proceedings and set a date for the jury trial during the hearing.[99]

Selection of Jury

The number of jurors depends on the crime the defendant is charged with and whether he/she admits his/her guilt. If the defendant is subject to capital punishment or life imprisonment, nine jurors are required in a participatory trial. If the defendant admits the charges, five jurors are required. In all other cases, seven jurors are required.[100] As in the USA, the parties in a participatory trial may challenge prospective jurors for bias or partiality. They also may exercise peremptory challenge through which parties can remove a prospective juror without grounds for the discharge. While the number of

---

[95] Id. 9.

[96] Criminal Procedure Act. Art. 266-1.

[97] Act on Citizen Participation in Criminal Trials. Art. 36.

[98] Criminal Procedure Act. Art. 266-13.

[99] Id. 266-9.

[100] Act on Citizen Participation in Criminal Trials. Art. 13.

Table 2 Number of peremptory challenges available in participatory trial

Number of jurors	Number of peremptory challenges available
9	5
7	4
5	3

prospective jurors for a cause is not provided for by the statute and interpreted as unlimited, the number of peremptory challenges depends on the composition of jury (Table 2).[101]

An impaneled jury has some rights and duties regarding a jury trial. In order to gain a clear understanding of the testimony, the jury may ask the judge to examine the defendants and witnesses on necessary matters. However, they cannot question directly them.[102] Jurors may also present opinions on the case and sentencing suitable for the defendant.[103]

Deliberation and Verdicts

Jurors taking part in a trial shall deliberate on whether a defendant is guilty after hearing the presiding judge's explanation on the case. During deliberation, the jury can hear opinions from judges who take part in the trial when a majority of jurors request such opinions.[104] If the jury does not reach a unanimous verdict of "guilty" or "not-guilty", judges provide their opinions on evidence and testimonies directly to the jurors except for a statement of 'guilty' or 'not guilty.'[105] After the judges and jurors have jointly discussed the guilt of the defendant, the jurors, again in the absence of the judges, render a verdict based on a simple majority. If the defendant is found guilty by the jury, the jurors shall discuss sentencing with the judges and shall express their opinions. Similar to the previous proceeding, the presiding judge shall explain the extent of punishment and conditions of sentencing before discussing sentencing.[106] This process is a departure from the U.S. model and more closely resembles the German system in which lay assessors and judges jointly discuss the defendant's guilt. Opinions of the jury both as to guilt or non-guilt and on sentencing have no binding authority on the court's judgment.[107]

[101] Id. 30.

[102] Id. 41.

[103] Id. 12.

[104] Id. 46(2).

[105] Id. 46(1).

[106] Id. 46(4).

[107] Id. 46(5).

3.3.2 Enhancement of Crime Victims' Status

Brief History of Enactment Relating to Victims of Crime

As in other countries, victims of crime in Korea have also been sidelined from criminal procedure for a long time. However, in the 1980s, citizens and the Government started becoming interested in victims' status and bringing them into criminal procedures. In 1981, the Government adopted a compensation order process in the criminal justice system under the Act on Special Cases concerning Expedition etc. of Legal Proceedings. According to this process, victims do not need to take civil action in addition to criminal proceedings when they desire compensation for any harm directly resulting from the crime. They might obtain compensation only from the criminal proceedings in which they were involved as victims. Six years later, the Korean Constitution granted citizens the right to receive aid for harm suffered from the Government[108] and to be heard at criminal proceedings.[109] In order to specify the right, the Korean National Assembly enacted the Crime Victim Aid Act and revised the code of criminal procedure interpolating provisions that courts should allow victims to testify upon their request.

Since the 1990s, the Korean criminal justice system showed significant changes in terms of protection and support of victims of crime. Their security, privacy and benefits were protected in terms of social welfare through a series of enactments, including the Act on Special Cases concerning the Punishment of Specific Violent Crimes, the Act on the Punishment of Sexual Crimes and Protection of Victims, the Act on the Prevention of Domestic Violence and Protection, etc. of Victims, and the Act on Protection of Specific Crime Informants.[110]

In the 2000s, an important stride for victims of crime was made regarding rape victims. The Korean Government started supporting such victims in their medical treatment. For example, when the Government interviews certain victims of sexual violence as witnesses, video conferencing apparatus should be used so that they can avoid confronting the offenders during trial. The Korean National Assembly passed a Bill for the "Act on the Prevention of Sexual Trafficking and Protection, etc. of Victims," which provides effective support for the victims of sex trafficking, such as the establishment of support institutions and counseling centers.

These series of enactments, however, were criticized in that they were not a system of comprehensive measures for all victims of crime, but only exceptional ones for limited victims of crime. For example, the laws focused mainly on a narrow category of vulnerable victims including females under 13 years old and disabled victims. This was because private organizations, rather than the

---

[108] Constitution, Art. 30, "Citizens who have suffered bodily injury or death due to criminal acts of others may receive aid from the State as prescribed by the Act."

[109] Id. 27(5), "A victim of crime shall be entitled to make a statement during the proceedings of the trial of the case involved as prescribed by the Act."

[110] Park et al. (2009).

Government, played a primary role in this achievement. The organizations noticed the rights of female victims and tried to put them into legislation without a blueprint for the synthetic protection of all victims. The Korean Government and civil organizations paid attention to this situation and kept expanding the scope of victims for support and protection.

New Status of Victims of Crimes in Criminal Trials

Responding to the huge demand of citizens to develop a support system for victims of crime and the necessity to overcome the above-mentioned criticism, the Ministry of Justice started to deploy new methods for victims' participation in criminal courts and set forth provisions giving the duty of victim protection to the Government and entitling victims with rights in criminal trials.

Notice to Victims

Upon request of a victim of crime or his/her legal representative, a public prosecutor shall inform them as to whether the indictment has been instituted for the crime, the time and place of the trial, the results of the trial, and whether suspects and defendants have been detained or are out on bail.[111] Unlike provisions in the United States, the Korean Criminal Procedure Act prescribes a request of appropriate persons as a prerequisite to notifying the district attorney. The Ministry of Justice explains that such a triggering mechanism was established to protect victim's privacy in cases where he/she does not desire information of victimization to be released to the public.[112]

Victims' Right to Review and Copy Litigation Records

In the criminal trial process, victims have been sidelined since they were unable to have opportunities to confer with the prosecutor. As a result, victims were unaware of the status of investigation or information before and during trial. During the trial process, there have even been instances in which victims were faced with the defendant's argument and could not respond to it effectively because of the lack of information relating to the case. In this sense, the right to review and copy records with which he or she is involved reflects the needs of victims for equivalent status in terms of information.[113] In addition, the records can be utilized as a helpful tool for victims who are willing to take civil action for any loss or harm resulting

[111] Criminal Procedure Act, Art. 259-2.

[112] Ministry of Justice, Criminal Procedure Act (amended), 2007, p. 132.

[113] Park et al. (2009).

from the crime. Plaintiffs may proffer powerful authority in civil suits seeking for remedies.[114]

According to the Criminal Procedure Act, victims or legitimate attorneys may file an application with the presiding judge[115] to view or copy litigation records. A prosecutor should be informed of such application. The judge may authorize the application upon satisfaction of the pre-requisites: First, it is necessary for the victim's remedies or there is any other justifiable ground. Second, the judge deems it proper in consideration of the nature of the crime involved, the status of the trial, and other circumstances.[116] The judge may allow the viewing and copying under certain conditions and victims may not appeal the court's decision of prohibition or condition. Although the current rights of victims are remarkably improved in terms of victims' participation in criminal trials, it is necessary for the scope of the records to be disclosed and the qualification of the limits to be specific. Korean practitioners and scholars have also acknowledged this need and have researched for a proper way to do so.[117]

Presence of Persons with Reliable Relationship

Some specialists or people having a close relationship with a victim may be seated next to the victim who is supposed to testify in court. Being together in trial, victims may feel more relaxed and less anxious and nervous. This may effectively help victims exercise their right to make a statement. This right already existed in the Korean criminal justice system only for vulnerable victims. For example, victims of sexual violence and sex trafficking, victims of child abuse, and elderly citizens were allowed to request the presence of persons close to them as victims in investigation or trial.[118] The criminal procedure code also required courts and law enforcement officers to arrange for a person having a stable relationship to be seated with a

---

[114] Lee (2008).

[115] Criminal Procedure Act, Art. 294-4. Victim's spouse, lineal relatives and siblings are also entitled to make an application if the victim is deceased or suffers from a substantial mental or physical disorder.

[116] Criminal Procedure Act, Art. 294-4.

[117] Investigation, *Research, and Evaluation of Judicial Reform and Criminal Policy (III)*. For the more appropriate measure of confining the scope and listing the requirements for view and copying, they refer to the practice of German Criminal Procedure. Victims in Germany can view and copy those files which are available to the court, those that would have to be submitted to the court if charges have been preferred, and officially inspect impounded evidence [German Criminal Procedure Act 147(1)]. In addition, the code provides that inspection of the files shall be refused (1) if overriding interests worthy of protection, either of the accused or of other persons, constitute an obstacle thereto; (2) if it appears that the purpose of the investigation would to be jeopardized or if the proceedings would be considerably delayed thereby [German Criminal Procedure Act 406(e)].

[118] Act on the Punishment of Sexual Crimes and Protection of Victims, Art. 22-3; Act on the Punishment of Acts of Arranging Sexual Traffic, Art. 8; Welfare of the Aged Act, Art. 39-8; Child Welfare Act, Art. 28.

victim when juveniles or the mentally disabled are the victims of sexual violence or trafficking, unless there were concerns about impediments in the proceedings or investigation by the court.

However, victims of crimes, other than sexual crimes, had not been entitled to such benefits. The Criminal Procedure Act of 2007 revised the code and extended the scope of victims of crime eligible for these benefits. Ordinary victims may request the presence of persons with stable relationships and the court may allow such request if they are likely to feel terribly uneasy or tense in light of their age, physical or mental condition, or any other circumstances. Without any request from a victim, the court shall allow a person who has a stable relationship with the victim to be seated in company if the victim is under 13 years of age, incompetent to discern right from wrong, or has a physical or mental disability. However, the court can refuse the company if it is likely to cause trouble in the proceedings.[119] The rules of criminal procedure define a person with a stable relationship as a person who can help with psychological stability and communication with a victim. Therefore, any counselor who is hired by a victim, a medical doctor, or an employer may be allowed to sit in company with the victim as well as his/her spouse, linear ascendants, siblings and cohabitants.[120]

Right of Victims to be Heard

Since 1987, the Constitution has provided victims with the right to make a statement in criminal court.[121] As a measure to fulfill the right to a substantive degree, criminal procedure allows a victim to make a statement about the case in which he or she is involved. Although the enactment was better in terms of guaranteeing the victims' rights, the practice still had some issues to be overcome. Upon victims' request, the court could grant the victims an opportunity to be heard when the court examined them as witnesses. If the court found that victims had enough opportunities to make a statement in the investigative processes, it could not allow them to make submissions in trial. In addition, the right was allowed to the victims themselves only, not their legal representatives or survivors.

The Criminal Procedure Act of 2007 eliminated the requirement of insufficient opportunities for victims to make a statement at the investigative stage and enlarge the scope of persons entitled to give their opinions in court to legal representatives, lineal relatives or siblings. In addition, the Act provided for three specific contents of the statement which they are allowed to make in trial: degree of harm and effect of the crime, opinions about sentencing or punishment, and other opinions relating to the case.[122]

[119] Criminal Procedure Act, Art. 163-2.

[120] Rules of Criminal Procedure, Art. 84-3 (2).

[121] Constitution, Art. 27(5).

[122] Criminal Procedure Act, Art. 294-2.

Non-disclosure of Victims' Statements

In principle, a criminal trial should proceed in open court, and it is the constitutional right of defendants. However, this may be limited under certain conditions. The Constitution and the Court Organization Act clarify the principle with some limitations, declaring that trials and decisions of the courts shall be open to the public, unless such disclosure undermines national security, public safety, or good social morals.[123] In criminal trials, there has been great demand for victims to testify in closed court to protect themselves or their privacy. The criminal justice system has granted this right to victims of sexual violence. Trials may not be open to the public in cases where closed trials would contribute to the protection of the victim's privacy.[124] However, recently practitioners and scholars in criminal procedure suggested the need for closed trials for victims of crimes other than sexual violence. They pointed out that victims of ordinary crimes were also concerned about the release of their private information and identity. With this demand, a new Bill was passed in 2007 to grant these rights to all victims. Victims, legal representatives, and prosecutors may submit petitions for a closed trial and the court should decide such in consideration of the reason for the petition.[125]

3.3.3 Petitions for Adjudication

The Korean criminal justice system permits only prosecutors to charge or file criminal cases and gives them great discretion in the decisions of the prosecution. Therefore, under their judgment, a suspect may be brought to a trial or walk away. From citizens' viewpoints (especially victims of crime), however, there should be checks on such discretion in cases where the prosecutor decides not to prosecute a case when the victim has a considerable interest in the treatment of the offender. In these situations, the victim may file a constitutional complaint,[126] appeal on prosecution,[127] or petition for adjudication.[128] However, none of these effectively satisfies the needs of victims. Although the Constitutional Court allows the prosecution not to charge a suspect, the victim's appeal does not compel the prosecution to charge the suspect. Moreover, these procedures cost victims time and money.

If victims are willing to file a complaint with regard with the Court, it takes considerable time because it goes through the Court, the final resort in the judiciary system. A complaint requires a very complicated process and paper work, so that victims need to hire a lawyer for it. The law concerning constitutional complaints

[123] Constitution, Art. 109; Court Organization Act, Art. 57.

[124] Act on the Prevention of Sexual Traffic and Protection, etc. of Victims, Art. 22(1); Act on the Punishment of Acts of Arranging Sexual Traffic, Art. 9.

[125] Criminal Procedure Act, Art. 294-3.

[126] Constitutional Court Act, Art. 68(1).

[127] Prosecutors' Office Act, Art. 10.

[128] Criminal Procedure Act, Art. 260.

also requires victims to retain a lawyer. On prosecution appeals, victims have criticized that there is no meaningful way to enforce them because they are raised against the very institution which already refused to charge. Appeals have no other binding authority to reconsider its exercise of discretion, but merely remain as internal affairs. Appeals for adjudication to courts also have proven ineffective in practice. Most of all, eligible cases are confined to crimes committed by public officials. The relevant Acts reflected concerns that the prosecutors' office is not likely to charge certain public officials and intended to limit the scope of crimes in which the prosecutors, who are public officials themselves, will have some bias or prejudice in investigation and prosecution.[129] Therefore, no victims of other crimes were considered eligible applicants for appeals, resulting in great criticism of the limitation.

The Criminal Procedure Act of 2007 revised the provisions relating to petitions, including the types of eligible cases. The main goal of the revision was to extend the right to appeal to all victims. However, the legislation had to consider the impact of the extension and the possibility of abuse and misuse of petitions. In order to reduce such concerns, the Act provided for three measures: First, it excluded complainants other than victims from the scope of eligible applicants for petitions. Second, the Act requires victims to proceed with appeals to prosecutors' office before petitioning the court.[130] It leads the prosecutors' office to review its previous decision and voluntarily overturn the decision not to prosecute before a court issues an order to prosecute. Third, the Act allows the court to require a petitioner to bear all or some of the expenses incurred in the proceedings for a petition in cases where the court denies the petition because it does not comply with the legal processes or lacks grounds, and when the petitioner withdraws the appeal.[131]

3.3.4 Exclusionary Rule

In 2007, the Korean National Assembly newly interpolated a provision preventing "evidence obtained in violation of due process" from being admitted in criminal trials.[132] The Korean Supreme Court previously admitted the legality of tainted evidence, stating that its evidentiary value would not be changed, even though it had been obtained illegally, and thus, legality of such evidence was compromised and admissible in criminal trials.

In accordance with the new legislation, however, the Korean Supreme Court overruled the 40-year-old precedent in one case. The defendant, a governor of Jeju Province, was alleged to have conducted an illegal election campaign. The prosecutor searching the defendant's office seized various documents held by the

[129] Including the crime of abuse of authority, Criminal Act, Art. 123.

[130] Criminal Procedure Act, Art. 260 (2).

[131] Id. 262-3.

[132] Id. 308-2.

defendant's secretary who visited the office. The documents were presented as primary evidence for the prosecutor. Defense counsel argued that the seizure was conducted in violation of search and seizure procedures. In addition, they went on to argue that secondary evidence (the "fruit of the poisonous tree") should also be excluded. The district court allowed acceptance of the evidence relying on the rationale of precedents without reviewing whether they involved any illegal process. The Korean Supreme Court overruled the precedents and overturned the guilty verdict which the district court judged based on tainted evidence.[133]

The Court stressed that "search and seizure shall be conducted in accordance with the procedures under the Constitution and the Criminal Procedure Act, because it raises no small concerns that search and seizure will infringe citizens' rights." The Court went on to say that evidence obtained in violation of the procedures under the Constitution and the Criminal Procedure Act is generally inadmissible evidence since it does not follow due process guaranteeing basic human and civil rights. Moreover, the Court argued that the most efficient method to reduce and prevent illegal search and seizure is to exclude illegally obtained evidence from incriminating evidence and to adopt the "fruit of poisonous tree" doctrine.

Regarding the method of exclusion, the Korean Supreme Court adopted a kind of "discretionary" exclusion of illegally obtained evidence rather than automatic and mandatory exclusion. The Court judged that such evidence should not be automatically excluded only because it was obtained in violation of search and seizure procedures. It argued that illegally obtained evidence may be admitted if the unlawful conduct of law enforcement officers does not violate "the substance of due process" in review of the totality of circumstances. In other words, if exclusion of evidence would result in disregard of justice through harmony of due process and substantive fact-finding, the evidence may come into trial as an exception to the rule.

The Court, as a guideline for practice of search and seizure as well as for court decisions on admissibility, listed facts for judgment of admissibility: legislative intent of the laws regulating search and seizure, the degree of violation, the specific process of violation, the likelihood of avoiding the violation, characteristics of the rights and legal rights which the procedure provision is intended to protect, connection between the defendant and the evidence, and causation between collecting the evidence and conduct in violation of laws. The expectation is that the legislation and the Court decision will reduce attempts of law enforcement officers to gather evidence illegally and will reinforce the spirit of the Constitution as to requiring warrants.

---

[133] 2007 Do 3061 (decided on Nov. 15, 2007).

3.3.5 Improvement of System Relating to Habeas Corpus

An investigative authority may take a person into custody for arrest and detention. According to the code revised in 1995, a judge may issue a warrant for detention if a suspect or defendant who is believed to have committed a crime has no legal address or there is any reasonable ground (similar to "probable cause" in U.S. criminal law) to believe that he/she may destroy evidence or attempt to flee.[134] In 2007, the Act was amended to impose a new duty on courts to take into consideration other circumstances in order for judges to be careful in issuing warrants: the seriousness of the crime, the possibility of recidivism, and the likelihood of harm to the victim or witnesses.

In respect to arrest, an investigative authority should obtain a warrant. A prosecutor may request the warrant if there is a good reason (probable cause) to believe that a suspect has committed a crime and will not comply with a request by the authority to appear at a police station.[135] However, an investigative authority may arrest a suspect without a warrant in two situations: arrest of flagrant offenders[136] and emergency arrest.[137]

The Criminal Procedure Act provides a device reducing concerns about the abuse of the emergency arrest exception. When a public prosecutor or judicial police officer has arrested a suspect in the absence of a warrant with intention to detain, the public prosecutor shall request a warrant for detention from a judge without delay.[138] When a warrant for detention is not requested or issued, an investigative authority should release the suspect immediately.[139] After release, the investigative authority may not re-arrest the person on the same criminal facts without a warrant.[140]

When a public prosecutor releases a suspect without requesting a warrant for detention, within 30 days from the date of release, he or she should give written notice to the court of the identity of the suspect released, time and place and specific grounds of the emergency arrest and release, respectively, and the identity of the prosecutor or police officer who made the arrest without a warrant and released the suspect.[141] In addition, the person who was released from emergency arrest, or his/her defense counsel, legal representatives, spouse, lineal relatives, or siblings may inspect or make copies of the notice and relevant documents.[142]

[134] Criminal Procedure Act, Art. 70.

[135] Id. 202-2.

[136] Id. 212.

[137] Id. 200-3.

[138] Id. 200-4(1).

[139] Id. 200-4(2).

[140] Id. 200-4(3).

[141] Id. 200-4(4).

[142] Id. 200-4(5); 201-2(4).

Anyone arrested or detained on a criminal charge shall be brought promptly before a judge. Upon a prosecutor's request for the issuance of a warrant for detention, the court shall hold a hearing without delay to decide whether to issue such warrant. Prosecutors and defense counsel may make submissions during the hearing. With respect to the legality of the arrest or detention, all persons arrested or detained have a right to habeas corpus. He or she, including defense counsel, a family member, a cohabitant and an employer, may submit a petition for judicial review of the legality, no matter whether the apprehension was carried out with or without a warrant.

4 Conclusion

Korea has developed its criminal justice system in many ways. As discussed above, Korea has endeavored to find effective and proper measures for punishment considering public security, including sentencing guidelines, the GPS monitoring system, and pharmacological treatment of sexual offenders. With respect to criminal procedure, it newly adopted citizen-participatory criminal trial which allows citizens to play a limited role as a juror. Even though the role of a jury is not the same in the United States or Germany, it is considered a meaningful effort to enhance the transparency of and democracy in trial proceedings by citizens who vigorously participate.

Victims of crime also have more rights in trial. The right to participate in a trial will vitalize victims who had been forgotten in the system, to be a more active player in the courts. The investigative authority will practice in a manner that better guarantees due process with the exclusionary rule and an enhanced system of habeas corpus. However, Korean criminal law and procedure have a long way to go beyond these accomplishments. These achievements are a substantial step for the Korean criminal justice system toward more effective crime control and enhanced due process.

References

Byun J-p (2007) The history and prospects of amendments to the Criminal Procedure Act. In: Databook for the Korean Criminal Law Association's 50th Anniversary Symposium

Huh I-t (2005) Reforms and development of Korean Penal Law. International Congress of Penal Law, p. 113

Kim Y-k et al (2011) New introduction to legal studies. Bobmunsa, Seoul, p 230

Lee S-j (2008) Evaluation and reform measures of the provisions on victims' protection in the amended Criminal Procedure Act. Comp Study Crim Law 10(2):156

Ministry of Justice (2007) Amended Criminal Procedure Act, Seoul, p 132

Park M-s et al (2009) Investigation, Research, and Evaluation of Judicial Reform and Criminal Policy (III). Korean Institute of Criminology

Shon D-k (2010) Criminal Procedure Act. Sechang Publishing, Seoul

Commercial Law

Chanho Park

1 Introduction

The nature of the Commercial Act of the Republic of Korea (hereinafter "Korea") is that of fundamental laws that focus on profitable business activities unlike the common law code. The Commercial Act comprises five parts in total, namely: (1) General Parts, (2) Commercial Activities, (3) Corporate Parts, (4) Insurance, and (5) Maritime Parts. The common view is that Part 1 and Part 2 are more likely a special aspect of the Civil Act.[1] What is commonly seen in many countries, including the USA, Japan and Germany, is that their Commercial Acts have been modified frequently in accordance with the local and global economic situation. The Korean Commercial Act has undergone a number of changes since the 1997 Financial Crisis, and there were some reforms in the corporate governance part and amendments in the merger & acquisition part to encourage corporate transparency. The Korean legal system is based on the civil law code, which is significantly different from the Corporate law (or Company Law) of the USA's or the UK's that have been established through case law.

However, the Korean Commercial Act (especially the Corporate Parts) has been amended in reflection of changes in the reality of the Korean corporations, economic policies and the international economic situation, therefore, it has resulted in changes in policies. In particular, the companies that chose to be in trading business because of the limits that the domestic market has have become multinational companies, moving from a simple export to setting up local entities. In fact, Korean companies had to change their corporate systems to fit the global standard and to secure transparency as their markets have extended to the international markets. This paper will give a description of the Korea's company policies and briefly review the basic structure of the Korean Commercial Act.

[1] Choi (2010), at 2.

C. Park (✉)
Korea Legislation Research Institute, Seoul, Republic of Korea
e-mail: pchlaw1972@gmail.com

Korea Legislation Research Institute, *Introduction to Korean Law*,
DOI 10.1007/978-3-642-31689-0_6,

2 General Parts

1. The Characteristics of the Korean Commercial Act The Korean Commercial Act regulates individual business activities, but practically regulates business enterprise[2] activities. As Korean economic development in the last 60 years shows, the Korean economy has developed centering around large-scale business enterprises so called 'Chaebul' and they have become the backbone of the economy. Lately, criticisms have been made claiming that the Korean Commercial Act overly protects business enterprises and there have been some discussions on introducing the concept of 'corporate social responsibility' into the Commercial Act.[3]

The Korean Commercial Act defines the concept of 'merchant'. A merchant, in legal definition, includes both natural persons and legal persons who engage in commercial activities. A merchant is separated into two concepts: 'Merchant by Nature of Business' and 'Merchant by Legal Construction'. The former concept means a person who engages in commercial activities in his/her own name. The latter concept, as described by Article 5(1), means that "a person who engages in a business in the manner of maintaining a shop or similar equipment shall be deemed a merchant, even if he does not engage in business activities." The Korean Commercial Act defines such concept because it doesn't have a separate law on legal entities like business enterprises or companies which pursue profits as the USA's and the UK's company laws do, but the Commercial Act covers the overall profit business activities. The criteria to be a 'merchant by nature of business' is business activities under Article 46. A merchant is a natural or legal person who engages in these business activities under one's name.[4] Korean enterprises are acting as a

---

[2] In this paper, 'Business Entity' includes all natural persons and legal entities involved in commercial activities. For a joint-stock company, it uses the term 'Corporation' that is commonly used in the Common Law. The term 'Business Enterprise' represents the four terms defined by the Korean Commercial Act, namely 'Limited Liability Company', 'Unlimited Partnership Company', 'Limited Liability Company' and 'Stock Company'.

[3] Chung (2010a), at 6.

[4] Article 46(Basic Commercial Activities) The following activities which are effected as business are called commercial activities: Provided , that this shall not apply to such activities as are effected by a person who manufactures goods or renders services solely for the purpose of earning wages:

1. Sale of movables, real estate, valuable instruments and any other properties;
2. Lease of movables, real estate, valuable instruments and any other properties;
3. Activities relating to the manufacturing, processing, or repairing;
4. Activities relating to the supply of electricity, electric wave, natural gas, or water;
5. Taking over the contract to complete works or to supply services;
6. Activities relating to publishing, printing, or photographing;
7. Activities relating to advertisements, communications, or information;
8. Receiving and providing credit, exchange, and other financial transactions;
9. Transaction by facilities used by the public;. . .and

22. Acceptance of payment settlement affairs using a credit card, electronic currency, etc.

social entity beyond the role of an economic agent pursuing profits. There are also a number of stakeholders in terms of corporate capital. As most Korean companies are incorporated, the Korean Commercial Act has provisions on corporate bonds and a range of stock systems in order to facilitate corporations to raise corporate capital. The corporate bonds and stocks are a system which shows the nature of enterprises as a social entity and actualized in terms of raising corporate capital and obtaining independency for corporations.

Raising corporate capital is inseparable from corporations, and stocks are one of the elements of corporate capital in Korea as it is in other countries.[5] The Commercial Act sticks to the principle of 'the value per stock shall be equal' but still prescribes that 'shareholder's liability shall be limited.'

It also has such provisions on stocks as corporate bonds,[6] redeemable stocks (Article 345), convertible stocks (Article 346) and bonds (Article 513), which facilitate corporations to raise capital through issuing a range of different types of stock.

Considering that raising capital usually involves risks, the Commercial Act sets forth the corporate system and shareholders' limited liability to mitigate the risks and diversify the corporate risks.

A business enterprise must be run independently from all stakeholders, including employees, directors, officers and shareholders. Thus, the Korean Commercial Act prescribes that all business enterprises shall be established as a legal entity (profit company). In addition, a corporation, under the Act, must have directors who are appointed by shareholders to run the business, which ensures a separation between ownership and control. A business enterprise can attract more capital from more shareholders depending on its financial situation, and the accountability rests with the legal entity. Limited liability works well to obtain professional managers and to attract more capital to the corporation. Put simply, the basic concept of a business enterprise, especially a stock company under the Korean Commercial Act is basically the same as the concepts of shareholders, board of directors and capital that are set forth by such countries where stock companies are common as USA and UK. However, the Korean companies have changed in a manner that a number of legal entities belong to one mother corporation and thus created 'Chaebul', the affiliates of which are connected financially. Such economic-scale has ensured the injection of an enormous amount of capital in a relatively short time to maximize manpower and productivity.

---

[5] Article 329 (Formation of Capital and Par Value per Stock).
(2) The capital of a corporation shall be divided into stocks.

[6] Article 469 (Offering of Bonds).
A corporation may offer bonds for subscription upon a resolution of the board of directors.
Article 470 (Limits on Total Amount):

(1) The total amount of bonds shall not exceed four times the amount of net assets of the corporation as shown by the latest balance sheet.

2. Increasing Corporate Transparency Korean companies (business enterprises) were the engine that has driven the economic growth of Korea which was the fastest in the world. Korean large corporations, so called *Chaebul*, have had direct and indirect influence on the Korean Commercial Act since then. Any changes in the Korean laws and policies with respect to corporations have focused on efficiency and growth and it has continued until the 1997 financial crisis. However, more Korean companies have changed to multinational companies and more money started flowing in from the international monetary market, the importance of corporate transparency has been emphasized. With the IMF's bailout that helped to overcome the financial crisis in 1997, more Korean companies have introduced and placed policies aiming to improve corporate transparency to follow the global standard, such as outsider directors, audit committees, and derivative suits.

3 Companies

1. Introduction The corporation represents the largest share of the countless enterprises existing today. The 21 basic business activities that Article 46 of the Korean Commercial Act lists are mostly the activities of corporations. Korea's Commercial Act defines four types of corporations. Article 170 of the Act categorizes corporations into four kinds, which are 'partnership companies', 'limited partnership companies', 'stock companies', and 'limited liability companies.' Kinds other than the four are not regarded as corporations. A stock company is the most active type and the Act also has the largest number of Articles regarding a stock company from Article 288 to 542. The listed companies (companies which list their stocks on the Korea Stock Exchange) account for the largest number of stock companies. The Commercial Act has 11 special cases that only apply to listed companies from Article 542(2) to 542(12).[7]

2. The Legal Concepts of Company The Commercial Act defines a 'company' as an 'association incorporated for the purpose of engaging in commercial activities and any other profitmaking activities' in Article 169 and sets forth that 'a company shall be a juristic person' in Article 171(1). Referring to both Articles, a company can be defined as 'an incorporated legal person for the purpose of profitmaking with three elements of commerciality, association and legal person.' In other words, a company is an association consisting of people who share the same purpose (association), an agent which can be independent from its members and obtain the rights and liabilities itself (legal person), and a person who engages in profitmaking activities (commerciality). A corporation should have the element of an association, but a stock company or limited liability company can be established

[7] Kim (2010), at 119–120.

and be comprised of as few as one person.[8] In addition, precedent cases ruled to allow 'piercing the corporate veil'. When a company is not treated as a separate legal person and has a legal dispute with a third party, the law may not allow the separate personhood but pierce the corporate veil by holding the person liable for the dispute that the company is involved in.[9]

A stock company is a type of corporation with individuals holding some shares of the stock of a company. Members of a company (shareholders) have liability for investment limited to the amount of the subscription price they paid and no liability for the company's debts. Shareholders are free to transfer their ownership of stocks without limitation, which makes it easy to recover the invested capital. Thus, stocks can largely attract investment, and a stock company enables a massive amount of capital to raise. A stock company is a suitable type for large-scale business that needs a large amount of fixed capital and the continous influx of capital.

The Korean Commercial Act also includes limited liability companies in the range of companies.

A limited liability company is a form of company where all members of the company have liability limited to their monetary contribution to the company, like a stock company. This is a suitable type for a small or medium sized company with a relatively small number of members. The strict and complicated rules and provisions on limited liability companies have been easier. Unlike a stock company, a limited liability company has characteristics of being private and closed. The characteristics that are different from those of a stock company are that the amount of shares to be transferred is limited and its members are liabile for the capital in some cases (the Commercial Act, Article 550, 593).

3. The Nature of Stock Companies A stock company is a type of company where a person becomes a member (shareholder) by subscribing for stocks or by acquiring issued stocks, and the members of a company have only limited liability for the company's debts to the value of the money they invested. Since the birth of different forms of company, a stock company has been the most successful form because of its unique capital structure that has stocks as the unit of capital and makes it easy to attract capital, and because of the limited liability of its shareholders that limits the risks of failure. Such characteristics can fully meet the objectives of an association. Thus, the key elements to a stock company are capital, shares and shareholders.[10]

The capital of a company refers to the total sum of the par value of all issued and outstanding shares.[11] The capital of a company is important to the stakeholders of a company and three principles apply for stable capital management. Under this

[8] Articles 288 and 543 (1); Supreme Court Decision 66Da1187 delivered on September 20, 1966 et al.

[9] Supreme Court Decision 87DaKa1671 delivered on November 22, 1988.

[10] Lee (2010), at 338.

[11] Article 451 (Capital) Unless otherwise provided for in this Act, the capital of a company shall be equal to the total sum of the par value of all issued and outstanding shares.

principle, capital stock and the investors of the capital stock shall be stated in the articles of incorporation. It is to provide stakeholders in transaction with the company with predictability in business and credibility of a company by stating and notifying the size of capital stock. Article 1 of the Commercial Act clarifies that a company shall prepare the number of shares to be issued at the time of incorporation and that all the shares shall be subscribed prior to incorporation.

Another important principle with respect to the capital of a company is that the net assets equivalent to the company's capital should actually be maintained. This principle means that transaction of a company's capital stock between a company and a shareholder should be prohibited. It is called 'the principle of maintenance of capital', and the principle basically intends to prohibit capital stock from feeding back to shareholders and to protect creditors of a company under the limited liability of shareholders. All of the shares to be issued at the time of incorporation should be paid for in full amount and all contributions in kind should be delivered.[12] When a company comes into existence, promoters and directors should take liability for subscription and payment of shares,[13] the issuance of shares below par should be restricted, and acquisition of the company's own shares should also be restricted.

As the capital of a company is divided into shares,[14] a share is the smallest unit consisting of the capital of a company and the unit for a member (shareholder) to invest. Thus, it should be noted that a stock company, with respect to a relationship between its members and capital, is totally different from a partnership company and a limited partnership company. A partnership company or a limited partnership

---

[12] Article 295 (Payment of Subscription Price and Performance of Contribution in Kind in Promotion of Incorporation) ①. Where promoters have subscribed for all of the shares to be issued at the time of incorporation, they shall, without delay, make full payment of the subscription price. In such cases, they shall designate a bank or other financial institution at which the subscription price is to be paid and the place for payment. Article 303 (Duties of Subscribers) A person who has subscribed for shares shall be responsible for the payment of the subscription price in accordance with the number of shares allotted to him by the promoters.

[13] Article 321 (Promoter's Warranty Liability for Subscription and Payment) ① Where, after the company comes into existence, any shares issued at the time of incorporation of the company are found not to have been subscribed or the subscription for certain shares has been revoked, the promoters shall be deemed to have subscribed for such shares jointly.

② Where, after the company comes into existence, the subscription price of shares in accordance with Article 295(1) or 305(1) has not been paid for in full amount, the promoters shall make such payment jointly and severally.

Article 428 (Director's Warranty Liability for Subscription) ① In cases where shares have not yet been subscribed for or the subscription of shares have been revoked after the registration of alteration due to the issuance of new shares was effected, directors shall be deemed to have jointly subscribed for such shares.

② Paragraph(1) shall not affect any claim for damage against directors.

[14] Article 329 (Formation of Capital and Par Value per Share) ① Deleted <2009.5.28>

②The capital of a stock company shall be divided into shares.

③The par value per share shall be equal.

④The par value per share shall be at least 100 won.

company has its members before the amount of investment and shares of each member are set up, whereas a stock company sets up the capital stock first and a person becomes a member by subscribing for the stocks. The reason for dividing the capital into shares is to facilitate raising capital. In other words, dividing the capital into a small unit enables people with small funds to subscribe for the stocks of a company. Shares are a means of attracting massive capital from the public. Investors are issued share certificates which can be free to be transferred and transacted in a market, which leads to easy recovery of the invested capital and consequently easy attraction of investors (shareholders).[15]

(1) Limited Liability of Shareholders Shareholders have limited liability up to the subscription price which the person has invested[16] and no obligation to make further investment in a company. It is called 'limited liability of shareholders'. Based on this principle, shareholders of a company are not liable for the company's debts and do not have to pay off with their own assets.[17] This prevents a possible risk arising from large-scale business, and economic agents in the capitalistic economy establish companies that have a separate and independent legal person by type, region and other factor, and invest in the businesses to create value and profits. Any loss arising from a business can be offset by providing the assets assigned for the business as collateral and the loss that the assigned assets do not cover should be borne by creditors rather than being extended to the other assets that the business holds.[18] A stock company is a corporation with a separate legal identity, but it is actually the shareholders of a company who are the agents of a company. Therefore, the limited liability system that may shift the loss arising from a business failure to a society is not free from ethical criticism. However, without the limited liability system, a shareholder may have to incur excessive expenses to oversee the management of a company, to check the financial status of other shareholders, and to pay constant attention to changes of other shareholders. If other shareholders are not in good financial shape, the company's debts that he has to be liable for would increase. Thus, the limited liability system is unavoidable to attract capital from the public which has become the basis of the capitalistic economy. In other words, the limited liability system is indispensable for realizing capitalism.

(2) Shares and Shareholders

1) Shares The term 'share' has two meanings. One is the unit of capital, the other one is a shareholder's right, the authority of a shareholder. A share should have par

[15] Lee (2010), at 340.

[16] Article 331 (Liability of Shareholder) The liability of a shareholder shall be limited to the subscription price which he has paid for his shares.

[17] In an extreme case, when a Company Law holds a shareholder liable for the company's debts, it may pierce the corporate veil. (see Supreme Court Decision 87DaKa1671 delivered on November 22, 1988).

[18] Kim (2010), at 133–134.

value printed on its face and the par value per share shall be equal. In addition, the par value per share should be at least 100 won.[19] Par value stock is a stock that has a certain amount of value printed on it.[20] Shares can mean the status of a shareholder including one's rights and responsibilities to the company. A shareholder has a range of rights and responsibilities according to one's status in the company. A shareholder is entitled to two rights: a self-interest right to receive economic benefits from the company and a public-interest right to participate in managing and operating the company. In addition, the responsibility to make contributions[21] is one of the responsibilities that shareholders should assume.[22]

2) The Principle of Shareholder Equality Shares imply the assets, corporate governance, and proportionate interest that a shareholder has. Proportionate interest means that the right of a shareholder is proportionate to the number of shares that he/she owns. It is called 'the principle of shareholder equality'. The Korean Commercial Act sets forth the principle of shareholder equality as individual rights, but it does not have specific provisions defining the principle.[23] Provisions of the articles of incorporation, resolutions at a shareholders' meeting or at a board of directors' meeting, or execution of work that do not follow the principle of shareholder equality are interpreted null and void. There is a Supreme Court case that declared a contract to be null and void because it violated the principle of shareholder equality.[24] A clear example of the principle of shareholder equality may be the exercise of the voting right at a general shareholders' meeting, which shows the equal treatment for each share. The principle of 'one share, one vote' was indeed derived from the equality of proportionate interests that shareholders have as to corporate governance. Article 369(1) of the Commercial Act prescribes that 'a shareholder shall have one vote for each share', claiming the principle of 'one share, one vote[25]' which is one of the few provisions forming the basis of corporate governance in the Korean corporations.[26]

The principle of shareholder equality may be excluded or limited by special provisions in the law. For example, there are some provisions exclusive from the

[19] See Article 329

[20] A non-par value stock is a stock that indicates only a certain proportion to the capital. The Korean Commercial Act only acknowledges par-value stock, but an investment company established by the Capital Market Act can exceptionally issue non-par value stocks. [the Capital Market Act, Article 196(1)].

[21] It is the liability of a shareholder. The liability of a shareholder shall be limited to the subscription price which he has paid for his shares (see Article 331).

[22] Son (2010), at 345–346.

[23] Kim (2010), at 148–149.

[24] See Supreme Court Decision 2006Da38161,38178 delivered on June 28, 2007. This is a court case where the company agreed to compensate for loss of paid-in capital in its entirety at the time of employees' severance from the company. The Supreme Court ruled that such agreement is invalid as a violation of the principle of shareholder equality.

[25] Article 369 (Votes) ① A shareholder shall have one vote for each share.

[26] Kim (2010), at 148–149.

principle of shareholder equality, including 'different classes of shares',[27] 'non-voting shares',[28] 'election of auditors',[29] 'minority shareholders',[30] and 'disposition of fractional shares.'[31] However, those exclusive provisions are just the other way to describe the methodological and technical aspect of the principle of shareholder equality.

3) Shareholders Shareholders are referred to members of a stock company. It is more accurate to say that a person becomes a member of a stock company not by investing, unlike other types of companies, but by acquiring shares that are units of the capital of a company. Acquiring a share or shares in a company is the premise for being a shareholder. A shareholder is granted a shareholder's right which is one of the rights given to the members of a company and becomes the basis of individual rights to the company.

---

[27] Article 344 (Different Classes of Shares) ① A company may issue two or more classes of shares which are different with respect to their particulars as to the dividends of profits or interest or the distribution of the surplus assets.

② In cases falling under paragraph(1), the articles of incorporation shall provide for the details and number of each class of shares and shall also provide for the minimum dividend rate with respect to a class of shares having any preferential right as to the dividend of profits. <Amended on Dec. 29, 1995>

③ If the company issues different classes of shares, special provisions may be made from class to class with respect to the subscription for new shares, the consolidation, split, or retirement of shares or the allotment of shares in consequence of a merger or split of companies, even where no such matters have been provided for in the articles of incorporation.

[28] Article 370 (Non-Voting Shares) ① Where a company issues different classes of shares, the articles of incorporation may state that a shareholder of a certain class of shares having preferential rights as to the dividend of profits shall not be entitled to vote: *Provided*, That such shareholder shall be entitled to vote from the general meeting subsequent to the general meeting where a resolution to disallow the preferred dividend as provided for in the articles of incorporation is adopted until the time of closing the general meeting where a resolution to allow such dividend is adopted.

② The total number of the shares having no voting rights shall not exceed 1/4 of the total issued and outstanding shares.

[29] Article 409 (Election) ① Auditors shall be elected at a general shareholders' meeting.

② Any shareholder who holds more than 3/100 of the total issued and outstanding shares, exclusive of non-voting shares, may not exercise his/her vote in respect to such shares exceeding the above limit, in the election of auditors under paragraph (1). <Amended on Apr, 10, 1984>

③ The articles of incorporation may provide for a lower ratio than referred to in paragraph (2).

[30] Article 366 (Demand for Convocation by Minority Shareholders) ① Shareholders who hold no less than 3/100 of the total number of shares issued may demand the convocation of an extraordinary general meeting, by filing with the board of directors a document or electronic document stating the subject matters of and the reasons for the convocation of the meeting.

[31] Article 443 (Disposal of Fractional Shares) ① If the number of shares makes them unfit for the consolidation, the new share issued for that portion unfit for the consolidation shall be sold by means of auction and the proceeds from which shall be delivered to the former shareholders in proportion to exchange at the price quoted thereat may be sold through such exchange and shares without an exchange quotation may be sold in a manner other than auction with permission of the court.

4. Corporate Governance The Korean Commercial Act categorizes the organs of corporations into essential organs and temporary organs. The shareholders' meeting, one of the essential organs, is a decision-making organ on basic matters of a company. A board of directors and a representative director is the organ to conduct corporate affairs. Auditors or the audit committee is an auditing organ over directors and financial matters of a company. An inspector, one of the temporary organs, may be appointed by a court or at a shareholders' meeting to investigate the establishment process of a company, the status of the company's property, or any necessary matters.[32]

(1) General Shareholders' Meeting and Voting Rights A shareholders' meeting is a regular meeting, at which shareholders attend to decide matters concerning the company. A shareholders' meeting can only pass resolutions as to matters provided for by the Commercial Act or the articles of incorporation.[33] In this sense, it is not an absolute body but the most important body.

A shareholders' meeting is convened not by shareholders, but by a board of directors (Article 362). Shareholders have the right to call for a shareholders' meeting to a board of directors [Article 366(1)]. If a board of directors does not convene a shareholders' meeting after the request of a shareholders' meeting, the shareholder who made such request may convene a shareholders' meeting with permission of the court [Article 366(2)]. When a company convenes a shareholders' meeting, it should give written notice to each shareholder or send electronic document to all shareholders after receiving the consent of each shareholder [Article 363(1)]. The notice must state the subject matters of the meeting [Article 363(2)]. A company, the total capital of which is less than one billion won and the number of the directors of which is one or two, may not have a board of directors.[34] In this case, each director must perform the function of such board of directors. Shareholders' meetings can be categorized into ordinary general meetings, convened once a year, and extraordinary general meetings, convened from time to time when necessary.[35] Resolutions of a general meeting should be passed by affirmative votes of a majority of the shareholders who have the voting rights at the meeting and representing one-quarter of the total issued and outstanding shares, unless

---

[32] Chung (2010a), at 376.

[33] Article361 (Power of General Shareholders' Meetings) At general shareholders' meetings, resolutions may be adopted as to matters provided for in this Act or the articles of incorporation.

[34] Article 383 (Number, Term of Office, etc.) ① Directors shall be at least three in number: Provided, That in case of a company, the total capital of which is less than one billion won, the number of the directors may be one or two.

[35] Article365 (Convocation of General Meetings) ① An ordinary general meeting shall be convened at least once a year at a fixed time.

② Where a company has determined the settlement of accounts to take place more than two times a year, a general meeting shall be convened with respect to each such period for the settlement of accounts.

③ An extraordinary general meeting shall be convened from time to time whenever it is necessary.

otherwise provided for by the Commercial Act or the articles of incorporation [Article 368(1)].

A voting right is the right of a shareholder to participate and cast a vote in resolutions at a shareholder's general meeting. Shareholders can participate in the management of a company by exercising their voting rights. A shareholder's voting right is the right that naturally belongs to a shareholder, which cannot be deprived or limited even by the articles of incorporation.[36] A shareholder should be allowed one vote for each share that he/she owns.[37] The Commercial Act has exceptional provisions that may restrict the principle of 'one share, one vote', however, which are non-voting shares,[38] shares of the company's,[39] shares of the parent and/or subsidiary companies' ,[40] shares of a person who has special interests,[41] and shares in the election.[42]

(2) Directors The board of directors makes decisions on matters of a company, but it cannot manage a company directly. A representative director represents and manages the company upon the decisions made by the board of directors. Each director at the board of directors except a representative director has the right to supervise the performance of duties by a representative director,[43] but they do not have the right to manage and represent the company. Thus, each director is merely a premise for being a representative director and it is not an organ of a company itself.[44]

Directors who are members of a board of directors participate in decision-making on matters of a company and supervise the performance of duties by a

---

[36] See Supreme Court Decision 2002Da54691 delivered on December 24, 2002.

[37] See Article 369 (1)

[38] Article 370 (Non-Voting Shares) ① Where a company issues different classes of shares, the articles of incorporation may provide that a shareholder of a certain class of shares having preferential rights as to the dividend of profits shall not be entitled to vote. Provided, That such shareholder shall be entitled to vote from the general meeting subsequent to the general meeting where a resolution of disallowing the preferred dividend as provided for in the articles of incorporation is adopted until the time of closing the general meeting where a resolution of allowing such dividend is adopted.

[39] Article 369 (Votes) ② The company shall not be entitled to vote in respect of its own shares.

[40] Article 369 (Votes) ③ In cases of a company, its parent company and its subsidiary company together, or its subsidiary company alone holds more than 1/10 of the total issued and outstanding shares in another company, the shares of the company or of the parent company held by such other company shall not be entitled to vote.

[41] Article 368 (Method of Adopting Resolutions and Exercise of Voting Rights) ④ A person who has special interest in the resolution of a general meeting may not exercise his voting rights thereupon.

[42] Article 409 (Election) ② Any shareholder who holds more than 3/100 of the total issued and outstanding shares, exclusive of non-voting shares, may not exercise his/her vote in respect of such shares exceeding the above limit, in the election of auditors under paragraph (1).

[43] Article 393 (Authorities of Board of Directors) ②The board of directors shall supervise the performance of duties by the directors.

[44] Son (2010), at 415.

representative director. Directors are appointed at a shareholders' meeting,[45] but they are not proxies or employees of the shareholders, but representatives of a company. Therefore, directors are not obliged to shareholders, but have duties and responsibilities for their company. The provisions of the Civil Act should apply to the relationship between the company and the directors.[46]

The Commercial Act classifies directors into inside directors, outside directors, and other directors who are not engaged in regular business. Outside directors are those not engaged in regular business of the company. Regular business means daily business and matters of the company.

The Commercial Act provides for the qualification as outside directors[47] and prescribes that listed companies should have a certain number of outside directors.

---

[45] Article 382 (Appointment of Directors, Relationship with Company and Outside Directors) ① Directors shall be appointed at a general shareholders' meeting.

[46] Article 382 (Appointment of Directors, Relationship with Company and Outside Directors) ② The provisions for delegation in the Civil Act shall apply *mutatis mutandis* to the relationship between the company and the directors.

[47] Article 382 (Appointment of Directors, Relationship with Company and Outside Directors) ③ Outside directors are not engaged in regular business of the relevant company, and do not fall under any of the following subparagraphs. Where outside directors fall under any of the following subparagraphs, they shall be removed from office:

1. Directors and employees who are engaged in regular business of the relevant company, or directors, auditors and employees who have been engaged in regular business of the relevant company within two years;
2. The principal, his spouse, lineal ascendants, and lineal descendants, in cases where the largest shareholder is a natural person;
3. Directors, auditors and employees of the corporation, in cases where the largest shareholder is a corporation;
4. Spouses, lineal ascendants, and lineal descendants of directors and auditors;
5. Directors, auditors and employees of a parent company or a subsidiary company of the relevant company;
6. Directors, auditors and employees of a corporation which has a significant interest in the relevant company, such as business relations with the company; and
7. Directors, auditors and employees of another corporation for which directors and employees of the relevant company work as directors.

Article 542–8 (Appointment of Outside Directors) ② No outside director of a listed company shall fall under any of the following subparagraphs and any subparagraphs of Article 382 (3), and if a director falls under one or more of the following, he/she shall be removed from office:

1. A minor, a person of incompetence, or a person of quasi-incompetence;
2. A person who has been adjudicated bankrupt and has not yet had his or her rights reinstated.
3. A person in whose case not more than two years have elapsed since his or her imprisonment without prison labor or a heavier punishment was completely executed or exempted;
4. A person for whom two years have not yet elapsed since he/she was dismissed or removed from office after he/she violated Acts separately determined by Presidential Decree;
5. In cases where a shareholder of a listed company and a party (hereinafter referred to as "related party") that has a special relationship with the shareholder as prescribed by Presidential Decree own the largest number of shares of stock issued, based on the total number of stocks-issued other than nonvoting stocks, the shareholder (hereinafter referred to as the "largest shareholder") and such related party:

The Act also has provisions on the selection process of outside directors for large listed companies.

Other directors who are not engaged in regular business do not include outside directors. Other terms were used in the industrial practice to indicate this type of director, such as part-time directors, but the terms were standardized in this legal term. The provisions concerning outside directors are not applied to this type of director and their legal status is the same as that of inside directors.[48]

The number of directors should not be less than three and the terms of office of directors do not exceed 3 years. Directors are usually appointed at a general shareholders' meeting upon its resolution, but the Korean Commercial Act accepts the cumulative voting system. The cumulative voting system allows one share to have multiple voting rights equivalent to the number of directors to appoint. For example, if the company has three openings for director position, a shareholder with one share can cast three votes, so that the shareholder can concentrate his/her full share of votes on a certain candidate or split the votes to a few candidates. Concentrated voting can be adopted only when a company appoints more than two directors.[49] If a company has only one opening, the concentrated voting system that allows the shareholders to concentrate their votes is meaningless. The Commercial Act does not enforce the concentrated voting system to companies, but has the provisions that allow companies to opt out a concentrate vote.[50]

The Civil Act prescribes that directors should have a duty of care and due diligence[51] for the company and the Commercial Act has provisions on the fiduciary duty.[52] The Commercial Act also prescribes three duties of directors in order to balance between the interests of directors and of the company, namely 'prohibition

---

6. A shareholder (hereinafter referred to as a "major shareholder") who owns more than 10/100 of the total number of issued stocks, other than nonvoting stocks, by his calculation regardless of the name of a shareholder, or exerts de facto influence on important matters related to the management of listed companies, including the appointment and dismissal of directors or auditors, and his spouse, lineal ascendants and lineal descendents; and

7. A person determined by Presidential Decree, who has difficulty in faithfully performing his duty as an outside director, or who may have an influence on the management of listed companies.

[48] Lee (2010), at 533.

[49] Article 382-2 (Concentrated Vote) ① Where a general meeting of a company is convened to elect two or more directors, shareholders who hold no less than 3/100 of the total shares, excluding nonvoting shares, may request that the company elect directors by means of a concentrated vote, except as otherwise prescribed by the articles of incorporation.

[50] Lee (2010), at 537–538.

[51] Article 382 (Appointment of Directors, Relationship with Company and Outside Directors) ② The provisions for delegation in the Civil Act shall apply *mutatis mutandis* to the relationship between the company and the directors.

Article 681 of the Civil Act (Mandatary's Duty of Care and Due Diligence) A mandatary shall manage the affairs entrusted to him with the care of a good manager in accordance with the tenor of the mandate.

[52] Article 382-3 (Fiduciary Duty) Directors shall perform their duties in good faith in the interests of the company in accordance with Acts, subordinate statues, and the articles of incorporation.

of competitive business' ,[53] 'transactions between directors and the company' ,[54] and 'duties of directors to maintain confidentiality.'[55] Directors also have the duty of reporting to auditors or the audit committee[56] in order to prevent any possible substantial loss on the company and enhance the efficiency of auditors or the audit committee. The Commercial Act does not prescribe it, but the court cases rule that directors should supervise the performance of duties by other directors.[57]

Liabilities of directors split to liabilities to the company and to the third persons, and the liabilities to the company are divided into the liability to damage concerning their performance[58] and the warranty liability for subscription.[59] The liability to third persons is usually the liability to damage arising from the performance of their duties. Particularly when a director causes loss to a third person due to neglect of his duty, (even though a company does not know the fact that the director is liable to such damage) the director usually does not hold the liability for the loss to the third person personally.

---

[53] Article 397 (Prohibition of Competitive Business) ① No director shall, without approval of the board of directors, effectuate for his own account or for the account of a third person any transaction which falls within the class of business of the company or become a member with unlimited liability or a director of any other company whose business purposes ear the same as those of the company. ② If any director has effectuated a transaction for his own account in contravention of paragraph (1), the company may, upon a resolution of the board of directors, deem such transaction as effectuated for account for the company and if he has effectuated a transaction for account of a third person, the company may demand the pertinent director to transfer any interest accrued therefrom. ③ The rights under paragraph (2) shall be extinct with the lapse of one year after the day on which such transaction has been effectuated.

[54] Article 398 (Transactions between Directors and Company) A director may effectuate a transaction with the company for his own account or for account of a third person only if he has obtained approval of the board of directors. In such cases, Article 124 of the Civil Act shall not apply.

[55] Article 382-4 (Duties of Directors to Maintain Confidentiality) No director shall divulge the business secret of the company, which has become aware of in the course of performing their duties, not only while in office but also after retirement.

[56] Article 412-2 (Director's Duty of Reporting) If a director finds any fact that is likely to inflict a substantial loss on the company, he shall immediately report such to the auditors.

[57] See Supreme Court Decision 2006Da68636 delivered on September 11, 2008.

[58] Article 399 (Liability to Company) ① If directors have acted in violation of any Acts and subordinate statutes or of the articles of incorporation or has neglected to perform their duties, they shall be jointly and severally liable for damage to the company.

② If any act mentioned in paragraph (1) has been done in accordance with the resolution of the board of directors, the directors who have assented to such resolution shall take the same liability.

③ The directors who have participated in the resolution mentioned in paragraph (2) and whose dissenting opinion has not been entered in the minutes shall be presumed to have assented to such resolution.

[59] Article 428 (Director's Warranty Liability for Subscription) ① In cases where shares have not yet been subscribed or the subscription of shares has been revoked after the registration of alteration due to the issuance of new shares was effected, directors shall be deemed to have jointly subscribed for such shares.

② Paragraph (1) shall not affect any claim for damage against a director.

The Commercial Act sets forth that a director should be liable for damage to a third person when he/she has neglected to perform the duties to protect the third person and to ensure directors perform their duties with care.[60]

(3) Board of Directors The board of directors is a body of directors which determines the activities of a company. It is an essential organ of a company. A small company, the capital of which is less than one billion won and the number of directors of which is one or two, does not have a board of directors, thus provisions on a board of directors do not apply to those companies. A board of directors is a body to hold meetings and it is not proper to perform the activities of a company. Thus, it is the role of the representative director to perform the activities that are decided by a board of directors. A board of directors makes a decision on the activities of a company by resolution and supervises the performance of duties by the directors.[61]

1) Subcommittees of Board of Directors The Commercial Act prescribes that a committee can be established within the board of directors pursuant to the articles of incorporation.[62] Such committee is subordinate to the board of directors to exercise the rights of the board of directors on the matters delegated by the board. The subcommittee of the board was introduced after referring to the American system for the purpose of efficient operation, objectivity and expertise of decision-making and included in the amended Commercial Act in 1999. A subcommittee of a board of directors under the Act is not compulsory. Companies can set up subcommittees based on their articles of incorporation.

A subcommittee of a board usually consists of more than two directors,[63] which means that no small company with less than one billion won of total capital and one or two directors may establish any subcommittee.[64] The type of a subcommittee to be established by the board is a matter of a decision by a company pursuant to its articles of incorporation. However, a listed company over a certain size[65] should have 'a committee for recommending candidates for outside directors' and 'an audit

---

[60] Article 401 (Liability to Third Persons) ① If a director has neglected to perform his/her duties willfully or by gross negligence, he/she shall be jointly and severally liable for damage to third person.

[61] Article 393 (Authorities of Board of Directors) ① Disposal and transfer of important property, borrowings of large scale assets, appointment or dismissal of managers, and management of affairs, such as establishment, transfer or abolition of branch offices, shall be made upon a resolution of the board of directors.

②The board of directors shall supervise the performance of duties by the directors.

[62] Article 393-2 (Subcommittees of Board of Directors) ① The board of directors may, as prescribed in the articles of incorporation, establish subcommittees.

[63] Article 393-2 (Subcommittees of Board of Directors) ③ A subcommittee shall be composed of not less than two directors.

[64] Chung (2010a), at 424–425.

[65] A listed company, the total assets of which are over two trillion won as at the end of the latest business year.

committee' to appoint outside directors. A committee for recommending candidates for outside directors should have outside directors representing at least half of its members, and an audit committee should have outside directors accounting for at least two-thirds of its members.

2) Representative Director A representative director has the authority to represent the company and implement the activities of the company. It is an essential body of a company. Theoretically, the authority to perform the activities of a company should belong to a board of directors but there are limits for a board of directors to perform practically. Thus, a board of director only makes decisions and a natural person performs the decided matters. In addition, a company has the authority, but it also takes a natural person who can actually obtain the authority and performs the duties on behalf of a company. Thus, the Commercial Act permits a company to appoint a representative director, who has the authority to perform the internal activities of the company and the authority to represent the company.[66] A representative director is, in principle, appointed upon a resolution of the board of directors, but he/she can also be appointed at a general meeting pursuant to its articles of incorporation.[67] Except the condition that a representative director should be one of the directors, there is no special qualification for a representative director. One or more of directors can be appointed as a representative director because there is no limit on its number. A representative director may retire upon termination of the term of office, dismissal or resignation. A representative director will be discharged from office when he/she loses the status of a director as it is deemed to lose the premise for a representative director. A board of directors or a general meeting which appointed a representative director can remove a representative director from office at any time.

(4) Derivative Suits by Shareholders This is a suit raised by a minority shareholder to hold a director liable for any loss to a company. Theoretically, an auditor or audit committee should file a suit against a company on behalf of the company,[68] but it is unrealistic due to the special connection between auditors/audit committees and directors. This may result in harm to the interests of a company and shareholders. Thus, the Commercial Act has the provisions that allow minority shareholders questioning the liability of directors by filing a law suit, which is the

---

[66] Lee (2010), at 564–565.

[67] Article 389 (Representative Director) ① A company shall appoint, upon a resolution of the board of directors, a director who shall represent the company: Provided, That the articles of incorporation may provide that such representative director shall be elected at a general shareholders' meeting.

[68] Article 394 (Representation in Action between Company and Directors) ① When a company files an action against a director and vice versa, the auditors shall represent the company in connection with such action. The same shall apply where a company is in receipt of a claim under Article 403 (1).

② In case where a member of the audit committee under Article 415-2 is a party to an action, the audit committee or a director shall request the court to elect a person to represent the company.

derivative suit system. In such lawsuit, a plaintiff would be a shareholder who holds not less than 1/100 of the total issued and outstanding shares of a company.[69] For a listed company in such cases, a plaintiff would be a shareholder who has held not less than 1/10,000 of the total issued and outstanding shares of a listed company for the last 6 months. The portion of shares that a minority shareholder, who files a suit, holds should be the same at the time of filing a suit, but this would not affect the suit if the portion of shares that he/she holds has reduced under 1/100 after the suite has been filed. However, a shareholder of a holding company cannot file a derivative suit (double derivative suit) against directors of a subsidiary company.[70] A defendant would be a director or a former director, including a person who is or was not a director but gives or gave directions and instructions on the activities of a company.[71]

Derivative suits started to be filed by civic groups after the financial crisis in 1997 for enhancing corporate governance. It is still rare to see a derivative suit in its original meaning, filed apart from the suits that were filed to attack the other party in the disputes over a control of a company. This tells that the derivative suit system is mostly used for enhancing corporate governance rather than relief of right.[72]

(5) Auditors and Audit Committee An auditor may audit the activities and performance of directors, demand the directors to report on the business, and investigate the activities and financial conditions of a company under Article 412 of the Commercial Act. A company has a supervising body on the management—auditors. The auditors have powerful authority. Directors should report to auditors any fact likely to cause a substantial loss to the company at any time (Article 412-2). Auditors may call for an extraordinary general shareholders' meeting by submitting to the board of directors a written statement specifying the subject matters and the reasoning of the convocation [Article 412(3)-1]. An auditor from a parent company may demand its subsidiary company to report on its business if necessary to carry out his duties [Article 412(4)-1]. An auditor of a parent company may investigate the business and financial status of a subsidiary company if the subsidiary company fails to submit such report promptly or it is required to verify the content of the report [Article 412(4)-2].

A subsidiary company cannot refuse such audit or report unless it has a justifiable ground [Article 412(4)-3]. An auditor should present the results of the audit and investigation on the agenda and the documents that directors have submitted to a general shareholders' meeting and give his opinion as to whether there are any violation of the Act, subordinate statutes or the articles of incorporation (Article 413). If an auditor with such powerful authority is a person who can easily be

---

[69] Article 403 (Derivative Suits by Shareholders) ① Any shareholder who holds not less than 1/100 of the total issued and outstanding shares may demand that the company file an action against directors to enforce their liability.

[70] See Supreme Court Decision 2003Da49221 delivered on September 23, 2004.

[71] Chung (2010a), at 467.

[72] Kim (2010), at 174–175.

influenced by the majority shareholders or the management, the audit system would become meaningless. Thus, the Commercial Act limits the voting right of a majority shareholder in the appointment of auditors at a general meeting. A shareholder who holds more than 3/100 of the total issued and outstanding shares excluding non-voting shares may not exercise the voting right in regard to the shares exceeding the limit at a time of appointing an auditor at a general meeting [Article 409(2)]. The ratio referred to in Article 409 (2) may be altered and got lower by the articles of incorporation [Article 409(3)].

The audit system under the Commercial Act is unique and rare in other countries. But it is unfortunate that the audit system in the past was merely a system existing only on the Act. Auditors were not active in a company and powerless. It was common to see auditors present at a general meeting to just read a report that was prepared by a company. They failed to check the management as expected by the Commercial Act. Korea has introduced the westernized audit system which western countries have had in place during the financial crisis in 1997 as those countries influenced the economic reform of Korea. An audit committee is a sub-committee of the board, which has a similar function as the one of an auditor's.[73] An audit committee is an operating committee of the board of directors which supervises and monitors the activities and performance of the management, and supervises the necessary activities for fair and accurate accounting and disclosure. It is an essential organ for corporate governance.

An audit committee has been introduced by the recommendation of the international financial organizations in 1999 as a part of the economic reform, but the practical reason for the introduction was to increase the oversight function on the management of companies as the previous audit system had failed to function properly.

Korea's audit committees have even stronger authority than that of audit committees in other countries because they hold authority over accounting as well as authority given to auditors under the Commercial Act. It means that they have more potential to enhance corporate governance depending on how they are used and operated. However, the legislation on the role of an audit committee in the aspect of corporate governance is still poor and it is important to develop best practices in this field. The articles of incorporation or the audit committee need to reflect any international best practices.[74] According to Article 415-2 (1) of the Commercial Act, a company, under the articles of incorporation, may establish an audit committee within the board of directors in lieu of individual auditors. When an audit committee is established, a company should not have any individual auditors. If the audit committee consists of only directors, it can affect the oversight function of the committee. Thus, the audit committee shall have outside directors who should account for more than 2/3 of the total number of members [Article 415-2(2)]. An audit committee should be established by the board of directors as a subcommittee

[73] Kim (2010), at 187–188.

[74] Kim (2010), at 188.

of the board. An audit committee may be set up when the majority of members of the board of directors vote for. However, the dismissal of a member of the audit committee requires the concurrent vote of 2/3 or more of the total number of directors [Article 415-2(3)]. The Commercial Act allows a company to determine whether it has auditors as in the past or it sets up an audit committee. However, the Act enforces a listed company with capital of not less than two trillion won to establish an audit committee in which the number of outside directors accounts for two-thirds of its members (Article 542-11).

4 Insurance

1. Introduction Insurance is a system where a number of people who may face economic risk arising from the same type of event (the insured event) form a group (a risk pool) and pool assets (fund) by paying a certain amount of money calculated based on the statistical method (premium). A person who is suffered from an accidental event (the insured event) is paid a certain amount of money from the shared fund (the insurance proceeds) to prepare for any unstable economic situation.[75]

An insurance contract law in a practical aspect means the law that regulates the matters and business in the private insurance sector (especially commercial insurance) and it means, in a formal aspect, the provisions concerning insurance in the Part IV of the Commercial Act.

2. Insurance Contracts Article 638 of the Commercial Act defines an insurance contract as a contract where one party pays the premium as agreed and the other provides a certain amount of money or its equivalent in kind when uncertain events against property, life or body of the insured person occur. It provides a consistent definition for damage insurance and personal insurance.

(1) Elements of Insurance Contracts The stakeholders of an insurance contract can be narrowed down to three types. First, the direct parties of an insurance contract, which are the insurer and the policyholder. Second, the policyholder, the insured, and the beneficiary when an insurance contract made by a policyholder is not for him/herself, but for a third person. Third, there are people supporting the policyholder, including an insurance agent, an insurance broker, and an insurance medical staff, etc.

Insured events are the incidents that actualize the liability of the insurer. Since insurance is to prepare against such incidents, insured events are essential element of an insurance contract. An insured event in damage insurance is also called 'a peril' under the Korean Commercial Act.[76] A peril is accurately the status of

---

[75] Chung (2010a), vol. II., at 483 (12th ed.).

being aware of the possibility of the occurrence of an insured event or the possibility of the occurrence of such event.[77]

In order to be accepted as an insured event, first it should be accidental. Being accidental means that the event should be uncertain in respect of the possibility or the time of occurrence as at the time the insurance contract is made.[78] Second, it should be an event that can occur. Thus, an insurance contract on an event that cannot occur or has already occurred, the contract should be null and void. This provision of the Commercial Contract is compulsory and makes a contract invalid even though such contract has been made by mutual consent. And an insured event should be objectively possible to occur and the insurer and an insured person shouldn't know if such event has already occurred or will never occur.[79]

(2) Making Insurance Contracts The Commercial Act imposes a duty of disclosure on the policyholder,[80] at the time of making the insurance contract, and a duty to deliver insurance policy and specify the insurance terms on the insurer.[81]

1) Duty of Disclosure With a duty of disclosure, a policyholder or the insured should disclose and not misrepresent any important matters and facts to the insurer upon the purchase of a policy (Article 651). The facts that a person with a duty of disclosure discloses are important in terms of making an insurance contract. The policyholder should disclose any matters and facts which can help the insurer to assess the risks of the occurrence of any insured event and to determine as to

---

[76] E.g., Article 647 (Request for Reduction of Premium upon Cessation of Certain Risks) Where the parties to an insurance contract agreed on the premium in consideration of certain risks, if such risks have ceased to exist during the period of insurance, the policyholder may request that the premium be reduced for the future.

[77] Article 652 (Notice on Alteration or Increase of Risks and Termination of Contract) ① If, during the cover period, the policyholder or the insured becomes aware of the fact that the possibility of the occurrence of the insured events has been substantially altered or increased, he shall give notice thereof to the insurer without delay. If the policyholder or the insured has neglected to do so, the insurer may terminate the contract within one month after it becomes aware of the fact.

[78] See Supreme Court Decision 2000Da20878 delivered on July 24, 2001.

[79] Article 644 (Effect on Preexisting Insured Events) If, at the time when an insurance contract is made, an insured event has already occurred or will never occur, such contract shall be null and void.

[80] Article 651 (Termination of Contract due to Breach of Duty of Disclosure) If, at the time of making an insurance contract, the policyholder or the insured, by fraud or gross negligence, fails to disclose or misrepresents material facts, the insurer may terminate the contract within one month after it knew the non-disclosure or misrepresentation or within 3 years after the contract was made: Provided, That this shall not apply where, at the time of making the insurance contract, the insurer knew the nondisclosure or misrepresentation or by gross negligence failed to do so.

[81] Article 640 (Issuance of Insurance Policy) ① When an insurance contract is made, the insurer shall prepare an insurance certificate and issue it to the policyholder without delay, except in cases where the policyholder fails to pay the whole premium or its first installment.

② Where an existing insurance contract is extended or altered, the insurer may be exempt from issuing an insurance certificate by writing down the extension or alteration on the existing insurance certificate.

entering an insurance contract or the conditions of the contract and which may cause the insurer not to enter the contract or to change the conditions of the contract if he/she is aware of the true fact.[82] Different types of insurance may require different types of important matters, thus it should follow the objective standard rather than subjective determination of the parties in the contract.

2) Duty to Deliver and Specify The insurer should deliver the standard insurance terms to the policyholder and specify the important provisions thereof at the time of entering the insurance contract.[83] This is to protect the policyholder from any legal issue by informing him/her of the contents of a contract that would bind the parties in the contract. It is imperative law to protect the interests of a policyholder. The insurer should inform the policyholder of any important content of a contract at the time of making a contract. The important contents referred to in above may be different for each type of insurance, but they are mainly the premium rate system, the content of the insurance policy, any changes of the content of the policy, grounds for termination, and grounds for exemption of the insurer. The insurer is not required to inform a policyholder of such matters as the content that the policyholder is aware of, a general and predictable matter, or matters provided for by law.[84]

3. Non-Life Insurance Non-life insurance involves a contract where the insurer promises to indemnify any loss to the property of the insured arising from an insured event and the policyholder promises to pay premium on such condition.[85] The types of non-life insurance under the Commercial Act are fire insurance, transport insurance, marine insurance, liability insurance and automobile insurance. Non-life insurance also requires insurance terms and conditions including the parties to the contract, the subject matter insured, and the insured events, etc. like other ordinary insurance contracts. The extraordinary element of non-life insurance is the interests going to the insured. If a non-life insurance contract remains valid, theoretically the insured event for the purpose of insurance should not occur so that the insured can have the economic interest. The Commercial Act describes such interest as "subject matter of an insurance contract,"[86] which is different from the

[82] See Supreme Court Decision 2004Da36215 delivered on July 14, 2005.

[83] Article 638-3 (Duty to Deliver and Specify Standard Insurance Terms) ① When an insurer enters into an insurance contract, it shall deliver the standard insurance terms to the policyholder, and inform him of their important contents.

② If the insurer violates the provisions of paragraph (1), the policyholder may cancel the contract within one month after the contract is made.

[84] See Supreme Court Decision 98Da32564 delivered on November 27, 1998; Supreme Court Decision 2007Da8044 delivered on May 27, 2010, et. al.

[85] Article 665 (Liability of Insurer of Non-Life Insurance) The insurer in a non-life insurance contract is liable to indemnify the insured against any loss to his property caused by the occurrence of the insured event.

[86] Article 668 (Subject Matters of Insurance Contract) Only such interests as can be estimated in a monetary sum may be subject matter of an insurance contract.

subject matter insured.[87] Subject matter of an insurance contract should be first, estimated in a monetary sum. Since non-life insurance covers the loss to the property, the loss should be estimated in a monetary sum. Second, it should be something that can be determined or has been determined by the social consensus as at the time of making an insurance contract. When the subject matter of an insurance contract is not determined by the time the insured event occurs, the loss cannot be determined therefore the insurance amount to be paid cannot be determined. Third, subject matter of an insurance contract should be legitimate. Thus, it shouldn't be something that may violate the social morals, any proceeds from tax evasion, burglary, gambling, or selling banned goods. The legitimacy of subject matter of an insurance contract should be determined in an objective manner regardless of good faith, ill will, or the competence of the person.

4. Personal Insurance Personal insurance involves a contract that the insurer is liable to pay the insured amount according to the contract when an insured event affects the life or body of the policyholder.[88] Personal insurance, where the insured is a person, is different from non-life insurance that indemnifies against any loss to property. Under the Commercial Act, life insurance and accident insurance are the representative personal insurance.

Life insurance is a type of personal insurance where the insurer is liable to pay the insured amount when an accident affects the life of the insured.[89] Life insurance is different from accident insurance because the payment is made upon the death of the insured person. It is also different from non-life insurance because the insured amount is fixed by a contract, whereas the insured amount of a non-life insurance does change by the degree of the loss or damage that has occurred.

It is a life insurance contract that a policyholder makes where a third party is the insured person, whereas a self-life insurance contract is an insurance contract where a policyholder becomes the insured person.

Accident insurance is a type of personal insurance where the insurer is liable to pay the insured amount and other benefits if the insured event causing the injury of the body takes place.[90] The other benefits referred to in the Act means non-cash matters, including treatment, medicine and medical supplies.

---

[87] Son (2010), at 1060.

[88] Article 727 (Liability of Insurer in Personal Insurance) The insurer in a personal insurance contract shall be liable to pay the insured amount and other benefits as the contract of insurance provides, in cases where the insured events may affect life or body.

[89] Article 730 (Liability of Insurer in Life Insurance) The insurer in a life insurance contract shall be bound to pay the insured amount agreed upon if the insured event affects the life of the insured.

[90] Article 737 (Liability of Insurer in Accident Insurance) The insurer in an accident insurance contract shall be liable to pay the insured amount and other benefits if the insured event causing the injury of the body occurs.

5 Marine Commerce

1. Introduction A marine commercial enterprise engages in commercial activities, using ships in the sea, and a marine transport enterprise is one of the key types of marine commercial enterprises. Marine commercial enterprises usually consist of material (ships) and personal (a marine commercial enterprise and its workers).

Although Marine Commerce is a part of Korea's Commercial Act, it has not seen many changes unlike the aforementioned corporate part. International law applies to many aspects of the Marine part, and International trade law applies to the Commercial part.

The term 'ship' in the marine commerce provisions of the Commercial Act, means a ship used for navigation for commercial activities or for other profit-making purposes (Article 740). The provisions of the Part V of the Act apply, not to only a ship being used for marine commercial activities, but also a ship for navigation that doesn't engage in profit making activities [Article 741(1)].

2. Marine Commercial Enterprises

(1) Personal Enterprise The Commercial Act indicates that the ordinary case is that a shipowner engages in running a marine commercial enterprise and prescribes its provisions mostly for a shipowner, but a shipowner under the Act includes a co-owner of a ship, a bareboat charterer, and a voyage charterer.

A shipowner is a person who has ownership of a ship under property law and uses the ship for the commercial and profit-making activities of his marine commercial enterprise.

A co-owner of a ship is a person who shares ownership in a ship and uses it for a joint marine commercial enterprise. The legal nature of co-ownership is not a mere shared ownership under the Civil Act, but should be a type of joint venture.

A contract of bareboat charter is made when a shipowner agrees to provide a ship to a charterer for the purpose of operation of a ship under the control of a charterer, and a charterer agrees to pay the charterage in return.[91] In this case, a bareboat charterer is the main agent of a marine commercial enterprise.

A voyage charter contract is made when a shipowner agrees to provide a charterer with a ship serviced by the crew on board and equipped with navigation facilities for a given period to be used for navigation and a charterer agrees to pay the fare fixed by the period in response thereto.[92] Voyage charter usually follows

---

[91] Article 847 (Meaning of Bareboat Charter) ① A bareboat charter shall come into effect when a shipowner agrees to provide a charterer with a ship for the purpose of operation thereof under the control of a charterer, and a charterer agrees to pay the charterage in response thereto.

[92] Article 842 (Meaning of Time Charter) A time charter shall come into effect by an agreement that a shipowner agrees to provide a charterer with a ship serviced by the crew on board and equipped with navigation facilities for a given period to be used for navigation, and a charterer agrees to pay the fare fixed by the period in response thereto.

the international standards and provisions, but the amended Commercial Act in 1991 set forth the minimum provisions on voyage charter in consideration of such standards and the practices, considering the fact that voyage charter contracts have been on the rise.[93]

(2) Limited Liability of Shipowner In 1962, the Commercial Act acceded to the international convention for the unification of certain rules of law of 1924 and reflected liability for the ship price and liability for price, but the amended 1991 Commercial Act acceded to the international convention for the unification of certain rules of law of 1976. The amended 2007 Commercial Act is in line with the 1991 Commercial Act, but it increased the cap on the liability for the deaths of passengers.

3. Marine Business Activities Marine transport under the Commercial Act prior to the amended Act in 2007 included charter (for navigation) and affreightment, but the 2007 Commercial Act excludes charter from marine transport. It classified navigation charter under the charter part, such as voyage charter and bareboat charter and has provided separate provisions.

The Commercial Act (Marine Transport) has acceded to the international convention for the unification of certain rules of law for international marine transport to a great degree in consideration of the reality of marine transport and international practice. The 1991 Commercial Act acceded to the Hague Rule in 1924 and reflected the 1968 Hague–Visby Rules and the 1978 Hamburg Rules, aligning with the international standard in terms of liability for loss and damage.
A contract of marine affreightment transport is made when a carrier agrees to transport individual goods by ship at sea and a consignor agrees to pay the freight for it.[94] The main parties in this type of contract are a carrier and a consignor and other parties to involve are a forwarding agent, a shipper and a consignee. A carrier should be liable for any loss occurring in the course of marine affreightment transport, so any marine enterprise engaging in marine affreightment transport may be the main party that takes liability. In other words, a shipowner as well as a bareboat charterer and a voyage charterer may take liability.[95]

The Commercial Act sets forth the provisions of flat-rate compensation on the liability of a carrier. Thus, if goods have been totally lost or arrival has been delayed, the amount of damages shall be determined by the price prevailing at the destination 'on the day on which they should have been delivered.' In cases of a partial loss of or damage to the goods, the amount of damages shall be determined by the price prevailing at the destination 'on the day on which they have been delivered'. This provision applies only where the loss of, damage to or delay of

[93] Chung (2010a), at 1025.

[94] Article 791 (Meaning of Contract of Affreightment in General Ship) A contract of affrieghtment in a general ship shall come into effect when a carrier agrees to transport individual goods by ship at sea and a consignor agrees to pay the freight for it.

[95] See Supreme Court Decision 2001Da12621 delivered on May 28, 2002.

arrival of the goods has arisen from a minor negligence of the carrier. If such case arises due to the willfulness or gross negligence of the carrier, the provision would not apply.

The Commercial Act has referred to the international convention for the unification of certain rules of law to limit the liability on its Article 797, which says that 'in cases where the damage to the cargo has occurred due to his intention or his reckless act or omission while recognizing the concern about the occurrence of damage, he should be liable for all damages. This provision limits the liability when such damage occurs due to the intentional act of a carrier. Thus, in cases where damage occurs due to the intentional act of other ship employees than a carrier, the limited liability is applied.[96]

A marine passenger transport contract comes into effect when a carrier agrees to transport the specific passengers from a place of departure to a place of arrival by ship on the sea and the other party pays the fare in response thereto.[97] The main parties in a marine passenger transport contract are a carrier who agrees to transport passengers and a passenger who pays the fare to a carrier in return.

4. Marine Transport Document A bill of lading is a document that acknowledges that specified goods have been received on board by a carrier and his duty to deliver such goods to the consignee who holds the bill at destination. A consignor[98] or a (navigation) charterer[99] can request the issuance of a bill of lading and the issuer would be a carrier or a shipowner. As more requests from the industry have been made for an electronic bill of lading system, new provisions on electronic bills of lading have been adopted.[100]

As the use of seaway bills has increased in the industry, the amended 2007 Commercial Act has new provisions on marine affreightment transport. A seaway bill is a document that a carrier (a shipowner) issues as a substitute for a bill of lading upon the request of a consignor (a charterer) where a carrier (a shipowner)

---

[96] See Supreme Court Decision 96Da31611 delivered on December 6, 1996; Supreme Court Decision 2004Da27082 delivered on October 26, 2006.

[97] Article 817 (Meaning of Marine Passenger Transport Contract) A marine passenger transport contract shall come into effect by the agreement that a carrier agrees to transport the specific passengers from a place of departure to a place of arrival by ship on the sea and the other party pays the fare in response thereto.

[98] Article 852 (Issuance of Bill of Lading) ① A carrier shall deliver, at the request of a consignor, a bill of lading in one or more copies after receipt of the cargo.

② A carrier shall deliver, at the request of a consignor, a shipped bill of lading in one or more copies after loading the cargo, or shall indicate such loading on a bill of lading referred to in paragraph(1)

[99] Article 855 (Charter Party and Bill of Lading) ① When requested by a charterer, a shipowner shall issue a bill of lading under Articles 852 and 853 after receipt of the cargo.

[100] Article 862 (Electronic Bill of Lading) ① A carrier may issue an electronic bill of lading by means of registration with the registry agency designated by the Minister of Justice with the consent of a consignor or a charterer in lieu of issuance of a bill of lading referred to in Article 852 or 855. In such cases, an electronic bill of lading shall have the same legal effect as a bill of lading referred to in Articles 852 and 855.

verifies receipt of goods on board and delivers such goods to a consignor or his proxy whose name is written thereon for limiting the liability.[101]
A person who can request the issuance of a seaway bill would be a consignor (in cases of an affreightment transport contract) or a charter (in cases of a charter contract), and the issuer would be a carrier (in cases of an affreightment transport contract) or a shipowner (in cases of a charter contract). A seaway bill is usually issued in writing, but it can be issued in an electronic form upon agreement.

5. Maritime Perils Marine commercial activities inevitably involve navigation on a sea, which may face a range of perils. The question here would be, how to deal with such risks related to marine activities and to adjust possible economic losses to each stakeholder. The Commercial Act has provisions to handle such perils, for example provisions on general averaging, collision of ships, salvage, and marine insurance. General averaging and salvage deals with maritime perils, proactively and collision of ships and marine insurance deals with maritime perils, passively.[102]
The Commercial Act defines general averaging as the damage and expenses which have arisen from the disposal of a ship or the cargo by a shipmaster in order to escape common peril of a ship and the cargo.[103]

It refers to such cases where collision occurs between seagoing ships or between a seagoing ship and a ship of inland navigation and provides for damage for a ship, or the goods or persons on board. The Act has some provisions in regard to collision of a ship, which includes Collision due to Force Majeure,[104] Collision due to Fault of One Party,[105] Collision due to Fault of Both Parties,[106] and Collision due to Fault of Pilot.[107]

---

[101] Article 863 (Issuance of Seaway Bill) ① If requested by a charterer or a consignor, a carrier may issue a seaway bill in lieu of a bill of lading referred to in Article 852 or 855. A seaway bill may be issued electronically according to the agreement between the parties.

[102] Chung (2010a), at 1102.

[103] Article 865 (Requirements of General Averaging) Damage and expenses which have arisen from the disposal of a ship or the cargo by a shipmaster in order to escape common peril of a ship and the cargo shall constitute general average.

[104] Article 877 (Collision due to Force Majeure) When a ship collides due to force majeure or the cause of the collision is unclear, a sufferer cannot claim damages due to the collision.

[105] Article 878 (Collision due to Fault of One Party) When a ship collides due to the fault of a crewman of one party, a shipowner of such party shall be liable to a sufferer for compensation for damages due to the collision.

[106] Article 879 (Collision due to Fault of Both Parties) ① When a ship collides due to the fault of the crew of both parties, each shipowner shall share the liability to compensate for damages according to the relative seriousness of faults of both parties. In such cases, when it is unable to judge the relative seriousness of such faults, the liability to compensate for damages shall be shared equally.

② In cases of paragraph (1), the shipowners of both parties shall be jointly and severally liable to compensate for damages to death and injury of a third party.

[107] Article 880 (Collision due to Fault of Pilot) In cases where a ship also collides due to the fault of a pilot, a shipowner shall be liable to compensate for damages in accordance with Articles 878 and 879.

The term "collision of a ship" here means that two or more ships in the course of operation, by act or omission, cause damage to each other, to another ship, or the goods or persons on board, and shall not inquire whether direct contact has arisen.[108] Damage occurring by collision of a ship should be able to verify a significant relationship with the collision.[109]

The requirement of salvage under the Commercial Act is that a person salvages a ship in distress or its cargo and other goods on board without any duty to do so. The Act prescribes that a person who, without any duty to do so, has salvaged a seagoing ship in distress or its cargo and goods, may claim suitable remuneration for such result and it shall apply between a seagoing ship and a ship of inland navigation.[110] In cases where the parties have made a salvage contract in advance and the salvage has been made pursuant to such contract, the same provisions of the Act shall imply the terms not stipulated in the contract, unless it is contrary to the nature of the contract.[111]

6 Conclusion

As discussed, the Korean Commercial Act covers a very broad range of commerce. That is one of the reasons why there has been a call in Korea for separating the 'company part' from the Act.

Theoretically, Korea's Commercial Act is still treated as a special Act of the civil law. However, Korea has adopted the company system over the last 60 years and modified the system in accordance with the Korea's situation. Many countries which study Korea's economic growth inevitably study Korea's distinctive company structure 'Chaebul', that has advantages and disadvantages. Such large corporation as Chaebul emerged based on utilizing the merit of a stock company/corporation that is a concentrated investment for a short time, but transparency of operation has become an issue.

[108] Article 876 (Provisions Applicable to Collision of Ship) ② The term "collision of a ship" in this Section means that two or more ships in their operation, by commission or omission, cause damage to each other, to another ship, or the goods or persons on board, and shall not inquire whether direct contact has arisen.

[109] See Supreme Court Decision 70Da213 delivered on June 13, 1972.

[110] Article 882 (Requirement of Salvage) A person who, without any duty to do so, has salvaged a seagoing ship in distress on certain waters, or its cargo and other goods, may claim suitable remuneration for such result. The same shall apply to the salvage between a seagoing ship and a ship of inland navigation.

[111] Article 887 (Agreement on Salvage) ① In cases where the parties have made a salvage contract in advance and the salvage has been performed pursuant to such contract, the matters not stipulated in the salvage contract shall be as prescribed by this Section, unless contrary to the contract's nature.

The modifications in Korea's Commercial Act, especially the company part has shown the process and changes of the Korean economy. The Korean economy has grown, led by the government, and then faced the financial crisis. As a result, extensive reformation for transparency has been implemented. Such realistic changes have brought theoretical conflicts in many aspects of the existing Commercial Act.

The parts of the Commercial Act, other than the company part, take more from the conventional theory of artificial person and follow the general systems, including international law. However, they also have been through changes due to market consolidation and other reasons.

The previous modifications of the Act were made mostly after the changes in market situation occurred. In other words, the law has followed after the market. Learning from the past, more efforts to change companies through policy and law, have been made these days. The Korean Commercial Act still expects to see a lot more changes, and in that sense, more discussions on how to develop the Korean style business operation should be made down the road.

References

Choi Junseon (2010) Commercial law, 6th edn.
Chung Chan-Hyung (2010a) Synopsis of lecture on commercial law, 9th edn.
Kim Hwa-Jin (2010) Commercial law
Korean Statutes in English (www.klri.re.kr)
Korean Supreme Court Decision (1966, 1988 et al., Korean Supreme Court Ed.)
Lee Chul song (2010) Lecture on commercial law, 11th edn.
Son Jinhwa (2010) Lecture on commercial law, 2nd edn.

Economic Law: Focusing on the Monopoly Regulation and Fair Trade Act

Youngsu Shin

1 Economic Order in the Constitution and Formation of Economic Law in Korea

Norms of economic law are not so familiar in Anglo-American legal cultures. Presumably, the expression of "economic law" might have derived from the continental legalistic environment, in which the notion can be defined as all statutes legislated to form fair economic order. Generally, the contents, structures, and legislative status of economic law depend on the economic order or system of the country in which the law is legislated. For that reason, economic law in each country has its own uniqueness. So is Korean economic law. Korean economic law is based on its economic order upon the Korean Constitution.

It is said that economic order can be divided into several types, but mainly into market economies and planned economies on the basis of the mechanisms by which they coordinate the economic activities of individual economic actors. Among them, economic order under the Korean Constitution is established on the basis of capitalism (Article 23)[1] and market economy (Article 119, subparagraph 1)[2], with some exceptions.

In this context, it has been called a social market economy, mixed economy or revised capitalism. However, even though Korean economic order belongs to the social market economy, it cannot be totally the same as that of Germany which is called to be such as well, because it is just reflecting characteristics of Korean economic policies.

[1] "The property right of all citizens must be guaranteed. The contents and limitations thereof shall be determined by Act".

[2] "The economic order of the Republic of Korea shall be based on respect for the freedom and creative imitativeness of enterprises and individuals in economic affairs".

Y. Shin (✉)
Kyungpook National University, Daegu, Republic of Korea
e-mail: shinys@knu.ac.kr

Korea Legislation Research Institute, *Introduction to Korean Law*, DOI 10.1007/978-3-642-31689-0_7, © Springer-Verlag Berlin Heidelberg 2013

In fact, Korea has been adapting capitalism and a market economy as its economic order since the founding of the country, but it had promoted a so-called command economy for several decades. It was in the early 1980s that Korea changed the direction of its economic order into market economic order, especially throughout the legislation of its competition law in 1980.

As a result, the current Korean economic law is comprised of three pillars, namely: (1) the competition law (or antitrust law) to regulate areas governed by the market economic order, (2) the laws of the regulated industries to revise the problems of market failures, and (3) a series of laws established to protect economically vulnerable. The positive law which belongs to the first category is the "Monopoly Regulation and Fair Trade Act" enacted in 1980. However, the laws covering the second class above are various according to the nature of the regulated industries. For example, the Communications Business Act, the Communications Basic Act in the communications sector, the Banking Act, the Act on the Structural Improvement of the Financial Industry in the financial area, and so forth fall within the second type of economic law in Korea. The last type of economic law is regarding the protection of the economically vulnerable, such as consumers and small-medium enterprises, and thus not a few Acts including the Framework Act on Consumers are related with this category. Among them, the most important economic law in Korea is the Monopoly Regulation and Fair Trade Act (hereinafter "Fair Trade Act", or "the Act").

This Chapter will focus on the Fair Trade Act as the core of Korean economic law, and analyze its substance and characteristics.

2 Enactment and Objectives of Korean Competition Law

2.1 Enactment and Development of Korean Competition Law

Although the Constitution of the Republic of Korea promotes the principles of a market economy as the core of its economic order, the economic activities of individual players have been continuously plagued by government intervention. This problem results primarily from the fact that the Korean government, through a series of economic development plans beginning in the 1960s, endeavored to overcome structural weaknesses and to reduce economic dependency on other countries by implementing export-oriented economic development policy. In order to accomplish these goals, the Korean government depended heavily on a small number of large-scale enterprises, and the government supported these enterprises through discriminating economic policy tools, such as tax exemptions and a favorable allocation of bank loans. At the same time, the Korean government itself played a significant role, directly or indirectly, in developing key industries and the overall economic infrastructure.

The effects of these policies were numerous and diverse. While Korea was emerged as a newly developed country due to such policies, most industrial sectors became monopolistic and only a few large-scale enterprises controlled the nation's main industries. Specifically, economic power was concentrated in the hands of a few large-scale firms and business conglomerates favored by the government during the economy's export-driven development years. Worse yet, the government's market intervention impaired the functioning of the market.

On the other hand, Korea had experienced undesirable influences of monopolistic behavior by some importers. For instance, so-called 'three powder (sugar, wheat flour, cement) troubles' occurred in 1963, and the second oil shock in 1972 plunged Korean society into rapid inflation. Amidst these hardships, the Korean government began to consider legislating competition law, and it actually submitted bills of competition law to the National Assembly in 1964, 1966, 1967, 1969, and 1972.

After many complications, Korea enacted the 'Monopoly Regulation and Fair Trade Act' in 1980, which was composed of prohibiting the abuse of market-dominant positions, anti-competitive mergers, cartels, and unfair trade practices[3]. It was also the second earliest competition legislation in Asia, after Japan. The Act was an attempt to simultaneously deregulate many important industries. In 1986, it was amended to introduce new provisions aimed at reducing excessive concentrations of economic power through heavier regulation of 'Cheabol.' Since then, the Act has been amended almost 40 times from 1986 through 2010, which amounts to more than once a year. But significant modifications including the whole amendment in 1990 have not been made frequently; it has been amended about in one and a half year intervals.

In terms of its appearance and structure, the Act is very similar to the Japanese Anti-Monopoly and Fair Trade Act. However, the substantive contents of the Act were affected by lots of competition laws in many countries, such as the GWB in Germany and the Sherman Act, the Clayton Act, the FTC Act in the U.S. etc.

2.2 *Purpose and Structure of the Fair Trade Act*

The Fair Trade Act pursues various objectives. According to Article 1, regarding the purposes of the Act, it seeks to promote fair and free competition, thereby encouraging creative enterprise activities, to protect consumers and to strive for balanced development of the national economy, by preventing any abuse of market-dominating positions by entrepreneurs and any excessive concentration of economic power, and by regulating undue collusion and unfair trade practices.

Upon this stipulation, the purposes of the Fair Trade Act are divided into the direct goal (to promote fair and free competition) and the ultimate goal (to encourage creative enterprise activities, to protect consumers, and to strive for balanced development of the national economy). As a matter of fact, however, in

[3] Act No. 3320. The Act was legislated on December 31, 1980 and came into force on April 1, 1981.

practice a more important objective of the Act is to promote the former one (fair and free competition).

In order to promote and ensure free competition in the market, the Fair Trade Act regulates economic players and activities that could undermine conditions of free competition, such as monopolies, oligopolies, mergers, collaborative activities, and cartels. With regard to monopolies and oligopolies, the Fair Trade Act does not explicitly prohibit the possession or acquisition of this sort of power. Instead, it forbids the abuse of a market-dominant position. In other words, the Act restricts anti-competitive or unfair behavior of market-dominant firms, rather than prohibiting monopolization or attempts to establish a monopoly. The Fair Trade Act also prohibits various anti-competitive methods and unfair trade practices under the rubric of "unfair business practices" in order to maintain fair competition and trade.

In this context, the substantive components of the Act can be divided into three categories on the basis of the objectives each seeks to achieve: (1) regulations to promote and ensure free competition; (2) regulations to ensure fair trade; and (3) regulations to reduce the concentration of economic power.

When it comes to the scope of the Act, in consideration of the fact that the purpose of the Fair Trade Act is to encourage creative business activities and protect consumers as well as facilitate balanced development of the national economy by promoting fair and free competition through the regulation of unfair collective activities of business operators (Article 1), the fact that the business operator who conducts unfair collective activities is stipulated to be the "operator of manufacturing business, service business and other businesses" and is not limited to domestic business operators (Article 2), and the fact that there is a need to include foreign business operators in the scope of the application of the Fair Trade Act in cases where an activity in a foreign country affects the domestic market, the Fair Trade Act shall be applied within the limit of the effect on the domestic market of a consensus, if a foreign business operator reaches a consensus jointly with another business operator to limit competition and that such consensus includes and affects the domestic market.[4] Furthermore, the Act made sure that it shall apply even to activities carried out overseas when they are deemed to affect the domestic market since 2005.

3 Regulation of Anti-Competitive Practices

3.1 *Prohibition of Abuse of Market-Dominant Position*

3.1.1 Definition of Market-Dominant Position

Under the Fair Trade Act, no market-dominant firm shall commit any abusive act. In the Act, a market-dominant firm refers to any enterprise enjoying market

[4] Supreme Court Decision 2004Du11275, March 24, 2006.

dominance and possibly determining, maintaining, or changing the prices, quantity, or quality of goods or services, or other terms and conditions of business as a supplier or customer in a particular business area, individually or jointly with other enterprises.

For the determination of market dominance, the relevant product market as the subject matter of transaction in a specific category of transactions associated with the competition issue and the relevant transactional and geographical market should all be delineated, and the potential for market dominance in that particular market should be determined. The 'relevant product market' encompasses a market consisting of a specific category of products in a competitive relationship which is generally able to suppress an exercise of market dominance by a market-dominant firm, and specifically refers to the totality of commodities which can be substituted in sale or purchase in response to a significant price increase or decrease for a reasonable period of time as to the currently traded goods. The scope of such a market is delineated in consideration of the price, function, and similarity of utility of traded goods, purchasers' recognition of the replacement, and related purchase behavior, as well as sellers' recognition of the replacement, and related management modes of decision, including a socially and economically acknowledged similarity and homogeneity of the business category. On top of that, the speed of technological development, other products necessary for the production of the commodities at issue, and the market situation of other commodities produced using the commodities at issue, and the ease of replacement in terms of time, economic, and legal factors are considered. The 'relevant geographical market' encompasses a regional area where firms in general competition are located. And specifically, it means an area to which a representative purchaser or seller turns for the alternative supplier or buyer when the prices in a specific locality increase or decrease significantly for a considerable period of time while the prices of all of the other localities remain uniform. The scope of the market is determined in consideration of prices, characteristics of the commodities at issue, production quantity, business capacity, transportation costs of the sellers, the purchasers' recognition of alternative places to purchase them and related business modes of decision, and the ease of changing places to purchase them in terms of time, economic and legal factors. In addition, technological speed, market situations, etc., such as other products necessary for the production of the commodities at issue, and the market situation of other commodities produced using the commodities at issue, should all be considered. Trends in free trade and globalization make free import and export more feasible, and related goods circulating in the domestic market include imported commodities from overseas in addition to domestic products. Where the importation of related commodities is not that difficult, then the possibility of such importation should be considered in determination of market dominance potential.

However, as it is not easy to assess whether a firm possesses a market-dominant position, the Fair Trade Act includes a presumptive clause that deems a firm to be market-dominant if it meets the conditions stated in Article 4.[5]

On the other hand, the Fair Trade Act requires that the Korea Fair Trade Commission (hereinafter, the "KFTC" or "Commission") be established and enforce measures designed to promote competition in markets where monopolies and oligopolies have long been entrenched. Korean economic policy reflects a clear understanding that it is impossible to render a market more competitive simply by forbidding the abuse of a market-dominant position (Article 3).

3.1.2 Abusive Behavior

The Act defines abusive behavior as any act of determining, maintaining, or changing the price of commodities or services unreasonably; unreasonably controlling the sale of commodities or provision of services; unreasonably interfering with the business activities of other enterprises; unreasonably impeding the participation of new competitors; unfairly excluding competitive enterprises; or considerably harming the interest of consumers.

Especially, the first two types of behavior (called 'explosive abuse') are referred to as the most remarkable characteristics of the Fair Trade Act in that such allows the competition authority to judge whether some price level is fair or not. In this context, the approach the Fair Trade Act takes toward monopoly is similar to that of the EU or German competition law, not to U.S. or Japanese.[6]

However, the types of abusive acts overlap with the unfair business practices in Article 23. For instance, for a refusal of transaction to constitute an act of status abuse by a market-dominant firm under subparagraph 3 of Article 3-2 (1) of the Fair Trade Act, it must be evaluated as to whether it is a conduct which unfairly restricts the business activities of another enterprise.

The "unfairness" here is different from unfairness of a refusal as an act of unfair transaction under subparagraph 1 of Article 23 (1) of the Fair Trade Act. Thus, the meaning of unfairness as it relates to a refusal of transaction by a market-dominant enterprise should be evaluated or interpreted independently in light of legislative purposes, such as "facilitation of competition in a monopolistic or oligopolistic market." It is not sufficient to identify unfairness in all cases where a market-dominant enterprise refuses a transaction with a specific enterprise, e.g., a partner of

[5] A firm with any of the following market shares in a particular business area (excluding an enterprise whose annual sales and/or purchases in a regular field of trade amount to less than KRW4 billion) shall be presumed to be a market-dominant firm:

1. The market share of one enterprise is 50/100 or more.
2. The total market share of three or less enterprises is 75/100 or more, excluding those whose market share is less than 10/100.

[6] As is well known, Article 2 of the Sherman Act prohibits monopolization itself, instead of regulating abusive behavior from a market-dominant position.

each transaction with an unfair intent or objective, or simply because a specific enterprise suffers a disadvantage, such that its business activities were restricted or likely to be restricted due to the refusal. Above all, unfairness should be recognized only where a refusal of transaction can be deemed perpetrated with an intent or objective of maintaining or reinforcing monopolistic status in the market, e.g., artificially influencing market order by restricting free competition in the market, and with determination that the refusal is likely to have an anti-competition effect, from an objective point of view. Therefore, since a defendant alleges that refusal of transaction by a market-dominant enterprise constitutes an abuse of a market dominance status, the defendant must prove that the refusal of transaction has the intent and objective as an act likely to affect the restriction of competition, such as a price increase of goods, decrease in output, harm to innovation, decrease in the number of capable competitors, decrease in diversity, etc. If any of the above effects is shown to have actually been materialized, it can be inferred that the act was likely to restrict competition, and such was intended or planned. Otherwise, upon considering various factors as a whole, such as the circumstance or motive of the refusal of transaction, attitudes, characteristics of the related market, degree of disadvantage due to the refusal, fluctuations in price or output, harm to innovation and reduction in diversity, etc., it should be determined whether the act of refusal had the intent or objective to effectively restrain competition. In addition, the related market affected by the restraint of competition should include not only the market to which a market-dominant enterprise or competitor belongs, but also the supply market providing raw materials, parts or half-finished parts for the production of the commodities of the market at issue, or the demand market which produces a new product upon receipt of the commodities from the market at issue.[7]

3.2 Merger Regulation

As for mergers, the Fair Trade Act prohibits those that would substantially restrict competition in a relevant market, while allowing mergers as an exception when the efficiency-enhancing effects of a merger far exceed the potential harms of restrained competition, or when the merger involves an enterprise whose paid-in-capital is less than the total assets on the balance sheet for a considerable period of time, thus deeming its revitalization impossible.[8] Like in other jurisdictions, the review of a merger in Korea requires a sophisticated process to accurately define the relevant market and assess anti-competitive effects. For the same reason, lots of economic analysis is fulfilled in the process of reviewing a merger.

---

[7] Supreme Court en banc Decision 2002Du8626, November 22, 2007 < Case concerning POSCO's Refusal to Supply Hot Rolled Steel Coils>.

[8] The justification under the Act follows the horizontal merger guideline of the US DOJ.

Under Article 7 (1) of the Act, the methods of mergers are classified into five types, namely: acquisition or ownership of stocks of other companies; an officer's concurrent holding of a position in another company (hereinafter referred to as "concurrent holding of an officer's position" by an officer or an employee (referring to a person who continues to engage in the affairs of the company although he/she is not an officer; the same shall apply hereinafter)); merger with another company; acquisition through transfer, lease, or acceptance by the mandate of the entire or main part of the business of another company or acquisition through the transfer of the whole or main part of the fixed assets used for the business of another company (hereinafter referred to as "acquisition through the transfer of business"); and participation in the establishment of a new company.

However, recognizing the difficulty of determining whether a merger substantially restrains competition, the Fair Trade Act has introduced a presumptive clause that made certain mergers presumptively illegal.[9]

3.3 *Prohibition of Cartels*

Like other competition legislation, the Fair Trade Act basically prohibits collaborative activities that unreasonably restrain competition, which is generally called a cartel or horizontal agreement in other jurisdictions. The attitude of enforcement toward cartel in Korea can be said to be quite strict. Administrative surcharges have been mainly imposed on cartels, particularly on such hardcore or naked cartels as horizontal price fixing, bid-rigging, market allocation, etc.

---

[9] Article 7 (4) raises the presumption that competition is substantially restrained in a particular business area in cases:

1. where the aggregate of the market share of a company taking part in a combination of enterprises (referring to the aggregate of market shares of the affiliated companies; the same shall apply herein) falls under any of the following categories:

   A. The aggregate market share of the company concerned satisfies the presumptive requirements for a market-dominant enterprise.
   B. The aggregate market share of the company concerned is the largest in the relevant business area.
   C. The aggregate market share of the company concerned exceeds the market share of the company with the second largest market share (referring to a company with the largest market share besides the company concerned) by not less than 25 % of the aggregate market share.

2. where a large company combines enterprises directly or through a person with special interest in accordance with the following requirements:

   A. A combination of enterprises in a particular business area where small or medium-sized companies covered by the Framework Act on Small and Medium Enterprises account for not less than two-thirds of the entire market share.
   B. A combination of enterprises wherein the combined company has a market share of not less than 5 %.

Meanwhile, the Act also defines moderate cartels, such as restricting the kinds and standards of goods or services, joint-venture, preventing the establishment or extension of facilities or the installation of equipment necessary for the production of goods under the same requirement for illegality.

However, in Korea, cartels may be permitted if deemed necessary for achieving certain desirable purposes, including: (1) industrial rationalization; (2) promotion of research and technological development; (3) resolution of economic depression; (4) promotion of industrial restructuring; (5) rationalization of terms of trade; and (6) strengthening the competitiveness of small-and medium-sized businesses. As proof of a meeting of the minds is both crucial and difficult in these cases, the Fair Trade Act provides that when two or more enterprises commit any of the acts listed in Article 19 (1), the parties shall be presumed to be in a cartel, and, therefore, substantially restraining competition (despite the absence of an explicit agreement to engage in such act).

However, under Article 19 (5), if two or more enterprises commit any of the acts listed in the subparagraphs of paragraph (1), it shall be assumed that the enterprises have agreed to conduct an act in association falling under any subparagraph of paragraph (1) when it is highly probable to reckon that they did the act in association regarding the characteristic of the relevant transaction, goods or services, economic reasons and ripple effects of the relevant activity, frequency, mode, etc. of contact among the enterprises. On the other hand, any firm subject to the presumption under Article 19 (5) of the Act may rebut the presumption by proving that an apparently identical or similar act from the other parties was done independently from each other under each business decision without any actual agreement to engage in a collusive act, or by demonstrating and proving circumstances justifying that an apparently identical or similar act was not an agreement to engage in a collusive act.[10]

3.4 *Prohibition of Unfair Trade Practices*

3.4.1 Overview of Prohibition of Unfair Trade Practices

The Fair Trade Act prohibits various anti-competitive methods and unfair trade practices under the rubric of "unfair business practices" in order to maintain fair competition and trade. The Act thereby forbids enterprises from engaging in any act listed under Article 23(1) that is likely to impede fair competition and/or trade or to cause affiliated corporations or other enterprises to commit such an act. In order to effectively prohibit these "unfair trades or practices," the types of, and criteria for, such trades or practices are clearly set forth by presidential decree. The area Article

[10] Supreme Court Decision 2002Du12052, January 28, 2005.

23 covers is very comprehensive so that around 70 % of cases the KFTC handles annually are related to unfair trade practices.[11]

The types of unfair business practices are specified in the provision of the Act. Those are acts of unfairly refusing to make any transaction or discriminative treatment against a certain trading party; acts designed to unfairly exclude competitors; unfairly coercing or inducing customers of competitors to deal with the enterprise in question; engaging in trade with a transacting party by unfairly taking advantage of its position in the business area; trading under terms and conditions that unfairly restrict or disrupt business activities; assisting a person with a special interest or other companies by providing advanced payment, loans, manpower, immovable assets, stocks and bonds, or intellectual property or by transacting under substantially favorable terms; any other act that threatens to impair fair trade, other than those listed in the above.

3.4.2 Discriminatory Treatment

The Enforcement Decree of the Act details 25 unfair practices. Among them, Article 36(1) of the Enforcement Decree states that 'price discrimination,' 'discrimination in trade terms and conditions,' and 'discrimination by groups' constitute unfair trade practices only when performed 'unfairly.' Among these, price discrimination means transacting at a significantly favorable or unfavorable price depending on trade region or trading party. So this offense will be constituted in cases where there is a significant difference in price depending on trade region or trading party, and such difference in price is so unfair as to create a concern of impeding fair trade in the market. Furthermore, considering the legislative intent of regulating price discrimination and the above provisions comprehensively, the determination of whether a price discrimination is unfair should depend on whether such price discrimination causes a concern that fair trade may be impeded, based on comprehensive consideration of various circumstances such as the degree of price discrimination, the degree of anticompetitive effect of the price discrimination on the business activities of the competitors or trading parties and on the market, necessity of resulting in the price discrimination in terms of business policy, the circumstances that led to the price discrimination, etc.[12]

On the other hand, subparagraph 3(b) in the same states that 'discrimination in favor of affiliates' constitutes an unfair trade practice unless there is a justifiable reason for such a practice. The legislative intent of this different style of provision is that: such a conduct may sustain the existence of enterprise groups' uncompetitive affiliates which will harm the effectiveness of the economy and cause additional concentration of economic power, and thereby is more likely to impede fair trade compared to other types of discriminatory conducts; therefore, if an act apparently

[11] The number of such cases from 1981 through 2010 is over 8,000. KFTC (2011), p.59.

[12] Supreme Court Decision 2004Du4703, December 7, 2006.

conforms with such a conduct, the act will automatically be deemed to be in danger of impeding fair trade and the party who has performed the act shall be burdened with the proof of proving otherwise.[13]

3.4.3 Unfairly Excluding Competitors

Article 23 (1) of the previous Monopoly Regulation and Fair Trade Act enumerates an 'act of unfairly excluding competitors' as one of the practices likely to impede fair trade, and Paragraph (2) 2 of the same Article determines its type. Article 36 (1) 1 of the Enforcement Decree of the Act stipulates unfair bargaining as one of the types of practice conforming to Article 23 (1) of the Act and defines it as the 'practices which are likely to exclude a competitor of one's own or subsidiary company by continuously supplying goods or services at a substantially lower price than the cost necessary for supply without justifiable grounds or by supplying goods or services at an unjustly lower price'.[14] A so-called ongoing unfair bargaining under the former part of subparagraph 1 (c) refers to an enterprise's continuous supply of goods or services at an unreasonably low price. If a practice falls under this category, it will likely to be deemed to impede fair trade 'without any good reason.' However, the so-called continuous unfair bargaining prescribed under the latter part of subparagraph 1 (c) shows that justifiable supply of goods or services at a low price is hardly considered an impediment to fair trade in itself. As a result, supply of goods or services at a low price is an act impeding fair trade only when it is done 'unfairly.' Whether there is unfairness should be decided according to the possibility of impeding fair trade after the overall review of various factors in a given situation, such as motives and objectives behind each unfair bargaining, the extent of low price, the possibility of repetition, the characteristics of goods or services in unfair bargaining and its market situation, the behavior's position in the market, the effect on competitors, etc.[15]

3.4.4 Abuse of Positions in Trade

In the meantime, the Fair Trade Act defines 'enterprise's abuse of a position in trade' instead as a type of unfair trade practices. This kind of unfair trade practice is frequently involved in civil disputes between private entities, so there have been some arguments that the Act should have not intervened these sorts of disputes in

---

[13] Supreme Court Decision 2000Du833, December 11, 2001.

[14] This act is treated like 'predatory pricing', but requirements for illegality of an unfair bargaining are different from those of predatory pricing in U.S. Supreme Court decisions in that the former doesn't ask to show the probability of recoupment. But the Korean Supreme Court decision regarding the requirement seems not to be clear. See Supreme Court Decision 99Du4688 delivered on June 12, 2001; Shin (2004).

[15] Supreme Court Decision 99Du4686, June 12, 2001.

Korea. But the Korean Supreme Court has ruled that, for the purposes of the Act, it cannot be viewed that the application of the Fair Trade Act shall be excluded solely on the ground that the pertinent case is a civil case which involves disputes concerning the interpretation of contract.[16]

The legislative intent was that an enterprise in a comparatively advantageous position should be prohibited from giving another party a transactional disadvantage by abusing its position, thus it establishes a fair trade between transactional parties who have a different economic standing. In determining whether a position is advantageous, the following factors should be considered: (a) market conditions, (b) differences between the parties' abilities to conduct business, and (c) the characteristics of the goods which are the subject matter of transaction. To determine whether a behavior of a party resulted in a transactional disadvantage to the other party by using his/her position, we should consider such factors as the intention, objective, effect and influence of the behavior, characteristics of the goods, situation of the transaction, degree of the prevailing position of the enterprise, and contents and degree of disadvantage to the other party. Furthermore, whether there was a deviation from the practice of normal transaction and whether it may impede a fair trade should be considered.[17]

Meanwhile, the Enforcement Decree of the Act subdivides abusive behavior into the following categories; (a) coercion to purchase: forcing other party to the transaction to purchase goods or services that the other party does not wish to purchase; (b) coercion to provide benefits: forcing the transaction party to provide economic benefits such as money, goods, or services; (c) imposing a sales target: imposing a target on the transaction party for transactions involving the goods or services you supply and forcing the other party to meet the target; (d) imposing disadvantages: establishing or modifying transaction conditions to the disadvantage of the transaction party or placing the other party at a disadvantage in the course of carrying out the transaction using methods other than those described in items (a) through (d); (e) interference in management: interfering in the management activities of the transaction party by requiring it to obtain approval or directions from you when it hires or fires officers or employees or by restricting the scope of goods, scale of facilities, quantity produced, or details of the transaction.

Among them, Article 23 (1) of the previous Monopoly Regulation and Fair Trade Act stipulated, in item (d), an 'act of making trade with a certain transaction party by unfairly taking advantage of his/her position in trade' as an unfair trade practice. Pursuant to Paragraph (2) of the same Article, the previous Enforcement Decree of the Fair Trade Act described the categories or standards for unfair trade practices. In addition, Article 36 (1) 4 (f) of the previous Enforcement Decree stated 'creation of disadvantages' (i.e. 'setting or changing the terms of business to the disadvantage of the transaction party in ways other than those stated in subparagraphs 1 through 3, and causing disadvantages in the process of

[16] Supreme Court Decision 2007Du20812, October 29, 2009.

[17] Supreme Court Decision 97Nu19427, June 9, 2000.

transaction') also as a practice under Article 23 (1) of Fair Trade Act. Accordingly, the mere fact that a practice is somewhat disadvantageous to the other party is not sufficient for a practice to constitute 'imposing a disadvantage' as described in item f (iv). In order for a practice to constitute 'imposing disadvantage,' terms of trade must be set or changed by the inappropriate use of business status, equal in effect to the acts prescribed in (a) through(c), i.e. forcing purchase, forcing payment of profits, forcing sales figures, etc. and such an act must potentially impede fair trade by inappropriately causing disadvantage to the other party, in light of the field's trade customs. Moreover, the decision of whether an act inappropriately gives disadvantage to the other party must be based on an overall consideration of the following matters; the nature and probability of the disadvantages that might affect the other party due to the terms of trade in question; the extent of limitations on competition that will arise between the parties in their ordinary business transactions; the business customs and business forms in the related field; effect on the general order of competition; and the provisions in the relevant statutes.[18]

3.5 Other Means to Regulate Anti-Competitive Practices

3.5.1 Prohibited Activities of Trade Organizations

No trade organization shall commit any of the following acts; (1) unfairly restricting competition including acts falling under the items in Article 19, (2) restricting the present or future number of firms in any business area, (3) unreasonably restricting the business matters or activities of member firms (referring to a firm as a member of the trade organization; the same shall apply hereinafter), (4) inducing a person to engage in unfair business practices under the subparagraphs of Article 23 (1) or to engage in practices of resale price setting under Article 29 or assist a person in committing such act. In numerous cases, trade associations have been involved in and even actually lead cartels in Korea.

A trade organization as an entity for promoting members' common interests is expected to restrict members' business activities to a certain extent to achieve its purposes. However, if its resolution undermines fair and free competition among members, then it constitutes an "act of unreasonably restricting the business contents or activities of member firms" under Article 26(1) 3 of the Fair Trade Act.

The legislative intent of providing an 'act unreasonably restricting the business terms or activities of member firms' as prohibited activities of trade organization stipulated in Article 26 (1) 3 of the Fair Trade Act.[19]

Meanwhile, when an act violates the provisions of Article 26, the KFTC may order corrective measures, not only upon the trade organization concerned, but, if necessary, also on the member enterprises.

---

[18] Supreme Court Decision 2000Du833, December 11, 2001.

[19] Supreme Court Decision 2001Du175, June 15, 2001 [Revocation of a Corrective Order, etc.].

3.5.2 Restrictions on Resale Price Maintenance

The Fair Trade Act also prohibits any act that can be considered as resale price maintenance (Article 29). However, this provision shall not apply to cases wherein there are justifiable reasons in terms of the maximum price maintenance preventing the transaction of commodities or services in excess of the specified prices. Remarkably, the Korean Supreme Court has recently made a decision that justifiable grounds should be considered, even in cases of minimum price maintenance.[20]

Additionally, certain resale price maintenance is allowed. Exceptions include situations where the actions are deemed justifiable, and those actions regarding publications specified in the Presidential Decree, or commodities meeting all of the conditions of Article 29(2) and that the KFTC has designated in advance as being eligible for Resale Price Maintenance.

3.5.3 Restrictions on Conclusion of Unfair International Contracts

Additionally, the Fair Trade Act prohibits firms or trade associations from entering into international agreements or contracts that provide for conduct constituting unreasonable restraints of competition, unfair trade or business practices, or resale price maintenance. When an act violates the provisions of Article 29 (1), the KFTC may order the relevant enterprise to discontinue such act, publicly announce the receipt of a corrective order, or take other necessary corrective measures against such conduct.

But it is known that there is no case infringe this provision so far.

4 Suppressing Concentration of Economic Power by Business Conglomerates (Chaebols)

4.1 Preliminary Observations of Chaebols

The business climate in Korea has been dominated by numerous pyramidal conglomerate groups which is called chaebol. Owing to the aid of financial affiliates and Government, they have been able to control the groups and specific industries for a few decades. Still, chaebols remain crucial drivers of Korea's economy, and each of them controls numerous listed and unlisted companies. For an instance, the top 30 chaebols currently account for roughly half of total corporate assets in Korea.

The reason how chaebols became so large, and how they have maintained their continued growth to this day is at least partially explained by their powerful ability.

---

[20] Supreme Court Decision 2009Du9543, November 25, 2010; Supreme Court Decision 2010Du9976, March, 10, 2011.

That is, controlling families have displayed in maintaining preferential terms of finance and large stores of internal capital markets through the progression of Korea's ever-changing financial environment. It all began in the early stages of Korea's economic development, when the chaebols enjoyed a virtual monopoly over capital.

In some aspects, it is true that there are some efficiency exists within chaebol structures, but it is also the fact that the efficiency has been eroded since the 1970s. The growth of the Chaebols soon became a burden to the Korean economic policy.

4.2 *Legislative Policies Against Chaebols in Korea: Past and Present*

During the later 1980s and throughout most of the 1990s, the Korean government tended to focus increasingly on regulating the concentration of economic power by chaebols. In 1986, the KFTC introduced a system that, on an annual basis, ranked chaebols according to their asset volume. Since 1992, cross-debt guarantees were prohibited. This prohibition was reinforced following the outbreak of the financial crisis in late of 1990s. Especially, the problem of a huge gap between ownership and voting rights within chaebols has been treated as a significant issue by Korea's law makers and regulators. In the wake of the crisis, a huge shakeout of the finance industry took place, with many nonbank financial institutions and banks being shut down, merged, or having their default assets bought out by the government's Korea Asset Management Corporation.[21] With the IMF urging, great strides were made in reducing mutual debt guarantees among chaebol affiliates. Lots of the impressive institutional progress, however, has occurred in the areas of investor protection and decision-making governance.[22] And these measures have not adequately addressed the vast gap between ownership and voting rights. In particular, because a controlling family often funnels control over its pyramid through a privately-owned firm, it is very difficult for outside shareholders to exert any influence on the pyramid structure as a whole.[23]

The government did occasionally look to policies aimed at enhancing the competitive environment. Particularly, some specific type of 'unfair trade practices' are specified in the Fair Trade Act which includes the act of assisting a person with special interest or other companies by providing advanced payment, loans,

---

[21] See id. at 192.

[22] See, Jwa and Lee (2004), and Song (2002). Suffice it to say that arguments have already arisen within legal academia that shareholders have been given too much power vis-a-vis directors. See, e.g., Park and Lee (2003).

[23] For example, control of the Samsung Group is channeled through Samsung Everland, a privately-held firm controlled by the son of the group's chairman.

manpower, immovable assets, stocks and bonds, or intellectual properties or by transacting under substantially favorable terms.[24]

4.3 Current Regulation of Chaebols by Fair Trade Act

The Fair Trade Act first defines "chaebol" as a large business group, and then establishes control over groups that fit this criteria provided therein. Subsidiaries belonging to these business groups are subject to the strict regulations provided for in the Fair Trade Act, including the prohibition of cross-shareholdings and debt guarantees for affiliated corporations. In addition, improper subsidies and other forms of subsidiary support that could hamper fair trade and competition are prohibited.

Currently, the Fair Trade Act controls holding companies and activities between subsidiaries belonging to large business groups in order to reduce the concentration of economic power. Its mechanisms of control include regulation of cross-shareholdings, debt guarantees for affiliated corporations, and anti-competitive subsidies.

The establishment of holding companies was prohibited in 1987, but has been allowed since 1999 in order to encourage company restructuring. However, there are still stringent restrictions on the establishment of holding companies because they can easily become a means to concentrate economic power. However, any company belonging to a Business Group whose total assets, etc., fall under some shall not acquire or own stocks of an affiliated company acquiring or owning its stock. And, any company belonging to a Business Group falling under some shall not give debt guarantees to its domestic affiliated companies, principally.

On the other, the stipulation regarding total amount of equity investment was deleted in 2009.

5 Enforcement and Remedies Under Fair Trade Act

5.1 Enforcement Agency: Korea Fair Trade Commission

The Fair Trade Act is enforced by the Korea Fair Trade Commission (hereinafter, the "KFTC" or "Commission"), a quasi-judicial regulatory agency. The Commission is established under the jurisdiction of the Prime Minister for the purpose of independently promoting the objectives of this Act.[25] The KFTC is composed of

---

[24] Sung-Hee Jwa, In-Kwon Lee, *id,* at 10–11.

[25] The Fair Trade Commission carries out its function as one of the central administrative organizations pursuant to Article 2 (Establishment and Structures of the Central Administrative Organization) of the Government Organization Act. <Amended on August 3, 2007>

nine commissioners, including a chairman, a vice-chairman, three standing, and four non-standing commissioners. The commissioners are appointed from among persons with experience or specialized knowledge in the field of monopoly regulation and fair trade or consumers and who meet the same qualifications. The President of Korea appoints the chairperson and vice chairperson at the recommendation of the Prime Minister, and the other commissioners at the recommendation of the chairperson.

Meetings of the Commission shall fall into the following two categories: meetings consisting of all members (hereinafter 'Plenary Session') and meetings consisting of three members, including a standing commissioner (hereinafter referred to as 'Chamber'). The Plenary Session shall deliberate on and determine the following matters: (1) matters related to the interpretation and application of Acts and subordinate statutes and public notices under the jurisdiction of the Fair Trade Commission, (2) matters involving an appeal, (3) matters whose resolutions have not been made in a Chamber, or those that have been decided to be referred to the Plenary Session by a Chamber, (4) matters required to establish or amend regulations or public notices, (5) matters having substantial economic impact or those that should be dealt with by the Plenary Session itself.

The Commission's jurisdiction encompasses virtually all antitrust enforcement in Korea. It investigates suspected violations and, when a violation of the Act is found, the KFTC issues corrective measures and attempts to ensure the violator's compliance with such measures; if necessary, surcharges are imposed, and criminal prosecution is pursued against the violator (of course by public prosecutors). Any party that wishes to claim damages resulting from a violation of the Fair Trade Act may bring a private suit against the violator after the Commission's corrective measures become definite and final. Furthermore, a public prosecutor may indict the violator for the violation of the Act.

A Secretariat within the Commission is responsible for the day-to-day affairs of the Commission, and consists of a secretary general, six bureaus, and four regional offices.

5.2 Administrative Procedures

5.2.1 Investigation Procedures

The enforcement procedures set forth in the Fair Trade Act include the investigation of suspected violations, the ability to order or recommend corrective measures, and the power to impose surcharges.

Under the Fair Trade Act, anyone who discovers a violation may report it to the Commission, and the Commission has the jurisdiction to conduct an investigation. However, an injured party has no legal right to require the Commission to undertake an investigation. Investigations are generally conducted by the Secretariat through authority delegated by the Commission. If it is deemed necessary, designated staff members of the Secretariat may take appropriate measures to collect information, examine materials at the suspected violator's place of business, or summon the parties to an investigative hearing.

When the Commission determines that there has been a violation, under certain circumstances, the Commission may simply recommend that the violator comply with specified corrective measures. The violator must notify the Commission of its intentions to comply with the suggested measures, and if it does so notify, corrective measures pursuant to the Fair Trade Act are a sufficient remedy. In cases where the alleged violator does not agree to take voluntary action, the Commission makes a final enforcement decision after giving the alleged violator and any interested third parties an opportunity to present their opinions. The final decision may include an administrative order for correction of the illegal conduct, a surcharge, or a criminal prosecution. Corrective orders include, among others, cease-and-desist orders, orders to lower prices, and public acknowledgment of violations. Surcharges can be imposed on those who violate most of the substantive provisions of the Fair Trade Act. In imposing surcharges, the Commission must take into account the nature and extent of a violation, the duration and frequency of that violation, and the resultant benefit accrued.

Interested parties may appeal the Commission's decisions to the Seoul High Court, and ultimately, to the Supreme Court.

5.2.2 Corrective Measures

If a violation of the Act has been committed, the Fair Trade Commission may establish the standards for correction and recommend that the relevant enterprise or enterprises' organization comply with those standards. Furthermore, the Commission can decide to issue an order of correction. Any party dissatisfied with the measures taken by the Fair Trade Commission pursuant to this Act may file an appeal stating the reasons with the Fair Trade Commission within 30 days of receiving notice of the said measure. And also, any person wishing to file a lawsuit in response to any measure taken by the Fair Trade Commission under this Act may do so within 30 days of the date of receipt of notice of the disposition in question or a written decision of the Fair Trade Commission against the appeal.

In the meantime, if an order of corrective measures under the Fair Trade Act is too specific, an Order would be meaningless as inapplicable to the daily numerous transactions with different details. Therefore, an order cannot avoid being inclusive or abstract due to its essential nature. Further, the purport of the system for order of corrective measures justifies an interpretation that an Order may not only suspend past acts of violations but also prohibit similarly patterned acts that may be repeated in the near future.[26]

[26] Supreme Court Full Bench Decision 2001Du5347, February 20, 2003.

5.2.3 Surcharges

The KFTC can impose surcharges upon violators. In imposing surcharges under this Act, the Fair Trade Commission must take into account the nature and extent of the unlawful practice, duration and frequency of the unlawful practice, benefit accrued by the unlawful practice. But in cases of mergers, the KFTC used to impose a fine to compel performance instead.

As for the scope of imposing surcharges, the Supreme Court said that where an enterprise engaged in so called unfair collaborative acts jointly with other enterprises, the Fair Trade Commission may impose a surcharge on such an enterprise on the basis of the sales revenue generated during the period of violation. The sales revenue should be adjusted by the rebate given due to inferior quality or damage of the goods. The scope of the goods or services of unfair collaborative conduct, which needs to be defined to obtain the sales revenue as a basis for a surcharge, should be determined on a case-by-case basis, in light of the following factors: the type and characteristics of the transaction, the territory in which sales took place, the transaction party, and the stage of transaction of the goods and services included in the agreement of enterprises engaged in unfair collaborative acts.[27]

5.3 *Private Actions*

A party who suffers loss by a violation of the Fair Trade Act can bring a private suit against the violators for damages. Under the Act, then, any enterprise or enterprises' organization violating the provisions of this Act and consequently causing loss to a person shall be liable to compensate such person's loss. If the enterprise itself or the enterprises' organization itself proves that it did not intend to commit any offense, and no error is found on its part, however, this does not apply.

When proving necessary facts to verify the amount of damage considering the characteristics of such facts is extremely difficult even though the occurrence of damage is deemed to be the result of a violation of the provision, the court shall decide the substantial amount of damage based on the result of evidentiary investigation and intent of overall pleading.

Meanwhile, the disputants can solve disputes related to acts in violation of Article 23 (1) (prohibition on unfair business practices) through mediation process established at the Korea Fair Trade Mediation Committee.[28]

---

[27] Supreme Court Decision 2001Du10387, January 10, 2003.

[28] In case mediation is realized, an agreement shall be deemed to have been reached as in the mediation protocol signed by the subjects of conflict and participating committee members.

5.4 Criminal Prosecution

In general, violations of the substantive provisions of the Fair Trade Act and failure to comply with resulting corrective measures are punishable by imprisonment of up to 2 years or fines not exceeding 150 million won. Serious offenses can be prosecuted through public action only after a complaint is filed by the Commission. If necessary, however, the KFTC shall file complaints together with the Prosecutor General for cases involving the serious offenses. Because the violation is deemed gross and considerable, it may substantially suppress competition. And the KFTC may not withdraw the complaint after prosecution has commenced.

6 Assessment on Effectiveness of Act

6.1 Preceding 30 Years of Korean Competition Law

It is 30 years since the Fair Trade Act was enacted in 1981. It is said that enforcement of the Act has greatly contributed to fair trade and free competition in the market, as well as to lessening anti-competitive or unfair trade practices. The Fair Trade Act and the KFTC are called as one of the most successful example in the world competition community which have developed in a short period of time (Shin 2011).

The Act, however, is not free from criticism—especially from academic and business circles. In general, the Act doesn't seem to be that successful in converting a monopolistic or oligopolistic market structure into a competitive one. Especially, since the deletion of the total amount of equity investment in 2009, the status of the concentration of economic power by Chaebol is getting more serious.

It can be started with the reason behind the Fair Trade Act's failure to reform the market structure. First, the Fair Trade Act is inherently flawed. Generally speaking, monopolization or oligopolization occurs when a fraction of existing competitors succeeds in gaining a controlling share of the market through a technological advancement or accumulation of capital. In Korea, however, the government is partly responsible for manifestation of monopolization as it was the government that created a number of monopolies through the favors it bestowed upon a few large-scale enterprises during the process of economic development. Moreover, while the United States has developed antitrust laws to prevent markets from becoming monopolized or oligopolized, the Korean government did not institute its own antitrust legislation until monopolization had permeated most domestic markets. Therefore, the Fair Trade Act faced serious obstacles from the very beginning.

Second, the Fair Trade Act might have been more effective had the government rigorously enforced the Fair Trade Act by regulating abuses of market power. Unfortunately, this did not happen. This becomes very clear when we compare the Korean experience with the implementation of antitrust legislation in Germany—a system that took an approach to antitrust regulation very similar to that of Korea. If we reflect on the past practices of the KFTC, we see that the Commission was not terribly aggressive in its regulation of monopolies, mergers, and collaborative activities until at least 1997.

There are many explanations for the Fair Trade Act's failure to reduce the concentration of economic power. The most persuasive reason is that the Fair Trade Act, in its current state, is inherently incapable of bringing about the desired reduction of concentration in economic power. To regulate the concentration of economic power effectively, careful study of the causes of concentration, and appropriate measures for reducing or alleviating such concentration should have been conducted before the Fair Trade Act was drafted. As a result of this failure, only a few means of accumulating economic power, such as establishment of holding companies, cross-shareholdings, and debt guarantees for affiliated corporations, were prohibited or regulated. Because the Fair Trade Act has not adopted any provisions regarding the dissolution of existing concentrations, the Fair Trade Act may be useful in preventing greater concentration of economic power. However, current measures provided by the Fair Trade Act cannot be expected to alleviate or resolve the concentration-of-economic-power problem itself.

Another sharp criticism of the current Fair Trade Act regulatory regime is that its measures are at odds with the primary aim of the legislation of ensuring and encouraging free competition and fair trade in the market. In other words, before regulating activities, such as the establishment of holding companies, cross shareholdings, total amount of equity investment, and debt guarantees for affiliated corporations, there must be some explanations as to why these activities are harmful to free competition and fair trade. The Fair Trade Act itself provides us with no justification for its regulations and, as a result, businesses are often skeptical of the Fair Trade Act's regulations.

6.2 Future Directions for Legislative Improvement of Korean Competition Law

For the Act to work more efficiently as the fundamental law of a Korean market economy, a number of revisions are suggested herein. These recommendations are grouped according to the substantive, agency-wide enforcement, and procedural aspects of the Act.

6.2.1 Substantive Aspects

First, the Fair Trade Act's criteria for determining whether a company has a market-dominant position are far too generous. Indeed, even those with market-dominant power are, in fact, seldom regulated. Hence, in order to make the Fair Trade Act more practically efficient, the presumptive criteria should be as stringent as those of German law.

Second, the Fair Trade Act's prohibitive criteria regarding mergers are set so high that they are virtually useless in practice. In order to enhance the efficiency of merger control, the criteria regarding horizontal mergers should be revised in a manner that has greater practical effect. Additionally, new provisions designed specifically to control conglomerate mergers should be introduced.

Furthermore, while the Fair Trade Act lists eight types of restricted anti-competitive cartels, this legislative approach does not provide for the new types of cartels that will inevitably arise with changes in the market and in sales techniques. From a practical standpoint, the Fair Trade Act should add a general inclusive clause regarding restricted anti-competitive cartels, rather than trying to define and list different specific types of cartels.

In addition, while the Fair Trade Act includes provisions regarding a meeting of the minds in cartel regulation, its provisions are written in such broad and unreasonable terms that it is of little practical use in regulating cartels. Legislation should be introduced to revise the Fair Trade Act in a manner that allows for more effective control over concerted actions.

Finally, the Fair Trade Act lists seven types of unfair trade or business practices. The Fair Trade Act states that the types of and criteria for such practices shall be determined by Presidential Decree. The problem with this approach, however, is that subjecting a violator to criminal charges when the elements of that crime are determined by presidential decree is that it may conflict with the principle of *nulla poena sine lege*. This approach may also render the Act ineffective in terms of regulating new types of unfair trade or business practices. In order to effectively regulate various unfair trade or business practices, it would be wiser to retain only the general provision in the Fair Trade Act that prohibits unfair trade or business practices, thereby allowing the specific types of outlawed practices to be decided by the Commission or the Court. Further, the provisions pertaining to restriction of international contracts, resale price maintenance, or trade associations should be deleted—there is simply no reason to regulate these aspects separately.

6.2.2 Enforcing the Agency-Wide Aspects

The KFTC is a quasi-judicial administrative agency in charge of the adjudication and development of antitrust policy. However, the Commission's current structure is not sufficiently organized effectively to execute its judicial functions. The Commission should be reorganized in a manner that strengthens its autonomy and enhances its expertise. More precisely, the Commission should be divided into two separate divisions, with one division taking charge of judicial decisions and the other handling the creation of the Nation's competition policy. Ideally, as with the German Bundeskartellamt, the judicial division would be further divided into seven and nine subdivisions, each responsible for a different industrial sector.

Each subdivision would be led by a commissioner, who would be aided by a division chairman and two assistant officers. The policy-making branch should be strictly limited to implementing long-term competition policies, repealing anti-trust statutes, and seeking cooperation with related organizations domestically and abroad. For the Commission's two divisions to perform optimally, the Commission as a whole should be staffed by lawyers and economists with expertise and experience in antitrust law and industrial organization.

6.2.3 Procedural Aspects

Public enforcement of the Fair Trade Act is primarily the responsibility of the Commission because the Commission analyzes and assesses market structure and performance—a process necessary for determination of whether a certain business practice is illegal or not. This is especially true in cases where there has been abuse of a market-dominant position or an anti-competitive merger. However, this same sort of detailed analysis and assessment is not required in cases involving unfair trade practices or hardcore cartels. This is because the legality of these actions is relatively easy to ascertain. The Commission should, therefore, concentrate its resources on controlling the abuse of market-dominant positions or anti-competitive mergers rather than on unfair trade practices or hardcore cartels. Because unfair trade practices and hardcore cartels can be more efficiently controlled through private enforcement or criminal procedure, limitations on these current methods should be dispelled, and new legal procedures such as injunctions and class actions should be made available.

References

Jwa S-H, Lee I-K (2004) Competition and Corporate Governance in Korea-Reforming and Restructuring the Chaebol. Edward Elgar, pp 12–13

Korea Fair Trade Commission (2011) 30 years' history of the KFTC, Korea Fair Trade Commission

Kwon, Oh-Seung (ed) (2011) Fair Trade Act 30 Years, Beobmunsa

Park JC-s, Lee D-a (2003) The Business Judgment Rule: A Missing Piece in the Developing Puzzle of Korean Corporate Governance Reform. J Korean Law 3(15):45–47

Shin Y-S (2004) The Yardstick for Judgment of Illegality on Unfair Bargaining and the Scope of Competitors under Korean Supreme Court Decisions. J Econ Law Precedent 1:251–291

Shin Y-S (2011) Changes and Development of the Fair Trade Act, Fair Trade Act 30 Years, Beobmunsa, p 160

Song O-r (2002) The Legacy of Controlling Minority Structure: A Kaleidoscope of Corporate Governance Reform in Korean Chaebol. Law Policy Int Bus 34:183, 225–226

Labour Law

Jaejin Shim

1 Introduction

Korean labour law is typically made up of two major branches: individual employment law and collective labour law. In addition, there arise new branches of labour law, such as work councils law, labour market law and labour relations committee law. Despite the advent of the new branches, given their dominance in labour law discipline, the focus of the chapter will be put on the two traditional branches of law. Given its importance, however, the chapter includes work councils law in explaining collective labour law although they can be differentiated in terms of their nature.

The chapter is designed to introduce the outline and the main features of labour law of Korea. It begins with a brief overview of the development of modern Korean labour law with a view to understanding current features of Korean labour in the Korea-specific historic context. Then it moves on to look at constitutional labour rights in order to show the constitutional framework which underpins Korean labour law. Then it explains the two main branches of labour law, respectively. While explaining them in detail, it intends to elaborate distinctive features of Korean labour law. Lastly before the concluding part, the chapter describes how enforcement and remedy system on labour law work. The features of enforcement and remedy system will hint at the extent that employment and labour rights are effective as a matter of fact in Korea. Conclusion tries to draw some characteristics of Korean labour law

J. Shim (✉)
College of Law, Daegu University, Daegu, Republic of Korea
e-mail: J.Shim@daegu.ac.kr

Korea Legislation Research Institute, *Introduction to Korean Law*,
DOI 10.1007/978-3-642-31689-0_8,

2 The Overview of the Development of Modern Labour Law

2.1 Foreign Influences on the Establishment of Labour Law

The First Constitution of Korea provides for two distinctive labour rights, namely, the right to work and the right to organize, to bargain collective and to strike. The section of 'the right to work' (a. 17) states that standards of working conditions shall be fixed by law, The section of the three collective labour rights (a. 18) stipulates that the scope and the extent of three collective rights have to be decided by law.[1] The endorsement of labour rights in the Constitution as contrasted with the absence of those in the US Constitution should be understood mainly in terms of the intense tension between socialism and capitalism of those days in Korea. In order to block the influence of socialism, drafters of the First Constitution of 1948 wanted to establish a social democratic regime similar to that of continental European countries where labour rights were constitutionally guaranteed.

Pursuant to the constitutional mandate above, the First Government enacted four main pieces of labour law in 1953: the Trade Union Act (the TUA), the Labour Dispute & Settlement Act (the LDSA), the Labour Relations Commission Act (the LRCA), and the Labour Standard Act (the LSA). Several important features of these laws remain in current labour law system, constituting its basic framework: validity of collective agreement over employment contact, the prohibition of unjust dismissal, remedy against unfair labour law practice, mediation through the Labour Relations Commission (the LRC) and cooling off period (later renamed as mediation period) before strikes. These features were a hybrid of those of both German and US labour law; the first two were originated from German labour law whereas the last two were from the US labour law. This was possible because the then Korean government relied on Japanese labour law, which was originally influenced by German labour law and to which features of the US labour law were added during the period of occupation by the US after the World War II.

Since the first enactment of modern labour law in 1953, labour law has had formidable changes. It is easy to describe these changes in terms of quantity. Currently there are more than 100 pieces of labour law in effect, beginning with four pieces in 1953. However, it is very difficult to value them in terms of quality. This task involves modern history of Korea which is lined with a couple of coups, rapid economic development, democratization and financial crisis. Despite this difficulty, most labour law scholars may agree that the turning point in the development of modern labour law is the year, 1987 when attitudes towards labour law under military regimes started to be changed under the pressure from massive

[1] Probably what was the most conspicuous provision in the First Constitution in relation to labour rights is 'employees' equal right to share profits of a private company' in the second sentence of a. 18. The second sentence was completely deleted when after the first military regime came to power, it comprehensively amended the First Constitution in 1963 (Lee HJ 2005).

demonstrations by citizens and national strikes by workers. For this reason, the two periods before and after 1987 will be explained separately as follows.

2.2 Development of Labour Law Before 1987

Although both individual employment law and collective labour law have changed significantly since 1953, they have been on different routes of change. To begin with, as the years that collective labour law was amended shows, military regimes put many restrictions on collective labour rights before 1987 each time they started a new government or a new constitutional order. According to the TUA of 1963, which the first military regime enacted 2 years after they came to power through a coup, multiple unions were no longer allowed to be organised in a company or a workplace. Moreover, the same law combined with the National Civil Servants Act (the NCSA) newly provided that civil servants were prohibited from organizing a trade union except for those actually doing manual labour as civil servants. In 1980, moreover, the second military regime, which seized the power after the leader of the first one was assassinated, introduced ban of any thirty party's intervention on labour disputes in the LDSA.

Conversely, individual employment law of 1953 did not deteriorate despite subsequent several occasions of amendment before 1987. Rather, it developed progressively towards better protection for workers. According to the amendment to the LSA in 1961, for instance, employers were obliged to pay workers severance pay when they retired or were dismissed. Moreover, the status of an employee as a preferential creditor in the event of his/her employer's insolvency was granted in 1974 and subsequently strengthened in 1980. In 1986, the National Minimum Wage Act (the NMWA) was enacted to protect low-paid workers.

The problem with individual employment law was not that it lacked sufficient provisions for workers' protection but that it was not effective as it was meant to be. Minimum standards set up in the LSA of 1953 were so high that they were not expected to be abided by. This was because the then Japanese labour law was taken as a legislative model in introducing modern employment law in Korea even though it was of too high standard for Korea under war in which no proper industry were established. In this respect, the ineffectiveness of the LSA of 1953 may be understandable. Even though Korean economy developed very rapidly in the 1960–1970s, however, the LSA did not become minimum standards as such.

2.3 Development of Labour Law Since 1987

After the military regime conceded to agree to amend the Constitution in order for a president to be directly elected, facing a series of massive national demonstrations in 1987, Korean labour suppressed by military regimes over almost three decades went on strikes all over the country in the midsummer of 1987. This was the turning point for the development of Korean labour law. Since 1987, there have been two dominant issues in labour law and relations: the first is the full realization of collective labour rights guaranteed in the Constitution. The second is the flexibilisation of labour, which has been demanded by employers and governments.

Since 1987, the restrictions on collective labour rights have been gradually removed in the course of substantive democratization in each sphere of Korean society. The prohibition of third parties' intervention in labour disputes, which was claimed to be in breach of the freedom of expression as well as constitutional labour rights, was replaced by the notification scheme in 1997 and its provisions were finally removed from labour law in 2006. Teachers and civil servants whose collective labour rights had been denied since 1963 were finally given the right to organize and to negotiate collectively by means of legislation in 1999 and 2006, respectively. However, they are still not allowed to go on a strike. Moreover, trade unions in public service who had to go through compulsory arbitration after they failed to reach an compromise in the mediation procedure, and as a result had no right to strike have been able to go on a strike from 2006, provided that they leave some workers working in order to maintain core functions of essential public services. Furthermore, two or more unions are finally allowed to be organised at one company or in one workplace from 2011. This shift resulted not from the Constitutional Court's rulings but from pressures from labour and international organizations, such as the ILO.

Since the 1990s, individual employment law has been at the forefront of the on-going battle between workers on the one side and employers and governments on the other side over the flexibilisation of employment, although it has been strengthened and sophisticated for better protection of workers in some respects. In the early 1990s, companies looked to flexibilise their workforce in order to reduce labour cost. As a result, they employed an increasing number of non-standard workers and outsourced part of their business to contractors. In addition, they wanted to accommodate fluctuating market by being able to reduce the number of workers more easily. This trend of flexibilisation became dominant after the financial crisis of Korean economy in 1997. Successive governments backed up these business demands even when they were administered by competing political parties.

In the course of flexibilisation of employment, firstly, economic dismissal was, for the first time in the history of modern Korean labour law, codified in the LSA in 1997. It had previously been regulated by means of case law. One year later, law of economic dismissal was amended in order to ensure that economic dismissal in the course of merger and acquisition with a view to preventing business from deteriorating could be allowed. Furthermore, new working hour systems, such as flexible working hour system and selective working hour system, which were supposed to be able to vary standard working hour in accordance with employers' business necessities, were permitted with certain restrictions under which employers were not able to introduce these systems in their workplace without a written agreement with employees' representatives. Simultaneously, the then Government pursued flexibilisation of employment in relation to temporary agency work. This effort brought about a new law, the Temporary Agency Work Act (the TAWA) 1998, which was, for the first time in the history of Korea's modern labour law, to permit temporary agency work in industries specified in the Act. Under the LSA, temporary agency work had been forbidden for several decades before the introduction of the Act.

3 Constitutional Labour Rights

Workers' labour rights in Korea have their constitutional grounds unlike those in, for instance, the US and the UK. Individual employment rights are constitutionally based on the right to work provision (a. 32). The provision imposes not only the state's duty to promote workers' employment (a. 32(1))[2] but also its duty to provide decent working conditions with workers with a view to guaranteeing their human dignity [a. 32(3)].[3] It can be said that the latter's duty gives all individual employment laws, such as the LSA and the NMWA, their constitutional legitimacy. In particular, protection from discrimination against female workers in a. 32(4)[4] is one of the constitutional bases for the Act on Equal Employment between Men and Women (the AEEMW).

Collective labour rights under labour law are mainly based on what is called the Three Labour Rights (the TLRs) provision (a. 33). The TLRs generally means three basic collective labour rights in a. 33(1),[5] namely, the right to independent association, the right to collective bargaining, and the right to collective action. The Constitutional TLRs are realised by means of the Trade Union and Labour Relations Settlements Act (the TULRSA). The TLRs has constitutional limitations for some workers in their scope. It is explicitly provided in the Constitution that two groups of workers can be denied the TLRs by means of an Act: civil servants and workers in defence industries [a. 33(2),[6] a. 33(3[7])]. As a matter of fact, civil servants who had been completely denied the TLRs for a long time are now entitled to the right to independent association and the right to collective bargaining with

---

[2] All citizens shall have the right to work. The State shall endeavor to promote the employment of workers and to guarantee optimum wages through social and economic means and shall enforce a minimum wage system under the conditions prescribed by an Act [a. 32(1)].

[3] Standards of working conditions shall be determined by an Act in such a way as to guarantee human dignity [a. 32(3)].

[4] Special protection shall be accorded to working women and they shall not be subjected to unjust discrimination in terms of employment, wages, and working conditions [a. 32(4)].

[5] To enhance working conditions, workers shall have the right to independent association, collective bargaining, and collective action [a. 33(1)].

[6] Only those civil servants, who are designated by an Act, shall have the right to association, collective bargaining, and collective action [a. 33(2)].

[7] The right to collective action of workers employed by important defence industries may be either restricted or denied under the conditions prescribed by an Act [a. 33(3)].

collective action still forbidden under the Act on the Establishment and Operation, etc. of Civil Servants' Trade Unions (the AEOCSTU) 2006. Similarly, workers employed in important defence industries are not able to enjoy the right to collective action. Although there is no explicit provision on the reservation of labour rights for teachers in the Constitution, moreover, similar to civil servants, teachers are interpreted to be able to be denied the TLRs in light of the right to education provision (a. 31), in subsection [a. 31(6)] of which it is stipulated that the status of teachers has to be determined by an Act.[8] Currently permanent teachers at universities are still denied the TLRs. However teachers at primary schools, middle schools and high schools are given the right to organise a trade union and the right to collective bargaining with some restrictions under the Act on the Establishment, Operation, etc. of Trade Unions for Teachers (the AEOTUT) after a decade-long pressure from labour movement, including teachers' organisations. Nonetheless, their right to industrial action is still deprived of.

Based on the constitutional labour rights, some statutory restrictions on labour rights have been challenged in the Constitutional Court. They include the complete prohibition of civil servants[9] and teachers[10] from enjoying the TLRs, the empowerment of a leader of a trade union only to conclude a collective agreement,[11] and the compulsory arbitration over labour dispute in essential public services.[12] It has been claimed in the Court that they are in breach of a. 32, or a. 33. However, most of such challenges have not been successful. Instead of being declared unconstitutional, some of them have been abolished or reformed by means of several occasions of amendment to statutory law through the Parliament.

4 Individual Employment Law

4.1 Scope

Individual employment law applies to employees, thus ruling out self-employed persons in its scope. All laws in relation to individual employment relationships have a unified concept of an employee as their definition of an employee refers to that in s. 2(1) of the LSA, which is defined as "a person who offers work to a business or workplace to earn wages, regardless of the kind of job he/she is engaged in." Case law regarding this definition has constructed it as a person who provides his(her) employer with defendant labour under his(her) direction.

[8] Constitutional Court Decision 89Hun-Ga106 Decided on July 22, 1991.

[9] Constitutional Court Decision 90Hun-Ba27 Decided on April 28, 1992.

[10] Constitutional Court Decision 89Hun-Ga106 Decided on July 22, 1991.

[11] Constitutional Court Decision 94Hun-Ba13, 26, 95Hun-Ba44 Decided on February 27, 1998; Constitutional Court Decision 2003Hun-Ba28 Decided on August 26, 2004.

[12] Constitutional Court Decision 2001Hun-Ga31 Decided on May, 15, 2003.

What has been the most controversial issue in relation to the definition is the distinction between an employee and a self-employed person. It has been under contention whether or not those who are not under specific direction from a company in relation to their performance of work and earn incomes according to their achievements, such as caddies, insurance salespersons, and private tutors using specific materials produced by a big education company are employees. As this group of workers, who are estimated to be as many as two million in Korea work exclusively for a particular company and under its control in its broad sense, it is not easily taken for granted that they are self-employed. Despite the affinity to the nature of an employee, however, the Supreme Court has consistently denied that the workers are employees as stipulated in the LSA.[13] Hence they have been completely excluded from almost all individual employment law except the IICIA. Pressure from labour movement made the government reluctantly amend the Industrial Injury Compensation Insurance Act (the IICIA) in 2006 to the effect that they are exceptionally allowed to apply to the Act (s. 125). Even this exceptional application is restricted as, unlike employees as defined in the LSA, however, the workers have to pay their contribution for the Industrial Injury Compensation Insurance (the IICI) and, on their request, they can withdraw from the compulsory IICI for employees.

Another issue in relation to the application of the LSA is its further restriction relying on the number of employees of a company. Not all employees are under protection of individual employment law although its scope has been gradually expanded. For instance, some important provisions of the LSA, such as the restriction of unjust dismissal, maximum working hours, the restriction of overtime work, overtime premium, and paid annual holidays do not apply to workplaces with fewer than five employees. The government argues that this exclusion is justified by financial burdens on small-sized companies and its administrative difficulties in extending the Act to them.

4.2 Working Conditions

4.2.1 Wages

Wages are defined as "any payment to an employee from an employer as remuneration for work, regardless of the term by which such payment is called" (s. 18, LSA). One of the most distinctive features of employment law in relation to wages is that several wages imposed on employers to pay as their duties are calculated on two different sub-conceptions of wages to pay: Average Wages (AWs) and Ordinary Wages (OWs).

[13] Supreme Court Decision 95Da20348 Decided on April 26, 1996; Supreme Court Decision 98Du9219 Decided on January 28, 2000; Supreme Court Decision 2002Da57959 Decided on January 10, 2003.

The OWs are basic wages for work for contractual working hours. Contractual working hours cannot exceed statutory daily (8 h) and weekly (40 h) working hour limit. The OWs can be calculated hourly, daily, weekly, or monthly, depending on what kinds of wages have to be paid. On the basis of the OWs, employers have to pay notice of dismissal allowance, and premium for overtime work, night work and holiday work.

The AWs are daily averages of total wages for the last three months. They are calculated by dividing the total amount of wages paid to an employee during three calendar months prior to the date on which the event necessitating such calculation occurred by the total number of the calendar days during those three calendar months. Unlike the OWs, hence, the AWs include, e.g., overtime payment in the three calendar months. This sub-conception of wages is designed to represent employees' ordinary actual average earnings for living. For this reason, the AWs have to be used to pay severance pay, a punitive reduction in wages and industrial injury compensation under the LSA and other relevant Acts.

Another of the most distinctive features in relation to wage regulation is the Statutory Severance Pay (the SSP). Employees who have been continuously employed by an employer for one year or more are entitled to the AW of 30 days per year when their employment is terminated. As there is no contribution from employees, the duty to pay the SSP is incumbent on their employer. For these reasons, the SSP is different from occupational pension scheme in developed countries. Recently amendments to the SSP were made to the effect that under the consent of employees an employer is able to change the SSP into retirement benefit scheme in which employees obtain pension instead of the SSP when they retire at a mandatory retirement age.

Generally speaking, individual employment law does not guarantee a substantive level of wages. In two exceptional circumstances, however, a certain level of wages may be paid to employees. Firstly, all employees are entitled to the National Minimum Wage (the NMW) or more under the NMWA. The NMW is annually determined on deliberation by the Minimum Wage Council, which consists of equal number of three different groups of members respectively representing workers, employers and the public interest. Secondly, when business is suspended for reasons attributable to an employer, employees have a right to guaranteed pay for that period, which is equivalent to at least 70 % of the AW (s. 46). Case law has been established to the effect that 'reasons attributable to an employer' is broad enough to cover a diminution in the requirements of business due to, e.g. decreases in sales and financial difficulties.

4.2.2 Working Hours

Under the LSA, an employee may not work more than 40 h per week and 8 h (7 h for an employee less than 18 years old) per day (s. 50) These hours may be extended by an agreement between the employee and his/her employer, by a maximum of 12 h (6 h per week for an employee less than 18 years olds). If an employee works continuously for at least 4 h, an employer must give him/her a 30-minute rest break (s. 54). As a matter of practice, this rest break time is normally used as a one-hour mealtime for an employee working 8 h per day.

An employee is entitled to a minimum of a paid weekly rest day (s. 55). Although Sunday is a customary weekly rest day, an employer is not legally obliged to give his/her employees Sunday as a weekly rest day. Moreover, the LSA provides for 15–25 days' paid annual leave for an employee whose attendance rate is 80 % or more for the previous year (s. 60). The days of paid annual leave depends on the period of service. When an employee has been working for the first year in employment, he/she may have 15 days' paid annual leave. Then one day accrues for every 2 years of service with the maximum of 25 days. Additionally, a female employee is entitled to menstrual leave of a day per month (s. 73).

When an employer wants an employee to work overtime, at night (10 pm to 06 am) or on a weekly rest day and public holidays, he/she has to pay the employee one and a half times his/her hourly OW rates (s. 56). By placing additional financial burden on an employer, this premium rule aims to discourage him/her from demanding an employee to work overtime, night work or on holidays. Since the rule does not apply when an employee is not able to take a paid annual leave, however, an employer needs only to pay his AW or OW for the unused days.[14]

As mentioned in the Section II, regulation on working time was amended in 1997 with a view to meeting flexibility from the employers' side. As a result, the LSA allows an employer to have employees work longer than 8 h for a specific day or 40 h for a specific week, on the condition that average working hours per week in a reference period of 3 months or less do not exceed 40 h (s. 51). This flexible working hour scheme is allowed only where the employer reaches an agreement in writing with a representative of employees on particular terms and conditions, such as a reference period and working days in the period and working hours for each working day. Likewise, the LSA provides for the selective working hour scheme in which employees can choose when to begin and finish work on the condition that average working hours per week in a reference period of one month or less do not exceed 40 h (s. 52). In order to introduce the latter scheme at his/her workplace, an employer has to reach an agreement with a representative of employees on, e.g., a reference period, total working hours, and fixed and variable working time. That those systems are allowed on certain conditions legally means that an employer is not obliged to pay e.g., overtime premium even if an employee works more than 40 h per week or 8 h per day nor is criminally punished for having the employee work over-time for a specific week or a day. However, the employer would have been so before the scheme was introduced.

---

[14] Supreme Court Decision 90Daka14758 Decided on June 28, 1991; Supreme Court Decision 90Daka11636 Decided on July 26, 1991.

4.2.3 Health and Safety

Health and safety are regulated under the Industrial Safety and Health Act (the ISHA). Under the ISHA, an employer has the duty to care for employees' health and safety. Separately from this statutory duty, the courts interpret the duty to care for employees' health and safety to be implied in an employment contract.[15] Even where the ISHA could not apply, hence, an employer would still have such duty.

The ISHA covers several health and safety issues in detail, such as management system on health and safety, safety and health measures and safety inspection. It is notable that particularly an employee is entitled to a medical check by a doctor every year or every other year, depending on the nature of the industry in which the employee works.

Under the IICIA, an employee is compensated for industrial injuries in terms of medical treatment, suspension of work, disabilities resulting from industrial incidents, and rehabilitation. When an employee dies from industrial injuries, moreover, his/her survivors are entitled to compensation under the IICIA. The IICIA is nearly universal in its scope as it applies to all the workplaces with a few ignorable exceptions whereas, as mentioned earlier, the application of important clauses in the LSA is confined to workplaces of five and more employees. The IICI is liability insurance which every employer is obliged to join on their full expenses and is operated by a state-owned institute. To the extent that the IICI compensates an employee for his/her industrial injuries, an employer is indemnified against his/her civil liability incurred when the injuries are caused by his/her negligent or intentional wrong. Most legal claims in relation to the IICIA pertain to whether the injury in question is work-caused. The criteria for determining work-causedness of a particular injury are enunciated in s. 37, IICIA and, in more detail, in s. 27 to s. 37, the Enforcement Decree of the IICIA.

4.2.4 Dismissal Etc.

With some exceptions, an employer has to give an employee one month's notice when he/she intends to dismiss the employee. However, the breach of this notice rule does not affect the validity of dismissal. It simply obliges an employer to pay the employee the OW of at least one month. Moreover an employer who intends to dismiss an employee, he/she has a duty to notify the employee of grounds for dismissal and the date of such dismissal in writing. Unlike the former notice provision regarding giving advance notice, the breach of the latter notice provision makes the dismissal void. The strictness of the latter provision in terms of validity is aimed at making an employer more scrupulous about dismissal and reducing possible disputes about the exact date of dismissal and the reason for dismissal.

[15] Supreme Court Decision 99Da47129 Decided on May 16, 2000.

It is notable that the coverage of the provision dealing with dismissal in the LSA is very broad. Under s. 23, the LSA, an employee is protected not only from dismissal but also from any detrimental treatment falling short of dismissal, such as job suspension, wage reduction and transfer of jobs in the workplace, whether or not it is made out of ordinary managerial considerations or disciplinary measures, as long as they are proven unjust. Comparatively, the scope of the provision is much broader than, for instance, that of the similar provisions under the UK labour law which deal only with dismissal.

It is also notable that the provision of dismissal etc. requires them to be 'just' as interpreted to demand stricter justification from an employer than to be 'reasonable' or 'fair'. As to 'just' dismissal, the courts have been of the view that dismissal of an employee is just "when from the standard of social common sense, there are grounds for dismissal that are as sufficient as for his/her employer not to continue an employment contract with the employee".[16] In relation to treatment falling short of dismissal, the courts has held that in principle, in order to decide whether such treatment is just or not, the extent of both business necessity and employee's disadvantages in relation to the treatment must be assessed in comparison with each other. As the courts themselves admit, however, the abstractness of the court's principled guidelines about judging whether treatment is just or not indicates that in a particular case, the courts have no choice but to decide it concretely by putting all the evidence concerned with the case together.

In order to be just, under the LSA, dismissal for economic reasons, which will be shortened as economic dismissal hereafter, has to meet what is called the four requirements: (1) urgent business needs, (2) prior efforts to avoid dismissal, (3) selection of candidates for redundancy by means of reasonable and fair criteria, (4) prior notification and consultation with representatives of employees (s. 24). It should be noted that when an employer intends to employ an employee for the same job that a dismissed employee was in charge of within 3 years after economic dismissal is made, the employer has a duty to reemploy the dismissed employee provided that the employee still wants the job (s. 25).

Although regulation on economic dismissal appears strict, it is not as strict as its literal interpretation. This argument can be backed up by the following observations. To begin with, the provision on economic dismissal additionally provides that economic dismissal for transfer and merger of undertakings aimed at preventing the deterioration of business has to be regarded as satisfying the first requirement [s. 24(1), LSA]. This provision was inserted in 1998 with a view to enhancing business restructuring. Moreover the courts have held that the 'urgent business needs' requirement is met when economic dismissal takes place as a precautionary measure to prevent possible business difficulties and is objectively reasonable.[17] Lastly given the courts' attitudes towards the fourth requirement

---

[16] Supreme Court Decision 91Da27518 Decided on May 12, 1992; Supreme Court Decision 93Da49192 Decided on February 11, 1994.

[17] Supreme Court Decision 2001Da29452 Decided on July 9, 2001.

before the statutory inclusion of economic dismissal,[18] it would not be surprising if economic dismissal failing to meet the fourth requirement but satisfying the other requirements was held not to be in breach of the provision on economic dismissal.

4.3 Mergers and Business Transfers and Employment Relationship

When a merger takes place, there is no doubt that contracts of employment, existing work rules and collective agreements at a merged company are maintained at a merging company. Hence, wages and other working conditions remain unchanged after a merger takes place. Moreover, the period of consecutive work at the merged company are not disconnected to work at the merging company for the purpose of, for instance, computing the SSP.

A business transfer has a similar legal effect on employment relationships. However, the way the courts construct the legal effects is different in light of employment. The Supreme Court held that in principle employment relationships with a transferee were transferred if there was no special agreement between the transferee and the transferor.[19] It went on to hold that although employment relationships were not transferred according to a special agreement of doing so, this agreement amounted to dismissal which was valid only if there were just grounds for the dismissal as stipulated in s. 23 or s. 24, LSA.

What is more contentious in Korea is the meaning and the scope of business transfer rather than its legal effect. Business has to be identical before and after it is transferred in order for such transaction to constitute business transfer. If the transaction turns out to be simple sales of assets, the transfer of employment relationships are not obligatory. The Supreme Court narrowly constructed the meaning and the scope of business transfer, thus e.g., excluding employment protection for employees who were selectively refused reemployment by a transferor.[20] Moreover, the Supreme Court upheld the decision of the court of second instance that a transaction in which one contractor subsequently succeeded another in a motor company was not a business transfer.[21]

[18] Supreme Court Decision 91Da19463 Decided on December 10, 1992.

[19] Supreme Court Decision 2000Du8455 Decided on March 29, 2002.

[20] Supreme Court Decision 99Du2680 Decided on July 27, 2001.

[21] Supreme Court Decision 2009Du19434 Decided on January 28, 2010.

4.4 Work Rules

Unlike in the western countries, it is not the case in Korea that an employment contract is a main legal source by means of which a dispute over working conditions and dismissal is settled. This is because legal practice in relation to employment is not centred on an employment contract due to Korea's traditional legal culture. Collective agreements are not a main legal source either as trade union density has been around 10 % over the last decade.[22] For these reasons, work rules are a main legal source and its legal significance is enormous.

An employer with ten or more employees has to formulate work rules and report them to the Ministry of Employment and Labour (s. 93, LSA). Matters which have to be written about in the work rules are listed in s. 93: the beginning and the end of business, break time, rest days, holidays; determination, calculation and means of payment of wages and reference period and payment day of wages; family allowances; retirement; severance pay, bonus and minimum wages; meal expenses and equipment of employees; educational facilities for employees; maternity protection and reconciliation of work and family, such as maternity protection and child care leave; workplace environments in relation to health and safety; reward and discipline; other matters applicable to all employees.

The legal effect of work rules is in the middle in the hierarchy of the three main legal sources, namely an employment, work rules, and a collective agreement. Work rules preside over employment contracts in terms of their legal effect. When the provisions dealing with employment conditions of employees in employment contracts fall short of those equivalent in work rules, the former are void and automatically replaced by the latter (s. 97, LSA). However, they are inferior to a collective agreement. Hence, a collective agreement has the same effect against work rules just as the latter do against an employment contract.

As mentioned already, formulating work rules is the legal responsibility of an employer. From another point of view, however, this means that an employer is entitled to determining working conditions of their employees unilaterally. For employees, their working conditions are changeable, sometimes unfavourably, whenever work rules are amended. For this reason, while Korean labour law bestows the right to establish work rules on an employer, it restricts the employer's power to establish or change work rules. Firstly, when an employer intends to amend work rules, he/she must consult a trade union whose members are more than half of all the employees or more than half employees where there is no such trade union [s. 94(1), LSA]. Although the employer may be punished for the breach of the duty to consult, however, work rules amended without consultation are still valid.[23] The reason was, the Court held, that, in principle, it was an employer who was entitled to establish or amend work rules.

[22] As of 2009, trade union density in Korea is 10.1 %, which is 0.4 % point lower than the previous year.

[23] Supreme Court Decision 94Nu3001 Decided on December 23, 1994; Supreme Court Decision 98Du6647 Decided on June 22, 1999.

Secondly, where an employer intends to amend work rules unfavourably against employees, he/she must obtain consent from a trade union whose members are more than half of all the employees or more than half employees where there is no such a trade union [s. 94(1), LSA]. In order to prevent an employer from easily changing working conditions unfavourably against employees where there is no trade union whose members are more than half of all the employees, the Supreme Court has held that the consent of more than half of all the employees is not individual but collective. The Court have been of the opinion that the collective consent requires the employees to agree with the unfavourable alteration of work rules by means of collective discussion as a whole or in each department.[24] As a matter of fact, however, the effect of requiring the collective consent was watered down when the Court held that it was not illegal that a company amended work rules unfavourably after almost all employees reluctantly signed up in a consent paper in their each department before their boss who explained and promoted the necessity of doing so to them.[25]

4.5 Prohibition of Discrimination in Employment

Discrimination in employment can be divided into two categories: discrimination on the grounds of personal traits and discrimination on the grounds of contractual status. The former takes place when an employer refuses to employ a candidate, dismisses, or otherwise treats less favourably, an employee on the grounds of, e.g., sex, race, religion, and nationality. The latter is concerned with e.g., part-time, fixed-term, and temporary work. Whereas the regulatory framework of the former is focused on the prohibition of discrimination, that of the latter is on both non-discrimination and the restriction of using such contractual status itself. For this reason, although those two categories are commonly considered discrimination in general, they have been very differently treated. Given such differences, regulation on non-standard work will be dealt with separately in the next sub-section.

The LSA provides in s. 6 that an employer is prohibited from discriminating against an employee on the basis of gender, nationality, religion, or social status. Since an employee under the LSA means only a person who is being employed, the LSA provision does not apply to the refusal of employment on such grounds. This had been the only provision on discrimination in individual employment law before the AEEMW came in force in 1988. Currently there are two additional anti-discrimination laws enacted recently: the Act on the Prohibition of Age Discrimination in Employment and the Promotion of Employment of the Aged (the APADEPEA) and the Act on the Prohibition of Disability Discrimination (the APDD). Unlike the LSA provision on discrimination, those discrimination laws

[24] Supreme Court Decision 90Do3031 Decided on March 27, 1991; Supreme Court Decision 92Da28556 Decided on June 24, 1994.

[25] Supreme Court Decision 2002Da23185 Decided on May 14, 2004.

on sex, age and disability regulate discrimination in application for a job as well as actual employment.

Discrimination in the three anti-discrimination laws above includes indirect discrimination as well as direct discrimination. Although the indirect discrimination provision was made in the amendment of the AEEMW in 2001, there have been few cases in relation to indirect discrimination. Moreover, the fact that the APADEPEA does not prohibit an employer from setting a retirement age at all shows that its regulation is not as strict as that was expected to be. Furthermore, the employers' duty of justifiable accommodation in the APDD has not been utilized as often as the equivalents in disability law of other countries have been. Overall, all the features mentioned above give us some doubts on the effectiveness of Korea's anti-discrimination laws.

4.6 Protection for Non-standard Workers

The proportion of nonstandard workers to the Korean workforce is significant. Based on the analysis of the periodical statistics produced by the Statistics Korea (the KOSTAT), the Ministry of Employment and Labour (the MEL) officially announced that, as of March, 2011, non-standard workers, such as fixed-term, part-time and temporary agency workers accounted for 33.8 % of all the Korean workers.[26] The significance of their number, combined with their unstable employment and poor working conditions, has made the protection of non-standard work one of the most controversial issues in Korea. The confrontation between trade unions and employers as to how to deal with the issue has been intense. As a compromise, a new law, the Act on the Protection of Fixed-term and Part-time Employees (the APFPE) came into being and amendments to the Temporary Agency Work Act (the TAWA) were made in 2006 with a view to protecting non-standard workers to a certain extent.

The protection for non-standard workers is twofold. One is aimed at regulating discrimination between them and standard workers and their poor working conditions. The other one is to prohibit the use of non-standard workers or limit its spread to a certain extent. The principal way of protecting them in the APFPE is the first one, combining it with the second one as a supplementary measure.

In terms of the first way, discrimination against fixed-term, part-time and temporary agency employees is prohibited under the APFPE and the TAWA. To prove that there is discrimination against them, it must be shown that they are less favourably treated than their comparators, namely, permanent, full-time employees

[26] The accurateness of this figure is doubted by trade unions and some scholars. From the same statistics, they contend that non-standard workers constitutes 48.7 % of the Korean workforce. There has been controversy about the size of non-standard workers between trade unions and some scholars, on the one hand and the governments, on the other hand.

and employees of a hirer, respectively, who are engaged in the similar work. In order to ensure their expedient and low-cost access to their anti-discrimination right, they are all given the right to seek protection from such discrimination through the LRC.

In relation to the second way, the position of part-time work is different from that of the other two. Under the protective laws for non-standard employees, there is no provision in relation to limiting the use of part-time work because the spread of the former is not considered problematic. However if a fixed-term employee has been employed more than two consecutive years by an employer, the employee is automatically deemed a permanent employee. Moreover, once a hirer has been using a temporary agency employee more than two consecutive years, he/she is obliged to employ the employee directly. The rationale for these provisions is that although fixed-term and temporary agency work are legitimately allowed to be used, they must not be overused to be exploited, or to replace standard employees.

There is another type of non-standard employees in Korea, who account for 3.6 % of all Korean workers.[27] They are contract workers who are employed by a contractor but works in a principal's company, which will be called in-house contract workers. In theory, they are not supposed to have any employment relation to a principal as they works for a contractor who provides goods or services to a principal. As a matter of practice in Korea's manufacture industry, however, they do the same work as employees of a principal in its premises under its direct or indirect direction on how to work. For this reason, recently the Supreme Court held in a seminal case, the type of work that contract workers carried on in a car manufacturer was temporary agency work, the use of which exceeding 1 year was forbidden in the manufacture industry under the TAWA.[28] In the same case, furthermore, the Supreme Court held that the car manufacturer was a direct employer of a contract worker under the TAWA as he had been in temporary agency work by the manufacturer for more than two consecutive years. According to the Court, contract workers working in a car manufacturer was under direct control of the human resource management of the company as they had been doing the same work as employees of the company under its direction.

5 Collective Labour Law

5.1 Scope

Collective labour law applies to employees as individual employment law does. Under the TULRSA, an employee means "a person who lives on wages, salary, or

[27] Kim Y (2011).

[28] Supreme Court Decision 2008Du4367 Decided on July 22, 2010.

other equivalents of income regardless of work he/she does" (2 ho, s. 2). As it can be seen, an employee is defined in slightly different wordings to those of the LSA. This difference makes the term "employee" include the unemployed as well as the employed whereas the equivalent in the LSA only covers the employed. In light of the employed, the courts are of the view that an employee in the TULRSA is the same as that in the LSA despite the possibility of extending the former's scope to include, e.g., caddies and insurance salespersons due to their different wordings. Unlike the LSA, moreover, the TULRSA does apply to all workplaces regardless of their size. As mentioned in the Section III, the scope of the TULRSA does not reach civil servants and teachers as their right to organize and to collective bargaining are protected through separate laws, namely, the AEOCSTU and the AEOTUT, respectively, with their right to collective action denied.

Under the TULRSA, it is an employer who has the duty of not committing an Unfair Labour Practice (ULP). Normally, an employer as a duty bearer has an employment relationship with an employee based on an employment contract between the employer and the employee. In-house contract employees as mentioned in the previous section have no, *de jure*, employment relationship with the principal as they works under an employment contract between them and a contractor. However, it is quite often the case that the company as a principal has, *de facto*, power to influence or control in-house contract employees in Korea. Where this is the case, there has been an issue whether the unfair labour practice scheme applies to the company as a principal. The Supreme Court held in a recent seminal case that, when a ship manufacturing company was in a position to control and determine working conditions of in-house contract workers, it was an employer of the workers, thus having a duty of not committing such a ULP against the in-house contract workers, to the extent controlling and interfering with trade union affairs as a ULP was concerned.[29]

5.2 *Trade Unions*

5.2.1 Trade Union: Definition and Requirements

A trade union means "an organization or associated organization of employees which is formed independently for the purpose of maintaining and improving working conditions, or improving the economic and social status of employees" (4 ho, s. 2, TULRSA). Hence, an organization must meet requirements needed by the definition of a trade union, such as its independence and having betterment of working conditions in a broad sense as its objective, in order to constitute a trade union under the TULRSA. However, these requirements as such are not as decisive as they seem to be because there are few objective tests of determining if an

[29] Supreme Court Decision 2007Du8881 Decided on March 25, 2010.

organisation satisfies such requirements. Hence, what matters in the process of registering a trade union are the following negative requirements, the meeting of any one of which makes an organisation automatically unqualified to be a trade union, thus being rejected the issuance of a certificate of establishment report by the relevant authority (4 ho, s. 2, TULRSA): (1) the organisation allows managerial employees to join it; (2) most of its expenditure is covered by an employer; (3) its objective is confined to fraternalism, self-discipline and other welfare activities only; (4) it allows a non-employee to join it (saving that a company union allows a person who has been dismissed by the company to join it from the time that he/she applied for a remedy order by the LRC to the time that the National LRC adjudicates); (5) it is mainly aimed at political movement. The second, the third and the fifth requirements are not controversial since meeting either of them necessarily leads to undermine the definition of a trade union mentioned above. However, because meeting the first or the fourth requirement does not always affect a trade union's independence or the fact that it is an organisation mainly made up of employees, some contend, the legitimacy of the two negative requirements may be doubted.

5.2.2 Establishment of a Trade Union

Employees are free to organize a trade union. When a trade union is established, it must be reported. When they decides that the trade union meets the requirements mentioned above, governmental administrative authorities issue a certificate of establishment report within three days after an application being accepted. When they decide that it fails to do so or that it does not correct a flawed application form within a specified period, they return the application form. If it is not reported and/or is not issued a certificate of establishment report, it is not a trade union under the TULRSA and accordingly is not entitled to some TULRSA-based concrete rights, such as application for both mediation procedure on collective bargaining and a remedial order against the ULPs (s. 7).

Korean trade unions are largely company unions the membership of which is confined to employees of a particular company. As multiple company unions having an overlapping membership basis in a company had not been allowed to be established, an application for a certificate of establishment report of a new company union had been rejected on the ground that it shared a membership basis with a pre-existing union in a company. Although this prohibition was said to aim to avoid rivalry between company unions and possible difficulties of collective bargaining on the side of an employer, its constitutionality had been doubted among many labour scholars because it in part denied employees the right to choose or organize such a trade union, as they want to join or establish in the workplace. As mentioned earlier, the prohibition of multiple unionism in the workplace was finally removed from the TULRSA on 1, July, 2011.

5.2.3 Operation of a Trade Union

Trade unions are organizations voluntarily established to improve employees' working conditions. Hence, they need to govern themselves independently from any external interference. In this regard, the first underlying principle in the operation of trade unions is autonomy. Furthermore, trade unions are able to regulate working conditions of their members through collective agreements, to go on a strike and to discipline the members for not complying with the rules or policies of trade unions. Given the trade unions' power over their members, it is necessary that trade unions should be operated democratically. In this sense, democracy is the second underlying principle. Therefore, the TULRSA provides for several provisions in relation to the two basic principles.

As to trade union's autonomy, trade unions are required to make rules and comply with them in their operation under the TULRSA. To begin with, when they make an application for a certificate of establishment report, they submit their rules along with the application form (s. 10). In addition, all matters specified in s. 11, such as objectives and activities, membership and membership fees, amendment to rules, dissolution, industrial action ballet, impeachment of representatives, election, and discipline and control, have to be included in the particulars of rules. Moreover, it is provided that trade unions have to comply with what is required in rules in relation to some other matters (s. 6, s. 17, s. 19, s. 22 and s. 23, TULRSA). When it comes to trade union democracy, every member of a trade union is entitled to equal participation in its all matters (s. 22). Furthermore, trade union members have not to be discriminated against on the grounds of race, religion, age, physical conditions, employment types, political party membership, and social status (s. 9, TULRSA). In addition, trade unions are required to make a decision on their important matters by means of a resolution adopted at a general meeting of trade union members. The matters include the establishment of, and the amendment to, rules, election and dismissal of trade union representatives, an amalgamation, a division and a dissolution of a trade union, collective agreement, financial matters, etc. [s. 16(1)]. In particular, resolutions on the first three matters, given their special importance, have to be made on the condition that more than half members are present and that two-thirds or more of those present are in favour of them. However, in order for those on other matters to be made, more than half members must be present and more than half of those present must be in favour of them [s. 16(2), TULRSA]. For the sake of trade union democracy, another provision requires that a trade union leader must notify its members of accounting records and current status of affairs and make them available for the members to peruse on their request (s. 26, TULRSA).

The principle of autonomy suggests that trade unions must not to be controlled or influenced by a government as well as employers. There used to be several provisions in labour law which made administrative authorities legitimately intervene in trade unions' affair. In fact, former military regimes controlled trade unions by means of such provisions. Some of them have been repealed and others amended in the process of the democratisation of Korea during the 1980s and the 1990s. Still, when administrative authorities decide that rules, resolutions, and dispositions of trade unions are in breach of labour law, they are able to order trade unions to correct such rules, resolutions and dispositions once they obtain a resolution of the LRC's made on their application (s. 21, TULRSA). Moreover, trade unions are obliged to report their accounting records and current status of affairs to administrative authorities where the authorities request so (s. 27, TULRSA).

Legal policy on forms of the closed shop under Korean labour law is difficult to grasp. Under the TULRSA, all forms of the closed shop are prohibited as a ULP except for the post-entry closed shop (union shop in the US context) meeting certain conditions. A post-entry closed shop is allowed only when a trade union organizing two-thirds or more of all employees at a workplace has a collective agreement in relation to the post-entry closed shop (2 ho, a81, TULRSA). However where the post-entry closed shop is allowed in such exceptional conditions, an employer must not treat an employee unfavourably on the grounds that he/she is expelled from a trade union or withdraws from a trade union and organises or joins another union (2 ho, a. 81, TULRSA). This means that even under a post-entry shop agreement, an employer dismiss, or otherwise treat unfavourably, an employee only when he/she withdraws from a trade union and remains not-affiliated with any trade union.

Providing, e.g., facilities for trade union representatives and trade union activities at a workplace level tends to be more at issue in Korean labour relations than in those of western countries. This is because trade unions in Korea, which are mostly company unions, need more accommodation from their employers for them to operate properly at a workplace level. It quite often takes place that under collective agreements, Korean companies provide a union office in their premises, time-off for trade union members and representatives and deductions of subscriptions from employees' pay. For employers to provide such accommodation for trade unions is exceptionally allowed, although under the TULRSA they are prohibited from providing financial support for trade union expenditure as a ULP (4 ho, s. 81).

One of the most controversial issues in collective labour law in the last decade has been whether the payment of full-time union officials by employers, which was not explicitly prohibited in the TULRSA and interpreted not to be a ULP in certain circumstances under case law, should be banned. Full-time union officials are mostly employees of the company in which their enterprise unions are organised. On the one hand, employers wanted it to be legally prohibited as a ULP, although as a matter of practice they were making payment of full-time union officials under collective agreements reluctantly reached due to heavy pressure from trade unions. On the other hand, trade unions contended that the matter should not be subject to legislative interference. In 2010 this long conflict ended up in the introduction of very complicated provisions in the TULRSA, which came into effect in July, 2011.

Currently the payment of union officials by employers are not allowed as it is the ULP explicitly prohibited under the TULRSA [4 ho, s. 81 and s. 24(2)]. Instead, a special kind of time-off scheme has been established to replace the payment of union officials by employers. In this scheme, despite the explicit prohibition of the payment by an employer to union officials, they may be engaged in activities in relation to trade union during working hours according to collective agreements without a wage reduction for the hours spent in trade union activities, subject to the maximum permissible time-off cap to be set by a governmental committee under the MEL [s. 24(4)]. The maximum permissible time-off cap varies depending on the numbers of trade union members. For instance, officials of a trade union of less than 50 members may have time-off for trade union activities up to 1,000 h per year (equivalent to 0.5 person as the number of full-time officials), and officials of a trade union of 15,000 and more members up to 36,000 h per year (equivalent to 18 persons as the number of full-time officials), if the union reaches an agreement with its employer. The maximum numbers of paid full-time officials (although they are not legally termed as such in the TULRSA) actually allowed in the new time-off scheme is smaller for most trade unions, much smaller for big-size unions, than those of paid full-time officials before the scheme was introduced in 2010. Moreover, their activities to be paid for is confined to internal ones of a company union or a company branch of an industrial union, thus excluding activities as an affiliate of associations of trade unions or the industrial union [s. 24(4), TULRSA]. For these reasons, it is arguable that the new scheme is evidently designed to weaken the power of trade unions in the workplace and to confine their activities to matters in a company or a workplace, not industrial or political ones.

5.3 *Collective Bargaining and Collective Agreements*

5.3.1 Collective Bargaining

The fact that trade unions in Korea are mostly enterprise unions determines how they carry out collective bargaining. Enterprise unions conduct collective bargaining with the companies on which they are based on. As the prohibition of multiple unionism at a workplace or enterprise level was abolished as of July, 2011, two or more enterprise unions (or an industrial union having members at the enterprise) would have been entitled to the right to separate collective bargaining for the sake of their respective members. However, this would have meant that the company on which the unions are based on have a lot of burden because of its duty to carry out collective bargaining in response to their separate demands. In order to avoid possible burdens on employers, compulsory single table collective bargaining at a workplace or enterprise level was introduced in July, 2011 simultaneously with the restoration of multiple unionism.

The process of arranging a single table for collective bargaining is stipulated in the TULRSA (s. 29.2–s. 29.5) and its Enforcement Decree in detail (s. 14.2–s. 14.12). Two or more enterprise unions (or an industrial union having members at the enterprise) have to decide their single representative entity for collective bargaining voluntarily. If they fail to in due course, a trade union (or an industrial union having members at the enterprise) of more than half of the whole trade union members of an enterprise or workplace is entitled to appoint all representatives for collective bargaining. Where there is no such union, each trade union is entitled to appoint representatives for the single entity up to the number calculated in relative proportion to the number of the members of each trade union within an enterprise or workplace. The LRC has jurisdiction over any dispute in relation to single representative entity.

It is the leader of a trade union that is entitled to conduct collective bargaining with an employer and to conclude a collective agreement with him/her under the TULRSA [s. 29(1)]. The leader of a trade union or an employer may authorize a third person to bargain and conclude collective agreements on their behalf [s. 29 (3)]. In relation to the authority to conclude collective agreements, there is an on-going issue in Korea despite the TULRSA's provisions. Conventionally, many Korean trade unions have a ballot for a collective agreement reached between their representatives and an employer before the leader of trade unions finally signs the agreement. If the ballot shows that more than half of the members who voted oppose the agreement, trade unions have to re-bargain for a better collective agreement. This practice is authorized by a trade union rule. Even before the clear enunciation of the effect of granting the authority to conclude collective agreements to the leader of a trade union in 1997, the courts held that a trade union rule or a provision in collective agreements providing for a preliminary ballot was illegal.[30] This means that, even if the leader signed a collective agreement before a ballot, the agreement would be valid. There has been criticism that the court's ruling and the subsequent amendment to the TULRSA to such an effect undermine democracy and autonomy of trade unionism.

5.3.2 Collective Agreements

A collective agreement is binding only when it is in written form and both an employer and the leader of a trade union sign, or affix their seals to, the agreement [s. 31(1), TULRSA]. Although both the parties to a collective agreements have to report the conclusion of collective agreements to the Administrative Authorities within 15 days after the date that such collective agreement is concluded [s. 31(2), TULRSA], the failure to do so does not affect the legal effect of a collective agreement but lead them to be administratively fined. The administrative authorities may order the parties to amend a collective agreement if they find the agreement unlawful [s. 31(3), TULRSA]. The authorities are able to do so only when they obtain a resolution to such effect from the LRC before they make such order.

The legal effect of a collective agreement is twofold. Firstly, collective agreements preside over employment contracts and workplace rules to the extent they are related to wages and other employment conditions. When the provisions covering employment conditions of employees in employment contracts or

[30] Supreme Court Decision 91Nu12257 Decided on April 27, 1993; Supreme Court Decision 91Nu10787 Decided on May 11, 1993.

workplace rules fall short of those equivalent in collective agreements, they are void and the former is automatically replaced by the latter (s. 33, TULRSA). This type of the legal effect of collective agreements is called "normative legal effect". Secondly, collective agreements have legal effect as one type of a contract. If either an employer or a trade union default on a provision in a collective agreement, the employer or the union is contractually liable to the other party. This type of the legal effect of collective agreements is called "contractual legal effect". This contractual effect of collective agreements is particularly relevant to provisions in collective agreements which deal with collective labour relations since they lack the first type of legal effect.

The normative legal effect of collective agreements may, in two certain circumstances, extend beyond the coverage to which the agreements are supposed to apply. Firstly, where a collective agreement applies to half or more of the employees in a workplace or an enterprise to which the agreement could be expected to apply to its utmost extent, its normative legal effect extends to cover the non-union employees in the workplace or the enterprise (s. 35). Secondly, where a collective agreement applies to two thirds or more of the employees in a certain geographical area to which the agreement could be expected to apply to its utmost extent, it presides over employment contracts or workplace rules of the employees in the area to which the agreement actually does not apply where administrative authorities obtain a resolution to that effect from the LRC (s. 36, TULRSA). The compulsory extension of the legal effect of collective agreements is designed to protect both minor non-union employees and trade unions as it enhances the former's working conditions and raises the effectiveness of collective agreements of the latter.

The period of validity of collective agreements may not exceed 2 years [s. 32(1), TULRSA]. Where a collective agreement has no provision on the period of validity or a provision of more than 2 years, its period of validity automatically change into 2 years [s. 32(2), TULRSA]. Where a collective agreement expires and no new agreement has been reached, the collective agreement remains valid for 3 months after its period of validity unless there is an agreement to different effect. If there is a provision in a collective agreement which provides that the collective agreement remain valid until a new collective agreement is concluded, hence, the provision is valid. Nonetheless, either party to the collective agreement may end it by giving the other party 6 months' notice before the day when the party wants to terminate it [s. 32(3), TULRSA]. Under the TULRSA, there is no explicit provision on what working conditions of trade union members will change into when 3 months passes after an existing collective agreement expires, or when either party gives the other party a notice of termination 6 months in advance and this period passes, and accordingly no collective agreement remains valid. The courts held that the working conditions in a collective bargaining which had so far applied to trade union members remained valid, as they had been already incorporated into contents of an employment contract of individual trade union members.[31]

[31] Supreme Court Decision 2007Da51758 Decided on December 27, 2007.

5.4 Collective Labour Dispute Settlement

When there arises a dispute over determining working conditions between a trade union and an employer, which is defined as 'collective labour dispute' under the TULRSA, either party has to apply for a mediation proceeding to the LRC. This mediation proceeding is compulsory in the sense that industrial action is prohibited from taking place without the proceeding completed, as stipulated in s. 45(2), TULRSA. The LRC has to form a tripartite mediation committee and complete the proceeding within 10 days (15 days for undertakings of public nature) when it receives an application for mediation.

Unlike a mediation proceeding, an arbitration proceeding must be agreed on by both parties or may be requested by either party if there exists a provision to that effect in a collective agreement (s. 62, TULRSA). It is conducted by an arbitration committee of the LRC, which is composed of three members representing the public. The committee has to complete an arbitration proceeding within 15 days once it receives an application for arbitration. The arbitrament which the committee makes as a result of the proceeding has the same legal effect as a collective agreement [s. 63 and s.70(2), the TULRSA]. The parties to collective bargaining are able to opt out a mediation proceeding, and an arbitration proceeding as operated by the LRC when they proceed through a third person who they want to take both mediation and arbitration in place of the LRC (s. 52. TULRSA).

5.5 Industrial Action

Probably one of the most distinctive features in relation to industrial action under Korean legal system is that all kinds of industrial action are activities for which employees organizing or joining them can be criminally punished under Korean Criminal Act unless they are otherwise justified. For instance, trade union leaders who organised a walk-out strike without committing any other criminal offence, such as the use of violence and illegal occupation of the premise of an employer, if the aim of the strike was not concerned with the determination of working conditions, were often charged with violating s. 314, Criminal Act. This provision stipulates that anyone who obstructed business by the use of force be punished with imprisonment of 5 years or less or fine of 15 million Won or less. Although the interpretation that collective refusal of work alone amounted to the use of force in s. 314, Criminal Act was often challenged in the courts, the Supreme Court upheld it[32] and the Constitutional Court declared it constitutionally legitimate.[33] Criminal sanction, as well as civil action based on tort law, for illegal stoppage of work itself in Korea is contrasted with the latter alone in most Western countries.

[32] Supreme Court Decision 90Do2771 Decided on Apri 23, 1991.

[33] Constitutional Court Decision 97Hun-Ba23 Decided on July 16, 1998; Constitutional Court Decision 2009Hun-Ba168 Decided on April 29, 2010.

Changing tack, however, the Supreme Court, for the first time, started to restrict the broad application of s. 314, Criminal Act to collective refusal of work in its recent decision.[34] It held that collective refusal to provide labour did not always constitutes violation of the crime of the obstruction of business. It went on to hold that it did so only "when it makes free intention of an employer frustrated by, for instance, causing immense disarray, or enormous damage to his/her operation of business due to its sudden occurrence at an unexpected time." As another recent decision of the Supreme Court's shows,[35] the seminal decision is likely to make the simple breach of an employment contract significantly less vulnerable to criminal sanction, although it does not completely make it free from the sanction

There are a variety of restrictions on industrial action, the violation of which, under the TULRSA, leads employees who organised or joined it to be criminally punished. Firstly, industrial action, in light of who has to organize it, has to be conducted by a trade union [s. 37(2)]. For instance, hence, industrial action organised by a temporary association of employees is prohibited.[36] Secondly, several restrictions on industrial action in light of its method must be complied with. Industrial action accompanied by violence and destruction has not to be conducted [s. 42(1), TULRSA]. Moreover, production facilities and other facilities in relation to main business must not be occupied in the course of industrial action [s. 42(1), TULRSA]. Unlike in western countries, as a matter of practice, a strike is often accompanied by the occupation of industrial places by strikers in Korea. It is established case law that occupation of the premises of an employer which is partial and does not disturb main business are allowed under the TULRSA. For instance, the Supreme Court held that the occupation of a conference room in a company which had not been often used was not illegal.[37] The maintenance and operation of security facilities of a workplace also must not be stopped, closed or interrupted [s. 42(2), TULRSA]. Even though a minority of employees are in breach of such restrictions, with trade unions not authorising it, however, this does not necessarily mean that industrial action as a whole becomes illegal.[38] Lastly, trade unions which intend to carry out industrial action have to follow certain procedures set by the TULRSA. Among other things, trade unions are prohibited from conducting industrial action unless it is supported by more than half members in a ballot (s. 41, TULRSA). Moreover, trade unions are able to proceed with industrial action only when they complete a mediation proceeding (s. 45, TULRSA). However, the courts held that the fact that the LRC neither accepted an application for mediation by a trade union because of insufficient collective bargaining between the parties, nor suggested a compromise because of a significant difference in both parties'

---

[34] Supreme Court Decision 2007Do482 Decided on March 17, 2011.

[35] Supreme Court Decision 2009Do11102 Decided on July 14, 2011.

[36] Supreme Court Decision 95Do748 Decided on April 22, 1997.

[37] Supreme Court Decision 2007Do5204 Decided on December 28, 2007.

[38] Supreme Court Decision 2003Du8906 Decided on December 26, 2003.

opinions during the proceeding did not make subsequent industrial action by the trade union illegal.[39]

In order to counteract industrial action by trade unions, an employer may conduct a lock-out. It is allowed only after industrial action by trade unions begins [s. 46(1)]. Moreover, a lock-out is not allowed to take place in such an aggressive manner that an employer intends to overwhelm or weaken a trade union.[40] The legal effect of an lock out is that, firstly, an employer is entitled to evict employees legally occupying his(her) premises, and that, secondly, he/she is exempted from his duty to pay wages to non-union members who are ready to work but are not able to work during industrial action. An employer is prohibited from hiring workers or outsourcing jobs in order to keep business normally operated in the course of industrial action (s. 44, TULRSA).

5.6 Employee Representational Participation (Works Council)

There are various forms of workers' participation in management around the world. Korea adopts the form of works council, which is called Labour-Management Council (LMC) under the Act concerning the Promotion of Workers Participation and Cooperation (the APWPC). An employer who employs 30 or more employees has the duty to establish an LMC. An LMC has to consist of an equal number of representatives of employees and an employer, with each side of representatives ranging between three and ten.

There are a great number of matters to be dealt with at the LMC. They are categorised into three types, depending on the scope of deliberation: matters for reporting, matters for consultation and matters for resolution. Firstly, an employer has to report and explain, e.g. economic and financial conditions and manpower plans of his/her enterprise. Secondly matters for consultation which the APWPC requires an LMC to discuss include improvement of productivity and gain sharing, hiring, posting, education and training of workers, handling of workers' grievance, improvement of industrial safety and health and other work environments and promotion of workers' health, institutional improvement for personnel and labour management, administration of working hours and recess hours, institutional improvement of wage payment methods, a wage structure, a wage system, etc., introduction of new machines and technologies or improvement of work processes and establishment or revision of work rules. Thirdly, an employer has not only to discuss but also to decide matters for resolution in an LMC. These are establishment of basic plans for the education and training and skills development of employees, setting up and management of welfare facilities, establishment of an employee welfare fund, matters not resolved by the Grievance Handling Committee,

[39] Supreme Court Decision 2000Do2871 Decided on June 26, 2001; Supreme Court Decision 2004Do746 Decided on September 11, 2008.

[40] Supreme Court Decision 98Da34331 Decided on May 26, 2000.

and establishment of various labour-management cooperative committees. An LMC needs at least two thirds of the members to vote in favour in order to decide such matters.

Given that a great majority of trade unions are enterprise unions in Korea, functions of trade unions are highly likely to overlap with those of LMCs. The APWPC resolves this potential problem by giving the power to appoint members of an LMC on employees' side to trade unions the number of whose members is more than half of all the employees in an undertaking. Otherwise, members of an LMC on employees' side are directly elected by the employees. Hence, a conflict may remain between an LMC and a trade union the number of whose members is half of all the employees or less in an undertaking. In principle, the APWPC explicitly provides that collective bargaining or any other activities of trade unions must not be affected by the APWPC (s. 5, APWPC).

6 Remedies

6.1 Inspection and Enforcement System

There are two traditional types of remedies for rights in the workplace. Firstly, provisions of protection for workers in relation to both individual employment and collective labour law are enforced through criminal sanctions accompanied by them. Although a few of provisions, such as provisions concerning unjust dismissal, have been decoupled from criminal sanction, still most of the employment and labour provisions in Korean labour law entail criminal sanction. Even when an employer violates provisions in a collective agreement in relation to working conditions, for instance, he/she is subject to criminal sanction (s. 92, TULRSA). In relation to collective labour law, furthermore, if an employer commits an ULP as defined in s81, TULRSA, he/she is criminally punished for the breach of the provision.

In order to ensure that such provisions involving criminal sanction are effectively enforced, there is a special policing system in the government where labour inspectors who belong to the MEL take place of police in relation to such provisions. Voluntarily or following accusations by employees or trade unions, the inspectors are entitled to inspect the workplaces or investigate such accusations.

Secondly, employees are able to bring an action to a civil court for the breach by an employer of individual employment law or a collective agreement. This is so because, where employment law provisions or provisions in the collective agreement in relation to working conditions of employees are more in favour of employees than such provisions in an employment contract, the latter become invalid and are automatically replaced with the former (s. 33, TULRSA; s. 15, LSA). For instance, hence, an employee is able to institute civil action to seek recovery of unpaid wages or to seek to declare an unjust dismissal void. Moreover, an employee may seek damages for a breach of an employment contract in a civil action.

6.2 Administrative Remedies: Labour Relations Committee

Korean labour law system provides employees with an additional type of remedy other than the two traditional ones mentioned above: administrative order by the LRC. This additional type of remedy is designed to overcome shortcomings of the latter which are too time-consuming and costly for employees to undergo. The remedy by the LRC differs from that through the Employment Tribunal in the UK or the Labour Court in Germany although it has similar functions to the latter agencies. It is an administrative body although it plays a quasi-judicial role in relation to employment and labour matters. When an employee or a trade union wants to appeal after they exhausted all the LRC procedures, hence, they have to bring an action to an administrative court of first instance. Moreover, a failure to comply with the order of the LRC places an employer under criminal sanction only when he/she does not appeal against it. Moreover, the order, even though it is obligatory because the employer does not appeal against it, has no legal effect on the civil law relationship between an employer and an employee.

6.2.1 Unjust Dismissal Etc.

As far as an individual employment relationship is concerned, an employee is able to make a claim to the LRC on the grounds that he/she is unjustly dismissed, suspended, transferred, given wage reduction, or taken other punitive measures against (s. 23, LSA). However, an employee is not able to make a claim to the LRC about other employment matters, such as wages in arrears. When the LRC upholds the employee's claim, it makes a restitution order to the respondent namely, his/her employer. If the employer fails to implement the restitution order, the LRC may impose non-compliance fees on the employer (s. 33, TULRSA). In 2007, the non-compliance fee scheme was introduced as an alternative to the criminal sanction for the violation of s.23.

6.2.2 Unfair Labour Practice

Since Korean trade unions are mainly enterprise-based, they are more vulnerable to interference of employers. With a view to ensuring that collective labour rights are fully enforced in the workplace, hence, there has been the Unfair Labour Practice Scheme as stipulated in s.81. The ULP Scheme differs to that of the US in that the former protects only employees and trade unions whereas the latter protects both sides.

Unfavourable treatment against an employee on the grounds that he/she has joined, or tries to join, a trade union, or has done just activities for business of the trade union is prohibited (1 ho, s. 81, TULRSA). Likewise, unfavourable treatment against an employee on the basis that he/she has joined a just collective action is not allowed to take place (5 ho, s. 81, TULRSA). Except for a post-entry union shop agreement between an employer and a trade union whose members are two-thirds or more of all the employees in an undertaking, an employer is banned from requiring an employee to defect, or join, or not to join, a particular union as a precondition of employing him/her (2 ho, s. 81, TULRSA). Moreover, employers' refusal to, negligence of, collective bargaining for unjust reasons is a prohibited ULP (3 ho, s. 81). Lastly not only employers' paying full-time union officials but also employers' controlling, or interfering with, employees' organisation and operation of trade union are a ULP (4 ho, s. 81, TULRSA).

6.2.3 Procedure

An employee or a trade union has to make a claim to a regional LRC within 3 months after, for instance, unjust dismissal or a ULP takes place. After investigation and hearing, a regional LRC may make a variety of remedy order, such as a restitution order in the case of unjust dismissal or an unfavourable-treatment-type ULP, banning order in the case of a control-interfere-type ULP or an immediate negotiation order in the case of the refusal of collective bargaining. These kinds of flexible remedial orders make them differentiated from the decisions of the courts. Either a claimant or an employer as a respondent may appeal to the National LRC against the decision of a Regional LRC within 10 days after they receive the documents of the decision. An appeal against the decision of the National LRC can be made to an administrative court within 15 days after its receipt.

7 Conclusion

As an introduction to Korean labour law, this article has summarised its general features and briefly analysed its characteristics where necessary. Thus far, this work has suggested several key factors which gave insight into the establishment and development of Korean labour law system.

Firstly, there was a decisive foreign influence on the formation of labour law system at the outset. As a result, Korean labour law system is a hybrid of those of both German and US labour law. Whereas current features of the TULRSA on collective agreement and prohibition of dismissal without just grounds are originated from German law, unfair labour law practice and the LRC derive from the US labour law. The infusion of two different, or sometimes conflicting, jurisdictions resulted from the historical influence of Japan and the US at the time modern Korean labour law, for the first time, was enacted.

Secondly, enterprise unionism is vital to understand collective labour law in Korea. Payment by an employer to full-time union officials, which is now prohibited as a ULP is a concession by an employer under the pressure from his/her enterprise union. It can be only understood in such context that although payment by an employer to full-time union officials are strictly forbidden, the new time-off scheme, *de facto,* maintains, albeit in a smaller scale, paid full-time officials. In the same vein, moreover, the restoration of multiple unionism at an enterprise level accompanied by the compulsory single-table bargaining scheme is aimed at regulating enterprise-based industrial relations effectively. This is shown by the fact that the compulsory single-table bargaining has been introduced despite the strong opposition that it would run the risk of violating the right to collective bargaining in the Constitution.

Thirdly, it is certain that democratisation explains the development of modern labour law. The removal of a variety of restrictions on labour rights has been made over the last several decades. There remain a few restrictions. For instance, the application of the crime of the obstruction of business in the Criminal Act to collective refusal to provide labour shows that the right to collective action is not completely recognised to be, *de facto*, a positive right in Korean labour law, although the right is explicitly provided for in the Constitution. However, the Supreme Court has shown a glimpse of change towards the substantivisation of the right to collective action.

Lastly, it is undeniable that there have been amendments of individual employment law designed to adopt flexibilsation of employment. In particular, most developments in individual employment law since 1997 have been made in response to the demand of flexibilisation of employment by employers. Such developments include flexible working hours scheme, temporary agency work, and economic dismissal law. It is notable that protection for non-standard workers has been made in the dominant trend of flexibilsation.

This article has confirmed that while Korean labour law has diverged in some respects and has converged in other respects in comparison with advanced Western countries. Probably the first two factors mentioned above shows sign of divergence and the other two sign of convergence. Arguably this trend will continue unless socio-legal factors influencing labour law, such as Korean industrial relations and the trend towards globalisation of Korean economy, radically change.

References

Araki T (2002) Labor and Employment Law in Japan. The Japan Institute of Labor, Tokyo

Blanpain R, Bromwich W, Rymkevich O, Spattini S (2009) The modernization of Labour Law and industrial relations in a comparative perspective. Kluwer Law International, Alphen ann den Rijn

Blanpain R, Bamber G, Pochet P (2010) Regulating employment relations, work and labour laws: international comparisons between key countries. Kluwer Law International, Alphen aan den Rijn

Cho KB (2011) Service provision change and transfer of the employment relationship. Democratic Jurisprudence 46

Deakin S, Morris G (2009) Labour Law. Hart Publishing, Oxford

Japan Institute for Labour Policy and Training (2004) The mechanism for establishing and changing terms and conditions of employment/the scope of Labor Law and the Notion of Employees. JILPT, Tokyo

Kim HB (2001) Labour law. Parkyoung-Sa, Seoul

Kim Y (2011) The numbers and situations of non-standard worker. Korea Labour & Society Institute, Seoul

Koilaf (2010) Labor Management Manual for Foreign Investors 2010. Koilaf, Seoul

Korea Labour Institute (ed) (2000) The amendments to labour law and labour relations in Korea. KLI, Seoul

Lee HJ (2005) Mr. Jeon's idea and role in ensuring "the equal right to share profits of the private company" in establishment of the constitution. SNU Law J 46(1)

Lee HJ (2009) The characteristic of labour law establishment and the role of Jin Han Jeon. SNU Law J 50(4)

Lee SW (2007) A long way to go: developments in protection of labour rights in Korea. Law Soc 34

Lee SW (2008) Changes in labour relations system since "1987 Labour Regime". Law Soc 32

Lim JR (2011) Labour law. Parkyoung-Sa, Seoul

Ministry of Employment and Labour (2010) Labour law for foreign CEOs Q & A. Koilaf, Seoul

Ministry of Labour (2006) The history of labour standards act. MOL, Seoul

Porges J (1990) The development of Korean Labor Law and the impact of the American system. Comp Labor Law J 12

Sugeno K (2002) Japanese Employment and Labour Law. California Academic Press. Durham

Private International Law

Hongsik Chung

1 Introduction

Private international law (or conflict of laws) is a set of rules of law that determine which court has jurisdiction and which law governs a given legal dispute. It also determines whether, and if so under what conditions, a judgment rendered by a foreign court will be recognized and enforced domestically. Private international law typically applies when a legal dispute has an international element.

South Korea has an economy at close to USD 1 trillion GDP and is positioned at 12th largest economy in the world. Korea recently entered into two historic and comprehensive free trade agreements with the United States and the European Union. Korea is the first single country ever to sign free trade agreements back to back with the two gigantic economic leaders in the world. The economic prospects from these free trade agreements are so promising, and more increased cross-border transactions of goods, services, and investment are naturally expected. In spite of these prospects, we may see many more foreign parties from U.S. and Europe being present in Korean court than before. Thus it is definitely necessary for foreign parties to study and explore Korean private international law.

The private international law of the Republic of Korea was originally created in 1962. It has been heavily criticized from its inception because the law was just modeled after then, Japanese private international law and did not take any necessary steps of extensive research of and comparative reviews with other representing countries' comparable laws. With advancement of technology and transportation and increase of trade, more complex legal issues have been arising internationally; however, the old law was not sufficient enough to address and resolve such

H. Chung
CHUNG-ANG University, School of Law, Seoul, Republic of Korea
e-mail: hschung@cau.ac.kr

Korea Legislation Research Institute, *Introduction to Korean Law*,
DOI 10.1007/978-3-642-31689-0_9,

complicated matters. Nevertheless, the old law had been in effect almost forty (40) years before it was first dramatically amended in 2001.[1] The amended law is still a current version as of July 2011.

The Law Amending the Conflict of Laws Act, named *Gukjesabeop* in Korean (the "Act")[2] was adopted in an effort to address many complicated emerging issues and reflect globally changing trends on private international law. As a result, the Act contains new features, including but not limited to: (1) inclusion of rules on international jurisdiction[3]; (2) diversification of connecting factors in determining applicable laws; (3) expansion of the principle of party autonomy in contracts and other areas; (4) adoption of protective rules for socio-economically disadvantaged groups, like consumers and individual employees; (5) attainment of gender equality in governing laws; and (6) adoption of the closest connection principle.

The drafters, in the course of creating the Act, referred to various international conventions and incorporated several relevant provisions thereof into the new Act. As for the international jurisdiction for consumer contracts and contracts of individual employment, for instance, the drafters took into account four different conventions and regulations: (1) the Convention on Jurisdiction and the Enforcement of Judgments in Civil and Commercial Matters of European Community of 1968 ("Brussel Convention"); (2) the Council Regulation (EC) NO 44/2001 of 22 December 2000 on Jurisdiction and the Recognition and Enforcement of Judgments in Civil and Commercial Matters ("Brussel Regulation"); (3) the Lugano Convention; and (4) the 1999 Preliminary Draft of the Convention on Jurisdiction and Foreign Judgments in Civil and Commercial Matters ("1999 Draft Convention"[4]). Furthermore, the contract part of the Act was inspired by both the Convention on the Law Applicable to Contractual Obligations of the European Community of 1980 ("Rome Convention") and the Inter-American Convention on the Law Applicable to International Contracts of 1994 and follows their general lines. In addition, the Act incorporated a substantial part of the Convention on the Law Applicable to Maintenance Obligations of 1973 and the Convention on the Conflicts of Laws Relating to the Form of Testamentary Dispositions of 1961 into the provisions regarding maintenance and will.

The purpose of the Act is specified in Article 1 thereof. The Act only sets forth international jurisdiction and determination of governing law for legal disputes

[1] The Law Amending the Conflict of Laws Act became effective as of July 1, 2001 and is still a current version. For a detail procedural history and background of amending the Conflict of Laws Act, *see* Ministry of Justice (2003), pp. 3–8.

[2] Law No. 6465 of April 7, 2001. Note that the terms, *conflict of laws* and *private international law* will be used interchangeably in this article.

[3] The international jurisdiction was not even dealt with from the old law.

[4] The effort to finalize the 1999 Draft Convention failed and instead resulted in adoption of the Convention on Choice of Court Agreements in 2005. Although not yet in force, it will probably be widely ratified. All the world's major economic powers took part in: the United States, the European Community, China, Japan, Russia, Canada, Australia, Brazil and many others (Hartley 2009, p. 201). However, Korea did not take part in the adoption of the Convention. It is known that the Convention was inspired by the Brussels I Regulation and follows its general provisions.

having foreign dimensions, not the recognition and enforcement of foreign judgments. The Act consists of sixty-two articles in total, which are allocated into nine separate chapters. Titles of all chapters and articles[5] are as follows:

CHAPTER 1. GENERAL PROVISIONS
Article 1. Purpose
Article 2. International Jurisdiction
Article 3. Law of Nationality (*Lex Patriae*)
Article 4. Law of Habitual Residence
Article 5. Application of Foreign Law
Article 6. Scope of the Governing Law
Article 7. Mandatory Application of Korean Law
Article 8. Exception to the Governing Law designated
Article 9. *Renvoi* in case of designation of foreign law
Article 10. Provisions of Foreign Law contrary to public order
CHAPTER 2. PERSON
Article 11. Capacity to be entitled to Rights
Article 12. Declaration of Disappearance
Article 13. Capacity to Act
Article 14. Declaration of Quasi-Incompetency and Incompetency
Article 15. Protection of Transactions
Article 16. Legal Persons and Associations
CHAPTER 3. JURIDICAL ACT
Article 17. Formal Validity of Juridical Acts
Article 18. Agency
CHAPTER 4. REAL RIGHTS (RIGHTS *in rem*)
Article 19. Law Governing Real Rights
Article 20. Means of Transportation
Article 21. Bearer Securities
Article 22. Res in transitu
Article 23. Contractual Security Interests over Claims, etc.
Article 24. Protection of Intellectual Property Rights
CHAPTER 5. CLAIMS (*Chaegwon*)
Article 25. Party Autonomy
Article 26. Objective Connection of Governing Law
Article 27. Consumer Contracts
Article 28. Employment Contracts
Article 29. Formation and Validity of Contracts
Article 30. Management of Affairs without Mandate
Article 31. Unjust Enrichment
Article 32. Tort
Article 33. Subsequent Agreement on Governing Law Article 34. Contractual Assignment of Claims (Chaegwon) and Assumption of Obligations
Article 35. Transfer of Claims (Chaegwon) by Operation of Law
CHAPTER 6. KINSHIP
Article 36. Formation of Marriage
Article 37. General Effects of Marriage
Article 38. Matrimonial Property Regime
Article 39. Divorce
Article 40. Relationships between Parents and Legitimate Children
Article 41. Relationships between Parents and Illegimate Children
Article 42. Legitimation of Illegitimate Children
Article 43. Adoption and its Dissolution
Article 44. Consent
Article 45. Legal Relationships between Parents and Children
Article 46. Maintenance
Article 47. Other Kinship
Article 48. Guardianship
CHAPTER 7. SUCCESSION
Article 49. Inheritance
Article 50. Wills
CHAPTER 8. BILLS OF EXCHANGE, PROMISSORY NOTES/CHECKS
Article 51. Capacity to Act
Article 52. Qualification of Payer of Check
Article 53. Form
Article 54. Effect
Article 55. Acquisition of Underlying Claims
Article 56. Partial Acceptance and Partial Payment
Article 57. Form of Acts for Exercising and Preserving Rights
Article 58. Loss or Theft
Article 59. Law of Place of Payment
CHAPTER 9. MARITIME COMMERCE
Article 60. Maritime Commerce
Article 61. Collision of Ships
Article 62. Salvage

---

[5] The titles of all chapters and articles in the Act are obtained from Suk (2003b), pp. 315–336, in which a full translation of the Act is separately contributed by Professor K. H. SUK, who is the most distinguished professor of law in the field of private international law in Korea.

This section is formatted to provide an overview of the Act, with a brief explanation of primary provisions and an introduction of recent Korean court decisions. Chapter II addresses jurisdictional issues. Chapter III deals with recognition and enforcement of foreign judgments although its rules are not included in the Act. Chapter IV covers core topics of choice of law, mainly general provisions, contracts, torts, property, intellectual property, etc.

2 International Jurisdiction

2.1 *General Principle*

Article 2 of the Act provides for a general principle about international jurisdiction.[6] Article 2(1) states that when the parties or the case in dispute has a *substantial connection* with the Republic of Korea, the courts shall have international jurisdiction with regard thereto. For determining the existence of a *substantial connection*, Article 2(1) further directs the courts to follow *a reasonable principle that is compatible with basic ideals for proper allocation of international jurisdiction.* (emphasis added)

Article 2(2) further provides for a guideline for interpretation of Article 2(1) although it is not particularly specific. Article 2(2) states that, for a purpose of determination of international jurisdiction, the court shall first refer to relevant provisions of the Korean Civil Procedure Act ("KCPA")[7] as to domestic venues[8]; however, the court is required to take into account the special characteristics of international jurisdiction, as distinguished from the domestic venue rules.

2.1.1 Interpretation of Article 2(1)

How *substantial* should the connection be, pursuant to Article 2(1), for the court to have the international jurisdiction? A lower court recently held that the connection between the parties or the case in dispute and Korea should be substantial enough to justify the exercise of international jurisdiction by the court. That is, a certain connecting factor with Korea should exist. For this purpose, the court shall take into account all of the circumstances surrounding each case.[9]

[6] For a general and comprehensive analysis of international jurisdiction in *Korean* language, *see* K. H. Suk, 「국제사법 해설」 p. 32 *et seq*.

[7] Act No. 9171, December 26, 2008.

[8] K. H. SUK, 「국제사법 해설」 pp. 43–44.

[9] Decision of 2007. 8. 30, 2006가합53066 (Seoul Central District Court).

With regard to the phrase, "basic ideals for proper allocation of international jurisdiction," pursuant to Article 2(1) of the Act does not provide for any definition of the basic ideals. However, the Supreme Court of Korea has previously stated that international jurisdiction shall be determined by *jori*[10] in accordance with basic ideals of equity between parties, and the propriety, swiftness and efficiency of the trial.[11] However, the drafters of the Act were afraid that the concept of the basic ideals would be limited to such view of the Supreme Court rendered prior to adoption of the new Act. Thus, Article 2(1) merely requires that the basic ideals shall be compatible with a *reasonable principle*.[12] In other words, the Act intends to encompass broader interpretation and application of the concept of the basic ideals to cases.

In 2005, the Supreme Court of Korea provided a rather specific interpretation of the basic ideals and the reasonable principle. In determining international jurisdiction, it held that the court shall follow the basic ideal that equity between the parties, and the propriety, swiftness and efficiency of the trial be promoted.[13] Specifically, the court should consider not only private interests, such as fairness, convenience and predictability for litigating parties, but also public interests in the propriety, swiftness, efficiency of the trial and the effectiveness of judgment. Which interests are more protected among these various interests should be reasonably determined based on both the substantial relationship between the forum and the parties in each specific case, and the substantial relationship between the forum and the disputed matters.[14]

2.1.2 Interpretation of Article 2(2)

With respect to Article 2(2), as mentioned earlier, the court shall look into relevant provisions of domestic territorial venues[15] in order to determine international jurisdiction. However, this is not to say that the court mechanically follows the provisions of the domestic territorial venues. Rather, Article 2(2) specifically requires the court to consider the *special characteristics* of international jurisdiction and then establish more detailed and refined rules on international jurisdiction. The premise for this is that both domestic venues and international jurisdiction share the same spirit of establishing a fair and efficient forum for dispute resolution. Thus, the drafters of the Act believed that the KCPA's provisions can at least provide a basis for international jurisdiction by way of analogy.[16]

---

[10] *Jori* means 'nature of the thing.'

[11] Decision of 1992. 7. 28, 91다41897 (the Supreme Court of Korea) and Decision of 1995. 11. 21, 93다39607 (the Supreme Court of Korea).

[12] K. H. SUK, 「국제사법 해설」 pp. 40–41.

[13] This is also the same principle that can be found from Article 1 of the Korea Civil Procedure Act ("KCPA").

[14] Decision of 2005. 01. 27, 2002다59788 (the Supreme Court of Korea).

[15] These provisions can be found from the KCPA, Articles 2 through Article 40.

[16] Kwon (2007), p. 125.

Pursuant to Articles 2 through 40 of the KCPA, there are a general venue and a special venue by which domestic territorial jurisdiction is decided. Articles 2 through 6 of the KCPA provide rules on the general venue. The court at the defendant's place of domicile[17] is competent to decide all claims.[18] In case the defendant has no domicile or his/her domicile is unknown, the general forum will be determined by the defendant's place of residence. When even the residence is undetermined or unknown, the general forum will be decided pursuant to the defendant's lastly known residence.[19]

The KCPA also provides for numerous special venues under Articles 7–24. Important among these special venues are: a workplace[20]; the place where an obligation is performed[21]; a location of the property in issue[22]; a place where a tortious act occurred[23]; and a place of registration.[24] Korean courts, in determining international jurisdiction, must first look into these domestic territorial venue clauses in the KCPA and, if necessary, attempt to apply or modify the domestic doctrines in light of special characteristics, if any.

2.1.3 Other Issues and Future Task

In the course of amending the Act, whether a specific rule on *forum non conveniens* should be created was discussed; however, such rule was not finally adopted.[25] Further, it appears that no case has been reported in which Korean courts allow a transfer of a case to another foreign court under the principle of *forum non conveniens*.

A future task for the international jurisdiction is to develop and refine rules on international jurisdiction and include them in the Act. The rules can be divided into two general categories, which are (1) general jurisdiction; and, (2) special jurisdiction. Further, the special jurisdiction should be sub-classified into various types of jurisdiction, such as contract, tort, intellectual property, jurisdiction agreement and exclusive jurisdiction. This task is left to the court and scholars.

---

[17] As for the concept of domicile and its different meaning from habitual residence, refer to Chapter IV, A. General Provisions, 2. habitual residence as a new connecting factor.

[18] KCPA, Art. 2.

[19] KCPA, Art. 3.

[20] KCPA, Art. 7.

[21] KCPA, Art. 8.

[22] KCPA, Art. 11.

[23] KCPA, Art. 18.

[24] KCPA, Art. 21.

[25] Ministry of Justice (2003) p. 25.

2.2 *Protection of Socio-Economically Disadvantaged Groups*

Korean legal systems take the view that consumers and individual employees, being in a weak bargaining position, need protection. This position is extended to the Act, which provides for special rules for consumer contracts and individual contracts for employment. The special rules cover both matters of jurisdiction and choice of law. These rules operate much more favorably for consumers and employees than for the other party and employers. These rules are modeled after Articles 13 through 15 of the Brussels Convention and Articles 15 through 17 of the Brussels Regulation.

2.2.1 Consumer Contracts

If a consumer sues the other party, he has an option to sue the other party in the country of his habitual residence.[26] Alternatively, the consumer may sue the other party in the country determined under Article 2. It could be the court of the country where the other party has its or his habitual residence or actually performs for the consumer. Thus, the consumer has two options to bring a lawsuit against the other party. One is under Article 27(4), and the other is under Article 2. Article 27(4) is significantly distinguishable in that the rule operates, clearly as contrary to the principle of *actor sequitur forum rei* (plaintiff is subject to the defendant's forum).[27]

If the other party sues a consumer, it or he may do so only in the courts of the country in which the consumer habitually resides.[28] This is an exclusive and limited jurisdiction available to the other party irrespective of any prior choice of court agreement between the parties.[29] If the parties choose the court in one of the parties' place of habitual residence, it would be void. It is sometimes very harsh against the other party to a consumer contract.

A court agreement on the choice between the parties is allowed, but only under limited circumstances.[30] Such court agreements on the choice are effective only in either of the following situations: (1) if such agreement is entered into *after* the dispute has arisen; or (2) if the agreement allows the consumer to bring an action before another court in addition to those having jurisdiction under Article 27. This is not to mention that Article 27(6) works more favorably for consumers than for manufacturers or suppliers.

---

[26] The Act, Art. 27(4).

[27] Ministry of Justice (2003) pp. 100–101; K. H. SUK, 「국제사법 해설」, p. 239.

[28] The Act, Art. 27(5).

[29] Ministry of Justice (2003) p. 101; K. H. SUK, 「국제사법 해설」, p. 240.

[30] The Act, Art. 27(6).

It should be noted that there is one important limitation on Article 27(4), (5) and (6). The three sections are only applicable to the type of consumer contract that falls under Article 27(1) of the Act. Although the nature of the consumer contract will be explained in Chapter IV, B. Contracts, it shall be a passive type of contract from the consumer's standpoint. In other words, if the contract was not made in a passive manner, the above three sections will be prohibited from applying. In the event it does not fall within the passive type of consumer contract, thus, Article 2 will determine the jurisdictional matters for the consumer contract.

2.2.2 Individual Employment Contracts

If an employee brings a lawsuit against an employer, the employee has two options as shown on Article 27 above. The first option is to bring a lawsuit against the employer in the country where the international jurisdiction is determined in accordance with Article 2. The jurisdiction could be the employer's place of residence or the place of performance. The second option is that the employee may sue the employer: (1) in the country in which the employee habitually carries out his/her work or in the last country where he did so; or, (2) if the employee does not or did not habitually carry out his/her work in any one country, in the country where the place of business that employed him is or was situated.[31]

This second option has two prongs. Under the first, jurisdiction is given to the country in which the employee habitually carries out his/her work. As the word 'habitually' makes clear, it is not necessary that all the work should be performed in one place. As long as the employee *habitually* works within the country concerned, it is irrelevant that the claim arose while he was temporarily employed elsewhere. If the first prong does not apply, the second prong comes into play. This allows the employee to sue the employer in the country where the business through which he was employed "is or was situated." If the location of that business has changed, the employee may sue where it *was* situated when the contract for employment was made or where it *is* situated at the time when the action is brought.[32] This is the meaning of the words, "is or was situated."

If the employer sues the employee, he may do so only in the country in which the employee habitually resides or in the country where the employee habitually carries out his work.[33] This is also an exclusive and limited jurisdiction, as seen from the consumer contracts, available to the employer irrespective of any prior choice of forum agreement between the parties. If the parties choose the court in the employer's habitual residence, it would be void.

Article 28(5) also allows the court agreement on the choice between the parties under some limited circumstances. Such agreement is effective only in either of the

[31] The Act, Art. 28(3).

[32] This is the meaning of the words, "is or was situated." Trevor, p. 68.

[33] The Act, Art. 28(4).

following situations: (1) if such agreement is entered into *after* the dispute has arisen; or (2) if the agreement allows the employee to bring an action before another court in addition to those having jurisdiction under Article 28.

3 Recognition and Enforcement of Foreign Judgments

Recognition is a precondition for both the *res judicata* and the enforcement of a foreign judgment in Korea. Thus, without domestic recognition, a foreign judgment neither has *res judicata* effect nor enforcement power domestically. The Act does not include provisions on the recognition and enforcement of foreign judgments in Korea. Relevant rules on the recognition and enforcement of foreign judgments are separated and included in the KCPA and the Korean Civil Execution Act ("KCEA"),[34] respectively. Article 217 of the KCPA governs recognition of all kinds of foreign civil (including family) and commercial matters. Articles 26 and 27 of the KCEA govern the execution of all kinds of foreign civil (including family) and commercial judgments and other equivalents of foreign judgments, including some arbitral awards.[35] Although the Act does not cover in itself the recognition and enforcement of foreign judgments, this Chapter III will briefly deal with the subject because it is very important from foreigners' perspective. It might be appropriate for the related provisions to be separated from the KCPA and the KCEA and then incorporated into the Act.

3.1 Recognition of Foreign Judgment

Pursuant to Article 217 of the KCPA, several requirements are to be met for the recognition of foreign judgments in Korea. It should be noted, however, that although recognition is a prerequisite for the enforcement of foreign judgments, no special judicial proceeding is needed to obtain certain recognition of a foreign judgment itself. Once the requirements for recognition under Article 217 are met and satisfied, the foreign judgment should automatically come into effect in Korea and be entitled to seek an execution judgment from Korean court.[36] In order to execute the foreign judgment within Korea, a judgment-creditor shall obtain from the court a separate judgment permitting the execution of the foreign judgment.

[34] Act No. 9525, March 29, 2009.

[35] These arbitral awards are governed by Articles 26 and 27 of the KCEA only if they are not subject to the Convention on Recognition and Enforcement of Foreign Arbitral Awards (the "New York Convention"). Since Korea is a contracting state to the New York Convention, recognition and enforcement of most foreign arbitral awards will be regulated by the New York Convention.

[36] Suk (2002), pp. 345–346.

Before the requirements for recognition are explained, a question naturally arises as to what types of judgments are entitled to consideration for recognition. Article 217 does not limit any specific kinds of judgments on its face. The recognizable judgments include not only monetary one but also specific performance in civil and commercial cases. However, criminal judgments, administrative judgments, and tax judgments are excluded from the scope of Article 217.[37] The requirements for recognition of foreign judgments are as follow:

3.1.1 Finality and Conclusiveness of Foreign Judgments

A foreign judgment is deemed final and conclusive when there is no possibility of further appeal under civil procedure. The judgment creditor has to prove either that no further appeal is possible or that the period for filing an appeal has already passed. Thus, foreign interim orders, foreign interlocutory judgments or foreign interim awards cannot be recognized under Article 217 of the KCPA. Whether or not this requirement of finality and conclusiveness has been met is determined in accordance with the foreign law by which the decision was rendered.[38]

3.1.2 Requirement of International Jurisdiction

The second requirement is that the jurisdiction of such foreign court should be recognized in accordance with the principles of international jurisdiction pursuant to the Act and subordinate statutes of Korea, or with the treaties on international jurisdiction.[39] This means that, because Korea has ratified neither bilateral nor multilateral treaty on international jurisdiction, the exercise of the international jurisdiction by the foreign court shall be compatible with Korean standards described in Chapter II above. In the event it is not compatible with the Korean standards, the foreign country judgment may be valid when rendered, but not entitled to recognition in Korea.

The timing for determining the existence of a foreign court's international jurisdiction requirement for recognition is not when the case is brought to the foreign court or when the judgment has become final in the foreign country. It should be when the foreign judgment is examined in a Korean court for recognition and enforcement.[40]

---

[37] Lee (2006), p. 115–116.

[38] K. H. SUK, 「국제사법과 국제소송 I」, p. 265.

[39] KCPA, Art. 217(1).

[40] K. H. SUK, 「국제사법과 국제소송 I」 p. 296; Lee (2006), p. 117.

3.1.3 Requirement of Lawful Service of Statement of Claim and Summons or Other Documents

The defendant in the original action must have been served with a copy of the statement of claim (or any equivalent document) and the summons or any orders in a lawful and timely manner for recognition in Korea.[41] The service shall be lawful and timely. The timely manner of service adequately informs the defendant of the nature of the claim and is given in sufficient time to afford the defendant an adequate opportunity to defend. Among the lawful means of service, however, Article 217(2) of the KCPA specifically excludes from recognition, a notice by publication to the defendant in the foreign court.

It should be noted that, if the defendant voluntarily responded to the lawsuit without the statement of claim and summons being properly served, this requirement is deemed to have been satisfied. Further, it is not necessary that the defendant in the original action should be a Korean national or entity for satisfaction of this requirement, while the old rule so required. Thus, Article 217 is applicable irrespective of the nationality of the defendant in the original action. Korea is a contracting state to the Hague Convention on Service Abroad of Judicial and Extrajudicial Documents in Civil and Commercial Matters since August 2000.

3.1.4 Requirement of Good Morals and Other Social Orderliness

The foreign judgment should not violate "good morals or other social orderliness." There is no statutory definition of good morals and other social orderliness, but the concept may correspond to a matter of "public policy". This requirement is to prevent a foreign judgment from being recognized and enforced in contravention of the public policy in Korea. What constitutes the violation of good morals and other social orderliness is left at the discretion of the competent court.

3.1.5 Requirement of Reciprocity

The last requirement is reciprocity between Korea and the country in which the original action was preceded. The foreign judgment is recognized and enforced only when Korean judgments are also recognized and enforced under the same or lenient conditions in the country of the original action concerned.[42] Lack of 'reciprocity' is a typical statutory ground for non-recognition of foreign judgments

[41] KCPA, Art. 217(2).

[42] Kwon,"Litigating in Korea" p. 141.

in many countries. However, the legal meaning of "reciprocity" is unclear, and most countries lack a special legal definition for such term.[43]

A question arises here as to when the reciprocity exists or as to the criteria for reciprocity. Korean courts now take a position that it would be sufficient enough when both of foreign system and Korean system do not substantially differ so as not to lose over-all balance, and when both systems are similar in important respects even if the recognition requirements of the foreign country should be neither equal to nor more lenient than those of Korea in each aspect.[44]

3.2 Execution of Foreign Judgments

Articles 26 & 27 of KCEA govern the execution of all kinds of foreign civil (including family) or commercial judgments. All foreign judgment creditors must obtain a judgment for enforcement from a competent Korean court. A compulsory execution based upon the judgment of a foreign court may be conducted only if a court of Korea has made a declaration of its legality by means of a judgment of execution.[45] A lawsuit for a judgment of execution shall be under the jurisdiction of the district court located at the judgment debtor's general forum, and if such general forum does not exist, it shall be under the jurisdiction of the court having jurisdiction over a lawsuit against the judgment debtor under the provisions of Article 11 of the KCPA.[46]

A judgment of execution shall be made without any examination as to the merits of the judgment.[47] Thus, the so-called "review de novo" is prohibited.[48] However, a lawsuit for a judgment of execution shall be dismissed (1) when it has not been proved that the judgment of a foreign court has become final and conclusive, or (2) when the foreign judgment fails to fulfill the conditions under Article 217 of the KCPA.[49] Therefore, all requirements of recognition provided for in Article 217 of the KCPA are mandatory for enforcing foreign judgments.

[43] Cf. Committee on Foreign and Comparative Law, Association of Bar, City of N.Y., Survey on Foreign Recognition of U.S. Money Judgments (July 2001) (reciting from L. S. Hoon, p. 126).

[44] Lee (2006), p. 133. (Decision of Oct. 28, 2004, 2002다74213 (the Supreme Court of Korea).

[45] KCEA, Art. 26(1).

[46] KCEA, Art. 26(2).

[47] KCEA, Art. 27(1).

[48] K. H. SUK, 「국제사법 국제소송 I」 p.348.

[49] KCEA, Art. 27(2).

4 Choice of Law

A choice of law problem arises when a court must decide which of multiple candidate laws will supply the rule of decisions for a case. In its most common form, this requires a court to choose between the laws of one or more countries. The Act imports the methodology based on categorization. When faced with a choice-of-law problem, we should start with a category, and then decide whether the particular law or issue at hand fits into that category. If so, we then derive a connecting factor that goes with the category—in the case of immovable property, a connecting factor is the place where the land is situated. The connecting factor will tell us what law is applicable. This structure gives the appearance of a logical mechanism capable of delivering certainty in solving choice-of-law cases. It can be shown as follows:

$$\text{Legal Category} \Rightarrow \text{Connecting Factor} \Rightarrow \text{Applicable Law}$$

For the first step, the difficult question is how to decide whether a given rule or issue should be regarded as fitting into a particular category. This process is known as 'characterization' or 'classification'. As regards the second step, there is often a problem in deciding how a connecting factor should be applied. How, for example, does one decide where a person is domiciled? What is the situs (location) of an intangible right. This process is known as 'determination of the connecting factor'. As regards the third step, once one knows what legal system applies, how does one discover what that law is?[50] Moreover, what should we do if we discover that, under the relevant foreign choice-of-law rule, the law of that country is not applicable? Should we ignore this, or should we apply the law that is applicable under the foreign choice-of-law rule?[51] Finally, if the foreign law is regarded as unfair or if it produces results that are regarded as unacceptable, should it be applied all the same?[52] These various matters will be considered further, below.

It should also be noted that the Act applies only to substantive law, never to procedural law. It is generally accepted in the Korea legal system that questions of procedures are always decided by the law of the court hearing the case. Exactly what constitutes procedure is sometimes controversial, and even complicated and difficult to decide.

[50] This is when the applicable law is a foreign law, and it is difficult to ascertain the foreign law.

[51] This question regards the problem of *renvoi*.

[52] This question is a matter of public policy.

4.1 General Provisions

These general provisions are common rules and applicable to all other provisions of the Act.[53] The general provisions deal with two important connecting factors, which are 'the law of nationality of a party' (*Lex Patriae*) and the law of habitual residence. Further, the Act covers various escape devices, which enables the court to avoid the normal effect of the choice-of-law rule it is applying, such as mandatory application of Korean law (Article 7) regardless of choice of law, exception to the governing law determined (Article 8), *Renvoi* (Article 9), and the public policy exception (Article 10).

4.1.1 Law of Nationality of Natural Person (*Lex Patriae*)

If, in cases where the *lex patriae* of a party governs and the party concerned has two or more nationalities, the *lex patriae* shall be the law of the country with which the party is most closely connected.[54] However, if one of the multiple nationalities is that of the Republic of Korea, the law of the Republic of Korea shall be the party's *lex patriae*.[55] In the event that a party has no nationality, or it is impossible to ascertain his/her nationality, the law of the country where he habitually resides shall govern; if it is impossible to ascertain his habitual residence, the law of the country where he resides shall govern.[56] In addition, if a governing law is determined to be the law of a country having separate tiers of the legal system, such as the United States of America, then the country's private international law (or conflict of law) shall determine a governing law. In the situation where the USA has no nation-wide mandatory conflict of law, Article 3(3) provides that the law of the local district with which the USA citizen party is most closely connected shall be the governing law.[57]

4.1.2 Habitual Residence as New Connecting Factor

If a party's habitual residence determines the governing law but it is impossible to ascertain his/her habitual residence, then the law of his/her residence shall govern.[58]

[53] Of course, the jurisdictional matters in Articles 2, 27 and 28 of the Act are not subject to the General Provisions here.

[54] The Act, Art. 3(1).

[55] *Id.*

[56] The Act, Art. 3(2).

[57] Ministry of Justice (2003) p. 29.

[58] The Act, Art. 4.

Although the Act does not define what habitual residence is, it is generally understood to be the place where the party has his/her 'center of life'[59] as disclosed by the facts of the individual's activities. Determining a party's habitual residence should be based on various factors, such as the duration and purpose of stay, and family and vocational relationships of the party.[60]

Habitual residence denotes actual residence plus some continuity and persistence, even though it does not denote the intended permanence or emphasis on expressed intent often associated with domicile.[61] In Korea, habitual residence is similar to the concept of domicile. Article 18(1) of the KCPA defines domicile as "the base and center of living of each person." The function of domicile in Korea is deemed to be as a legal headquarters by which all persons are allocated to governmental units for legal purposes. Thus, the difference between habitual residence and domicile is that the former is a factual concept and the latter is a legal concept.

4.1.3 Examination and Proof of Foreign Law

When a foreign law is to be applied, a question arises as to how the court has to discover what the law is. Different countries adopt different approaches, though they mostly fall into one or two categories. The first approach is to treat the foreign law in much the same way as forum law: it may be more difficult to ascertain, but it is still the court's role to ascertain it. The other possibility is to treat the foreign law as fact, not law: it must be pleaded and proved by the party wishing to rely on it. Article 5 takes a combining position of both approaches. Article 5 requires that the foreign law be applied by the court of its own motion, even if it is not pleaded by either party. However, the court is able to request the party to provide any 'cooperation' in finding a source of the foreign law and any governing foreign cases. Thus, the party does not have a burden of proof on the foreign law to be applied.[62]

Prior to the adoption of the Act, the Korean court maintained a very conservative position in examining and applying the foreign law, even if, under the old private international law, a foreign law was applicable. However, recent cases rendered after the adoption of the Act indicate that Korean courts have been taking the opposite view. Some recent Supreme Court cases dismissed lower courts' decisions on the ground that the lower courts did not endeavor to find and apply the designated foreign law and just simply applied the domestic law.[63]

---

[59] K. H. SUK, 「국제사법 해설」 p. 81.

[60] *Id.*

[61] Scoles et al. (2004), §4.14.

[62] K. H. SUK, 「국제사법 해설」 p. 85–86.

[63] Decision of 2008. 1. 31, 2004다26454 (the Supreme Court of Korea); Decision of 2010. 3. 25, 2008다88375 (the Supreme Court of Korea).

4.1.4 Scope of Designated Governing Law

It was generally regarded that the applicable foreign law must be private law, not public law. Recently, however, the distinction between private and public laws tends to be unclear and ambiguous. The criteria for such distinction vary from country to country. Thus, Article 6 states that the application of a provision of foreign law shall not be precluded only because the provision is attributed the character of public law. Accordingly, mandatory laws of the foreign law, such as the Foreign Exchange Transaction Act[64] or the Foreign Trade Act[65] can be applied to resolve the dispute in a Korean court. It is not necessary, however, that such public law be applied mandatorily to the dispute. In other words, it means that the public type of foreign law could be applied if it is reasonable to do so, based upon an appropriate interpretation of the Act.[66]

4.1.5 Mandatory Application of Korean Laws

Article 7 expressly provides that provisions of a 'mandatory law of Korea', which in view of its legislative purpose is applicable irrespective of the governing law, shall apply, even if a foreign law is designated as applicable under the Act.[67] The term 'mandatory law of Korea'[68] pursuant to Article 7, is the rules that must be applied regardless of the law applicable to the contract. It shall be also distinguished from the so-called "ordinary mandatory rules of law" which cannot be derogated from by mere agreement. Scholars and drafters of the Act refer to the Article 7 rules as "international mandatory rules." Thus, international mandatory rules are rules that cannot be derogated from by agreement and shall be applied even when a foreign law

---

[64] Act No. 9374, January 30, 2009.

[65] Act No. 9630, April 22, 2009.

[66] K. H. SUK, 「국제사법 해설」 p. 90.

[67] Article 7 of the Act modeled after Article 18 of Swiss PIL Act (this Code does not prevent the application of those mandatory provisions of Swiss law which, by reason of their particular purpose, are applicable regardless of the law designated by this Code), and Article 7(2) of the Rome Convention. ("Nothing in this Convention shall restrict the application of the rules of the law of the forum in a situation where they are mandatory irrespective of the law otherwise applicable to the contract.")

[68] This type of law is also referred to 'overriding mandatory provisions' under Article 9(1) of the Rome Regulation I (Regulation 593/2008), which are "provisions, the respect for which is regarded as crucial by a country for safeguarding its public interests, such as its political, social or economic organization, to such an extent that they are applicable to any situation falling within their scope, irrespective of the law otherwise applicable to the contract under this Regulation". The Rome Regulation I was negotiated during 2007, and formally adopted on 17 June 2008. It came into force August of 2008 and applies to contracts concluded after 17 December 2009. Contracts concluded prior to that date will still be governed by the Convention. (Hartley, p. 571).

is designated as the *lex causae*.[69] Examples of such international mandatory rules in Korea include, but are not limited to, the Foreign Exchange Transaction Act, the Foreign Trade Act, and the Monopoly Regulation and Fair Trade Act.[70]

International mandatory rules are generally classified into three categories: international rules pertaining to *lex causae*, international mandatory rules of the forum, and international mandatory rules of third countries. The Act contains provisions only on mandatory rules in the first two categories.[71] The Act does not accept the third category, contrary to the position that the Rome Convention and Rome Regulation I have.

4.1.6 Exception Clause; Escape Clause

Even though the Act adopts a principle of the closest connection in the course of determining governing laws, there may be situations where, in light of all circumstances, it is manifest that the case has only a very limited connection with the law designated by the Act and has a much closer connection with another law. As an escape device in that situation, Article 8(1) provides that the law designated by the Act shall not be applied in those exceptional situations. Instead, the law of another country having a much closer connection with the legal relationship shall apply. However, this exception clause shall be strictly invoked and exercised where such exceptional situation is *unequivocally* clear. If there is any question as to the application of the exception clause, then it shall not be invoked. This clause probably can be applied to cases, such as special types of tort cases or where a flag of convenience is involved in a maritime case.[72] No cases have been reported that application of the exceptional clause was at issue.

Article 8(2) provides that the exception clause is not applicable in cases of a choice of law made by the parties. Thus, a voluntary choice of law by the parties should prevail over the exception clause in any case.

4.1.7 Renvoi

The application of *renvoi*[73] is regarded as another type of escape device. Let us assume a case comes before a Korean court, and Korean choice-of-law rule states that English law applies. However, the English choice-of-law rule dictates that

---

[69] *Lex causae* refers to the law that would be applicable in the absence of choice of law by the parties. (Scoles, §18.4 p. 957).

[70] Act No. 9554, March 25, 2009.

[71] Suk (2003b) p. 110. (Although it is not expressly mentioned, Article 6 of the Act deals with international mandatory rules pertaining to *lex causae*. Under Article 6, one may argue that international mandatory rules of *lex causae* should apply as part of *lex causae*.)

[72] K. H. SUK, 「국제사법 해설」 pp. 102–104.

[73] *Renvoi* means in French ‘sending back’.

Korean law applies. Under that situation, it should be decided whether the Korean court should ignore the English choice-of-law rule and just apply English law, or should accept the *renvoi* and apply Korean law. Article 9(1) of the Act provides an answer to this question: the Korean court should accept the *renvoi* and apply the Korean law. This rule is only effective where the foreign choice-of-law rule refers back to the law of the forum. In the event the foreign choice-of-law rule refers to the law of a third country (in the case of transmission), this rule is not applicable, except Article 51(1)[74] only.

It should be noted, as an exception, that Article 9(2) enlists several situations where the rule of *renvoi* is not applicable. Pursuant to Article 9(2), *renvoi* is not permitted in cases, including, but not limited to, where: (1) the parties have chosen the governing law; (2) the law governing a contract is designated by the Act; or (3) allowing *renvoi* would be contrary to the very purpose of any specific provision under the Act. The above third situation can be controversial[75] because it depends on an interpretation of the specific provision.

4.2 Contracts

Provisions for contracts (Articles 25 through 29) modeled after the Rome Convention. Any subsequent changes by the Rome Regulation I have not yet been reflected in the relevant provisions. Generally, the Act takes a three-step approach in the course of determining law in contract. The first step is to determine whether there is an express choice of law. If there is, the expressly chosen law applies. If there is no express choice, the court must consider whether there is an implied choice. If there is, such implicitly chosen law will decide the case. However, the concept of an implied choice is restricted to cases in which the court believes that the parties had genuinely considered the matter. If there is no implied choice, the court would apply the objective test of the closest and most real connection.

4.2.1 Principle of Party Autonomy

Express Choice of Law

The Act recognizes the right of the parties to expressly choose the applicable law.[76] There is no requirement that the law chosen should have any connection with the

[74] Article 51(1) of the Act provides that the capacity of a person who assumes obligations under a bill of exchange, promissory note or check shall be governed by *lex patriae* of such person. If *lex patriae* provides that such capacity shall be governed by the law of another country, the law of that country shall apply.

[75] For further in depth analysis thereof, refer to K. H. SUK, 「국제사법 해설」, pp. 113–115.

[76] The Act, Art. 25(1).

parties or the contract. Any neutral type of law can be chosen. Thus, the choice is completely free. As seen above, the parties' express choice of law is not subject to the exception clause under Article 8. However, one Supreme Court case has a view that if the parties' choice of law is clearly unreasonable and unfair, it would be made in contravention of public policy.[77] As a result of this decision, though the complete free choice of law by the parties is acknowledged, it can be said that it ought to be reasonable and fair to some extent.

Article 25(2) expressly permits *depecage* which is the practice of using more than one law in deciding a single case—that is, of deciding some issues under one law and others under another. Further, Article 25(3) allows parties to change the governing law at any time after the contract is concluded.

Implied Choice of Law

In addition to the express choice of law, Article 25(1) permits an implied choice of law by the parties. However, the implied choice may be acknowledged only when it is reasonable to do so in light of the terms of the contract or the circumstances of the case. The implied choice is interpreted to mean that both of the parties thought about the matter, that they both thought the answer was so obvious that it was not necessary to state it, and that they had the same view as to what the answer was.[78]

Other Various Issues

The chosen law may expressly or implicitly include a 'rule of law' that was not in force in any country. The rule of law may include various types, such as a code drawn up by some international body, but never adopted. One example of the rule of law is UNIDROIT[79]'s Principles of International Commercial Contract ("PICC").

The law applied under this choice-of-law clause is the law as it exists from time to time. Relevant changes after the contract is made are applied. On the other hand, the parties are not prevented from incorporating by reference, such a code (or any other set of rules) into their contract. Where a set of rules is incorporated by reference into a contract, it is as if those rules were set out in the contract. Where a set of rules is incorporated by reference, subsequent changes are not taken into account.[80]

It is questionable whether the parties were free to designate a foreign law where all relevant elements were connected with another country, that is, the forum country. Article 25(4)'s answer is that, even if all the elements 'relevant to the

[77] Decision of 1997. 9. 9, 96다20093 (the Supreme Court of Korea).

[78] Trevor, p. 567.

[79] UNIDROIT stands for "International Institute for the Unification of Private Law."

[80] Trevor, pp. 573–574.

case' are connected with only one country,[81] the parties are free to select the law of another country as the governing law of the contract. However, the application of the ordinary mandatory rules of the law of the former country cannot be excluded in such cases.[82] Thus, Article 25(4) applies only where all relevant elements (other than a choice of law or a choice of court) are connected with a single country.

The purpose of this provision is to ensure application of the ordinary mandatory rules of the country with which all the elements are connected other than the choice of law.[83] The Act, like the Rome Convention, does not clarify what elements are to be regarded as 'relevant to the case' for the purposes of Article 25(4). The habitual residence and residence of the parties and the place or places of performance would clearly be relevant; on the other hand, some connections would be of such minor importance that they would be disregarded. The determination as to what elements are relevant is for the national court.[84]

4.2.2 Applicable Law in Absence of Choice (Objective Governing Law)

Article 26(1) provides that if there was no express or implied choice of law, the contract would be governed by the law of the country with which it was most closely connected. Unlike Article 25(1), it should be noted that the law of the country to be determined pursuant to Article 26(1) should not be a "rule of law" including *lex mercatoria*.

Articles 26(2) and 26(3) then try to provide more predictability by laying down a presumption as to what that law should be. This was based on the theory of 'characteristic performance', a doctrine invented by the Rome Convention and Swiss private international law. Under that theory, a contract is presumed most closely connected with the country of the party who is to affect the characteristic performance.[85] The characteristic performance doctrine is based on the idea that, in most types of contract, one party undertakes to do no more than pay money. Since this payment of money is common to most kinds of contract, it should be disregarded. Instead, the characteristic performance must, therefore, be that of the other party.[86]

---

[81] This means that it is a purely domestic contract.

[82] This rule is derived from Article 3(3) of the Rome Convention. Article 3(3) of the Rome Convention was apparently the result of a compromise. Some delegations wanted the Convention to provide that the parties could not make a valid choice of law in the case of a purely domestic contract; the delegates, notably that of the United Kingdom, were opposed to this limitation on the parties' freedom of choice. The compromise was to allow a free choice, but not to exclude the ordinary mandatory rules from the operation of the choice of law. (Trevor, p. 601).

[83] Suk (2003b), p. 123.

[84] Philip (1982) at p. 95 (*recitation* from Trevor, p. 601).

[85] Trevor, p. 581.

[86] *Id.*

Pursuant to Article 26(2), a contract is presumed most closely connected with the country where the party who carries out one of the following performance, habitually resides at the time of the conclusion of the contract:

(1) In a contract for the sale of goods (or for transfer), the performance of the seller (or of transferor);
(2) In a contract for the provision of services (or for granting the use of a thing or a right), the performance of the service provider (or of the party granting the use); or
(3) In mandate contracts, independent contracts (or contracts for completion of work) and similar contracts for services, the performance of the party providing the services.

One noteworthy point is that the presumptive provisions provided do not refer to the law of the country in which the characteristic performance is to be actually *carried out*, but to the law of the country in which the party who is to carry out that performance, habitually resides.[87] For example, if a Korean company agrees to sell goods to a U.S. company and delivery is to take place in the USA, the applicable law is the law of Korea, not that of the USA.

Two things should be clarified further at this point. First, if the party carrying out the performance is a legal entity or an organization, it should be the law of the country in which the characteristic performer has its principal place of business, not the place of incorporation.[88] However, where under the terms of the contract, the performance was to be effected through a place of business (like a branch office) other than the principal place of business in the course of the party's profession or business activity, the law of the country where the place of business[89] was situated, shall be presumed most closely connected with the contract.[90]

The second point is that some contracts may not have characteristic performance. This was recognized by the Rome Convention as well, providing that the presumption would not apply if the characteristic performance could not be determined.[91] After all, it was only a presumption itself. Thus, the presumption should be disregarded if it substantially appeared from the circumstances that the contract was more closely connected with another country.[92] The result was that the principle

[87] The Act, Art. 26(2).

[88] *Id.*

[89] This place of business refers to the place of the branch office.

[90] *Id.*

[91] Although the Act does not specifically mention, it should be consistently interpreted with the Rome Convention, Article 4, paragraph 5.

[92] The contents of this sentence are similar to the Rome Convention, Article 4, paragraph 5; however, this paragraph was not adopted in the Act because the general exception clause under Article 8 of the Act applies. From the author's perspective, it would be better to specifically include this rule in Article 26, not only because the parties may miss the general exception clause under Article 8, but because this rule may be able to clarify the presumption which is always rebuttable if possible.

was that of the closest connection; there was a presumption based on the characteristic performance doctrine; but it was made clear that this was to be rebutted if in fact the contract was more closely connected with another country.[93]

Article 26(3) provides that a contract relating to a right *in rem* in immovable property shall be governed by the law of the country where the property is situated. The Rome Convention provides that the right *in rem* in immovable property also includes a right to a tenancy of immovable property.[94] The Act should be interpreted accordingly.

4.2.3 Consumer Contracts and Individual Employment Contracts

The basic principle of contract law is to give effect to the intention of the parties. However, there is another principle. In certain circumstances, the law rejects what the parties have agreed on, or it insists that the contract should be subject to terms they did not agree on. This is because the law pursues policy aims, even against the will of the parties. In many cases, the justification for imposing such legal rules on the parties is that the interests of society outweigh those of an individual; in others, it is simply the desire to help parties regarded as being in a weak bargaining position in making a contract (for example, consumers and individual employees). In all situations, the result is the same: what the parties agreed on is overridden by the law. In cases of consumer contracts and individual employment contracts, thus, certain ordinary mandatory rules override a choice of law in a wider range of circumstances.

Consumer Contracts

Article 27 contains special rules on consumer contracts. A consumer contract is made between a consumer and a professional (non-consumer or the other party). A 'consumer' is a person acting for a purpose outside his/her trade or profession; a professional is someone acting in the exercise of his/her profession or business activity. Article 27 addresses two different situations: the first is when both a consumer and a professional chose a law in their contract; and the second is in the absence of the choice of law.

Article 27(1) governs the first situation. The general idea is that any ordinary mandatory rules of the country of the consumer's habitual residence shall be applied irrespective of the choice of law by the parties. For example, even if a choice of law was agreed upon with a foreign law, any mandatory rules[95] protecting

[93] Trevor, pp. 581–582.

[94] The Rome Convention, Article 4, paragraph 3.

[95] These mandatory rules cannot be derogated from by agreement, and should be distinguished from the international mandatory rules under Article 7 of the Act. (Ministry of Justice (2003), p. 99–100).

the consumers in Korea shall be applied to any dispute arising out of the consumer contract. Here, the parties' choice of law is overridden by the mandatory rules that were designed to protect the consumers in the country thereof. Of course, if the choice of law was Korean law, then the protective measures for consumers would certainly be secured.

Article 27(2) regulates the second situation. In the absence of choice of law, the consumer contract shall be governed by the law of the country of the consumer's habitual residence regardless of the standards of the objective governing law under Article 26.

One important point to consider is that the provisions under Article 27(1) and (2) are only effective, provided that:

1) Where, prior to the conclusion of a contract, the professional engaged in or directed to the country of the consumer's habitual residence any professional or business activities, including soliciting business through advertisement, and the consumer had taken in that country any steps necessary for the conclusion of the contract;
2) Where the professional received the consumer's order in the country of the consumer's habitual residence; or
3) Where the professional induced the consumer to go abroad to place his/her order there.

Consumers in this context are regarded 'passive consumers' while the professional actively targeted the consumer's country in some way. The contract was concluded within the framework of that targeting. Article 27(1) originally modeled after Article 5(2) of the Rome Convention, but has been slightly modified to cover consumer contracts via the Internet.[96] The drafters of the Act also intended the *consumer contract* (though not specifically defined) to cover broader than that of Article 5 of the Rome Convention and even Article 120[97] of the Swiss Private International Law Act.[98]

Individual Employment Contracts

Individual employment contracts follow a similar pattern of consumer contracts. Article 28(2) specifies the law applicable in the absence of the choice of law, while Article 28(1) says that, although the parties may choose another law, such choice

---

[96] Suk (2003b), p. 125.

[97] Contracts relating to the provision of ordinary goods and services intended for the personal or family use of the consumer and which are not associated with the professional or commercial activities of the consumer shall be governed by the law of the state in which the consumer habitually resides:(a) If the supplier received the order in that state; (b) If the conclusion of the contract was preceded in that state by an offer or an advertisement and the consumer performed there the necessary acts to conclude the contract; or (c) If the consumer was induced by the supplier to go abroad to place his/her order there.

[98] Suk (2003b), p. 125.

will not prevent the application of the ordinary mandatory rules that would have been applicable in the absence of the choice of law. The difference from the consumer contract is a way of determining a governing law in the absence of the choice of law. Notwithstanding the provisions of Article 26, an employment contract shall be governed by the law of the country in which the employee habitually performs his work, or if the employee does not habitually perform his work in any one country, by the law of the country where the place of business that employed him is situated.[99]

The following example will illustrate the position. Let us assume that a U.S. company employs a man who habitually resides in Korea as its sales representative in China and Japan as well as Korea. The office of the sales representative is in Korea, where his wife answers the phone and deals with e-mails. He spends most of the week in his sales territory, particularly in China and Japan. Since he does not habitually perform his work *in* any one country, but does habitually carry it out *from* his base in Korea, the applicable law in the absence of the choice of law will be that of Korea. A Korean court will also have jurisdiction over an employment-law claim by him against his employer. If the parties had chosen U.S. law to govern the contract, this choice, although valid, would not deprive the employee of the protection of the ordinary mandatory rules[100] of Korean law. It would seem that he could also invoke the employee-protection rules of U.S. law, unless they were incompatible with those of Korean law. So he might enjoy double protection.

Tort

General Rules

The general rule laid down in Article 32(1) is that the applicable law is that of the country in which the tort was committed. It has been problematic where the wrongful act of the defendant takes place in one country and the damage occurs in another. Article 32, however, does not clearly address the situation. This issue should be resolved by court decisions and scholarly opinions.

The Korean Supreme Court rendered its opinion on that issue prior to the enactment of the Act. It held that the 'place of the tort' included the place of the tortious act as well as the place of injury.[101] It is not clear, however, whether the injured party may be able to select the law more favorable to him or whether it is up to the court to select *ex officio* the law more favorable to the injured party. Lower courts recently decided that the injured party has an option to select the law more

[99] The Act, Art. 28(2).

[100] Like Article 27, these mandatory rules cannot be derogated from by agreement, and should be distinguished from the international mandatory rules under Article 7 of the Act. (Ministry of Justice (2003), pp. 104–5).

[101] Decision of 1983. 3. 22, 82다카1533 (the Supreme Court of Korea); Decision of 1985. 5.28, 84다카966 (the Supreme Court of Korea).

favorable to himself.[102] Thus, it is the Korean court's position that the injured party has to actively raise to the court either law that is more favorable to himself.

If the tortfeasor becomes a corporation, then a question arises as to how the corporation's habitual residence should be determined. It seems that a majority view is the corporation's principal place of business, although another view contends that it should be the place of incorporation.[103]

Limitation of Damages

There is one limitation under Article 32(4), however. It provides that in cases where a tort is governed by a foreign law under Articles 32(1) through 32(3), damages arising out of the tort shall not be awarded in either situation: (1) if the nature of the damage is not appropriate so as to merit compensation to the injured party; OR (2) if the damages so awarded would substantially exceed the amount of compensation deemed appropriate in the particular case.

The typical examples of the former are punitive damages and treble damages recognized by various statutes and U.S. courts. Such punitive damages and exemplary damages are not recognized by Korean courts because it focuses on punishment or retribution. Instead, as a form of monetary compensation, Korean laws, in principle, only consider and permit the compensatory damage that is to properly compensate the victim and, hence, are proportional to the victim's harm or loss.

An example of the latter is the 'grossly excessive damages' awarded by foreign courts. It should be noted that the latter case is applied only if the damages awarded under the foreign law substantially exceed the amount of compensation deemed appropriate under Korean standards. In other words, this means that if the damages awarded under the foreign law do not substantially exceed the amount of appropriate compensation under Korean law, such awarded damages can be acknowledged.[104]

Exception to General Rule

As an exception to Article 32(1), notwithstanding Article 32(1), Article 32(2) provides that if the tortfeasor and the victim had their habitual residence[105] in the same country at the time the tort occurred, the law of that country will be the governing law. Article 32(2) will be generally applicable when both parties having their habitual residences in Korea involved in tort in a foreign country. This rule is based on a rationale that Korean law is most closely connected with such situation.

---

[102] Decision of 2002. 5. 23, 99가합84123 (Seoul District Court); Decision of 2006. 1. 26. 2002나32662 (Seoul High Court).

[103] K. H. SUK, 「국제사법 해설」 pp. 286–287.

[104] K. H. SUK, 「국제사법 해설」 p. 291.

[105] Note that it is not the parties' nationality here.

The result is the same, regardless of whether both parties had any pre-existing relationship.

Notwithstanding Articles 32(1) and 32(2), Article 32(3) states that, when the tortious act constitutes a violation of a pre-existing legal relationship between the tortfeasor and the injured party, claims found on this act are governed by the law applicable to the legal relationship. In other words, the law that governs the parties' pre-existing legal relationship displaces the law that would otherwise govern the tort. Such pre-existing legal relationship is called the 'accessory connecting factor'. Accordingly, if the existing relationship, such as a contractual relationship between the parties, is prejudiced by a tortious act, the tort is subject to the governing law of the contract. The governing law in this case is the tort law of the country whose contract law is applicable to the contract.[106] The rule under Article 32(3) takes priority over Articles 32(1) and 32(2).

Article 33 allows a choice of law by agreement in the case of non-contractual obligations, including management of affairs without mandate (Article 30), unjust enrichment (Article 31), and tort (Article 32). Normally, the choice of law by agreement is possible only *after* the occurrence of the tort. Further it is available only when Korean law is agreed upon; provided, however, that the rights of third parties must not be prejudiced by such agreement.[107] This requirement is intended to protect any interests of third parties, such as an insurance company. Thus, even if the parties agree with Korean law after the occurrence of the tort, the insurance company would be liable for damages to the extent that the objectively determined law, not the Korean law, provides.

Overall, we should consider a priority among the above mentioned provisions [Articles 32(1), 32(2), 32(3) and 33]. If an agreement stipulates a choice of law under Article 33, it shall apply first, then the law governing the pre-existing relationship under Article 32(3), if any. If no foregoing method is available, the law of the country of the same habitual residence under Article 32(2), if any, shall apply. Lastly, the law of the country where the tort occurred under Article 32(1) shall apply.

Unjust Enrichment

The general rule laid down in Article 31 is that the applicable law is that of the country in which the unjust enrichment took place. Like tort under Article 32(3), when unjust enrichment results from a violation of a pre-existing legal relationship between the parties, claims founded on this Article are governed by the law applicable to the legal relationship. In other words, the law that governs the parties' pre-existing legal relationship displaces the law that would otherwise govern the unjust enrichment. Such pre-existing legal relationship is called the 'accessory

[106] Suk (2003b), p. 128.

[107] The Act, Art. 33.

connecting factor'. Accordingly, if the existing relationship, such as a contractual relationship between the parties, is prejudiced by the unjust enrichment, the unjust enrichment is subject to the governing law of the contract.

In addition, as described under Article 33, the choice of Korean law by agreement between the parties is allowed only after an unjust enrichment has occurred; provided, however, that the rights of third parties must not be prejudiced by such agreement.[108] As to a priority of applicable law, the law chosen by the parties, if any, shall apply first, then the accessory connecting factor, if any. In the event the foregoing methods are not available, the law of the country where the unjust enrichment took place shall apply.

Property

A general view is widely held that property matters are governed by the *lex situs*, the law of the country where the property is situated. However, it was suggested that, while this works well in the case of tangible property, it is unsatisfactory when applied to intangible rights, such as security interests over claims, shares and other rights, bank accounts, bonds, certificates of deposit, letters of credit and other financial instruments.

Acquisition and Transfer of Tangible Property (Movables and Immovables)

Tangible property may be either movables (goods and chattels) or immovables (land). The application of the *lex situs* to land is so obvious that almost nothing further needs to be said: all property rights (rights in rem) in land are governed by the law of the country in which the land is located.[109]

Movable property is more problematic, since it may be moved from one country to another. The basic rule—the *lex situs* rule—is that the question whether property rights are acquired in goods depends on the law of the place where the goods are situated at the time the act or event occurred as a result of which it is claimed that the rights are acquired.

Article 19(1) generally provides that the principle of *lex situs* is also applied to all movable property. When the interest in movable property is acquired or lost, such acquisition and loss of interest in the movable property shall be governed by the law of the place where the property was located at the time the fact existed from which the acquisition or the loss derives.[110] Article 19(2) often applies to a cross-border transaction of goods between Korea and a foreign country. In a case of export of goods from Korean to Japan, for example, let us assume that, when a contract for sale of the goods is made, the goods are still located in Korea. If so,

[108] The Act, Art. 33.

[109] The Act, Art. 19(1).

[110] The Act, Art. 19(2).

Korean law applies to the transfer of title in the goods. Pursuant to Korean law, possession by the buyer of the goods is a necessary element for the transfer of title in the goods. The transfer of title in the goods to the buyer does not occur until after the Japanese buyer possesses the goods, even if the buyer has already paid for the goods prior to the possession thereof. In a converse situation where the goods are imported from Japan to Korea, pursuant to contract, the goods are located in Japan. Because possession is not a required element for the transfer of title under Japanese law, the title in the goods is simultaneously transferred to the Korean buyer at the time of execution of the contract.

Means of Transportation

A new connecting factor is introduced for means of transportation, such as aircraft and railway vehicles, since the *lex situs* of a means of transportation changes constantly. Under Article 20 of the Act, property rights in the aircraft are governed by the law of its nationality, and property rights in the railway vehicles by the law of the country approving its transportation services. There is a separate provision as to the governing law to be applicable to the property rights in a ship under Article 60.

Property in Transit (Res in Transit)

Article 22 of the Act provides that the acquisition, loss and change of interests in movable property in transit based on a legal transaction shall be governed by the law of the country of destination. Article 22 addresses the situation where the movable property is disposed of by transferring ownership interest, or placing a pledge or security interest thereover, while in transit. If the adopted connecting factor of the *lex situs* is applied to the movable property in transit, then the connecting factor would constantly change as movable property is disposed of while in transit.[111] This will cause instability in determining the governing law for the movable property in transit. Considering this situation, the country of destination is adopted as a connecting factor to increase a stability and predictability. Thus, the law of the country of destination governs the acquisition, loss and change of interests in movable property in transit.

Bearer Securities (Unregistered Securities)

Bearer securities are negotiable instruments and are treated as movables. Generally, bearer securities are subject to the law of the country where the securities are located (*lex carte sitae*). Article 21 provides that the acquisition, loss and change of rights concerning bearer securities shall be governed by the law of the site (*lex situs*) of such security at the time of the completion of the causal action or event. The term

[111] Ministry of Justice (2003), p. 81; K. H. SUK, 「국제사법 해설」 p. 179.

'rights concerning bearer securities' refers to both the rights represented by the bearer securities and the rights to the security certificate itself.[112]

It should be noted that the question as to whether a certain instrument is a bearer security should be determined by the law governing the right represented by the bearer securities. Further, although the acquisition and disposition of a right to a bearer securities certificate is a matter to be governed by the *lex cartae sitae*, the change of the right represented by a bearer security should be governed by the law governing the right itself, not by the *lex cartae sitae*. In this regard, Article 21 may be a little misleading and should be so interpreted.[113]

Article 21 is intended to apply to securities that exist in the form of a certificate and are directly held by investors. Thus, Article 21 should not apply to cases where investors hold their securities indirectly through intermediaries, and cross-border securities transactions are concluded by a mere account transfer. In such cases, the bearer securities cannot be treated as movables; instead, the law of the place of the relevant intermediary should apply.[114] This is so-called "place of the relevant intermediary 'approach' (PRIMA)".[115]

Contractual Security Interests Over Claims, Shares and Other Rights

Article 23 provides that, with respect to contractual security interests over claims (*chaegwon*), shares, other rights, or the securities representing or embodying such claims, shares and other rights, the law applicable to the right over which such security interest is created shall govern. It should be noted that Article 23 designates the law governing the right represented by a security certificate only, not the law governing the right to the certificate itself. The latter is governed by *lex cartae sitae*. In addition, as described in the bearer securities, Article 23 is also intended to apply to securities existing in the form of a certificate and held directly by investors. Thus, it should not apply in cases where an investor holds his securities indirectly through an intermediary, nor where a cross-border security transaction is effected by a mere account transfer, in which case the PRIMA would apply.[116]

Intellectual Property

The essence of an intellectual property right is that it grants a monopoly: the holder can do something that others may not do. If another person infringes that monopoly,

---

[112] Suk (2003b), p. 119.

[113] Suk (2003b), p. 120.

[114] Determining the governing law raises a difficult issue if the two places of relevant intermediary are different, i.e., the place where the rights of the security interest provider are registered and the place where the rights of the security interest holder are registered (Reciting from Suk (2003b) p. 120).

[115] *Id.*

[116] Suk (2003b) p. 121.

the holder of the right may sue the infringer. The alleged infringer can normally defend himself in two ways: he can claim that what he was doing does not constitute an infringement (because it is outside the scope of the monopoly); or he can argue that the intellectual property right is invalid.

There are various ways in which the latter option may be pursued. The validity of the intellectual-property right may be raised as a defence in the infringement action, in which case it will have to be decided before judgment for the alleged infringement is given. In some legal systems, the court hearing the infringement action may decide it as a preliminary issue; in others, it may have to be decided in separate proceedings. In the case of a patent, for example, proceedings may have to be brought before the national patent office. Where the validity of the right is decided in separate proceedings, the infringement proceedings will have to be stayed (suspended) to await their outcome.[117]

Article 24 adopts the principle of the law of the protecting country (*lex loci protectionis*). The protection of intellectual property rights shall be subject to the law where the right was infringed.[118] It should be noted that the language of Article 24 is a little different from the relevant provision in other countries' private international laws having the same principle. For instance, Article 110 of Swiss Private International Law says, "intellectual property rights shall be governed by the law of the state in which protection of the intellectual property is sought." The reasons are as follows. First, if the phrase, "the law of the State in which protection of the intellectual property is sought," is written in Korean language, then it may be misunderstood that the law of forum state should govern due to language nuance. Second, since the infringement of intellectual property rights is the most problematic issue raising the question of the governing law, the language of Article 24 is written as it is ("the law where the right is infringed").[119] Regardless of the superficial meaning of the language in Article 24, accordingly, it should be interpreted that the law of the protecting country, not the law of forum state, governs the matters of intellectual property.

The law of the protecting country is sometimes equivalent to that of the forum state; however, it is not necessarily the same. For example, if an infringee brings a lawsuit against a Korean national in a Korean court for an alleged infringement that was occurred in United Kingdom, then the law of the protecting country is the law of the United Kingdom even though the forum state is Korea. Further, it should be noted that the protecting country is not the same one as where the intellectual property at issue was registered. Sometimes, the countries of the registration, the protecting country, and the forum country, respectively, can be different. In addition, it is not necessary that the protecting country is the same one as where the infringement was made. In cases of infringement of patent rights, the protecting country will be the same as the infringed country. However, if any party seeks

[117] Trevor, pp. 288–289.

[118] The Act, Art. 24.

[119] Ministry of Justice (2003), pp. 86-7; K. H. SUK, 「국제사법 해설」 p. 191.

another type of protection other than the infringement, like transfer of intellectual property rights, then the protecting country in the lawsuit will be the one where such protection is sought, not the one where the infringement was made. In sum, the drafters of the Act and scholars have a view that Article 24 is designed to govern most types of intellectual property matters including creation, transfer and infringement of intellectual property rights.

A categorization as to infringement of intellectual property does matter because it can be characterized as tortious action that is governed under Article 34. Since the Act is separating the rule of the infringement of intellectual property from that of tort, such infringement should be governed by Article 24, not by Article 32. However, it should be noted that limitation of damages provided for under Article 32(4) can be invoked into the infringement matter.[120] Thus, damages arising out of the infringement may not be awarded in either situation: (1) if the nature of damage is not appropriate so as to merit compensation to the infringee; or (2) if the damages so awarded would substantially exceed the amount of compensation deemed appropriate in the particular case. An infringer in the infringement lawsuit may want to utilize Article 32(4) in his/her case in order to lessen the amount of damages.

Matters Common to Contractual and Non-contractual Claims

Law Governing the Assignment of Claims

Article 34 deals with the applicable law for voluntary assignment of claims and assumption of obligations. The legal relationship between an assignor and an assignee under a voluntary assignment of claims shall be governed by the law that applies the contract between the assignor and assignee.[121] It appears that the party's autonomy is adopted to resolve any dispute between the assignor and assignee.

Article 34(1) further deals with the legal position of the debtor. It covers the matters, including but not limited to: (1) assignability of claims; (2) the relationship between the assignee and the debtor; (3) the relationship between the third party and the debtor; (4) the conditions under which the assignment can be invoked against the debtor; (5) whether the debtor's obligations have been discharged; and (6) which assignment has priority in case of double assignments by the assignor.[122] These matters shall be governed by the law governing the claim assigned.[123]

It is most likely that there would be two voluntary assignments to different assignees. Let us assume that A is the creditor and that he/she has a claim against

---

[120] Ministry of Justice (2003), p. 87; K. H. SUK, 「국제사법 해설」 p. 194.

[121] The Act, Art. 34(1), first sentence.

[122] K. H. SUK, 「국제사법 해설」 p. 303.

[123] The Act, Art. 34(1), second sentence.

B (the debtor). A assigns this claim first to one assignee (C-1) and then to another (C-2). If either, or both, of the assignees approaches B demanding payment, the question whom B must pay is resolved by the law governing the claim assigned.

Presumably, one assignee will get paid; the other will not. Let us assume further that C-1 is entitled to payment. C-2 will not be able to do anything more as regards B. C-2 might then turn to A for recourse. If he claims a remedy from A—perhaps rescission or damage, the law governing the contract of assignment between the two of them (A and C-2) will apply.

Let us assume that C-2 gets no satisfaction from A. Perhaps the latter is bankrupt. The only remaining option is for C-2 to sue C-1. The issue would now be one of priority of rights. The law governing the assigned claim would determine which assignment has priority, because the applicable law should be neutral as between the two assignees. For this reason, it would be wrong to apply the law governing the contract of assignment for determination of priority of rights. Under the law governing the assigned claim, if the assignment to C-2 has priority over that to C-1, the latter would have to transfer payment to the former.

Law Governing the Assumption of Obligations

In addition to the assignment of contractual rights, the delegator may wish to delegate all or some of his/her obligations under the contract. A delegatee will assume the contractual obligations transferred by the delegator. Although the assumption of obligations may be regarded as contrary to the assignment of claims, Article 34(2) of the Act provides that the provisions on the assignment of claims shall apply *mutatis mutandis* to the assumption of obligations. Article 34(2) is applicable to the assumption of both contractual and non-contractual obligations.

Transfer of Claims by Operation of Law

Article 35 deals with the transfer of claims by operation of law, such as subrogation by an insurance company which makes payment on behalf of its insured client and then sues the party which the injured person claims caused the damages to him. The insurance company is subrogated to the rights of the insured client.

The transfer of a claim by operation of law is subject to the law governing the underlying legal relationship between the former creditor and the new creditor,[124] which is the applicable law in the insurance contract in the above case. However, if there is any provision in the law governing the claim, itself, to be transferred, that protects the debtor, such provision shall take precedence over the law determined under the first sentence of Article 35(1).[125] Obviously, this exception is intended to protect the debtor.

[124] The Act, Art. 35(1), first sentence.

[125] The Act, Art. 35(1), second sentence.

In the absence of such legal relationship, the transfer of a claim by operation of law shall be subject to the law governing the claim, itself, to be transferred.[126] For example, if a third-party makes payment on behalf of another without any contractual obligations, the law governing the claim itself will determine any dispute arising out of such transfer. The rational is that the transfer of a claim by operation of law is the effect or consequence of payment of the claim.[127]

Kinship

Chapter 6 of the Act (Articles 36 through 48) broadly covers issues of governing laws concerning marriages (Articles 36 through 39), parent-child relationships (Articles 40 through 45), maintenance (Article 46), and guardianship (Article 48).

Marriage

Formation of Marriage A substantive requirement of a marriage is deemed to be validly met as long as each party meets requirements for the marriage pursuant to the law of nationality of one of the parties thereto (*lex patriae*).[128] Each party does not need to meet the requirements for the substantive requirement of a marriage of the other party. The *lex patriae* herein means the law in effect at the time of marriage and does not consider that party's subsequent change of nationality thereafter.

Subject to one exception, the formal validity of a marriage is determined either by the law of the place of marriage ceremony or by the *lex patriae* of each party.[129] The one exception is, if the marriage ceremony took place in Korea, and one of the parties is Korean national, then the formal validity of such marriage shall be determined by the law of Korea.[130]

General Effects of Marriage The Act presents multiple governing laws for general effects of marriage. The general effects of marriage shall be governed in the following order: (1) by the *same lex patriae* of the spouses, if any; (2) by the law of the same habitual residence of the spouses, if any; and (3) by the law of the place with which the spouses are most closely connected.[131] It should be noted that the 'same' *lex patriae* of the spouses is different meaning of the 'common' *lex patriae*.[132] Let us assume that, if a husband has Korean nationality, and a wife

[126] The Act, Art. 35(2).
[127] Suk (2003b) p. 130.
[128] The Act, Art. 36(1).
[129] The Act, Art. 36(2).
[130] The Act, Art. 36(2).
[131] The Act, Art. 37.
[132] Ministry of Justice (2003), p. 133; K. H. SUK, 「국제사법 해설」 p. 318.

maintains both Korean and U.S. nationalities at the same time. It could be said that the spouses have a common nationality of Korea, not the same *lex patriae*. In order to determine the wife's *lex patriae*, Article 3 of the Act shall be applied. If the wife's *lex patriae* is determined to be "Korea" pursuant to Article 3, then the husband and wife are deemed to have the 'same' *lex patriae*, and the Korean law shall govern matters of their general effects of marriage. In the event the wife's *lex patriae* is determined to be USA, then the spouses have no same *lex patriae*. Then, they should consider, as the next step, as to whether they have the same habitual residence. This Article 37 broadly governs most of effects of marriage, except maintenance obligations between spouses under Article 46.

Matrimonial Property Regime Conflict of laws questions arise concerning both property owned by the parties at the time of marriage and that acquired subsequently. These questions may occur either during the marriage, for example, in actions concerning title or proceedings by creditors, or on termination of the marriage by divorce or death. Basically, the matrimonial property regime is governed by the law applicable to the general effects of marriage under Article 37.[133] This is because the matrimonial property is closely related to the present marriage.

Exceptionally, however, the Act allows party autonomy with some restrictions.[134] If the parties to the marriage expressly agree to resolve any marital property issues to one of the following laws: (1) the law of nationality of one of the parties to the marriage; (2) the law of habitual residence of one of the parties to the marriage; or (3) the law of the place where the land is located, then the selected law shall be respected, provided, however, that the agreement between the parties to the marriage were validly executed, in writing, with their signatures. Guaranteeing such party autonomy in matrimonial property regime follows the Hague Convention on the Law Applicable to Matrimonial Property Regime of 1978 and similar codification of other countries.[135]

Divorce Article 39 also subjects divorce to the law governing the general effects of marriage under Article 37. As an exception, however, if one of the parties to the marriage is a Korean national having his/her habitual residence in Korea, then the divorce shall be governed by Korean law.[136] Without this exception, there will be a practical burden on a Korean family registration officer to determine a law governing the divorce based under a default rule of Article 39. This exception is designed to relieve such burden.

[133] The Act, Art. 38(1).

[134] The Act, Art. 38(2).

[135] Ministry of Justice (2003), p. 137; K. H. SUK, 「국제사법 해설」 p. 324.

[136] The Act, Art. 39.

Law of Parent–Child Relationships

Formation of Parent–Child relationships The Act makes a distinction between the relationship of a parent and a legitimate child and that of a parent and an illegitimate child, providing different connecting factors. Under Article 40, *lex patriae* of either parent at the time of the child's birth is the law governing the formation of the parent and legitimate child relationship. As a result, such formation of the above relationship can be more easily made. As for the formation of a parent and illegitimate child relationship, on the other hand, the mother's lex partriae at the time of the illegitimate child's birth is the law governing such formation of the relationship.[137] If the formation of a father and illegitimate child relationship is at issue, one of the following two governing laws can be freely selected: (1) the law of the father's *lex patriae* at the time of the child's birth; or (2) the law of the child's current habitual residence.

With respect to recognition of a child, Article 41(2) provides that such recognition shall be governed either by the law generally applicable to the formation of a relationship between a parent and an illegitimate child or by the recognizing party's *lex patriae* at the time of recognition. As a result, if the recognizing party is a mother, the recognition is to be governed by: (1) the mother's *lex patriae* at the time of the child's birth; or, (2) the mother's *lex patriae* at the time of recognition. On the other hand, if the recognizing party is a father, the recognition is to be governed by one of the following four laws: (1) the mother's *lex patriae* at the time of the child's birth; (2) the father's *lex patriae* at the time of the child's birth; (3) the father's *lex patriae* at the time of recognition; or (4) the law of the child's habitual residence at the time of recognition.

Article 42 deals with legitimation of an illegitimate child. Under Article 42, such legitimation shall be governed by the *lex patriae* of the father or the mother, or by the law of the illegitimate child's habitual residence, at the time when an event constituting the legitimation is completed. Thus, the Act intends to make the legitimation being easily made.

As for adoption, Article 43 provides that requirements, formation, effects, and dissolution of adoption shall be governed by the *lex patriae* of the adoptive parents at the time of adoption. The rationale underlying this connecting factor is that the adopted child becomes a member of the family of the adoptive parents and that the adoptive parents' country usually constitutes a center of life of the adoptive child.[138] However, if the child's *lex patriae* requires the child's or any third party's consent or approval as to the formation of the parent-child relationship, Article 44 provides that such requirements must be satisfied. Obviously, this requirement is to protect the child's interests.

Rights and Obligations of Parent–Child Once the parent–child relationship is formed as described above, Article 45 provides that the rights and obligations of the

[137] The Act, Art. 41(1).

[138] Suk (2003b) p. 134.

parents and child shall be determined by the law of the child's habitual residence. Exceptionally, however, if the child's *lex patriae* is the same as that of both father and mother, then such *lex patriae* shall govern.

Law of Maintenance

Following rules under the Hague Convention on the Law Applicable to Maintenance Obligations of 1973, Article 46 has adopted a unified approach in which maintenance obligation shall be governed by the law of habitual residence of the maintenance creditor. However, if the maintenance creditor is unable to obtain maintenance from the debtor under such law, then the law of their common nationality shall apply.[139] This exception is intended to protect interests of the maintenance creditor. As for maintenance obligations arising out of divorce, Article 46(2) provides that if the divorce is granted or recognized in Korea, the maintenance obligation shall be governed by the law that actually applied to the divorce, not the law under Article 46(1). A reason providing a different connecting factor in the maintenance obligation arising out of the divorce is that the issue of maintenance is closely connected with the dissolution of marriage so that both matters of divorce and maintenance should be governed by the same law.

Law of Guardianship

Generally, matters of guardianship shall be governed by the ward's *lex patriae* under Article 48(1). Article 48 does not treat minors and adults differently. However, if a foreigner having his/her habitual residence or domicile in Korea becomes physically or mentally incompetent, Korean laws shall apply in one of the following situations: (1) where there is no person who can perform duties of guardianship determined under the *lex patriae* of the ward, or a determined person cannot perform the duties of guardianship for whatever reasons; (2) where a Korean court declares incompetency; or (3) where there is an otherwise urgent need to protect the ward.

Succession

This Chapter identifies the law mainly applicable to the succession of property at the death of citizens of the Republic of Korea, who die while living abroad for an extended time for business, personal or retirement reasons; and of citizens of other countries who come to Korea and die therein leaving their assets in Korea and/or in the nation of their citizenship. Korea is not yet a contracting state to the Multilateral

[139] The Act, Art. 46(1).

Convention on the Law Applicable to Succession to the Estates of Deceased Persons which was adopted without dissent at the Sixteenth Session of the Hague Conference on Private International Law October 20, 1988.[140]

General Issues

As to emigrating citizens, when they do not indicate another preference, it is assumed that they would prefer to retain their ties with their nation, at least until they have become substantially integrated into the foreign country. Consistent with this general principle, Article 49(1) provides that the succession of assets at death shall be governed by the *lex patriae* of the decedent as of the time of his/her death, unless indicated otherwise in a will of the decedent. This rule adopts the 'principle of unity' under which the entire estate of the decedent shall be governed by one single same law, regardless of whether the estate comprises of immovable and/or movable properties. Further, the same law should determine both the persons who succeed to the estate and the shares they receive even though assets are located in different countries, i.e., the estate should be treated as a unit, and the location of assets should not change the successors.

Under Article 49(2), however, the testamentary control by the decedent is recognized in a limited extent. That is, the decedent's designation of one of the following two laws is permitted and recognized only if it is validly made under his/her will: (1) the law of the nation of his/her habitual residence at the time of such designation; or, (2) the law of the situs of immovables as to disposition of the immovables only. However, it should be noted that in order for the former law to be applied, the decedent has to maintain his/her habitual residence in the nation until death.

Issues Relating to Wills

Pursuant to Article 50(1), the *lex patriae* of the testator as he/she executed the will shall govern most issues relating to the will, such as formation and effect of the will, other than the issue as regards the form of the will. In addition, amendment or revocation of the will shall also be governed by the *lex patriae* of the testator at the time of the amendment or the revocation.[141]

With respect to matters of form in a will, the Act follows the principles of the Hague Convention on the Conflicts of Laws Relating to the Form of Testamentary Disposition of 1961. Article 50(3) provides that the form of the will shall be governed by one of the following various laws: (1) the law of the nationality of the testator either when the will was made or at the time of his/her death; (2) the law of the testator's habitual residence, either when the will was made or at the time of

[140] For more details on the Convention, *see* Scoles (1994).

[141] The Act, Art. 50(2).

his/her death; (3) the law of the place where the will was made; or, (4) as far as immovables are concerned, the law of the place where they are situated.

Promissory Notes and Checks

Chapter 8 of the Act (Articles 51 through 59) deals with governing laws regarding bills of exchange, promissory notes and checks. These articles directly borrowed the principles laid down in the "Convention for the Settlement of Certain Conflicts of Laws in connection with Bills of Exchange and Promissory Notes of 7 June 1930" and the "Convention for the Settlement of Certain Conflicts of Laws in connection with Cheques of 19 March 1931." These conventions were created to unify relevant rules on conflict of laws.

Maritime Commerce

Generally, the Act takes a position that various matters of maritime commerce should be governed by the "law of the country of the ship's registration."[142] The matters of maritime commerce to be governed by the law of the country of the ship's registration may include, but are not limited to the following:

① Ownership, mortgages, maritime liens, and other real rights (rights *in rem*) of a ship;

② Priority rights of an encumbered ship;

③ Extent of shipowner's liability arising out of the acts committed by the captain and sailors of the ship;

④ Whether a shipowner, charterer, manager, operator or any other user of the ship is entitled to invoke into the limitation of liability and the scope of such limitation of liability.[143]

However, it should be noted that such determined law of the country of ship's registration would not be conclusive to the aforementioned matters if the registration of the ship was made as a result of a flag of convenience and that no other links with the country of registration may exist. If it is found, Article 8, one of the exception clauses in the Act, may apply. As described earlier, because Article 8 can be invoked in a very limited circumstance, a careful case-by-case analysis for the flag of convenience should be made.

---

[142] The country of the ship's registration should be distinguished from the countries of, the flag or the home port, of a ship.

[143] The Act, Art. 60

References

Hartley TC (2009) International Commercial Litigation – text, cases and materials on Private International Law. New York, USA: Cambridge University Press

Kwon Y (2007) Litigating in Korea: a general overview of the Korean Civil Procedure. J Korean Law 7(1)

Lee SH (2006) Foreign judgment recognition and enforcement system of Korea. J Korean Law 6(1)

Ministry of Justice (2003) 「국제사법 해설」 법무부

Philip (1982) Mandatory Rules, Public Law (Political Rules) and Choice of Law in the EEC Convention on the Law Applicable to Contractual Obligations. In: North PM (ed) Contract conflicts. North-Holland Publishing Company, Amsterdam

Scoles EF (1994) The Hague covention on succession. Am J Comp Law 42:85

Scoles EF, Hay P, Borchers PJ, Symeonides SC (2004) Conflict of Law, 4th ed. West, St Paul

Suk KH (2002) 「국제사법과 국제소송 I」 박영사

Suk KH (2003) 「국제사법 해설」 2d ed., 지산

Suk KH (2003b) The new conflict of Laws Act of the Republic of Korea, vol V, Yearbook of Private International Law. Kluwer Law International

Printed by Printforce, the Netherlands